OXFORD WORLD'S CLASSICS

A SENTIMENTAL EDUCATION

GUSTAVE FLAUBERT was born in 1821 in Rouen, where his father was chief surgeon at the hospital. From 1840 to 1844 he studied law in Paris, but gave up that career for writing, and set up house at Croisset in 1846 with his mother and niece. Notwithstanding his attachment to them (and to a number of other women), his art was the centre of Flaubert's existence, and he devoted his life to it. His first published novel, *Madame Bovary*, appeared in 1856 in serial form, and involved Flaubert in a trial for irreligion and immorality. On his acquittal the book enjoyed a *succès de scandale*, and its author's reputation was established.

Flaubert has been considered a realist. It is true that he took enormous trouble over the documentation of his novels—his next, *Salammbô* (1862), involved a trip to North Africa to gather local colour. But Flaubert's true obsession was with style and form, in which he continually sought perfection, recasting and reading aloud draft after draft.

While enjoying a brilliant social life as a literary celebrity, he completed a second version of *L'Éducation sentimentale* in 1869. *La Tentation de Saint Antoine* was published in 1874 and *Trois contes* in 1877. Flaubert died in 1880, leaving his last work, *Bouvard et Pécuchet*, to be published the following year.

DOUGLAS PARMÉE studied at Trinity College, Cambridge, the University of Bonn, and the Sorbonne. He later served in RAF Intelligence before returning to teach in Cambridge, where he was a Fellow and Director of Studies at Queens' College. He now lives in Adelaide, South Australia. He has written widely on French Studies and is a prize-winning translator from French, German, and Italian.

OXFORD WORLD'S CLASSICS

For over 100 years Oxford World's Classics have brought
readers closer to the world's great literature. Now with over 700
titles—from the 4,000-year-old myths of Mesopotamia to the
twentieth century's greatest novels—the series makes available
lesser-known as well as celebrated writing.

The pocket-sized hardbacks of the early years contained
introductions by Virginia Woolf, T. S. Eliot, Graham Greene,
and other literary figures which enriched the experience of reading.
Today the series is recognized for its fine scholarship and
reliability in texts that span world literature, drama and poetry,
religion, philosophy and politics. Each edition includes perceptive
commentary and essential background information to meet the
changing needs of readers.

OXFORD WORLD'S CLASSICS

GUSTAVE FLAUBERT

A Sentimental Education

The Story of a Young Man

Translated with an Introduction and Notes by
DOUGLAS PARMÉE

OXFORD
UNIVERSITY PRESS

OXFORD

UNIVERSITY PRESS

Great Clarendon Street, Oxford OX2 6DP

Oxford University Press is a department of the University of Oxford.
It furthers the University's objective of excellence in research, scholarship,
and education by publishing worldwide in

Oxford New York

Auckland Bangkok Buenos Aires Cape Town Chennai
Dar es Salaam Delhi Hong Kong Istanbul Karachi Kolkata
Kuala Lumpur Madrid Melbourne Mexico City Mumbai Nairobi
São Paulo Shanghai Taipei Tokyo Toronto

Oxford is a registered trade mark of Oxford University Press
in the UK and in certain other countries

Published in the United States
by Oxford University Press Inc., New York

Introduction, Main Characters, Select Bibliography,
Chronology, Translation, Historical Sketch, Explanatory Notes
© Douglas Parmée 1989

The moral rights of the author have been asserted

Database right Oxford University Press (maker)

First published as a World's Classics paperback 1989
Reissued as an Oxford World's Classics paperback 2000
Reissued 2008

British Library Cataloguing in Publication Data

Data available

Library of Congress Cataloging in Publication Data

Flaubert, Gustave, 1821–1880.
[Education sentimentale. English]
A sentimental education: the story of a young man / Gustave Flaubert;
translated with an introduction and notes by Douglas Parmée.
p. cm.—(Oxford world's classics)
Translation of: L'éducation sentimentale.
Bibliography: p.
I. Title. II. Series.
PQ2246.E413 1989   843'.8—dc19   89–3252

ISBN 978–0–19–954031–0

1

Printed in Great Britain by
Clays Ltd, St Ives plc

CONTENTS

INTRODUCTION

Some thoughts of Flaubert on *L'Éducation sentimentale*, novel-writing, and life:

I want to write the moral history—sentimental would be more accurate—of the men of my generation . . . It's about love and passion . . . but inactive passion . . . A profoundly true subject but for that reason probably not very amusing. (These last words are far too modest: his novel would prove very amusing, but this quotation dates from 1864, before he was properly launched into the novel and before he had realized the great possibilities of the historical background.)

In my view, the novelist has no right to express his opinions on the things of this world. In creating, he must imitate God: do his job and then shut up.

A novel must be scientific, that is, remain within the bounds of general probability.

I've not been painting a flattering picture of the democrats . . . but I assure you I haven't spared the conservatives.

There's a fundamental stupidity in mankind which is as eternal as life itself.

The infinite stupidity of the masses makes me tolerant towards individuality.

I'm grateful to you for magnifying the individual so diminished in these days by Democrasserie (words addressed to the writer and critic H. Taine (1828–93), referring to the latter's book on Italy; *crasse* in French means both 'filth' and 'a dirty trick').

Oh, if only we could get used to living without dogmatic principles, what a progress that would be!

You're always having to deal with bastards, being lied to, deceived, slandered and ridiculed, but that's to be expected and you must thank heaven when you meet the exception. That's

why I never forget the tiniest scrap of happiness that comes my
way, such as a friendly handshake or a smile.

I don't know what the two words mind and matter mean.
Nobody has any experience of either. Maybe they're two
abstractions created by our intelligence? In a word, I consider
materialism and spiritualism both equally absurd assumptions.

First, the title: sentimental in the sense of allowing
feeling to predominate over reason or deliberately indulging
in emotions is a familiar concept and although Frédéric
Moreau's family and school upbringing is very staid, his
personal education through his taste for poetry and novels
primarily concerned with passionate love must certainly
predispose him to lead a life excessively swayed by sentiment rather than reason. He is not alone in the novel;
others surrounding him suffer from a similar predilection,
although this may not always show itself in love relationships: political views can similarly be based on the dictates
of the heart rather than the head. There is, however, in the
novel an important extension of the term education; a
reader quickly discovers Flaubert's liking for multiple
meanings and the novel, as well as being an investigation of
romanticism in love and politics, is an account of an
emotional apprenticeship, an education of the feelings of a
romantic young man in the school of Paris society during
the turbulent period leading up to the 1848 Revolution.
This is the heart of the novel; it is a poignant and sometimes
devastating experience.

L'Éducation sentimentale first appeared in 1869, some five
years after Flaubert first started on it. He had needed every
minute. First, as he conceived the novel as 'the scientific
form of life', he had undertaken meticulous research to
ensure that all verifiable details were exact, even insignificant ones—though 'insignificant' is perhaps not the appropriate word, since, like a skilful detective story writer,
Flaubert would slip in details that were only apparently
trivial. But he was insistent that a novelist should remain,
in his words, 'within general probability', though his conception of probability did not exclude chance or coincidence, albeit to a smaller degree than in real life. The artist

creates like God but Flaubert thought the work of art should represent a greater logic; he imposes a pattern on his fictional reality, though never at the expense of acceptable truth to life. He must retain the reader's confidence through plausibility; any detectable error would destroy the illusion of reality.

A further reason for the years he spent on this and all his novels was his concern with style, which has become legendary. He wished his prose to have the rhythm of poetry and the accuracy of a scientific text; the words he used, if occasionally technical—he was a surgeon's son—were not extraordinary but their ordering and juxtaposition would convey an individual conception and vision. To discover if he had achieved this correlation between sound and sense, he would declaim it as if it were a piece of verse. The result, at its best—clearly not all passages reach or demand such intensity—is a text of complex mental, emotional and sensual reverberations. It must be hoped that not too much of this effect is lost in transposing these reverberations, over a time-gap so large and a cultural gap even larger, into a language whose sound and structure differ so greatly. Fortunately, a couple of Flaubert's stylistic devices go nicely into English: first, his extensive use of indirect, reported speech in which, instead of: She said: *'He's coming to see me'*, you write: *He was coming to see her*, leaving it unclear whether this is an objective statement by the author or an expectation of a character. This device is easily adaptable to make dreams, memories, or hallucinations appear not imagined but real, obviously useful in dealing, for example, with such a fantasizer as Frédéric Moreau. Secondly, Flaubert's favourite tense, the imperfect, translates excellently into English, which provides 'he went', 'was going', 'would go', and other forms. Proust called Flaubert 'the man of the imperfect', and a tense used to express incomplete or concurrent actions is admirably suited to convey the confused round of constantly recurring events and situations, similar but never identical, which forms a basic pattern of the novel.

Much critical—and too much uncritical—ink has been

spilt to prove the autobiographical nature of the novel, based on the premise of a similar starting-point: Flaubert's 'vision' at the age of fourteen on a Trouville beach of Élisa, 26 years old and shortly to become Madame Schlesinger, matches Frédéric Moreau's first sight of Marie Arnoux on the boat to Montereau. The parallel can be developed: Flaubert was also a provincial with a bossy mother, under her financial sway, unable to form stable relationships—luckily for us: otherwise we'd all have been deprived of his masterpieces, and critics (whom Flaubert disliked) of a highly lucrative industry. But the biographical aspect cannot be sustained: Élisa had an illegitimate child, and eventually became deranged (she must have lacked Marie's resilience in coping with an impossible husband). But although not an autobiography, *L'Éducation sentimentale* shows Frédéric Moreau with enough temperamental similarities, including even hints of homosexuality in his relationships with Deslauriers and Arnoux, to enable his creator to identify, even in ironical distaste, with this bewildered dreamer, incapable of enjoying any but prospective and retrospective pleasures, and to give intensity and depth of feeling to Frédéric's rather banal predicament—raw young men in love with beautiful older married women are two-a-penny, in fact and fiction. These similarities may well explain why, with all his silliness and conceit, Frédéric is still rather engaging, generous and kind, like his creator, and until thoroughly 'educated' by the sophistications of the metropolis, a relatively upright young man, though he can never nerve himself to be truthful to his mother: but moral cowardice is a relatively consistent trait in all the characters.

These characters are mainly far less pleasant: all liars, usually cheats, and often callous. They are largely middle-class, sometimes of the raffish sort; Flaubert found this sort of bourgeois less boring than most; there are also a few aristocrats, often even more dubious, whose talents of dissembling make it easy, when necessary, for them to parade as middle-class; no peasants, apart from the occasional, usually uncomplimentary reference; a few members of the working classes, with a definitely sympathetic glimpse at desperate, unemployed, and famished manual labourers. With his private income, Flaubert was himself a member of the bourgeoisie—a reluctant one—and he wisely sticks to depicting the class he knew best. In any case, he was of the opinion that in modern times there was little moral difference between the classes, all equally selfish, avid for material gain and philistine, and thus, by his definition, bourgeois. Flaubert has frequently been accused of painting his characters too black, though post-Hitler, post-Stalin generations might have some justification for finding his view of humanity rather rosy. One can adopt a less dramatic level: are his characters not merely putting into practice the normal moral standards of any strictly commercial society? Of course, we can see that none of *us* could behave like that; but are we so sure of our colleagues, our neighbours, even—horrible thought—some of our friends?

In fact, Flaubert was all too well aware of the aesthetic dangers of painting an excessively black picture of mankind in a novel; he himself wrote that a novelist must not feel hatred, pity, or anger towards his characters, but he could never feel too much sympathy. His insistence on the importance of creating his characters from the inside, of 'getting under their skin', was in itself a sort of guarantee of sympathy; few people find themselves detestable. The most disagreeable are thus shown with redeeming features: even Roque adores his daughter. Others can plead extenuating circumstances: both Deslauriers and Rosanette have suffered deprived childhoods which would satisfy the most exacting psychiatrist. Similarly, the most virtuous are flawed: the loyal Dussardier, brave as a lion, is like putty in the hands of the tough feminist and part-time money-lender and procuress Vatnaz, who has also, incidentally, not had an easy early life. This idealistic but dim Dussardier is a particularly good example of a truth which emerges quite convincingly during the novel: sentimentality, by losing touch with reality, leads to an inflexible belief in abstract principles; thus, the 'democrats' Sénécal and Deslauriers show no love of ordinary people. Even the virtuous Madame Arnoux is dogmatically conventional to the point of dullness—can this be why her husband has a weakness for lively tarts? Not that her shortcomings make her less touching: Flaubert's impartial sympathy ensures that, however imperfect his characters may be morally, they are always to be viewed as human beings, which is something the characters find rather difficult to do between themselves: the novel abounds in derogatory references to 'that other man (or woman)', as tiresome or hateful. As Sartre has pointed out: 'Hell is other people'.

Any choice of character by an author is clearly biased, but Flaubert does present his characters in a way calculated to produce a plausible semblance of impartiality. After a brief physical description, the sort of first impression we might have on meeting someone in real life, the reader gets to know them in stages, by their words, gestures and actions, as it were externally, again as in real life, and often through the eyes and ears of the somewhat naïve Frédéric. Readers are thus required to be particularly alert and interpret for themselves signs which he fails to pick up. These signs are often disconcerting; words and actions do not necessarily match and it thus becomes difficult or impossible to grasp people's motives. Can we even then be sure that the characters themselves know exactly what they're doing or why they're doing it? We can well begin to think that self-ignorance as much as self-interest is the basis of much human behaviour. Certainly it appears that some feelings or thoughts are either too dimly or perhaps too strongly perceived to be capable of communication; there seems to be an inaccessible core, an individual source of feeling, of joy or suffering, perhaps the most valuable part, within even the most ordinary people. Indeed, in Flaubert's aesthetic canon, there are no such people as ordinary persons. 'We can only produce an ideal if we respect what is true and truth only by generalizing', he wrote, and as a result, his characters, while being types, are also, at the same time, abundantly individual: Arnoux, who seems to have taken a good deal of his truth to life from the highly individual Monsieur Schlesinger, the husband of Élisa and whom Flaubert knew quite well, is a splendidly flamboyant example of this blend of general and particular.

Flaubert's characters certainly have one general trait in common: their inconsistency. This can obviously get them into trouble, but the constant disparity not only between words and actions but between hopes or ambitions and achievement is a prime source of humorous irony: Arnoux's antics in combining art and business, wife and mistresses, or Frédéric's in combining girlfriend with fiancée and a grand passion are very funny, which doesn't prevent them from being sad as well; on a broader canvas, Deslauriers' efforts to fulfil his personal ambitions while remaining true to his democratic principles in a highly fluid political situation are also comic, if similarly disheartening. And in the whole novel there is no more hilarious and at the same time chilling episode than the sentimental, blinkered clap-trap passing as serious democratic debate at the appalling meeting of the republican *Club de l'Intelligence*. But we note that these discrepancies between theory and practice are only pathetic, never tragic. In this basically bourgeois world, tragedy would imply and involve a greater commitment and depth of feeling than Flaubert's characters are capable of. Only very rarely, as in the case of Madame Arnoux, are we deeply moved. How could characters so self-centred and inconsistent hope to appear as, at best, superior clowns?

Flaubert's questioning of our motives goes deep. If Frédéric loves Madame Arnoux as deeply as he thinks, how do we explain the visit he makes as soon as he first arrives in Paris as a student? Does his final gesture towards Madame Dambreuse spring purely from that love? Constant irony makes it hard to see if irony is intended and when readers are treated purely as spectators or eavesdroppers, when sensible comments are placed in the mouths of otherwise plainly unreliable characters, or vice versa, they hardly know what to think. Frédéric's romantic rigmarole to Madame Arnoux in Chapter VI of Part 3 is clearly a smoke-screen, even if it may well, in part, represent some of his past feelings; but is the scene in his Paris garden, when he offers Marie its solitary rose, an impromptu gesture of real affection, part of a seduction technique or a parody of a romantic stereotype? Or is it all three, in problematical proportions? Similar riddles are posed throughout the novel and indeed provide much of its fascination.

It's an amusing irony that Flaubert himself complained that his characters were boring, largely because they were so middle-class. As he once wrote: 'Nothing is as bloody as the country except the middle classes and when you get both together, the bloodiness is complete.' But he did also write that 'wit and charm are the almost exclusive apanage of Bohemians' and he does depict Arnoux's circle of friends and helpers, who are largely middle-class Bohemians, as mostly amusing and lively. Despite this, he seems to have toyed with the idea of giving his novel the title of *Les Fruits Secs*, which is fruit failing to fulfil its early promise or, more bluntly, failures. He didn't eventually use the title, perhaps because it would have made too explicit the ironical fact that worldly success in the novel goes to people such as Hussonnet, the frivolous time-serving buffoon of a journalist (Flaubert disliked newspapers) or the morally ambiguous and extraordinarily astute Martinon, the complete rationalist amongst so many romantics. But we need not be surprised at this; Flaubert's private view of public recognition was, as he wrote, that 'honours disgrace you' (though he himself accepted the Legion of Honour!), 'a title is degrading, and official position stultifying'. This attitude may explain the undercurrent of subversion, gentle rather than violent, a teasing view of those in authority—particularly in politics and finance—which deflates them without ever suggesting that the world can exist without some sort of authority; it is a sort of quietist anarchy, tinged with humour and occasionally a little desperation.

But what of Frédéric himself? Is he not to be judged a failure? He certainly never brings his own dreams of various sorts of fame to fruition, but these are all presented as silly anyway, particularly in a character whose inadequacies are pretty plain, so their non-fulfilment can scarcely be deemed failure. More positively, his rejection of a hypocritical and corrupt 'smart' society can be read as a moral victory, even a sign of wisdom and not too inglorious. With Flaubert little is certain but is he not suggesting that success and failure are imposters? He himself wrote: 'We must laugh and cry, enjoy and suffer, in a word, vibrate to our full capacity . . . I think that's what being really human means.' Frédéric has lived in this way and in his old age will surely have many happy events to recall, as well as sad ones to embellish; blissful moments in the course of his love of Marie which, Flaubert tells us, he would not have exchanged for the most glamorous love affair. And in point of fact, where glamorous women are concerned, he doesn't do too badly either: for both men and women, he has charisma—and, of course, plenty of money. He'll have more happy memories than most men. Flaubert once wrote of himself as experiencing, on 'sunny' days of enthusiasm, glimpses of a state of mind higher than life, in which fame would be of no account and even happiness pointless, and Frédéric is also shown as enjoying similar glimpses. Even the 'mental stagnation' mentioned at the end of the novel is rather belied by the liveliness of his last conversation with Deslauriers. So the reader would be wise not to 'write him off'; Flaubert's openness as a novelist is so extensive that peremptory judgements are very dangerous. And, after all, like almost all the other characters, he *survives*, an important factor in those revolutionary days and one which we in modern times are increasingly growing to appreciate.

Those revolutionary days form an essential part of Flaubert's novel. Having transformed his own Byronic rebellion into a wrily ironic and probing psychological exploration of personal relationships, the novelist entwines it with extraordinary virtuosity with a highly personal, thought-provoking account of the 1848 Revolution in France, which was to be crucial for the future development of European society, specifically in the evolution of socialism and capitalism. It is an account which puts the novel on a different plane from most, setting it side by side with Stendhal's *La Chartreuse de Parme* and even with that heroic sacred cow *War and Peace*, an aristocratic masterpiece which, like many master-pieces, requires heroism to read to the end; Flaubert's novel is certainly less of an adolescent fantasy than the first and even funnier; far less sermonizing and shorter than the second; and far more relevant to the current human condition than either. Flaubert had thought deeply about politics and undertook such painstaking research—original and secondary sources of books, articles, pamphlets, newspapers, periodicals, eyewitnesses (of whom he was one)—that professional historians recognize *L'Éducation sentimentale* as a valuable contribution to the history of the period: 'my foregrounds are imaginary, my backgrounds real', he wrote. They are vivid as well as accurate, enlivened by exact, individual details; we feel we are actually present: we know it is twenty past one when the Tuileries Palace is occupied, that in the Palais Royal later on there are *seven* bonfires burning. It is a fabric of minute observation of small events and objects, not all necessarily 'significant', nor even directly relevant, but rendered with great care for sound and rhythm which charms, like the simple details of a Chinese poem; a blend of imagined and real, satisfying in its authenticity and compelling in its immediacy.

Though its main events and protagonists are referred to, Flaubert makes no attempt to give a complete picture of the Revolution; he is a novelist, not an historian. In his choice of incident, he maintains his customary ironic slant: one of the main events he records, which Frédéric witnesses quite by chance—typically, he'd been heading off in the wrong direction—is the heroic attack on a building by insurgents to release prisoners from government custody, who, however, had unfortunately been transferred elsewhere; and as we read on, we see the high-minded struggle of the republicans quickly degenerate into looting and drunken rioting. Not surprisingly, Frédéric's enthusiasm soon turns to disgust and, ironically, just as he misses the February Revolution because of amorous preoccupations, so he misses the most crucial event of the entire Revolution, the desperate, failed workers' June uprising, by retreating into the country, though he does see some of its dreadful results when he returns to Paris generously hoping to come to the help of a wounded friend (Part 3, Chapter I)—one of Flaubert's most vivid pictures and a sinister foresight of bombed twentieth-century cities. For the modern reader, of course, as for the contemporary reader, the whole struggle is sheer dramatic irony: we know that the cause being fought for so spiritedly by the republicans is doomed.

Since political opinions, indeed views on every subject, are voiced not by the author but through the mouths of characters and are thus often conflicting and inconsistent, we cannot expect any one single explicit statement. On one occasion, however, Flaubert surprisingly appears to break his rule of impartiality to speak approvingly of the humanitarian liberalism of the early republican government set up immediately following the February Revolution. Nevertheless, the general impression that emerges is that public and private affairs follow a similar course; in all of them, there are certain underlying causes, often based on false or trivial evidence, prejudice or misunderstanding as well as on legitimate grounds; but in history, as in people's lives, random events and odd, even absurd, chances and coincidences play an often considerable role. Thus, in the 1848 Revolution, certain events, such as a crop failure, were clearly unpredictable and unavoidable; even the eventual uprising in February was triggered off by an unforeseen incident, the shooting of rioters in the boulevard des Capucines and not by design. Flaubert leaves us with an ironical paradox: the perhaps avoidable February uprising led to the humanitarian Second Republic whereas the workers' uprising in June, in many ways justified by desperate unemployment and broken promises, led to the destruction not only of socialism but of democratic principles. The power of the human will is limited; facts, however absurd they may seem, cannot be changed by sentimental platitudes or abstract principles. Within the wide parameters of general probability, chance and coincidence can be decisive; there is, of course, a wide gap between such a belief and a belief in causeless nihilism and this is a leap that Flaubert does not make.

Flaubert's research was not confined to history and politics; in his concern for authenticity, he checked on everything necessary: financial operations on the Paris Bourse, race meetings (he used the names of real race-horses), society funerals, croup, restaurant menus, the manufacture of ceramics, women's clothes, available means of transport between Paris and Fontainebleau at a given period; he even visited Chartres which eventually receives only the slightest passing mention. But this sort of accuracy is not half the story: for Flaubert, just as characters had to be individual as well as typical, so description needed a personal imprint; he told his disciple Maupassant that he must make his reader aware how, in any cab rank, one horse is different from the fifty others behind or in front of it; he should forget everything he'd ever seen or heard about horses and render his personal vision. Flaubert possessed this gift to an extraordinary degree. He once informed the writer and critic Taine that while writing, he would have a sudden vivid glimpse of, say, a roomful of furniture, including the stains on one piece, only to find eventually that he didn't need to use any of it. His imaginative inner eye had visualized, as it were, for the sake of visualizing; and he spoke, too, of the joy which accompanied such visions. Transcribed in such a state of excitement with the full armoury of his stylistic resources, it is not surprising that even trivial details have an extraordinary impact and create such persuasive moods. It is a descriptive power which makes nonsense of the criticism that 'not enough happens' in the novel: for alert readers, something is impinging on their consciousness all the time; and Flaubert is so subtle and so mischievous that if you are not careful, you may fail to see the point or miss some of the fun. Perhaps this is why on every rereading, one finds some hitherto unnoticed delight.

Flaubert badly needed a heroine; deeply touching as Marie Arnoux is, she is very much a creation of Frédéric's own vision of her. The novelist found what he wanted in

Paris, to some extent also a creation of Frédéric's as he moped drearily around Nogent, but also existing very much in her own right in her cosmopolitan sophistication, bustling boulevards lined with trees and luxury restaurants, cafés and casinos (the brothels, only hinted at, must be in the side-streets), stimulating intellectuality and political activity, fine gardens and monuments, elegantly alluring women. But all that glitters is, naturally, not gold. Paris also makes a good anti-heroine: Frédéric finds the grand evening carriage parade on the Champs-Elysées less glamorous when he's part of it; luxury restaurants can be the expensive scene of squabbles, sickening humiliations and sordid seduction; the surface of the lovely Seine, gleaming as in a future Impressionist painting, can inspire suicidal thoughts; the alluring women are tricky and costly to bed, the fine Tuileries Palace can be taken over by a mob and the leafy terrace of its gardens houses below it haggard, famished insurgents. Above all, there is universal greed; the basic reality of this polished society is money, rarely honestly come by: property speculation; Stock Exchange gambling (did no one warn Frédéric that shares can go down as well as up?), with special interest in the 'sunrise' industries of the age, gas and railways; shady art deals; smear journalism; and, as expected, the oldest trade of all, thoroughly explored by Flaubert, who was quite an expert—prostitution. It is ironical that in a novel entitled *A Sentimental Education*, the main basis of relations between the sexes is financial; Flaubert was happy to show that there may not be a very big gap between venal and 'respectable' love. Rosanette is an excellent example of a blurring of such distinctions. She is a representative of a very widespread Parisian breed, the superior kept woman or *lorette*, a name derived, charmingly, from Our Lady of Loretto, the patron saint of the local church in the Bréda quarter where such ladies congregated in the 1840s. The lower income bracket, students, impecunious journalists, and so on, make do with the cheaper, semi-amateur working-class or shop-assistant *grisette*: Hussonnet, Martinon, and Deslauriers all find them handy at various times. For greater speed or convenience, there are plenty of ordinary street whores.

In this connection, one incident in the novel has aroused in the past a good deal of controversy. In the last chapter, in the course of happily reminiscing with Deslauriers, Frédéric says that the best moment in his life is an abortive visit, as a schoolboy, to a Nogent brothel—he took fright and flight at the door. He may, of course, have been half-joking, for many of Flaubert's characters say things they don't mean. But assuming he is speaking seriously, may he not merely be suggesting, rather tritely—he is something of a specialist in triteness—that anticipation is better than realization? Or, more interestingly, may not Flaubert be hinting that despite his 'sentimental' apprenticeship in Paris, where he has learned rather nasty habits, Frédéric has remained impenitently an idealist with a hankering after the lost innocence of youth? We shall never know, nor do we need to. One thing in his life, however, seems pretty certain: since one of his friends, anxious to 'become a man', goes to him for help, it is very likely that even while languishing for his 'great love', Frédéric's sexual hygiene will have included more easily available females.

Another major, perhaps even more expensive pleasure than love, and possibly preferred by many, is eating and its normal French concomitant, drinking. Meals of many kinds form one principal thread in the pattern of the novel. Some are nasty, student-style meals in the Latin Quarter or worse; one of Deslauriers's golden dreams is to be rich enough to buy a decent meal—a noble dream for a vehement anti-bourgeois—and how he envies Frédéric, one of whose first thoughts on becoming rich is to eat luxuriously; Hussonnet gets round the problem by cadging meals, like any sensible reporter before the expense account had become a recognized institution. But it is the extravagant, large-scale blow-out that is central to the novel, the established gastronomic ritual of lavish middle-class luncheon and dinner parties, so useful for making friends and influencing people, showing off your wealth—conspicuous consumption was not a twentieth-century invention—clinching a deal, achieving prestige, indulging your greed in a generally acceptable fashion.

For the novelist, it is the perfect vehicle for gathering people together who provide, often unwittingly, information about their emotions and attitudes, advancing the narrative, particularly useful when direct portrayal of action is being avoided, and, of course, showing people making pigs of themselves. By using parallel meals, Flaubert can also provide a structure for the novel and hint at contrasts or similarities between different milieux. The quintessential entrepreneur Arnoux provides flashy food and lively conversation while the aristocratic banker Dambreuse and his elegant wife lay on meals in exquisite taste to the accompaniment, alas, of dull social chit-chat and money-talk; Cisy's 'smart' party is over-lavish, particularly in the drink, and disastrous, as might be expected from such a silly man; Frédéric's house-warming brings out his friendliness and the envy and selfishness of most of his friends, competitors in the Parisian rat-race. We must always remember that these were peculiarly unsettled times, offering many dangers as well as many opportunities, a free-for-all with the devil taking the hindmost, and that such conditions bring out the worst (Sénécal) as well as the best (Dussardier) in anyone. One thing is certain: whatever else it may be, Frédéric's Paris is too vigorous to be decadent; these self-indulgent bourgeois are tough; perhaps the most remarkable trait of middle class and aristocrat alike is their determination to survive. In her corruption as in her dynamic gaiety and luxury, we are forced to accept Paris, warts and all.

Another example of this irresistible energy is that very Parisian occasion, the public or private dance or ball, which forms a similar pattern in the novel to the accounts of meals. Arnoux again scores highly: the dance at Rosanette's is a splendid romp, all the more sparkling since it is viewed through the unsophisticated eyes of a still innocent Frédéric. It is a fancy-dress ball, an excellent opportunity for people (dissatisfied with their lives or their status) to let their hair down and play out their fantasies: middle-class women got up as marchionesses, or simple (innocent?) village girls, their generally ageing partners as navvies or macho dockers; there's even a consumptive good-time girl, pathetically coughing her lungs up, an anticipation—with hindsight—of a future Romantic cliché with Mimi Pinson in Murger's *Scènes de la Vie de Bohème* and *La Dame aux Camélias*, both of which appeared in 1848.

Rosanette's frolic contrasts markedly with the Dambreuses' white-tie affair, though the ladies' low-cut dresses do suggest a hint of more fun off-stage (a hint later confirmed) and, as further evidence of hypocrisy, smutty talk does appear in due course; we do not expect Flaubert to resist the chance of a dig at any pious façade of respectability. The public ball attended by Frédéric, Arnoux and various friends, also useful in introducing the mountebank Delmar, is a romp even more tumultuous than Rosanette's and of considerable social interest as well as enlightening us further on several characters; here the tone is given by the frenetic music—Offenbach is not far away—and by the splendidly vulgar blend of exotic architecture: Moorish and Gothic, a touch of China in the roof and Venetian lamps, of course.

In this hectic metropolis people dash about in all directions. Carriages are essential, the smarter the better, clearly a status symbol as important as the modern motor car and one that Flaubert was obviously fascinated by. Not to have one, and the most luxurious possible, is a grave solecism and Frédéric actually has his girl snapped up under his nose by a rival who can offer her a lift home. He is in any case continually being frustrated and bewildered by going to the wrong place or arriving at the wrong time. Flaubert is plainly anxious to foster a similar confusion as to time in the minds of his readers: how else can we explain the odd fact that in an historical novel, firm dates are so sparse? Indicating time by mention of some notorious scandal or crime, the performance of a play or some vague phrase such as 'in May', 'that June', with no indication of the year, could hardly have been enlightening, even for a contemporary reader; but it is a deliberate reminder that the period is chaotic and liable to make people lose track of the succession of events; it also ingeniously hints that when people are so selfishly absorbed in personal concerns, chronological time tends to become obscured.

Frédéric is the perfect example of this self-absorbed *perpetuum mobile*. His solitary walks round Paris at all hours of the day and night, in all weathers, are, in Sartre's barbarous phrase, a superb 'objectivization of the subjective' in their blend of inner and outer worlds. Two longer trips, described in great detail, have especial importance and illustrate not only Flaubert's technique of describing parallel events but his use of description as metaphor representing much more than its face value. His river trip at the beginning of Part One during which he experiences his vision of Marie Arnoux supplies in many of its particulars a prefiguration of the course of the novel: the initial bustle, the ensuing routine, aspects of landscape, the thoughts and actions of the passengers, the glimpses of Arnoux, philandering yet considerate, business-like yet impulsive, the expectancy, romantic dreams, bursts of hope, elation, gloom, frustration, even resignation. Similarly, at the beginning of Part Two, his parallel journey in the opposite direction, and especially his drive through the southern suburbs of Paris, gives warning that his intoxicating city is a flawed heroine; many details—the midwife's establishment and the massive fortifications are obvious examples—turn out to be prophetically sinister.

These two journeys are particularly meaningful but there are numerous other themes and situations which act both as metaphors and as strands in the web of patterns that replaces the conventional story-line: music—the harpist on the Montereau boat, Madame Arnoux's pure voice singing drawing-room ballads which would be sloppy for anyone other than a star-struck lover, Delmar's bellowing, equally conventional but so representative of the times, Madame Dambreuse's soulless piano playing (life is less easy to control than a keyboard); journalism and the Press—Deslauriers and his confounded newspaper, Hussonnet, who makes a living and a whole career out of bluff and buffoonery, Frédéric, who makes one grotesque incursion into journalism, Vatnaz, with her pathetic yearning to be printed (as a feminist, she could in any case hardly expect fair treatment from Flaubert); art-dealing—Pellerin, the idealistic faker, the interesting aesthetician but lousy painter, though in the end the joke is on his creator who failed to foresee the prestigious success of the art form to which Pellerin finally turns, Arnoux, the brash southerner, the modern man, the compulsive liar who's already trying to turn art into a saleable commodity and ends up selling hideous and sentimental religious objects; bastardy, involving the Roques and the Dambreuses as well as Frédéric and Rosanette; religion, which was for Flaubert largely a social smoke-screen, strangely involving the different pieties of Madame Dambreuse and Marie Arnoux as well as her husband and having odd affinities with dogmatic politics—Sénécal's views on religion are particularly interesting; the provinces and Paris, contrasting in life-style and politics, with the provincial National Guards rushing to quell the uprising of the Paris workers; wills and legacies affecting the lives of all the main characters—Frédéric, who without his inherited wealth would not count for much, Deslauriers, who by his rigid views on the subject of succession ruins any chance of an academic career, which would have transformed his life, Martinon, who needs money for a successful career in politics, the Dambreuses; venality—it's difficult to meet anyone who's not open to some form of bribery; plays and theatre-going, clearly, in different ways, one of the most important aspects of cultural, social, and even political life; various aspects of male and female lust, which are thoroughly explored; protectionism and free trade, a persistent theme and as modern as the 45 per cent income tax introduced by the Second Republic; usury—everyone is always borrowing or lending: indeed, the climactic anti-climax of the novel turns on debt as much as love.

Human artefacts and natural scenery are also important in the pattern of the novel. Carefully, even lovingly, described rooms with their furniture and furnishings, ornaments, pictures, and even books enable the reader to compare or, more often, contrast the social and particularly the financial situation of their occupants while, superimposed on the general impression, tiny personal touches reveal individual tastes; when people are present, Flaubert often further personalizes his interiors by creating specific moods, like a skilled cameraman, with long shots, close-ups, stills, quick shifts, soft focus, and particularly lighting—he's continually drawing our attention to windows and lamps. Single objects often assume disproportionate significance; the Renaissance casket shuttling between Arnoux's wife and one of his mistresses is the most striking example but there are a number of others: a broken parasol throws light on both Frédéric and Arnoux; Rosanette's portrait by Pellerin has a metaphorical importance far beyond its artistic interest; the different colours of women's eyes draw Frédéric's attention as much as their boots and slippers (he's obviously a foot fetishist); the almost ethereal beauty of Madame Arnoux's hands as personalized by Frédéric's loving gaze contrasts with Vatnaz's claws; cashmere shawls give a lot of pleasure and cause even greater trouble—cashmere clearly stands for luxury, just as cigars seem to represent vulgarity; North African furnishings are smart and its materials chic—so, ironically, does Flaubert remind us of the bloody conquest of Algeria by the French. We must, however, be careful not to exaggerate the importance in the work of 'symbolic' objects; hunting the symbol can easily become undignified; Flaubert loved depicting and we can enjoy his descriptions as we can enjoy a painting without trying to find a 'deeper' meaning in every detail.

Similarly, natural scenery exists in the novel, both in its own right and to provide particular strands in the web of the overall pattern: the Seine flows throughout the novel, sometimes beautiful but indifferent, sometimes charmingly delicate (the waterfall at Nogent, when Frédéric is with Louise), and even once, at Saint Cloud, nearly sinking the feckless Arnoux's skiff; the sun's glare, impersonal and all-powerful, tires out the restless city but beautifies its parade of carriages down the Champs-Elysées; the landscape of Nogent is dull and domesticated and damp in winter (Frédéric is used to that: it's usually raining on him in

Paris, too) and there's also a hint of danger from Roque's wolves; Auteuil, the scene of another of Frédéric's idylls, is pretty rather than grand—almost too pretty and with a touch of autumn melancholy. But the set-piece—Flaubert claimed he wanted to avoid set-pieces but his visual exuberance clearly got the upper hand—is the idyll in the Forest of Fontainebleau, carefully organized but with all the immediacy of notes taken on the spot: solemnity and exhilaration, a painterly chiaroscuro with cinematic long shots and close-ups, lurking danger (monstrous rocks, smells of decay, leafless branches in midsummer), the delicacy of gossamer and butterflies, glittering water and greenery of every shade, sun and sudden showers, hills and valleys, low bushes and towering trees, details matching, hinting at or even generating their many moods, at times with humour (how can one find solitude?), at others with pathos (Rosanette's sad childhood), set in the present yet containing many hints of the past and the future.

The reader of *L'Éducation sentimentale* need not therefore be much concerned by the ostensible framework of the novel—three parts, divided into six chapters, plus one extra chapter forming a sort of epilogue in Part 3; nor even by the love of Frédéric and Marie. The essence of the novel lies in an intricate, endlessly suggestive play of mirrors reflecting a bewildered age, not too unlike ours, and casting light, often ironical, on large areas of life without ever robbing them of their mystery; nor is emotion always ridiculed and even the fun is hardly ever cruel. But it was too puzzling a blend for Flaubert's contemporaries; the critics largely savaged it and the public held off. Anti-heroes were not yet in fashion; the humorous undermining of both left and right—and most people in the middle—flicked too many readers on the raw; and like many truths, cool light cast on inconstancy in even a 'grand passion' is not comforting. Flaubert's friend, not always a loyal one, Maxime du Camp, probably hit the nail on the head when he wrote that the public wanted only works which said 'yes' and 'no' whereas Flaubert prefers to throw out hints; it's interesting how often the expression 'no doubt' occurs—

meaning, of course, that there is a great deal of doubt. The sophistication of twentieth-century culture has better prepared us to appreciate Flaubert's disillusioned world, still half-embedded in romanticism (aren't we all, willy-nilly?), recognizably modern in many ways while remote enough to have great nostalgic charm. Flaubert himself tells us how to approach the novel: 'Don't read like children, for diversion, nor for instruction, like ambitious persons; no, read it in order to live'—meaning, of course, imaginatively, in our minds; at the time he was writing Madame Bovary, he'd even said that his purpose was to set people dreaming. It is to be an aesthetic and dispassionate appreciation ('stupidity lies in wanting to draw conclusions'), penetrating into a stylized world, so much preferred by Flaubert to the real one, but which still retains in its characters and events and even more in its backgrounds, plausible links with the world of ordinary experience.

Culler (see Bibliography) reports Ford Madox Ford's opinion that people cannot consider themselves educated until they've read *L'Éducation sentimentale* fourteen times. This number seems perhaps excessive; but if you do, it is pretty certain that, on each occasion, further thoughts will come into your mind, new details will strike you, a little nudge from Flaubert will affect your mood and set you off in new directions. It is an extremely addictive novel; all one needs to do is to relax and give oneself over to the wiles of this elusive persuader. Remember to sip, not gulp; this is vintage stuff.

MAIN CHARACTERS

Frédéric Moreau: the provincial 'young man' of the sub-title; his 'education' in Paris is a major theme of the novel.

Madame Moreau: his widowed mother, most respectable; has ambitions for her son.

Monsieur Arnoux: an entrepreneur, speculator and womanizer.

Marie Arnoux: his wife, mother of two children, Frédéric's 'grand amour'.

Deslauriers: Frédéric's close friend, bright, ambitious, aggressive.

Martinon: a farmer's son, a clever, hard-working careerist; a man of reason.

de Cisy: a viscount from Brittany, dapper, with social pretensions.

Hussonnet: journalist, dramatic critic, and clown.

Pellerin: a painter with more aesthetic theories than talent.

Dussardier: a 'nice young man', modestly employed, an idealistic republican.

Sénécal: uncompromising, puritanical, a sometime mathematics teacher, an egg-head.

Regimbart: a boozy revolutionary chauvinist, a great pal of Arnoux's.

Mademoiselle Vatnaz: a frustrated feminist with literary pretensions.

Rose-Annette Bron (the 'Marshal'): an attractive, lively tart.

Delmar: singer, showman; later cashes in on playing revolutionary parts on the stage.

Monsieur Dambreuse: an aristocratic politician, time-server, and financier.

Madame Dambreuse: his considerably younger, exquisitely elegant, and very determined wife.

Monsieur Roque: Dambreuse's unsavoury agent.

Louise Roque: his impulsive, unsophisticated, red-headed daughter.

SELECT BIBLIOGRAPHY

Numerous modern French editions of *L'Éducation sentimentale*, either as separate editions or as part of collected works, include: *Belles Lettres* (latest edition 1958), introduction and notes by R. Dumesnil; Gallimard, *Folio* (1965), preface by A. Thibaudet; *Club de l'Honnête Homme* (1971), edited by M. Bardèche; *Lettres françaises* (1979), introduction and notes by A. Raitt; *Classiques* Garnier (1984), introduction and notes by W. M. Wetherill; the Flammarion edition (1985), introduction and notes by C. Gothot-Mersh. I wish to record a debt to these editors and also to the late Pierre Larousse for his invaluable *Grand Dictionnaire Universel du XIXe Siècle*.

There are various editions of Flaubert's correspondence; Francis Steegmuller has provided an American translation of parts of it: *Letters of Gustave Flaubert 1830–1857* (Harvard University Press, 1980).

General critical works on Flaubert are legion; those on *L'Éducation sentimentale* alone are too numerous to list and in any case largely in French, even when they come from the pens of English-speaking experts such as Fairlie, Raitt, or Wetherill. A selection of relatively recent works in English or American, likely to be in print or available in libraries and of interest to a non-specialist, would include:

J. Barnes, *Flaubert's Parrot* (Jonathan Cape, 1984 also in Picador).

V. Brombert, *The Novels of Flaubert, Themes and Techniques* (Princeton University Press, 1966).

P. Cortland, *The Sentimental Adventure* (Mouton, 1967).

J. Culler, *The Uses of Uncertainty* (Paul Elek, 1974).

A. Fairlie, *Imagination and Language* (Cambridge University Press, 1981).

H. Levin, *The Gates of Horn: a Study of Five French Realists* (New York, Oxford University Press, 1963).

H. Lottman, *Flaubert* (Methuen, 1989).

M. Nadeau, *The Greatness of Flaubert* (Alcove Press, 1972; translated from the French).

R. J. Sherrington, *Three novels by Flaubert* (Oxford University Press, 1970).

E. Starkie, *Flaubert, the Making of the Master*, and *Flaubert, the Master: A Critical and Biographical Study* (both Weidenfeld and Nicholson, 1967 and 1971 respectively).

A. Thorlby, *Flaubert and the Art of Realism* (Bowes and Bowes, 1956).

S. Ullmann, *Style in the French Novel* (Blackwell, 1960).

Readers wishing to pursue in greater detail the social, political, and historical aspects of the novel briefly touched on in the Introduction, Historical Sketch, and Notes of this edition will obviously face a wide choice. Everything relevant from the pen of Theodore Zeldin will be informative and stimulating; further reading could usefully include:

E. L. Newman and R. L. Simpson, *Historical Dictionary of France from the 1815 Restoration to the Second Empire*, 2 vols. (Greenwood Press, Westport, Connecticut, and Aldwych Press, London, 1987).

J. Plamenatz, *The Revolutionary Movement in France, 1815–71* (Longmans, 1965).

A CHRONOLOGY OF GUSTAVE FLAUBERT

1821   Born in Hôtel-Dieu Hospital, Rouen, where his father was chief surgeon.

1835   Starts writing (short tales, some historical); spends holidays in Nogent-sur-Seine with an uncle; makes frequent later visits.

1836   Is spellbound by a vision of Élisa Foucault on a Trouville beach (c.f. Frédéric's vision of Marie Arnoux on the boat to Montereau, p. 6; Élisa is at the time living with Maurice Schlesinger, whose life and character were to offer material for Monsieur Arnoux; Maurice married Élisa in 1840 when her husband died).

1837–8   At school in Rouen continues writing, often stories of morbid, wild Romanticism (e.g. Titles such as 'Dream of Hell', 'Memoirs of a Madman'; one story is of a savage rape by a man/ape). He is already reading and enjoying Shakespeare, Cervantes (Don Quixote will remain a favourite book), and the Marquis de Sade. Writes a five-act historical drama entitled *Loys XI*.

1841   Enters Law Faculty of the Sorbonne; during his studies frequents the Schlesingers and Pradiers (c.f. p. 60).

1843   Starts writing *L'Éducation sentimentale* (first version); fails his second law examination (first one passed in 1842).

1844   Mysterious seizure of an epileptic nature; gives up law.

1845   Finishes *L'Éducation sentimentale* (extremely autobiographical with little similarity to the later version).

1846   Father and sister die; settles with his mother and, until her marriage, his niece, in a large eighteenth-century property in Croisset, close to Rouen. Starts a protracted, intermittent (Mummy disapproves!), and fairly stormy affair with attractive, well-known poet, novelist, and dramatist Louise Colet (born 1810, long-standing and unfaithful mistress of Victor Cousin, see pp. 15, 286); her affair with Flaubert (her only title to fame) finally ended in 1854.

1848   With friend Maxime du Camp and particularly well-loved fellow-writer Bouilhet witnesses the February Revolution, including sack of the Palais Royal (see p. 316); Maxime later wounded in June riots.

1849–51 Finishes *La Tentation de St Antoine* (first version); reads it to Maxime who advises him to burn it; leaves with him for Near East, always alluring to the Romantic generation; visits Egypt (where he's likely to have acquired his syphilis), the Holy Land, Rhodes, Constantinople, Athens, the Pelopponese, Naples, Pompeii, Rome, Florence, Venice, Cologne, Brussels, and back in Paris in time to see Louis Napoleon's coup of 2 December. Has started on *Madame Bovary*.

1855   Rents a flat in Paris where he henceforth often resides.

1856   Starts on second version of *La Tentation de St Antoine*, of which a few fragments are published in a review. Publication of *Madame Bovary* begins in serial form.

1857   Flaubert acquitted of charge of publishing an immoral work. Published now as a book, *Madame Bovary* is a great success. Starts work on historical novel *Salammbô*. Lively social life in Paris begins, at first mainly with writers (the critic Sainte-Beuve, the Goncourt brothers, the poet and critic Théophile Gautier, Renan). Goes to Tunis to research his novel, which is set in ancient Carthage.

1862   *Salammbô* published; a great success.

1863   His period of 'smart' society *salon* life takes off, particularly a growing friendship with Princess Mathilde, Napoleon III's cousin; he meets Turgenev; the Goncourts visit him in Croisset.

1864   Begins documentation, planning, and research for final version of *L'Éducation sentimentale*, which he starts writing. Visits Sens, Montereau.

1866   Awarded the Legion of Honour; George Sand, a constant correspondent, twice visits him in Croisset.

1869   Publication of *L'Éducation sentimentale*, which is not well received by public or critics.

1870   During Franco-Prussian War becomes lieutenant in National Guard.

1872	Grief-stricken by death of mother; completes third and final version of *La Tentation de St Antoine*.
1874	*La Tentation de St Antoine* published; well received. Starts work on *Bouvard et Pécuchet*.
1875	His generous financial arrangement with his niece and her husband leads Flaubert to great impoverishment.
1876–7	Composes and publishes *Trois contes* (*Hérodias*, *La Légende de St Julien l'Hospitalier*, *Un Coeur simple*); a considerable success.
1880	Dies with the last chapter of *Bouvard et Pécuchet* uncompleted (it is published in 1881).

A SENTIMENTAL EDUCATION

The Story of a Young Man

PART ONE

CHAPTER I

On the morning of 15 September 1840 the *Ville de Montereau* was lying alongside the quai Saint-Bernard* belching clouds of smoke, all ready to sail.

It was six o'clock and late arrivals were scurrying up out of breath dodging round barrels and hawsers and laundry baskets; the crew were turning a deaf ear to any enquiries; there was a lot of bumping and jostling; baggage was piling up between the two paddle-boxes; and through all this racket the hiss of steam could be heard escaping through the iron plates and covering everything in a whitish pall. The ship's bell was clanging away in the bows.

Finally the vessel cast off and the two banks of the river, packed with warehouses, yards and factories, began to unwind like two broad lengths of ribbon.

Standing motionless beside the helm was a long-haired youth of eighteen holding a sketchbook under his arm. Through the haze he was observing church towers and other notable buildings whose names he didn't know. Then, as Paris slipped swiftly away behind him, he cast one final backward glance over the Île-Saint-Louis, the Cité and Notre-Dame and breathed a heavy sigh.

Frédéric Moreau had recently matriculated and was on his way home to Nogent-sur-Seine* where he'd be kicking his heels for the next couple of months before returning to embark on his legal studies. His mother, having provided him with just sufficient to cover his expenses, had packed him off to Le Havre to visit an uncle who, she hoped, would be putting her son in his will; Frédéric had left him only the previous day, and to compensate for not being able to spend longer in the capital was returning to his home in the provinces by the longest possible route.

The hubbub was subsiding; everyone had settled on a place; a few were clustered round the engine-room, keeping warm; the funnel was puffing steadily away, laboriously gasping out black plumes of smoke; tiny drops of moisture trickled down the brasswork; the deck vibrated under the gentle throbbing from below, and the two paddle wheels churned up the water as they spun round.

The river was bordered on both sides by sandbanks. Rafts of logs heaved quietly up and down in the ship's wash; or you could see the dim figure of a man sitting in a boat, fishing; then, gradually, as the swirling mists lifted, the sun came out, the hill on the right bank of the Seine dropped out of sight, and another one loomed up closer on the opposite side.

This hill was topped by trees dotted between bungalows with hipped roofs. They had sloping gardens separated by newly built walls, iron gates, lawns, greenhouses, and pots of geraniums set at regular intervals on terraces with parapets to lean on and enjoy the view. As they caught glimpses of these small country villas, so charming and peaceful, more than one of the passengers thought longingly of owning one and living out the rest of his days up there, with a nice billiard-room, their own motor launch, a wife, or some such dream. The novel pleasure of a cruise was making people unbend; practical jokers were already getting up to their tricks; there was a good deal of singing. People were in high spirits. All around, glasses were being filled.

Frédéric was thinking of the room he'd be living in in Paris, of an idea for a play, of subjects for a painting, of future passionate affairs of the heart. He felt that the happiness owed to such a pre-eminently sensitive soul as himself was slow in coming. He declaimed a few melancholy lines of verse under his breath as he paced round the deck. He made his way forward, beside the ship's bell, and in the middle of a circle of passengers and crew saw a gentleman busily flirting with a young country girl as he fingered the gold cross she was wearing on her breast. He was a burly fellow, fortyish, with crisp curly hair, his stocky frame squeezed into a velvet morning coat; his cambric shirt had two flashing emerald studs and his baggy white trousers fell

4

over a bizarre pair of red Russian leather boots trimmed in blue.

Unperturbed by Frédéric's presence, he turned several times to give him a quizzical wink. Next he offered cigars all round. Then, no doubt bored by the company, he walked away. Frédéric followed him.

First they discussed the merits of different sorts of tobacco and from there by natural progression turned to women. The man in the red boots proffered the young man advice, expounded theories, told a story or two, quoted himself as an example, all in a friendly way and with an amusingly shameless candour.

He was a republican; much travelled; knew all about the theatre, restaurants and newspaper offices from the inside; was on good terms with all the leading actors and actresses, whom he referred to familiarly by their first names. Frédéric soon found himself confiding his own projects to him; he approved but broke off to peer up at the funnel, then hurriedly mumbled a lengthy calculation under his breath to work out 'how much every stroke of the piston at so many r.p.m. would . . . etc.' Having found the answer, he started admiring the scenery. He confessed he was glad to have got away from the office.

Frédéric was beginning to warm towards him and couldn't resist asking him his name. In one breath the stranger replied:

'Jacques Arnoux, owner of *L'Art industriel*, boulevard Montmartre.'

A servant came up in a gold-braided cap:

'Please sir, would you mind coming below? Missy's crying.'

He disappeared.

L'Art industriel was a hybrid organization, half art magazine, half art gallery. Frédéric had seen huge advertising posters about it a number of times in his local bookshop, with Jacques Arnoux's name prominently displayed.

The sun was beating down, glinting on the iron stancheons, the plates of the rails and the surface of the water, through which the prow was slicing a double wash that

5

surged out towards the banks of the meadows; at every bend in the river the same screen of pale poplars could be seen. The landscape was completely empty. In the sky, tiny white clouds hovered in suspended animation; a vague all-pervasive sense of boredom seemed to be sapping the boat's energy, making those aboard even more insignificant.

Apart from the handful of wealthier first class passengers, the rest were workers and shopkeepers accompanied by their wives and children. As the habit at that time was to travel in shabby clothes, almost all had on old skull-caps or faded hats, threadbare black coats frayed at the elbows from rubbing on desks or frock-coats with button tops ragged from constant wear at work in the shop; you could see the occasional shawl-collared sleeveless jacket over a coffee-stained cotton shirt; a pinchbeck tiepin stuck in a tattered necktie; list slippers held on by stitched-on trouser-straps; two or three suspicious-looking characters carrying bamboo sticks with leather loops and casting furtive glances around them; fathers eyeing their families with disapproval. People were chatting, on their feet or squatting down on their luggage; others had dropped off to sleep in a corner; a number were busily eating. The deck was littered with walnut shells and cigar stubs, pear skins and left-overs of cold meat produced from paper wrappings; three cabinet-makers in smocks had stationed themselves at the refreshment bar; a ragged harp-player was relaxing with his elbows resting on his instrument; now and again you could hear the roar of the coal in the ship's furnace, a burst of shouting, laughter; and all the while the captain kept pacing to and fro on the bridge between the paddles. Making his way back to his seat, Frédéric pushed open the iron door of the first class section, disturbing a couple of sportsmen with their dogs.

It was like a vision from another world:

She was sitting in the middle of a bench seat, all alone; or at least he was so bedazzled by her eyes that he was not aware of anyone else. As he walked past her, she looked up and involuntarily he bowed his shoulders; then, moving

6

further along on the same side, he stopped and looked back.

She had on a wide-brimmed hat whose pink ribbons fluttered behind her in the wind. Parted in the middle, her black hair curved round the tip of her arched eyebrows and swept down very low as if lovingly framing her oval face. The voluminous folds of her pale spotted muslin dress flared out all around her. She was working on a piece of embroidery; her straight nose, her chin, her whole body, was silhouetted against the airy blue background.

As she remained sitting in this same attitude, he walked around a few times on both sides to disguise his manoeuvre and then took up his post close beside her sunshade, pretending to be watching a motor boat on the river.

Never had he beheld such a magnificent brown skin, so entrancing a figure, such dainty, transparent fingers. He stood gazing in wonder at her work-basket as if it was something extraordinary. What was her name? Where did she live and what sort of life did she lead? What was her past? He wanted to know what furniture she had in her bedroom, the dresses she wore, the people she knew; even his physical desire for her gave way to a deeper yearning, a boundless, aching curiosity.

A black woman with her hair tied in a silk headscarf came up holding the hand of a little girl who already looked quite grown-up. She'd just woken up and her eyes were full of tears. She took her on to her lap. 'Missy had been naughty and her nearly turned seven, too! Her mother wouldn't love her any more! She got away with all her fads and fancies too easily!' Frédéric was delighted to hear all these remarks, rather as if he'd just made a find or acquired something.

He supposed she might be from Andalusia or possibly from the West Indies? Had she brought that black woman back with her from some tropical island? Meanwhile a long purple-striped shawl dangled over the brass handrail behind her back. How often, on damp evenings during long sea voyages, she must have wrapped it round her, covered her

7

feet with it, even slept in it! But its fringes were dragging it overboard; Frédéric sprang forward and retrieved it.

She thanked him. Their eyes met.

'Are you ready, wife of mine!' It was that man Arnoux shouting from the companionway where he'd just appeared.

Mademoiselle Marthe ran up to him, flung her arms round his neck, and started tugging at the ends of his moustache. The sudden twang of a harp came echoing along the deck and Marthe demanded to see the band; shortly afterwards the black maid showed the harpist into the first class. Arnoux recognized him as a former artist's model and surprised the bystanders by the extremely familiar way he addressed him. Finally the harpist tossed his long hair back over his shoulders, stretched out his arms and started to play.

It was a sentimental ballad about the mysterious East, complete with daggers and flowers and stars. The ragged player sang in a harsh, strident voice; the throb of the engines was upsetting the flow of the tune; he plucked harder at the metal strings and they vibrated more loudly as if sobbing a lament for a proud, defeated love. On both sides of the river, woods sloped down to the water's edge; there was a gust of cool air; Madame Arnoux was staring into the distance. When the music stopped, she blinked several times as though coming out of a dream.

The harp-player came up deferentially holding out his cap. While Arnoux was feeling in his pocket for some change, Frédéric held out his closed hand, opened his fingers, and discreetly dropped a twenty-franc gold piece into the cap, not out of vanity but impulsively, as a heartfelt, almost religious benefaction, in her name.

Arnoux pointed towards the dining-room and amiably suggested they might go down to lunch. Frédéric assured him he'd already eaten; in fact, he felt ravenous but hadn't a single sou left in his pocket.

Then he thought that after all he had the same right as anyone else to sit in the saloon.

At the round tables, middle-class passengers sat eating, with a waiter in attendance; the Arnoux were at the back, on the right; Frédéric sat down on the long plush upholstered seat and picked up a newspaper that was lying there.

At Montereau they would be catching the Châlons stagecoach. Their trip to Switzerland was going to last a month. Madame Arnoux told her husband off for being so soft with his daughter. He whispered a few words into her ear, doubtless something endearing for she gave a smile. Then he stopped eating to get up and draw the curtains behind her head.

The light reflected from the low white ceiling was extremely glaring and from where he was sitting opposite her, Frédéric could make out the shadows cast by her eyelashes. She was putting her glass to her lips and crumbling a crust between her fingers; from time to time the lapis lazuli medallion on a thin gold chain round her wrist tinkled against her plate. Yet the people around didn't seem to notice her.

Now and again the side of a boat could be seen through the portholes as it came alongside to pick up or drop passengers. The people at table kept leaning forward and looking out of the window to identify the riverside villages.

Arnoux was complaining about the food; he took strong exception to the size of the bill and managed to get it reduced. Then he took the young man up to the bows for a grog. But Frédéric soon made his way back to the awning where Madame Arnoux had also returned. She was reading a slim volume in a grey binding. From time to time the corners of her mouth would twitch and her face light up with pleasure. Frédéric felt jealous of this man who'd thought up these things which seemed to be interesting her. The longer he watched the more he felt a gulf widening between them. He was thinking that presently he'd have to leave her for good, never to meet again, without extracting a single word from her, not even leaving her a single memory of himself!

On the right was a broad plain, on the left grazing land rising gently up towards a hill with vineyards and walnut trees and a mill set amidst greenery; little paths zigzagged up the pale rock to the skyline. How wonderful to walk up there together side by side with his arm round her waist while her skirt swept over the yellow leaves, listening to the sound of her voice, basking in the radiance of her eyes! The boat might stop, they'd only have to go ashore; yet such a simple act was no easier than making the sun stand still!

A little further on a grand house appeared with square turrets and a high-pitched roof. Extensive flowerbeds stretched out in front and arched avenues of lime trees led away into the distance. In his mind's eye he could see her passing through this leafy green shade. At that moment a young man and woman appeared on the terrace between the tubs of orange trees. Then the whole scene slipped out of sight.

The little girl was playing round him. He tried to give her a kiss. She took refuge behind her nanny; her mother scolded her for not being nice to the man who'd rescued her shawl. Was this an indirect approach?

'Is she going to speak to me at last?' he wondered.

Time was running out. How could he get an invitation out of Arnoux? Yet the only thing he could think of was to draw attention to the autumn tints!

'Winter'll soon be here. What a lot of dances and dinner parties!'

But Arnoux was busy with his luggage. The heights of Surville loomed up as they approached the two bridges, passing a rope-works and then a row of squat cottages; below were pots of tar and wood chips; little boys scampered along the sand turning cartwheels. Recognizing a man wearing a sleeved waistcoat Frédéric shouted:

'Get a move on!'

They were arriving. With great difficulty he managed to find Arnoux in the throng of passengers. Shaking Frédéric's hand, he said:

'Lovely knowing you, my dear fellow! We must meet again sometime!'

On the quayside Frédéric turned back. She was standing beside the helm. He threw her a look meant to express his whole soul; she gave no sign of having seen him. Then, ignoring his servant's greeting, he snapped:

'Why didn't you bring the carriage up to here?'

The poor man started apologizing.

'Trust you to muck things up! Give me some money!'

And he went off to eat at the inn.

Fifteen minutes later he felt an urge to go, as if by chance, into the coachyard. Maybe he'd see her again?

'Oh, what's the point!' he said to himself.

And Isidore drove him off in the buggy. The horses were not both his mother's; she'd borrowed one from Monsieur Chambrion the tax-collector to hitch up with her own. The driver had left the day before, rested at Bray till the evening and then spent the night at Montereau, so both horses were fresh and kept up a brisk trot.

Fields of stubble stretched away endlessly; the road was lined with trees on both sides; one pile of stones followed another. Gradually the whole journey began to come back to him, Villeneuve-Saint-Georges, Ablon, Châtillon, Corbeil and all the other villages, so vividly that he was now able to recall fresh details and more personal peculiarities: on her foot peeping out from under the bottom flounce of her dress she'd been wearing a dainty, dark red silk bootee; the wide canvas awning above her head formed a sort of canopy and all the time its fringe of tiny red tassels quivered in the breeze.

She looked exactly like the women in romantic novels. He wouldn't have wanted to add to or take away one single detail of her; the universe had suddenly become more spacious and *She* was the glittering focus of it all. So, lulled by the motion of the carriage and gazing up at the clouds with half-closed eyes, he surrendered to his dreams of never-ending bliss.

In Bray he didn't wait for the horses to finish their oats but walked on ahead along the road by himself. Arnoux had called her Marie. Loudly he called 'Marie!' His voice was lost in the air. A broad sweep of crimson glowed in the western sky. Across the stubble-fields great stacks of wheat were casting giant shadows. In the distance a farm dog started barking. Seized by an inexplicable foreboding, Frédéric felt a shiver run down his spine.

When Isidore caught up with him, he picked up the reins himself. His moment of weakness had passed. By hook or by crook he was determined to gain entry into the Arnoux's home and make their closer acquaintance. It must be an amusing household and he liked Arnoux anyway; and after that, who knows? At this thought the blood rushed to his head, he felt a drumming in his temples; he cracked his whip, shook the reins, and set the horses going at such a pace that the old coachman kept saying:

'Easy does it! Easy does it! You'll make them broken-winded!'

Gradually Frédéric calmed down and listened to what his servant was saying.

Everyone was eagerly awaiting the master's homecoming. Mademoiselle Louise had been in tears, wanting to come along in the carriage.

'Who's Louise?'

'You know her, she's Monsieur Roque's daughter.'

'Oh yes, I'd forgotten,' he replied off-handedly.

Meanwhile the horses were ready to drop; they were both lame and it was striking nine at Saint-Laurent's when he drew up in front of his mother's house in the place d'Armes; Madame Moreau's spacious mansion, with its garden backing on to open country, was yet another source of prestige for her: she was the most respected person in the town.

She came from an old aristocratic family, now extinct. Her plebeian husband, whom her parents had forced her to marry, had died from a sword wound during her pregnancy, leaving her in some financial difficulty. She had an 'at home' three times a week and gave the occasional grand dinner party. But the number of candles would be carefully worked out in advance and she was never slow to collect her farm rents. These straitened circumstances, which she kept secret like some vice, had made her serious-minded, but she practised her virtues without any display of primness or acrimony. The widow gave her mite with the air of a Lady Bountiful. People would consult her on the choice of servants, the upbringing of girls, and jam-making; on his diocesan rounds, the bishop was put up in her house.

She had lofty ambitions for her son and, to avoid risk, disliked hearing any criticism of the government: someone would be needed to take her son under his wing at the outset; afterwards, thanks to his own ability, he'd become a member of the Conseil d'État,* an Ambassador, a Minister of the Crown. His outstanding record at his school in Sens justified her pride: he'd won the prize for 'Best Pupil of the Year'.

When he went into the drawing-room there was a great flurry and everyone stood up; he was kissed and hugged and then they formed a large semi-circle of seats and armchairs round the fire. Monsieur Gamblin immediately asked him what he thought about Madame Lafarge.* This question on a topic of such burning interest didn't fail to arouse heated argument; to Monsieur Gamblin's disappointment, Madame Moreau put a stop to it; he'd been thinking it would be useful for the young man in his future role as legal expert and left the room in a huff.

They shouldn't have been surprised at anything from a friend of Monsieur Roque! In connection with old Roque, Monsieur Dambreuse's name came up; he'd just bought the large La Fortrelle property. But the tax-collector had taken Frédéric aside to discover what he thought of Monsieur Guizot's latest book.* Everybody was keen to learn about his business; Madame Benoît craftily set the ball rolling by enquiring after his uncle. How was that nice old gentleman? He never gave any news of himself these days. Hadn't he got a distant cousin somewhere in America?

The cook came in to announce that the master's soup was on the table. The others discreetly withdrew. As soon as they were alone his mother said to him in a low voice:

'Well?'

The old gentleman had given him a very friendly welcome but no hint of his intentions.

Madame Moreau gave a sigh.

'Where is *She* now?' he was wondering.

The coach would be on its way and in the front compartment, no doubt wrapped in her shawl, she'd be leaning her lovely head against the cloth upholstery, fast asleep.

Just as they were going upstairs to bed a letter was delivered by one of the servants from the Cygne de la Croix.*.

'What is it?'

'It's from Deslauriers. He wants me to do something for him.'

'Ah, your old school friend!' remarked Madame Moreau caustically. 'I must say he picks his time well!'

Frédéric hesitated but the claims of friendship won the day. He picked up his hat.

'Well don't be too long anyway!' said his mother.

CHAPTER II

Charles Deslauriers's father was a former army captain who'd resigned his commission in 1818, gone back to Nogent, married, and with the money from his wife's dowry bought a position as bailiff which barely provided a living. Soured by years of injustice, still suffering from old wounds, and heart-broken for his emperor, he vented his pent-up rage on his immediate family. Few people were ever more soundly thrashed than Charles but the lad refused to be cowed. When his mother attempted to intervene, she got a taste of the same medicine. In the end the captain took his son into his own office and kept him slaving away all day long copying legal documents, which made his right shoulder noticeably more muscular than the left.

In 1833 the captain was invited by the presiding judge to resign and he sold his bailiffship. His wife died of cancer. He moved to Dijon and there set up as a 'trafficker in men'* in Troyes; he managed to get a bursary for his son and sent him to the grammar school in Sens where he met Frédéric. But one of the boys was twelve, the other fifteen, and in any case there were a hundred and one differences of birth and temperament to keep them apart. Frédéric had all sorts of little delicacies and luxuries in his locker, such as a dressing case. He liked to lie in bed late, watch the swallows, read plays; missing his home comforts, he found life at school hard. The bailiff's son liked it.

He worked so hard that at the end of his second year he was moved up to the Third Form.* All the same, either because he was poor or because he was quarrelsome, he met a good deal of veiled animosity. But once when a servant called him a beggar's brat in front of everyone in the Middle School playground, he flung himself at his throat and but for the intervention of three masters would have strangled him. Frédéric was full of admiration and couldn't resist giving him a hug. From then on they were inseparable. This affection from a 'big boy' no doubt flattered the younger one's vanity, while for Charles the offer of loyalty was a godsend.

During the holidays his father left him at school. Chancing on a translation of Plato he was carried away by enthusiasm and fell in love with metaphysics. Since he approached it with youthful energy and the blissful confidence of a mind casting off its shackles, he made rapid progress. Everything in the library was grist to his mill: Jouffroy, Cousin, Laromiguière, Malebranche, the Scottish school.* To obtain access to the books he had to steal the key.

Frédéric's pastimes were less earnest. He drew Christ's family tree in the rue des Trois-Rois, carving it first on a post and then on the door of the cathedral. From medieval drama he moved on to memoirs: Froissart, Commynes, l'Étoile, Brantôme.*

He became so obsessed by the images conjured up in his mind by his reading that he felt an urge to imitate them: he dreamt of becoming the future French Walter Scott. Deslauriers's dream was to create a vast philosophical system with the most far-reaching ramifications.

They'd discuss all this in the playground during recreation, facing the school motto inscribed below the clock, exchange whispers on the subject in chapel, under the gaze of Saint-Louis, and dream about it in the dormitory overlooking a churchyard. On school walks, they would bring up the rear and rattle on endlessly about what they'd do once they'd left school. First they'd set off on a Grand Tour financed by an advance on Frédéric's future inheritance when he came of age. Then Paris, where they'd work together and never leave each other; as a relaxation from work they'd have love affairs with princesses in satin bedrooms or torrid orgies with illustrious ladies of the town. These high-flown hopes were followed by spasms of doubt. After manic bursts of verbal exuberance they'd relapse into utter silence.

On summer evenings when they'd been walking for a long time along stony paths beside vineyards or on the open road miles out in the country and the wheat was dancing in the sun while the rich scent of angelica wafted through the air, half-suffocating, in a sort of intoxication, with their heads swimming, they'd stretch out on their backs; the other boys would be in their shirt-sleeves playing tig or flying kites. The master would call to them and they'd all troop back beside the gardens crossed by little streams and then along the broad boulevards under the shadows of old walls. Their footsteps echoed through the deserted streets, the gates would open, they'd go upstairs and they'd feel sad, as if they'd had an orgy.

The headmaster considered them a disturbing influence on each other, yet it was thanks to his friend's urgings that Frédéric worked hard in the Upper School. In the summer holidays of 1837 he took him home to his mother's.

Madame Moreau took a dislike to the young man. He ate inordinately, declined to go to church on Sunday, and professed republican sentiments; to crown it all she suspected him of luring her son along to houses of ill fame. A close eye was kept on their relationship. This only increased their fondness for each other and it was a sad moment when they parted the following year and Deslauriers left to study law in Paris.

Frédéric was looking forward to joining him there. They hadn't seen each other for two years, and after exchanging greetings and hugs they went off down to the bridges to talk undisturbed.

When he'd demanded to see the accounts of his father's guardianship, the captain, now running a billiards saloon in Villenauxe, had seen red and cut off Charles's allowance on the spot. But as he wished to apply for a teaching post later on and was penniless, he was going to take a job as chief clerk in a solicitor's office in Troyes. By pinching and scraping he'd be able to save four thousand francs, so even if he didn't get a bean from his mother's estate, he'd still have enough to live on and work independently while waiting to be offered a post. So they'd have to give up their long-cherished plans of living together, at least for a while.

Frédéric's face fell. Here was the first of his dreams coming to grief.

'Cheer up!' said his friend. 'While there's life there's hope. We're young, I can still come and join you later. Stop worrying!'

He gave him a shake and to change the subject asked him about his trip.

Frédéric hadn't much to tell. But as the memory of Madame Arnoux came back, his sadness vanished. Bashfulness prevented him from mentioning her but instead he talked at length about Arnoux, reporting his remarks, his behaviour, his connections. Deslauriers strongly recommended him to cultivate the acquaintance.

Frédéric hadn't written anything recently, his literary tastes had changed: what he now valued most highly was passion; his enthusiasm was almost equally divided between Werther, René, Franck, Lara, Lélia,* and other more mundane heroes and heroines. There were times when he felt music was the only art capable of expressing the turmoil of his inner life; then he'd have dreams of writing symphonies; or else he found his interests focusing on the surface of things and he wanted to become a painter. However, he had composed some poetry, which Deslauriers pronounced 'splendid stuff', without asking to hear any more.

For his part, he'd lost interest in metaphysics. His concern was with the economic bases of society and the French Revolution. He was now a tall young man of twenty-two, thin, with a big mouth and a determined expression. That evening he was wearing a shabby coat of hard-wearing material and his shoes were white with dust, for he'd walked all the way from Villenauxe to see Frédéric.

Isidore came up to them. Madam would like the master to come back in and she'd sent him his coat as she was afraid he might be feeling cold.

'Don't go yet!' said Deslauriers.

So they continued to walk from one end to the other of the two bridges which met on the narrow island lying between the river and the canal. Facing them on the Nogent side was a cluster of slightly rickety houses; on the right they could see the church behind the wooden water-mills, their sluices now closed, and, along the river bank to the left, hedgerows at the bottom of gardens now practically invisible. But in the direction of Paris the main road ran straight downhill and in the distance the meadows were lost to sight in the evening mist. It was a still night lit by a whitish glow; scents of damp leaves came wafting up towards them; from the sluice between the river and the canal a hundred yards away came the strong, gentle murmur of water rippling in the dark.

Deslauriers stopped and spoke:

'It's funny, all those simple folk sleeping so peacefully! Just wait! There's another '89 on the way! People are fed up with new constitutions and charters, quibbles and lies! Oh, if only I had a newspaper or some sort of forum, what a shake-up I'd give everything! But to get anything done you need money! What a curse to be the son of a publican and waste your youth having to earn enough to survive on!'

He hung his head, biting his lips; he was shivering in his thin overcoat.

Frédéric threw half his own coat over his shoulders. They wrapped it round themselves and walked along together under it, holding each other round the waist.

'How do you think I'm going to be able to live there without you?' Frédéric said. His friend's bitterness had revived his own black mood. 'With a woman who loved me I'd have been able to achieve something. Why are you laughing? Genius feeds on love, it's the air it needs in order to breathe. To produce really outstanding works you've got to feel grand emotions. As for trying to find the woman I

18

need, I give up! Even if I ever do find her, she'll turn me down. I'm the sort of man who's doomed to be a failure and I'll go to my grave without ever knowing whether I was real gold or just tinsel!'

A long shadow fell across the roadway and they heard a respectful voice say:

'A very good evening to you, gentlemen.'

The speaker was a little man in a voluminous brown frock-coat with a pointed nose poking out from under his peaked cap.

'Monsieur Roque?' asked Frédéric.

'The same,' the voice replied.

Frédéric's fellow townsman explained that he had just been inspecting the wolf traps in his riverside garden.

'So you've returned to these parts? Splendid! My little girl told me. I trust you're still in good health? You'll be staying with us for a while?'

And he went on his way, no doubt somewhat discouraged by Frédéric's lukewarm reception.

In fact Madame Moreau refused to have anything to do with him: old Roque was living in sin with his maid and people had a very poor opinion of him in spite of the fact that, as Monsieur Dambreuse's agent, he was the election-rigger for the district.

'Is that the banker who lives in the rue d'Anjou?' asked Deslauriers. 'Do you know what you should do, old man?'

Isidore again came up and interrupted them. Madam was worried that he was staying out so long and he had strict orders to see that he came home.

'All right, all right, we're on our way!' said Deslauriers, 'he's not going to spend the night on the tiles!'

And when the man had gone off:

'You should ask the old man to introduce you to the Dambreuses. What's better than rich contacts? You've got evening dress and white gloves, so make the most of them! You simply have to know that sort of person. Later on you can introduce me too. Just imagine, a millionaire! Get him to take a fancy to you, and his wife as well! Get her to go to bed with you!'

Frédéric protested.

'It's only normal procedure, old man! Remember Rastignac* in the *Comédie humaine*! I'm sure you can pull it off!'

Frédéric had such confidence in Deslauriers that he could feel his scruples crumbling. Forgetting Madame Arnoux or else including her in the proposed strategy towards Madame Dambreuse, he couldn't help smiling.

'Final tip: take your exams. A degree's always useful and for God's sake forget your Catholic and Satanic poets.* Their view of life hasn't ever got beyond the Middle Ages! You're stupid to be discouraged. There've been some very great individuals whose start in life was harder than yours, starting with Mirabeau*, for instance. Anyway we'll not be separated for long. I'll make my crook of a father cough up. Goodbye, I must be off! Have you got ten francs to pay for my dinner?'

Frédéric handed over the ten francs, all that was left from what Isidore had given him that morning.

Meanwhile, a stone's throw from the bridges, on the left bank, a light was shining from the attic window of a low house.

Deslauriers saw it and sweeping off his hat he solemnly declaimed:

'Oh Venus, Queen of the Heavens, behold thy humble servants. But Penury is the mother of Wisdom! Mercy me, what malignity did we not suffer for that . . .'

They were tickled by this reference to a joint escapade and burst out laughing in the street.

Then, having settled his bill at the inn, Deslauriers accompanied Frédéric back to the Hôtel-Dieu crossroads and after one long last hug the two friends parted.

CHAPTER III

Two months later, having got off the coach that very morning in the rue Coq-Héron,* Frédéric at once thought of paying his all-important call.

Luck had favoured him. Old Roque had brought round a packet of papers with the request that he should deliver them by hand to Monsieur Dambreuse, and he'd also given him an unsealed note of introduction to his fellow townsman.

Madame Moreau seemed surprised at this action. Frédéric concealed the pleasure he felt.

Monsieur Dambreuse was really the Comte d'Ambreuse but from 1835 onwards he had gradually dropped his title and his party, turned his mind to industry and, keeping his ear always close to the ground, with a finger in every pie and an eye for a bargain, as wily as a Greek and as hard-working as any native of the Auvergne, he'd amassed what was said to be a considerable fortune. In addition he was an officer of the Legion of Honour, a member of the Departmental Council of the Aube as well as of the Chamber of Deputies, and in line for a peerage. And always ready to oblige as well: the Minister was growing tired of his continual requests for help of various sorts, decorations or tobacco licences; in addition, with his reservations against the government, he inclined to be left of centre. His attractive wife, whose name appeared in fashion magazines, chaired various charitable committees. By gently humouring duchesses she was successfully mollifying the ill will of their aristocratic neighbours and holding out hopes that Monsieur Dambreuse might yet repent and prove useful.

On his way to the rue d'Anjou* the young man had been feeling uneasy.

'I should have put on my tail-coat. I suppose I'll be invited to their dance next week. What'll they have to say to me?'

Then the thought that Monsieur Dambreuse was just a bourgeois restored his confidence and he sprang out of his cab on to the pavement of the rue d'Anjou with a jaunty air.

Pushing open one of the double carriage gates he crossed the courtyard, and went up the front steps and into an entrance hall paved in coloured marble.

Between the high glossy white stucco walls, a red-carpeted double stairway with brass stair-rods led straight upstairs. At its foot stood a banana plant whose broad leaves

21

drooped over the velvet of the balustrade. Two bronze candelabra with porcelain globes hung on chains from the ceiling; gusts of hot stuffy air were pouring out of the vents in the open stoves; the only sound was the ticking of a grandfather clock standing under a wall-trophy at the far end of the hall.

A bell rang, a footman appeared and showed Frédéric into a small room in which he could make out two strong-boxes and rows of pigeon-holes containing cardboard boxes. Monsieur Dambreuse was writing at a roll-top desk in the middle of the room.

He ran his eye over old Roque's letter, slit open the canvas bag containing the papers, and examined them.

From a distance, thanks to his slim build, he might still have been taken for a young man but his sparse white hair, his frail limbs, and above all the extraordinary pallor of his face betrayed the dilapidated state of his health. His pale green eyes, colder than any glass ones, were filled with ruthless energy. His cheek bones were prominent, his knuckles gnarled.

Finally he rose to his feet and questioned the young man about common acquaintances, Nogent, and his studies; then he gave a bow to indicate that the conversation was at an end. Frédéric went out through another corridor and found himself down in the courtyard next to the coach-house.

A blue brougham drawn by a black horse was standing by the front steps. The door was opened, a lady got in, and the carriage began to rumble slowly over the sand-covered drive. Coming from the other direction Frédéric arrived at the gateway at the same time as the brougham. The young woman was leaning out of the window saying something in a low voice to the porter; he could see only her back covered in a violet cloak. However, he could look right inside the brougham, which was upholstered in blue rep with silk braid and fringes; the entire space was occupied by her clothes, and from the tiny padded box there came a fragrance of lilies and a vague general scent of elegant womanhood. The driver slackened the reins, the horse

22

suddenly brushed against the corner-stone, and the whole outfit disappeared.

Frédéric made his way home along the boulevards.

He was sorry not to have been able to get a proper look at Madame Dambreuse.

Just beyond the rue Montmartre a traffic jam made him look round and on the opposite side of the street he saw a marble plaque which read:

JACQUES ARNOUX

Why hadn't he thought of her before? It was Deslauriers's fault! He crossed over to the shop but didn't go in: he waited for *Her* to appear.

Behind the tall, clear glass windows was a skilfully arranged display of statuettes, drawings, engravings, catalogues and copies of *L'Art industriel*; the subscription price was also printed on the door, the centre of which was adorned with the editor's monogram. On the walls were large, glossily varnished paintings and at the back two low chests covered in ceramics, bronzes and enticing curios; between them was a small staircase closed off at the top by a velvet curtain; a Meissen chandelier, a green rug and a marquetry table made the place look more like a drawing-room than a shop.

Frédéric pretended to be examining the drawings. After prolonged hesitation he went in.

An assistant emerged from behind the curtain and informed him that Monsieur Arnoux wouldn't be coming 'into the shop' until five o'clock. Could he take a message?

'No, I'll come back,' said Frédéric meekly.

He spent the next few days looking for lodgings and finally decided on a second-floor room in a residential hotel in the rue Saint-Hyacinthe.

Clasping a brand-new blotting pad under one arm he went off to the opening lecture. Three hundred bare-headed young men were packed into tier upon tier of a lecture hall where an old man in a red gown held forth in a dreary monotone; there was a scratching of quills on paper. Here once again he was faced by the dusty classroom smell, the same kind of lectern and just as much boredom! He continued to attend for a fortnight but before they'd reached Article 3 of the Civil Code he'd given up and abandoned the Institutes of Justinian at the *Summa divisio personarum*.

The joys he had expected were not forthcoming, and after exhausting the resources of a public library, going round the Louvre, and spending several nights in succession at the theatre, he lapsed into utter idleness.

There were a hundred and one other things to depress him even more: he had to make out laundry lists and put up with the porter, a bumpkin with the build of a medical orderly, who came up to make his bed in the morning, full of grumbles and reeking of spirits; he couldn't stand his room with its ornamental alabaster clock; the partition walls were flimsy and he could hear students next door making punch, laughing and singing.

Fed up with being alone, he sought out one of his former schoolmates, Baptiste Martinon, and found him living in a boarding house in the rue Saint-Jacques swotting up his rules of procedure in front of a coal fire.

Opposite him a woman in a print cotton dress was sitting darning his socks.

Martinon was what is known as a fine figure of a man, tall and chubby with regular features and bulging eyes of a bluish tinge; his father, a big farmer, wanted him to join the state legal system, and in his eagerness to prove how staid and sober he already was, Martinon wore a neatly trimmed fringe beard.

As Frédéric had no rational grounds for his woes and couldn't claim to be suffering from any disability, Martinon failed to understand why he was complaining about life. He himself went off to Law School every morning, then took a stroll round the Luxembourg Gardens, spent the evening in a café over a small cup of coffee, and with his fifteen hundred francs a year and his loving little working-class girlfriend felt perfectly happy.

'A fine sort of happiness!' exclaimed Frédéric to himself.

24

At Law School he'd made another acquaintance, a Monsieur de Cisy, a young man of excellent family who was so genteel as to be almost ladylike.

Monsieur de Cisy enjoyed sketching and admired Gothic art. Together they went several times to look at the Sainte-Chapelle and Notre-Dame. But this aristocratic young man's distinguished manners concealed a very weak intelligence. He was surprised at everything; the slightest joke would send him into fits of laughter and he seemed such a complete simpleton that at first Frédéric suspected him of pulling his leg; eventually he realized that he was just very dim.

So there was no one to whom he could open his heart. He was still waiting for his invitation from the Dambreuses.

On New Year's Day, he left his cards on them but got none in return.

He had called again at *L'Art industriel*.

He went back a third time and finally saw Arnoux, who was in the middle of an argument with four or five people and barely acknowledged his greeting; Frédéric felt offended. All the same he was still wondering how he might manage to meet *Her*.

His first idea was to call often and discuss buying paintings. Then he thought of slipping a few *frightfully good* articles (written by himself) into the gallery's letter-box, thereby establishing contact. Perhaps the best plan would be to come straight to the point and declare his love? So he composed a twelve-page letter full of lyrical outbursts and invocations; he then tore it up, did nothing, and made no attempt to do anything, paralysed by fear of failure.

Above Arnoux's gallery there were three first-floor windows, brilliantly lit every evening, through which shadows could be seen moving around, one in particular—*Hers*—and he'd go miles out of his way to watch those windows and observe that shadow.

One day he came across a black woman in the Tuileries holding a little girl by the hand and he was reminded of Madame Arnoux's maid. She must come here like the others, so every time he walked through the Tuileries his heart would beat faster in his hope of meeting her. When it was sunny he'd continue his walk to the top of the Champs-Elysées.

Lolling in their low-slung barouches with their veils fluttering in the wind, women would drive nonchalantly past close beside him, imperceptibly swaying on the glossy leather seats which creaked to the rhythm of the horses' hooves. As the number of carriages increased and they slowed down on approaching the Rond-Point, they would occupy the whole roadway, jammed mane to mane and lamp to lamp. The steel stirrups, the silver curbs and the brass buckles glinted amongst the breeches, the white gloves and the fur rugs dangling over the coats of arms on the carriage doors. He felt as if lost in a remote world. As his eyes wandered over these female faces, vague similarities would bring Madame Arnoux to mind, and he'd imagine her sitting there with the others in one of those little broughams like the one used by Madame Dambreuse. But the sun set and a cold wind was whirling up clouds of dust. The drivers sank their chins into their neck-cloths, the wheels started to turn faster, rasping on the asphalt, and off the carriages went down the avenue at a brisk trot, wheel to wheel, swerving, overtaking, and finally dispersing at the place de la Concorde. Behind the Tuileries the sky turned slate-grey; in the garden the trees formed two huge clumps topped with indigo; the gas jets were lighting up and the Seine, greenish in colour over its whole expanse, was shredded into shimmering silver against the piers of the bridges.

He'd go off to dine at a restaurant in the rue de la Harpe where a set of meal tickets cost just forty-three sous. He'd sit there looking scornfully at the old mahogany cash desk, the grubby table-napkins, the dirty cutlery and the hats hanging on the wall. He was surrounded by students like himself, discussing their professors or their girlfriends. What did he care about professors? Had he got a girlfriend? To avoid their boisterous conviviality, he'd arrive as late as possible; the tables would be all littered with left-overs, with two tired waiters drowsing in a corner and the empty room stinking of cooking, oil lamps and tobacco smoke.

Afterwards he'd walk slowly back home. The lamps swayed to and fro and long yellowish reflections were dancing in the mud underfoot. Shadowy figures sidled along the pavements carrying umbrellas; the cobbles were greasy, the mists were coming down, and he seemed to feel the damp and gloom wrapping themselves round him and penetrating deeper and deeper into his heart.

Seized by a fit of remorse, he started attending lectures again; but since he was completely ignorant of the topics being explained, the simplest things left him at a loss.

He began on a novel entitled 'Sylvio, the fisherman's son'. It was set in Venice. The hero was himself, the heroine, Madame Arnoux. She was called Antonia and in order to get her, he murdered a number of noblemen, burnt down part of the city, and serenaded under her balcony where, fluttering in the breeze, were the red damask curtains from the boulevard Montmartre. He was depressed at recognizing so many personal reminiscences. He gave up writing and became even more idle.

He wrote begging Deslauriers to come and share his room with him. They'd work out how to live on his allowance of five thousand francs a year; anything would be better than this unbearable existence. But Deslauriers wasn't yet able to leave Troyes; he urged him to find some form of distraction and to keep in touch with Sénécal.

Sénécal was a very junior assistant maths master, self-opinionated and a dyed-in-the-wool republican; an up-and-coming Saint Just,* Deslauriers claimed. Three times Frédéric had climbed the five flights of stairs up to his room but he had never received a return visit. He gave up trying.

He decided to enjoy himself and went to the Opéra balls. But the rowdy high spirits made his heart sink as soon as he went through the door. Furthermore he was inhibited by fear of financial humiliation, imagining that suppers with masked ladies would be grand adventures entailing vast expense.

Yet he felt he deserved to be loved. Sometimes he'd wake

27

up full of hope, dress carefully as if in preparation for an assignment with a woman, and spend hours scouring the streets of Paris on foot. Each time he saw a woman in front or coming towards him he'd say to himself: 'That's *Her*!' Time and again he was disappointed. Thinking about Madame Arnoux intensified these desires even more. Perhaps he'd meet her on his way? And to enable him to speak to her he'd dream up complicated series of lucky coincidences or else dread perils from which he'd rescue her.

And so the days slipped by in the same pattern of frustration and boring rituals. He'd thumb through the booklets under the Odéon* arcades, go to the café to read the *Revue des deux mondes*,* drop in at the Collège de France* for an hour to listen to a lecture on Chinese or economics. Every week he wrote a long letter to Deslauriers; occasionally he dined with Martinon, and saw Monsieur de Cisy now and again.

He hired a piano and composed German waltzes.

One evening at the Palais-Royal Theatre he spotted Arnoux sitting beside a woman in a stage box. Was it *Her*? The woman's face was hidden by the green taffeta screen at the edge of the box. Eventually the curtain rose and the screen was drawn aside. She was a lanky woman about thirty years old with a faded look and thick lips which, when she laughed, revealed magnificent teeth. She was chatting familiarly with Arnoux, rapping him over the knuckles with her fan. Then a blonde girl, with slightly red eyes as if she'd been crying, came and sat down between them. Arnoux half leant on her shoulder and kept on talking to her for quite a while as she listened in silence. Frédéric was racking his brains to figure out what sort of women these were, in their modest black dresses with flat turn-down collars.

At the end of the performance, he rushed out into the corridor; it was packed with people. Arnoux was going downstairs ahead of him, one step at a time, offering an arm to each of the women.

Suddenly a beam of gas-light lit up his head. He was wearing a black crêpe on his hat. Perhaps *She* was dead?

Frédéric was so tortured by the thought that the very next day he dashed round to *L'Art industriel*, hurriedly paid for one of the prints on show in the window, and enquired after Monsieur Arnoux.

The assistant, somewhat surprised, replied:

'He's very well.'

Frédéric went pale.

'And how's Madame Arnoux?'

'She's very well too.'

Frédéric went away, forgetting to pick up his print.

Winter came to an end. In the spring he felt less depressed and started working for his examinations, which he passed successfully. After that he went home to Nogent.

To avoid arousing comment from his mother he didn't visit his friend in Troyes. When he returned to Paris to resume his studies, he gave up his lodgings and took two rooms on the quai Napoléon* which he furnished himself. He'd given up hope of an invitation to the Dambreuses; his grand passion for Madame Arnoux was beginning to peter out.

CHAPTER IV

One December morning as he was on his way to his lecture on legal procedure, he thought he detected more activity than usual on the rue Saint-Jacques. Students were dashing out of cafés or calling to each other from house windows; people were putting up their shutters; and when he arrived at the rue Soufflot he saw a large crowd gathered round the Panthéon.*

Young men were walking about in small groups of some five to a dozen and going up to larger groups scattered round the square; at the far end, with their backs to the railings, men in workers' smocks were haranguing the onlookers while policemen prowled along the walls with their three-cornered hats cocked over one ear and their hands behind their backs, their heavy boots thudding on the flagstones. Everyone was looking perplexed and secretive.

There was clearly something afoot; an unspoken query was on everybody's lips.

Frédéric found himself standing next to a fair-haired, pleasant-looking young man with a moustache and Van Dyke beard in the style of young dandies in Louis XIII's day. He asked him what the trouble was.

'I've no idea,' the young man replied, 'and neither have they! It's the fashionable thing to do! What a lark!'

He gave a loud guffaw.

For the last six months, petitions in favour of Reform, which the National Guard* were being persuaded to sign, in addition to Humann's* scheme for new forms of tax return, and various other events had been leading to puzzling demonstrations in Paris; they had indeed become so common that the newspapers had stopped reporting them.

'It's got no style or colour,' Frédéric's neighbour went on. 'Methinks, good sir, we are become degenerate! Gramercy, in ye good olde days of Louis XI, nay even of Benjamin Constant*, there was greater sedition amongst the bookmen who now, stap me, are as meek as lambs, as addle-pated as donkeys, and fit only to be grocers. And this is supposed to be the cream of our youth, by Our Lady!'

He spread out his arms in a flamboyant gesture, like Frédérick Lemaître in *Robert Macaire*.*

Then, apostrophizing a rag-and-bone merchant busily rummaging through oyster shells outside a wine-shop:

'Tell me, my good man, dost thou belong to the cream of our youth?'

The old man looked up; in the middle of a hideously ugly face you could see, half hidden by a grey beard, a red nose and two drink-sodden eyes.

'Nay, thou seemst to me to be one of those of gallow's bird aspect who may be seen, in divers groups, scattering gold! Oh, scatter on, old patriarch, scatter on! Corrupt me with the treasure of perfidious Albion! Do you speak English?* I do not reject Artaxerxes'* gifts! Let us discuss the Customs Union!'*

30

Frédéric felt a tap on his shoulder. He swung round. It was Martinon. He was ghastly pale.

'Well, another riot,' he said, giving a deep sigh. He was full of moans, scared stiff of getting caught up in something. Above all, he was worried about the men in smocks, workers who were members of secret societies.*

'Do such things as secret societies exist?' asked the young man with the moustache. 'It's just a wheeze on the part of the government to scare the life out of the middle classes!'

Martinon urged him to lower his voice, for fear of the police.

'Do you still believe in the police yourself? And by the way, how d'you know I'm not a police spy?'

And he gave Martinon such a disturbing look that for a moment he didn't realize it was a joke. The crowd was jostling them and all three had been forced into the little stairway of a corridor leading to the new lecture-room.

A moment later the throng parted of its own accord and a number of men raised their hats to greet the arrival of the illustrious Professor Samuel Rondelot who, wrapped in his voluminous frock-coat, holding his silver-rimmed spectacles in the air and wheezing asthmatically, was making his way sedately towards the lecture-room. The professor was one of the legal luminaries of the nineteenth century, rivalling men like Zachariae and Rudorff.* His recent elevation to the peerage had not affected his way of life in the slightest; well known to be a poor man, he was highly regarded in all quarters.

Meanwhile voices could be heard shouting from the edge of the square:

'Down with Guizot!'

'Down with Pritchard!'*

'Down with traitors!'

'Down with Louis-Philippe!'

The crowd surged forward, pressing against the closed entrance to the courtyard and preventing the professor from going any further. He stopped at the foot of the stairway and then could be seen at the top of the three steps. He said something which was drowned by a roar of voices; now that

31

he represented Authority, his earlier popularity had been replaced by hatred. Each time he tried to make himself heard, the shouting started up again. He waved his arm high in the air, inviting the students to follow him. This action was greeted by jeers and yells on every side. He gave a scornful shrug of his shoulders and strode off into the passage. Martinon had taken advantage of his predicament to make himself scarce at the same time.

'Coward!' exclaimed Frédéric.

'Just careful!' replied the other man.

The crowd broke into triumphant cheers: they'd made the professor retreat. People were peering out of every window. Some of the crowd struck up the 'Marseillaise'*; others suggested going to Béranger's house.

'To Laffitte's!'

'To Chateaubriand's!'

'To Voltaire's!'* yelled the young man with the blond moustache.

The police were trying to keep the crowd moving, saying as gently as they could:

'Come along now, gents, move along, no loitering!'

Someone shouted:

'Down with the thugs!'

This had become the standard term of abuse ever since the September troubles.* Everyone took up the cry. Pursued by boos and catcalls, the guardians of the peace began to go pale; one of them cracked under the strain and gave a youth who came right up to him and openly sneered in his face such a violent shove that he went staggering back a couple of yards and fell down in front of the wine-shop. Everybody drew back but almost at once the policeman was himself bowled over by a sort of colossus whose hair stuck out like a bundle of tow from under his oilcloth cap.

He'd been standing watching the scene for some few minutes at the corner of the rue Saint-Jacques and now, quickly dropping a large cardboard box he was carrying, he flung himself on the policeman, holding him down and pummeling his face with his fists. The other officers rushed up. The formidable young man was so strong that it took at least four of them to bring him under control. Two were tugging at his collar, two others hung on to his arms, a fifth kneed him vigorously in the back, and they were all calling him a thug, a murderer, and a hooligan. With his shirt ripped open and his clothes in tatters, he protested his innocence: he couldn't just stand by in cold blood and see a child being beaten up.

'My name's Dussardier, I work for Valincourt Bros. Drapery in the rue de Cléry. What's happened to my box? I want my box!' He kept repeating: 'Dussardier, rue de Cléry. Where's my box?'

However, he calmed down and allowed himself to be taken without resisting to the police station in the rue Descartes. A crowd followed him. Frédéric and the young man with the moustache walked immediately behind, full of admiration for this young shop assistant who'd been revolted by the violence of the representatives of law and order.

As they made their way to the police station, the crowd dwindled. From time to time the policemen kept turning round with a scowl, and as the agitators had nothing further to do and the onlookers nothing further to see, they all gradually melted away. Passers-by were looking at Dussardier and making loud and offensive comments; one old woman standing in her doorway even exclaimed that he'd stolen a loaf, which unjust accusation increased the two friends' annoyance. Finally they arrived at the guardroom. Only a score of people remained and the sight of the soldiers was enough to convince them to beat a retreat.

Undaunted, Frédéric and his friend demanded to see the prisoner. The duty officer threatened to lock them up too, if they persisted. They asked to see the officer in charge, giving their names and stating that they were law students, like the prisoner.

They were shown into a completely bare room containing four benches set against the smoke-blackened plaster walls. At the end of this room, a small wicket opened and Dussardier's rugged face appeared; with his tousled hair, his tiny guileless eyes and flat nose, he looked vaguely like a friendly pug.

'Don't you recognize us?' asked Hussonet, as the man with the moustache was called.

'But I . . .' stammered Dussardier.

'Stop being idiotic,' the other man went on. 'They know you're a law student like us.'

In spite of their winks, Dussardier failed to grasp what was happening. He seemed to be collecting his thoughts and then suddenly:

'Have they found my box?'

Frédéric raised his eyes to the ceiling in despair. Hussonet replied:

'Oh, you mean the box you keep your lecture notes in? Yes, don't worry.'

They continued their charade and, finally realizing that they'd come to help him, Dussardier kept quiet for fear of compromising them. In any case, he felt rather bashful at being elevated to the status of student, on a par with these young men whose hands were so white.

'Would you like us to let anyone know?' asked Frédéric.

'No thanks.'

'How about your family?'

He hung his head and didn't reply; the poor young man was illegitimate. The two friends were surprised by his silence.

'Have you got anything to smoke?' Frédéric asked.

Dussardier fumbled in his pockets and pulled out the broken remains of a pipe, a fine meerschaum pipe with a blackwood stem, a silver lid and an amber mouthpiece.

He had been working hard for the last three years to turn it into the perfect pipe. He'd been careful to keep the bowl permanently wrapped in a chamois leather bag and smoke it as slowly as possible, never putting it down on marble and hanging it on his bed-post every night. And now he turned the bits over in his hand, with bleeding fingernails, staring wide-eyed at this wreckage of his pride and joy with an expression of unutterable misery.

'Suppose we give him some cigars?' whispered Hussonet, reaching for his pocket.

Frédéric had already placed a full cigar-case on the sill of the wicket window.

'Here, take these. And keep your pecker up!'

Dussardier reached out, eagerly shook the two hands he was being offered and, quite over-wrought, said in a voice shaking with sobs:

'What, are those really for me? Me?'

The two friends brushed aside his thanks and went off to have lunch together at the Café Tabourey opposite the Luxembourg Gardens.

As he cut into his steak Hussonet informed his companion that he worked for fashion papers and wrote advertisements for *L'Art industriel*.

'For Jacques Arnoux,' said Frédéric.

'Do you know him?'

'Well . . . yes and no. That's to say, I've seen him and spoken to him.'

Casually he asked Hussonet if he sometimes saw his wife.

'Now and again,' the young man replied.

Frédéric didn't dare to pursue his questions: this young Bohemian had suddenly assumed an enormous importance in his life; he settled the lunch bill with no sign of protest from the other man.

They felt mutually attracted, exchanged addresses, and Hussonet amiably suggested Frédéric might care to come along with him as far as the rue de Fleurus. Half-way across the gardens, the man who worked for Arnoux held his breath, contorted his face into an extraordinary grimace and started crowing like a cock. In reply, all the roosters in the vicinity set up a prolonged chorus.

'It's a signal,' explained Hussonet.

They stopped near the Bobino Theatre, in front of a house approached through a side-alley. At an attic window adorned with pots of nasturtiums and sweet peas, a young woman appeared in her bodice, hatless and resting her elbows on the edge of the gutter.

35

'Hullo, my pet! Hullo, my little chickabiddy!' said Hussonet, throwing kisses.

He kicked open the gate and went in.

Frédéric waited the whole of next week for him to re-surface, not daring to call on him for fear of appearing anxious to receive a return luncheon invitation; but he did search for him all over the Latin Quarter. He caught up with him one evening and took him round to his flat in the quai Napoléon.

They talked for hours, heart to heart. Hussonet's ambition was to achieve the fame and fortune to be found in the theatre. He was collaborating in vaudevilles—never performed—, 'had heaps of plans', and wrote lyrics for songs which he sometimes sang. Then, noticing a volume of Hugo and another of Lamartine on the bookshelves, he launched into a scathing attack on the Romantics: those poets lacked common sense, wrote incorrectly and, above all, weren't French. He boasted of his own knowledge of the language and proceeded to pick examples of their finest writings to pieces, with the mixture of virulence and pedantry typical of frivolous people discussing serious art.

With his own tastes under attack, Frédéric felt he needed to change the subject: why not take the bull by the horns and make the request on which his whole happiness depended? He asked the would-be man of letters if he'd take him along to Arnoux's gallery.

No problem at all; they agreed to meet the very next day.

Hussonet failed to turn up and let him down on three further occasions. One Saturday afternoon he did appear, at about four o'clock, but to take advantage of the cab he first called in at the Comédie-Française to pick up a box-ticket, stopped off at a tailor's and a dressmaker's, and scribbled a few notes in various porters' lodges before they finally arrived at the boulevard Montmartre. Frédéric went through the shop and up the stairs. Arnoux recognized him in the mirror standing in front of his desk and held out his hand over his shoulder, still continuing to write.

Five or six people were crowded into the narrow room, which was lit by a single window overlooking the courtyard;

at the far end a brown wool damask sofa stood in a recess between two door-curtains of the same material. On the mantelshelf littered with papers there was a bronze Venus; two lampstands with pink candles stood in identical positions on either side of the fireplace. In an armchair on the right next to a filing cabinet a man sat reading a paper, still with his hat on; the walls were covered with prints and pictures, valuable engravings or sketches by well-known contemporary artists, adorned by dedications professing their sincere affection for Jacques Arnoux.

'Everything still going all right?' he said, turning towards Frédéric, and without waiting for an answer whispered to Hussonet:

'What's your friend's name?'

Then more loudly:

'Do help yourself to a cigar on the filing cabinet over there.'

Situated in the heart of Paris, *L'Art industriel* was a convenient meeting place, a sort of neutral territory where competing interests could rub shoulders in a free-and-easy atmosphere. On that particular day you could have met Anténor Braive, the painter of royalty, Jules Burrieu, whose drawings were beginning to popularize the Algerian war; the cartoonist Sembaz, the sculptor Vourdat, and others, and not one of them corresponded to the student's preconceived ideas. They were simple in manner, outspoken in their speech. The other-worldly Lovarias told a dirty story while the inventor of oriental landscape-painting, the famous Dittmer, was wearing a knitted spencer under his waistcoat and went home by bus.

First they talked about a woman by the name of Apollonie, a former model, whom Burrieu claimed to have seen driving along the boulevards in a coach and four with two postilions. Hussonet explained this metamorphosis by the string of men who'd been keeping her.

'What an expert on Paris tarts this young fellow is!' exclaimed Arnoux.

'After you, sire, if there are any left,' the Bohemian

replied, giving him a salute to mimic the grenadier offering Napoleon his water-bottle.

They went on to discuss certain paintings in which Apollonie had sat for the head. Absent fellow painters came in for criticism, and surprise was expressed at the prices their works were fetching. Everybody was complaining about not earning enough money when in came a man of medium height wearing a coat fastened by a single button; he had bright eyes and a rather wild look.

'What a prize bunch of shopkeepers!' he exclaimed. 'What on earth does it matter? Those old masters who produced masterpieces didn't worry about earning huge sums, Correggio, Murillo . . .'

'Not forgetting Pellerin!' Sambaz interposed.

Ignoring the witticism the other man continued discoursing with such vehemence that Arnoux had to repeat twice:

'My wife's relying on you for next Thursday. Don't forget!'

These words reminded Frédéric of Madame Arnoux. The way to her apartment must be through the small room beside the divan? Arnoux had just opened the door on his way to fetch a handkerchief from the back. Frédéric had caught a glimpse of a wash-basin. But a sort of growl was coming from the corner of the fireplace; it was the newspaper reader in his armchair. He was five feet nine inches tall, had slightly drooping eyelids, grey hair and a majestic look. His name was Regimbart.

'What's the matter, Citizen?' enquired Arnoux.

'Another bit of skullduggery by the government!'

A primary school teacher had been sacked. Pellerin continued to develop his parallel between Michelangelo and Shakespeare. Dittmer was making his way out; Arnoux went after him and pressed two banknotes into his hand. Thinking this an opportune moment, Hussonnet said:

'Any chance of an advance, guv?'

But Arnoux had already sat down again and was telling off a seedy-looking old man wearing blue spectacles.

'Well, what a bright boy you are, old Isaac! That makes three works completely discredited and on the scrap heap!

Everyone's laughing at me! What am I going to do with them now people know all about them, I ask you! I'll have to ship them over to California! To hell with it! No, I won't listen to you!'

This character's speciality was providing such pictures with old masters' signatures. Arnoux was refusing to pay him and sent him packing with a flea in his ear. Then, with a complete change of manner, he greeted a pompous-looking gentleman wearing a decoration, a white necktie and whiskers.

Resting his elbow against the window-latch, he spoke to him at length, exuding charm; and then finally exploded:

'My dear count, I'm not short of willing helpers, you know!'

The count gave in, Arnoux slipped him twenty-five louis,* and as soon as he had left:

'God, these noble lords get on your nerves!'

'A pack of rogues the whole lot. of 'em!' muttered Regimbart.

As the afternoon wore on Arnoux's activity became more and more hectic; he was sorting articles, opening letters, drawing up accounts; hearing the sound of hammering in the shop, he went down to supervise some packing and then returned to his other tasks; all the time he kept scribbling away with his steel pen while parrying people's witticisms. That evening he was due to have dinner with his lawyer before leaving next morning for Belgium.

The others were chatting about current events: Cherubini's portrait, the new lecture theatre at the Beaux-Arts,* a coming exhibition. Pellerin was inveighing against the Institut.* Tittle-tattle and argument were tossed to and fro. The low-ceilinged room was packed like a sardine tin and the candles shone through the haze of cigar smoke like sunlight filtering through a mist.

The door next to the divan opened and a woman came out; she was tall and thin and her jerky movements made her watch charms tinkle against her black taffeta dress.

It was the woman he'd spotted last summer at the Palais-Royal. Some of the men greeted her by name and shook hands. Hussonnet had finally succeeded in extracting fifty francs or so out of Arnoux; the clock struck seven; everybody left. Arnoux told Pellerin to stay and took Mademoiselle Vatnaz into the back room.

They were whispering together; Frédéric couldn't hear what was being said. Then the woman raised her voice:

'The business was settled six months ago and I'm still waiting!'

There was a long pause, then Mademoiselle Vatnaz came back in. Arnoux had made her further promises.

'Oh well, we'll see later on.'

'Goodbye, happy man!' she said as she left.

Arnoux hastily went back into the dressing-room, plastered some brilliantine on his moustache, shortened his braces to tauten his trouser-straps, and then, as he was washing his hands:

'I'd like two paintings over the doors at two fifty apiece, sort of Boucher* style, right?'

'Very well,' replied the painter, pink in the face.

'Good! And don't forget my wife!'

Frédéric accompanied Pellerin to the top of the Faubourg-Poissonnière* and asked if he might be allowed to call on him sometimes; the painter graciously agreed.

Pellerin had read every book on aesthetics he could lay hands on, being convinced that once he'd discovered the secret of True Beauty he'd be able to produce masterpieces. He'd collected every imaginable aid—drawings, plaster casts, models, engravings—and his search was causing him agonies. He'd blame the weather, his nerves, his studio, would go out to seek inspiration in the streets, leap for joy when he'd found it . . . and then abandon the work and dream of producing something more beautiful.

He had a desperate longing to be famous, yet would fritter away his time in argument, believing in all sorts of rubbish, in systems, critics, the importance of regulating or reforming art; he'd reached the age of fifty without producing anything more than sketches. Pride and pigheadedness kept him from losing heart but he was always in a state of irritability, the sort of feverish excitement, half natural and half assumed, which is peculiar to actors.

On going into his studio you'd notice two large white canvases on which preliminary tones of brown, red and blue had been splashed here and there; over these a network of lines had been chalked in, like the mesh of a much-repaired fishing net. It was impossible to deduce the slightest idea of his intentions in these paintings and Pellerin would explain their subjects by indicating the missing parts with his thumb: one was going to be 'The Madness of Nebuchadnezzar', the other one, 'Nero Setting Fire to Rome'.

Frédéric expressed admiration, as he did also for studies of dishevelled nude women, landscapes swarming with tree trunks writhing under stormy winds, and above all fantastic pen and ink sketches reminiscent of Callot,* Rembrandt or Goya, models unknown to Frédéric. Pellerin no longer considered these youthful works at all important; now he was all for the *grand manner* and laid down the law with much eloquence on the subject of Phidias and Winckel-mann.* The objects all around underlined the forcefulness of his words: a skull resting on a prayer-stool, a few yataghans, a monk's robe—Frédéric slipped it on himself.

Whenever Frédéric arrived early he would find Pellerin still lying on his miserable old camp-bed which he kept hidden under a tatty bit of tapestry—he was an inveterate theatre-goer and went to bed late. He was looked after by a ragged old woman, took his meals in cheap eating-houses and didn't keep a mistress. The hit-or-miss quality of his information gave an amusing flavour to his paradoxes. His hatred of all that was common or middle class would erupt into scathing comments couched in richly lyrical language and his cult of the old masters was strong enough to bring him up to their level, or almost.

But why didn't he ever mention Madame Arnoux? Her husband he'd sometimes refer to as a good chap, at others as a charlatan. Frédéric was waiting to hear his revelations.

One day he was thumbing through one of his portfolios and came across the portrait of a gypsy who reminded him

41

rather of Mademoiselle Vatnaz, and as she intrigued him, he asked what her position was.

Pellerin thought she'd been a country schoolmistress in her younger days; now she gave private lessons and was trying to get published in some of the little magazines.

Judging by her attitude towards Arnoux Frédéric supposed she was his mistress?

'Good Lord, no, he's got plenty without her!'

Turning his face away to hide the blushes caused by such an unworthy thought the young man added jauntily:

'And no doubt she gives him tit for tat?'

'Not at all! She's as straight as a die!'

Frédéric felt guilty; he stepped up his visits to *L'Art industriel*.

Arnoux's name in large capital letters over the shop-front seemed to him something very special and significant, rather like Holy Writ. The broad pavement sloping down towards it helped him on his way and when the door opened, almost of its own accord, its handle, smooth to the touch, had the soft, sympathetic understanding of a hand held in his own. By slow degrees he became as regular in his habits as Regimbart.

Every day the latter would settle down in his armchair by the fireside, pick up *Le National*,* and monopolize it, expressing his reactions by exclaiming out loud or merely shrugging his shoulders. From time to time he'd wipe his forehead with a handkerchief which he kept tightly rolled and stuffed between the two top buttons of his green frock-coat. He wore trousers with creases, bootees, and a flowing cravat; his hat with its turned-up brim made him conspicuous from afar in any crowd.

At eight o'clock in the morning he would descend from the heights of Montmartre to partake of a little white wine in the rue Notre-Dame-des-Victoires. Lunch, followed by several games of billiards, saw him through till three, when he'd make his way towards the passage des Panoramas for a glass of absinthe. After his sessions at Arnoux's he'd drop in at the Bordelais Tavern for a vermouth and then, instead of going back home to his wife, he often preferred to dine alone in a little café in the place Gaillon where he insisted on being served with 'good home cooking, none of your fancy muck!' Finally he'd be driven to another billiard saloon where he'd stay till midnight or one o'clock, when the exhausted owner, having turned out the gas lights and put up the shutters, would beg him to leave.

However, it was not his fondness for drink that attracted Citizen Regimbart to these haunts but his ingrained habit of talking politics in such places; now his exuberance had succumbed to age and he would maintain a moody silence. Watching his solemn expression you'd have thought world affairs were churning round inside his head. Nothing ever emerged, and even amongst his friends no one could recall his having held any sort of a job, though he gave people to believe that he ran some kind of business advisory service.

Arnoux seemed to think very highly of him. One day he said to Frédéric:

'That man knows what's what, you know! He's a remarkable person!'

Another time Regimbart put down on his desk papers concerning some china clay mines in Brittany. Arnoux trusted his expertise.

Frédéric started showing Regimbart greater respect, even treating him to the occasional absinthe, and although he thought him stupid he'd often spend an hour or more with him merely because he was Jacques Arnoux's friend.

The art dealer had launched some contemporary painters and as a Man of Progress had been endeavouring to further his own financial interests while still preserving the appearance of artistic integrity; he was aiming to emancipate the arts and looking to get Great Art on the cheap. His influence, which covered the whole Paris luxury trade, was beneficial to the lightweights and the ruination of any sort of greatness. With his mania for pandering to public taste he perverted artists of ability, corrupted the strong-minded, wore down the weak, and brought fame to second-raters; his power over them lay in his contacts and his magazine. Bad painters were eager to see their daubs displayed in his gallery and upholsterers copied his furnishings. Frédéric

43

looked on him as a millionaire, a dilettante and a man of action rolled into one. However, there were many things which surprised him, for in his business deals, friend Arnoux was naughty.

He'd give fifteen hundred francs for a painting imported from some remote corner of Germany or Italy and then produce an invoice for four thousand to resell it, as a special favour, of course, for three thousand five hundred. One of his favourite tricks with painters was to demand a sweetener in the form of a smaller copy of their picture, on the pretext of making an engraving of it; he'd sell the copy and no print would ever appear. Any protest at this exploitation would be countered by a gentle dig in the ribs. With all this, he was most kind-hearted, very free with his cigars, extremely friendly, and quite unceremonious with strangers, liable to take a fancy to a work or a person, when he'd let nothing stand in his way and spare no trouble to help by advertising, writing letters or going the rounds. He considered himself an extremely honest man and his compulsive ebullience led him in all innocence to speak quite openly of his shady deals.

On one occasion, in order to rile a fellow art dealer who was giving a big party to launch a rival art magazine, only a few hours before it was due to take place, he asked Frédéric to write cancelling the invitations, then and there.

'As you'll appreciate, there's nothing dishonourable involved, is there?'

And the young man didn't dare refuse him the favour.

Next day, as he went into the office with Hussonnet, he saw the hem of a skirt disappearing through the doorway beside the staircase.

'Sorry!' apologized Hussonnet. 'If I'd known there were women about . . .'

'Oh, it's only my wife,' replied Arnoux. 'She happened to be passing so she dropped in to see me.'

'Dropped in?' said Frédéric.

'Yes, she's going home now.'

Abruptly the charm of the surroundings evaporated. The vague aura which he'd felt all around had vanished into

44

thin air or, rather, had never actually existed. It was like a bolt from the blue, an agonizing stab in the back.

Arnoux was fumbling in a drawer with a smile on his face. Was he laughing at him? The assistant put a bundle of damp sheets of paper down on the table.

'Aha! The proofs of the poster!' exclaimed Arnoux. 'I'm going to be very late for dinner tonight.'

Regimbart was collecting his hat.

'What, are you going to desert me?'

'It's seven o'clock!' retorted Regimbart.

Frédéric followed him out.

At the corner of the rue Montmartre he turned to look up at the first-floor windows and laughed self-pityingly to himself as he recalled the loving glances he'd so often cast towards them! So where did she live? How would he ever manage to meet her now? Once more he was alone in his longing and even lonelier than before.

'D'you feel like having . . . ?'

'Who, what?' said Frédéric, taken by surprise.

'An absinthe, of course!'

So Frédéric humoured his craving and let himself be taken along to the Bordelais Tavern. His companion settled his elbows on the table with his eyes fastened on the decanter while Frédéric cast a glance round the room and, spying Pellerin as he passed along the pavement outside, tapped on the window. Before the painter even had time to sit down, Regimbart was asking him why no one ever saw him at *L'Art industriel* these days.

'I'd sooner starve than go back there! The man's a monster, a philistine, a scoundrel, a criminal!'

For Frédéric, furious himself, this abuse was like music to his ears. At the same time he felt offended as it somehow seemed to reflect on Madame Arnoux herself.

'What on earth has he been doing to you?' asked Regimbart.

Pellerin's only reply was to stamp his foot and snort.

He was in the habit of undertaking, surreptitiously, a certain amount of work—charcoal and chalk portraits,

45

imitations of famous paintings—for sale to unwary collectors, and as he felt this sort of work degrading he preferred on the whole to keep it quiet. But Arnoux's 'dirty trick' was more then he could stand; he found relief in words: in fulfilment of a commission, agreed on in Frédéric's hearing, Pellerin had brought round the two pictures; and the dealer had had the cheek to criticize them! He'd expressed disapproval of the composition, the colours, and the draughtsmanship, particularly the latter; in a word, he'd declined to take them at any price. Then a debt had fallen due and Pellerin had been forced to let that old Jew Isaac have them; a fortnight later Arnoux had himself sold them to a Spaniard for two thousand francs.

'Not a penny less! What a dirty trick! And he's done lots of things like that, blast him! One of these days he'll find himself in the dock!'

'Oh, you're going too far!' said Frédéric in a timid voice.

'So I'm going too far, am I?' exclaimed the painter, thumping the table.

This violent outburst completely restored Frédéric's composure. Of course people could behave better but if Arnoux really had thought the paintings . . .

'Were no good! Out with it, don't be afraid to say what you think! Have you seen them? Do you know anything about painting? Well, let me tell you, my boy, I don't have any truck with amateurs!'

'Well, it's none of my business,' said Frédéric.

'If that's the case, then why are you so interested in standing up for him?' Pellerin asked coldly.

'Well I . . . because I'm his friend,' stammered Frédéric.

'Then give him my kind regards! Goodnight!'

And the painter stamped out, naturally ignoring any question of paying for his drink.

In defending Arnoux, Frédéric had convinced himself. Carried away by his own eloquence, he felt a sudden affection for this kind and clever man, maligned by his friends, who was now being left to work on, all alone, deserted by everyone. He couldn't resist a strange impulse

46

to go and see him at once. Ten minutes later he was pushing open the door of the art gallery.

Arnoux was working with his assistants on the layout of some enormous posters for an exhibition of paintings.

'Good Lord, what's brought you back here?'

Frédéric was embarrassed by this straightforward question; not knowing how to answer he asked if anyone had found his notebook, a small blue leather memorandum.

'The one you use to keep your love-letters in?' said Arnoux.

Blushing like a schoolgirl, Frédéric denied any such imputation.

'Your poetry then?' the dealer said.

He was handling the sample copies spread out around him and discussing their format, their colours, their margins; Frédéric was growing more and more irritated by his air of deliberation and above all by his hands as he ran them over the posters—large, rather flabby hands with spatulate finger-nails.

Finally Arnoux rose to his feet and as he said: 'Well, that's that,' chucked Frédéric familiarly under the chin; the young man recoiled and in disgust stalked out of the office for the last time in his life, as he thought. Even Madame Arnoux seemed cheapened by this display of impudent vulgarity on the part of her husband.

That same week he got a letter from Deslauriers announcing his arrival in Paris the following Thursday, and he eagerly jumped at the chance of changing over to more decent and honest, friendlier company: a man like that was worth all your women! He'd no longer need to meet Regimbart, Pellerin, Hussonnet or anybody else! Being anxious to put his friend up in comfort, he bought an iron bunk-bedstead, a second easy chair and extra bed-linen. On Thursday morning, as he was getting dressed to go and meet Deslauriers, his door-bell rang. In came Arnoux.

'Just a flying visit, that's all. Yesterday I was sent a superb trout from Geneva. We'll look forward to seeing you this evening, seven o'clock sharp, 24B, rue de Choiseul* . . . Don't forget!'

47

Frédéric's legs turned to jelly. He was forced to sit down. He kept repeating: 'At last! At last!' Then he wrote off to his tailor, his hatter and his boot-maker and had the notes delivered by three separate messengers. The key turned in the lock and the doorkeeper appeared with a trunk on his shoulder.

At the sight of Deslauriers Frédéric started to tremble like an unfaithful wife facing her husband.

'What on earth's up with you?' asked Deslauriers. 'You must have got my letter?'

Frédéric was too unnerved to lie.

He flung himself into his friend's arms.

Later, the lawyer's clerk told him his story. His father had refused to render an account of his guardianship, under the impression that this was required only once every ten years. But being an expert on procedure Deslauriers had succeeded in extracting every penny of his mother's money, seven thousand francs in all; and he'd got them on him, in an old wallet.

'It's something to fall back on if the worst comes to the worst. I must see about investing it and find a job for myself straightaway tomorrow morning. But today's a holiday and I'm all yours, old chap!'

'Oh, you mustn't put yourself out,' said Frédéric. 'If you've got anything important to do this evening . . .'

'Good God, man, if I did a thing like that I'd feel a real rat!'

This expression, with its unintentionally offensive implications, stung Frédéric on the raw.

On the table beside the fire the porter had set out a few cutlets, some galantine, a lobster, dessert and two bottles of claret. Deslauriers was touched by the warmth of his welcome.

'My word, you're treating me like a lord!'

They talked about their past, the future, and from time to time clasped hands and looked affectionately in each other's eyes for a minute. Then a messenger brought in a new hat. Deslauriers commented on its shiny top.

Next the tailor came in person to deliver the new dress-coat, just pressed by his own hands.

'Anyone'd think you were getting married!' said Deslauriers.

An hour later a third man appeared and out of a bag produced a quite magnificent pair of patent leather boots. While Frédéric was trying them on the boot-maker slyly noted the condition of the footwear of this man up from the country:

'Would the gentleman be needing anything himself?'

'No, thank you,' the lawyer's clerk replied, tucking his old lace-up shoes out of sight under his chair.

Frédéric was embarrassed at seeing his friend humiliated. He felt reluctant to make his confession. Finally he exclaimed loudly, as if the thought had only just occurred to him:

'Good heavens, I was forgetting!'

'What?'

'I'm going out to dinner tonight!'

'To the Dambreuses? Why haven't you ever mentioned them in your letters?'

It wasn't with the Dambreuses but the Arnouxs.

'You might have warned me!' said Deslauriers. 'I'd have come a day later.'

'I couldn't,' replied Frédéric. 'I only got the invitation this morning, just a short while ago.'

And to make amends for his omission and encourage his friend to overlook it, he undid the tangle of cords round his trunk, arranged all his belongings in the chest of drawers and offered him his own bed; he'd sleep in the lumber room. At four o'clock he started to get dressed.

'You've got loads of time!' said Deslauriers.

Finally he was dressed and left.

'How like the rich!' thought his friend.

And went off to dine in a little restaurant in the rue Saint-Jacques kept by someone he knew.

As he climbed up the stairs Frédéric's heart was pounding so fast that he had to stop several times. One of his gloves was too tight and split; while he was tucking the torn piece under his shirt-cuff, Arnoux, coming up behind him, took his arm and escorted him in.

The entrance hall was decorated in the Chinese style with a painted lantern hanging from the ceiling and bamboo plants in the corners. Going across the drawing-room, Frédéric stumbled over a tiger skin. The candelabra hadn't been lit but two lamps were alight at the far end of the room.

Mademoiselle Marthe came in to say her mother was getting dressed. Arnoux lifted her up to give her a kiss and then went off to select some special bottles from his cellar, leaving Frédéric alone with the girl.

She'd shot up since the trip to Montereau. Her brown hair fell in ringlets over her bare arms. Her dress, more flared than a ballerina's skirt, revealed a pair of pink calves and her whole charming person smelt as fresh as a bunch of flowers. She accepted the gentleman's compliments with a flirtatious look, solemnly inspected him, slithered round the furniture like a kitten, and vanished.

All his embarrassment had disappeared. The embossed paper lampshades were casting a subdued pearly light which softened the mauve of the satin wall-hangings. Through the slats of the large fan-shaped fireguard there was a glimpse of coal in the grate; next to the clock stood a casket with silver clasps. The room was littered with personal belongings: a doll in the middle of a small sofa, a lace shawl slung over a chair back, and on the work-table a piece of woollen knitting with two ivory needles hanging points down. It was altogether a peaceful, decent, homely scene.

Arnoux came back and from behind the other door curtain Madame Arnoux appeared. As she was in the shadow, at first Frédéric could make out only her head. She was wearing a black velvet dress and in her hair a long Algerian red silk net twined round her comb and dangling down over her left shoulder.

Arnoux introduced Frédéric.

'Oh, I remember Monsieur Moreau very well,' she replied.

Then all the guests arrived almost simultaneously: Dittmer, Lovarias, Burrieu, the composer Rosenwald, Théophile Lorris the poet, two art critic colleagues, a paper manufacturer, and finally the celebrated Pierre Paul Mensius, the last survivor of the grand manner in painting who bore not only his fame and his fourscore years but also his large paunch very stylishly.

When they went into dinner, Madame Arnoux took his arm. There was a vacant chair for Pellerin; although quite ready to exploit him, Arnoux was fond of him. Moreover, he was scared of his powers of invective, so much so that in order to placate him, he'd published his portrait in *L'Art industriel* together with an article praising him to the skies; and being more susceptible to fame than money, at about eight o'clock in came Pellerin, quite out of breath. Frédéric assumed they'd made it up some time ago.

He was finding the company, the food and everything else to his liking. The room was large and panelled with embossed leather like a medieval hall; behind a Dutch whatnot there was a pipe-rack full of chibouks; and round the table, amongst the flowers and bowls of fruit, the different colours of the Bohemian glasses sparkled like fairy lights.

He faced a choice of ten different sorts of mustard. He ate daspachio, curry, ginger, blackbirds from Corsica, Roman lasagnas, and drank some extraordinary wines, Lipfraoli* and Tokay. Indeed, Arnoux prided himself on his hospitality and with his table in mind used to keep in with all the mail-coach drivers; he was also on friendly terms with the cooks of the great houses who passed on recipes for sauces.

But it was the conversation which Frédéric found most fascinating. His appetite for travel was whetted by Dittmer's talk of the East; his curiosity concerning the theatre was appeased by Rosenwald's comments on the Opéra; and Hussonnet's account of spending a whole winter subsisting on nothing but Dutch cheese made the grim life of Bohemia seem funny. Then an argument between Lovarias and Burrieu on Florentine painting broadened his horizons by opening his eyes to certain masterpieces; and he had difficulty in restraining his delight when he heard Pellerin exclaim:

'Do stop going on about your wretched "reality". What does the word mean anyway? Some people see things black, others see them blue, and the mob sees them stupid! What could be less natural than Michelangelo, yet what could be more wonderful? All this concern for externals is the hallmark of our loathsome modern world and if things go on being like this art'll become a sort of stale joke, less poetic than religion and duller than politics! You'll never achieve its real goal, yes, its goal, which is to create a kind of impersonal state of ecstasy, if you go for minor works, however cleverly they're executed. Take Bassolier's painting, for instance: it's pretty, it's stylish, neat and tidy—and it adds up to damn all! It slips nicely into the pocket, you can take it with you on a journey, lawyers will pay you twenty thousand for it and it contains roughly two-penn'orth of ideas—and without ideas great art is impossible and without greatness there's no beauty! Olympus is a mountain! The most staggering monument in the world will always be the Pyramids. Exuberance is better than all your good taste, a desert than a city pavement, and a primitive savage preferable to a barber!'

As he listened Frédéric was watching Madame Arnoux and the words poured into his mind like molten metal into a furnace, fuelling his passion and generating love.

He was sitting three places below her on the same side of the table. From time to time she would lean forward slightly, turning her head to say a few words to her little girl and give her a smile; then a dimple would form in her cheek, adding a touch of tenderness to the kindness in her face.

When liqueurs were served she left the room. The talk became very bawdy. Arnoux was a past master in this art. Frédéric was amazed at the cynicism shown by these men. All the same their obsession with women established a sort of camaraderie between him and them and heightened his own self-esteem.

To hide his shyness, when he went back into the drawing-room he picked up one of the albums lying on the table. A number of leading artists of the day had illustrated it with drawings, written little pieces of verse or prose, or else merely signed their autographs; many unknown names mingled with those of the famous and the more ingenious ones were swamped in worthless trivia; they all contained more or less overt expressions of admiration for Madame Arnoux; Frédéric wouldn't have dared to write anything of his own beside them.

She went over to fetch the little silver-clasped casket which Frédéric had noticed on the mantelshelf of her boudoir. It was a Renaissance piece, a present from her husband. His friends made complimentary noises and she herself said how much she appreciated it; he became affectionate and kissed her on the forehead in front of everybody.

After that they split up into groups and chatted; old Mensius was sitting in a wing-chair beside the fireplace, next to Madame Arnoux; she was leaning over to speak in his ear, their heads touching, and Frédéric yearned to be deaf, ugly, infirm, provided he could have a famous name and white hair, anything to establish him on such intimate terms. His heart ached with frustration: why did he have to be so young?

But she came over to the corner where he was sitting, asked him if he knew certain of the guests, whether he was fond of painting, how long he'd been studying in Paris. Every word she uttered seemed to him something original, her own exclusive property. He was watching intently the loose strands of hair lightly brushing against her bare shoulder; he couldn't take his eyes off them, projecting his whole being into this white feminine flesh. But he didn't dare look her squarely in the face.

They were interrupted by Rosenwald coming up to ask Madame Arnoux to sing something. She stood waiting while he played the opening bars; her lips parted and a long, pure, liquid sound rose into the air.

Frédéric couldn't understand a single word of Italian.

She began slowly and solemnly, like a hymn, burst into a series of lively crescendos and then suddenly sank in a dying fall; the melody returned in a broad, tender, lingering, flowing rhythm.

She was standing by the keyboard with her arms hanging down at her sides and her gaze lost in space. Now and again she'd blink her eyes and peer forward for a second in order to read the music. In the lower register her contralto took on a darker, chilling tone and her lovely face with its bold eyebrows would tilt sideways towards her shoulder; her bosom heaved, she flung out both her arms and lovingly, as though caressed by a gentle breeze, she threw back her head and a stream of notes burst from her throat; her voice rose to three piercing trills, dropped, soared again still higher to one single note, and then, after a pause, ended with a final flourish.

Rosenwald remained sitting at the piano and continued to play for himself. One by one the guests took their leave. At eleven o'clock, as the last of them were going, Arnoux went out with Pellerin on the pretext of seeing him home. He was one of those people who complain of not feeling fit unless they've taken their after-dinner constitutional.

Madame Arnoux had come out into the hall; Dittmer and Hussonnet were saying goodnight; she shook hands with them and held out her hand to Frédéric as well; a sort of tingling sensation ran over every inch of his body.

He took leave of his friends; his heart was overflowing, he had to be alone. What was the significance of this proffered hand? Was it a purely formal gesture? Or was it an encouragement? 'Oh, come on, man, you're mad!' Anyway, what did it matter, now that he'd be able to see her any time he liked and bask in the light of her presence?

The streets were deserted. From time to time a heavy cart went lumbering past over the cobbles. One grey housefront followed the other; and Frédéric thought scornfully of all those human beings asleep behind those walls and shuttered windows, living out their lives without ever seeing *Her*, not one of whom even suspected she existed! He was oblivious to his surroundings, to space and time, to every-thing; he strode on blindly, pounding the pavement with his boots and rapping the shop-shutters with his stick, swept along in a daze. Suddenly damp air came swirling round him and he realized he'd reached the river.

The lights of the street-lamps stretched out into the distance in two straight lines, and long red flames shimmered in the depths of the slate-grey water while the paler sky above seemed to be resting on great shadowy masses rising up on either side of the river. Noble buildings, hidden from view, deepened the darkness. Beyond, over the roof-tops, hovered a luminous haze; all sounds were hushed into one single hum; a light breeze was blowing.

He'd come to a halt in the middle of the Pont-Neuf; baring his chest and hatless, he filled his lungs with air. At the same time he could feel a surge of inexhaustible power rising from the depths of his being, a flood of tenderness which set his nerves vibrating like the lapping waves before his eyes. A church clock struck slowly, like a voice calling to him.

Thrills ran through his body; he felt he was being lifted into a higher world. He'd been vouchsafed some extraordinary faculty of whose purpose he had no idea. He wondered, seriously, whether to become a great poet or a great painter; he opted for painting: that profession would be bound to bring him closer to Madame Arnoux. So he'd discovered his vocation! Now the purpose of his life was plain, his future assured.

As he was shutting his door he heard the sound of snoring coming from the dark little room next to his bedroom. It was that other man. He'd forgotten all about him. Out of the mirror he saw his own face watching him. He was, he thought, good-looking . . . And for a minute he stood there, gazing at himself.

CHAPTER V

By noon next day he'd bought himself a box of paints, some brushes and an easel. Pellerin agreed to give him lessons and Frédéric took him round to his rooms to see if there was anything lacking in his paraphernalia.

Deslauriers was back and the second armchair was occupied by another young man. The lawyer's clerk pointed to him:

'Here's the man! It's Sénécal!'

The young man did not attract Frédéric. His short-cropped hair made his forehead stick out, his grey eyes had a sort of steely glint, and his long frock-coat and whole get-up smacked of pedagogue and preacher.

They started chatting about the latest happenings, Rossini's *Stabat Mater** amongst others; on being questioned Sénécal stated that he never went to the theatre. Pellerin opened the paint box..

'Is that yours?' enquired Deslauriers.

'Of course it is!'

'Goodness me, what a funny idea!'

And he leaned over the table where the mathematics teacher was thumbing through a volume of Louis Blanc's works which he had brought along himself and reading passages under his breath while Pellerin and Frédéric examined the palette, the brushes and bladders. They started to talk about Arnoux's dinner-party.

'Is that the art dealer?' enquired Sénécal. 'There's a fine chap for you!'

'Why do you say that?' asked Pellerin.

'A man making money hand over fist by degrading political tricks!'

And he mentioned a very well-known lithograph depicting the entire royal family engaged in edifying pursuits: Louis-Philippe was holding a copy of the *Code civil*, the queen had a prayer-book, the princesses were busy embroidering, the Duc de Nemours was buckling on his sword, Monsieur de Joinville was showing his younger brothers a map, while in the background there was a glimpse of a double bed. This picture entitled 'A Nice Family' had delighted the middle classes and infuriated the patriots. Pellerin retorted, as sharply as if he had produced it himself, that everybody had a right to his own opinions. Sénécal couldn't agree: the sole aim of art was to edify the masses and the only valid subjects were those conducive to good behaviour; anything else was pernicious.

'But surely that depends on the way it's done?' exclaimed Pellerin. 'I may be producing masterpieces!'

'That's your bad luck then! No one's got the right . . .'

'What's that?'

'No, sir, you haven't the right to interest me in things I disapprove of! What's the point of all those finicky little works, those Venuses, for instance, who appear in all your landscapes? I fail to see what moral lessons there are for the People in them! You ought to show us how wretched they are, get us involved in their sacrifices! There's no shortage of subjects, for Christ's sake! Farm labourers, factory workers!'

Pellerin was speechless with rage; then, thinking he could clinch the argument:

'All right then, how about Molière?'

'Certainly,' replied Sénécal. 'I admire him, as a forerunner of the French Revolution!'

'Ah, the Revolution! Revolutionary art! There's never been a more barren period!'

'There's never been a greater one, sir!'

Pellerin folded his arms and looked him straight in the eyes.

'I get the impression you'd make a fine National Guardsman!'

His challenger was used to arguing. He retorted:

'I'm not one and I loathe them just as much as you do! But principles such as yours corrupt the masses! What's more, you're playing into the hands of the government. They wouldn't be so powerful if they didn't have the secret support of irresponsible clowns like Arnoux!'

Pellerin was so exasperated at hearing this that he

launched into a defence of Arnoux, even claiming that he had a heart of pure gold, that he was a trusty friend and devoted to his wife.

'Do you really think so? If you offered him enough he'd let you have her as a model!'

Frédéric's face went livid.

'He's obviously treated you very badly at some time or other?'

'Me? Not a bit, I once saw him in a café with a friend, that's all!'

This was true but the advertisements put out regularly, every day, by *L'Art industriel* got on his nerves. In his eyes, Arnoux was a representative of a society which would bring about the downfall of democracy. As a confirmed republican, he smelt corruption in any sign of elegant living, being himself completely undemanding and uncompromisingly honest.

Conversation lapsed. The painter hastily remembered an appointment and the schoolmaster his pupils; when they had gone Deslauriers asked various questions about Arnoux.

'You will introduce me later on, won't you, old chap?'

'Certainly,' Frédéric replied.

They started to work out their living arrangements. Deslauriers hadn't had any trouble in finding a job as second clerk in a solicitor's office, had signed on at the Law School and bought the books he'd be needing. So the life of which they'd long dreamt now began.

The glamour of youth made it a delightful one. As Deslauriers hadn't mentioned any financial arrangement, Frédéric kept quiet on the subject. He paid for everything, kept the wardrobe tidy, and saw to the household chores; but if the hall porter needed telling off, it was Deslauriers who undertook to do it, continuing his role as Frédéric's senior and mentor.

During the day they saw nothing of each other but they met in the evening when they would both settle down to work in their respective chairs beside the fire. But not for long. They'd exchange endless confidences, go into fits of laughter for no reason, sometimes squabble over a smoking lamp or a mislaid book and quickly make it up with a joke.

They would leave the door open between their two rooms and chat together from their separate beds.

In the morning they would stroll about on their terrace in shirt-sleeves; the sun would be rising, a slight haze moving along over the river, shrill cries coming up from the flower market; the smoke swirled from their pipes into the pure air which refreshed their eyes, still puffy with sleep, and they'd draw it into their lungs filled with a sense of boundless hope.

On Sundays when it wasn't raining they'd go out and walk along together arm in arm through the streets. Almost always the same thought would come into their minds at the very same moment or else they would chatter away, oblivious to their surroundings. Deslauriers's ambition was to become wealthy in order to achieve power. He wanted to stir things up, make a great splash, employ three secretaries, and give a grand political dinner party every week. Frédéric was busy setting up a Moorish palace for himself; he was going to spend his life on cashmere-covered divans to the sound of babbling fountains, waited upon by young blackamoors; and these dreams came to be so vivid that he'd grow depressed, as if such things had really existed and had now been lost.

'What's the point of talking about all this,' he'd say, 'when we're never going to get them!'

'Who knows?' Deslauriers replied.

In spite of his democratic views he kept urging Frédéric to renew his links with the Dambreuses. Frédéric pointed out that he'd already tried.

'What's that got to do with it! Have another go! You'll get that invitation!'

Towards the middle of March, amongst some other fairly stiff bills, they received one from the restaurant which sent up their evening meal. Not having the money to pay, Frédéric borrowed five hundred francs from Deslauriers; a fortnight later he repeated the request and the lawyer's clerk remonstrated with him for spending so much at Arnoux's gallery.

Frédéric was indeed spending excessively there. With a view of Venice, one of Naples and another of Constantinople in the middle of each of the three walls, paintings by Alfred de Dreux all over the place, a sculpture group by Pradier* on the mantelshelf, copies of *L'Art industriel* lying about on the piano, and art folders in the corners on the floor, the flat was so cluttered up that there was hardly any room to spread your elbows or put a book down. Frédéric claimed that he needed all this for his painting.

He was working at Pellerin's place. But Pellerin was often out and about, being in the habit of showing his face at all funerals and other events that would be reported in the Press, so Frédéric spent many long hours by himself in the studio. The calm of this large room—the only sound was the scampering of mice—the light falling from the ceiling and even the roaring of the stove at first plunged him into a sort of intellectual euphoria. Then he'd look up from his painting and run his eyes over the peeling walls, the knick-knacks on the whatnot, the torsos with their accumulated dust producing a sort of tattered plush effect; and, like a traveller lost in the forest, where every path keeps bringing him back again and again to the same place, behind every thought the memory of Madame Arnoux loomed up.

He fixed certain days when he'd call on her and, having reached the second floor, he'd stand in front of her door hesitating whether to knock. Footsteps were heard approaching, the door was opened, and the words 'Madam is not at home' brought deliverance, leaving him as it were with one less weight on his heart.

Yet he did meet her. The first time there were three other ladies with her; on another afternoon Marthe's writing teacher appeared on the scene. In any case the men invited to Madame Arnoux's dinner parties never paid her casual calls. Frédéric decided it would be more tactful to put a stop to his own.

But he never missed going round to *L'Art industriel* every

Wednesday without fail, so as to be invited to her Thursday night dinners, and he'd stay on longer than anyone else, longer than Regimbart, to the last possible minute, pretending to be examining a print or glancing through a newspaper. Eventually Arnoux would say: 'Are you doing anything tomorrow night?' and he'd accept before the words were out of his mouth. Arnoux seemed to be taking a fancy to him. He was showing him how to recognize wines, make a hot punch, cook woodcock in a wine and mushroom sauce; Frédéric would meekly follow his advice: he loved anything connected with Madame Arnoux—her furniture, her servants, her house, her street.

During these dinner parties he hardly ever opened his mouth; he just gazed at her. She had a tiny beauty spot near her right temple; over her forehead and beside her cheeks her hair was darker than elswhere and always looked a little damp at the edges; from time to time she'd stroke it lightly, with just two fingers. He knew the exact shape of each of her nails, the swish of her silk dress as she passed through a doorway filled him with delight, he'd furtively sniff the scent of her handkerchief; for him her comb, her gloves, her rings, were something utterly special, as remarkable as any work of art, possessing a personality of their own that was almost human; and all these things were wrapping themselves round his heart and fuelling his passion.

He'd been unable to resist revealing his love to Deslauriers. When he came back from Madame Arnoux's he'd wake him up, as if accidentally, in order to talk about her.

Deslauriers was sleeping in the lumber-room next to the water tap; he'd give an enormous yawn. Frédéric would sit down on the end of the bed. First he'd talk about the dinner and then go on to mention dozens of petty details in which he detected signs of disdain or affection. For instance, she'd once declined to accept his arm and taken Dittmer's instead; Frédéric had been upset.

'What rubbish!'

Or else she'd addressed him as her 'friend'.

'So what are you waiting for then?'

'I don't dare,' Frédéric would say.

'All right then, forget about it! Good-night!'

Deslauriers would roll over and go to sleep. He couldn't understand Frédéric's love in the least, seeing it as a terminal disease of adolescence; and doubtless finding Frédéric's exclusive company inadequate, he hit on the idea of inviting their common friends round once a week.

They'd start arriving at about nine every Saturday evening. The three Algerian cotton curtains were carefully drawn, the lamp and four candles were lit, and in the centre of the table the tobacco jar and a large selection of pipes were surrounded by bottles of beer, the tea-pot, a flask of rum and an assortment of cakes. They'd discuss the immortality of the soul and compare views on their professors.

One evening Hussonnet brought along a tall embarrassed-looking young man dressed in a frock-coat which was too short in the sleeves. It was the young fellow they'd tried to rescue from the police station the year before.

He'd been accused of theft and threatened with prosecution when he'd been unable to return to his employer the cardboard box containing lace lost in the course of the scuffle; he was now a clerk in a firm of carriers. Hussonnet had run into him that morning on a street corner and had brought him along because Dussardier wanted to express his thanks to 'the other man'.

He gave Frédéric back his cigar-case, still full, which he'd religiously kept in the hope of being able to return it one day. The young men invited him to come again and he continued to do so.

They all had a lot in common. In the first place none of them had a moment's doubt that the government was repulsive; the only one who made any effort to defend Louis-Philippe was Martinon. They'd bombard him with the stock ideas retailed in the Press: 'new Bastilles'* were being built 'directed against the masses'; the September Laws; Pritchard: Lord Guizot*; for fear of giving offence, Martinon kept quiet. In the whole of his seven years in secondary school, he had never once been given an imposition and he was well thought of in the Law Faculty. He normally wore a large beige frock-coat and rubber galoshes but one evening he turned up dressed fit to kill: double-breasted velvet waistcoat, white tie and gold chain.

They were even more surprised to learn that he'd just come from the Dambreuses. The banker had in fact recently bought a large parcel of land from Martinon senior; the old fellow had introduced his son to him and they'd both been invited to dinner.

'Were there lots of truffles?' asked Deslauriers. 'And did you slip your arm round his wife's waist, as you ought?'

Whereupon the conversation turned to the subject of women. Pellerin couldn't agree that there was such a thing as a lovely woman (he preferred tigers); anyway the human female ranked aesthetically low in the hierarchy of creation.

'The things that attract you about her—her breasts, her hair—are precisely those things that debase her as an Idea.'

'All the same,' objected Frédéric, 'long black hair and big black eyes . . .'

'Oh, don't bother to go on!' exclaimed Hussonnet. 'Ladies of Spain, I abhor you! And classical beauties? Include me out! After all, let's face it, tarts are more fun than the Venus de Milo! Isn't our national emblem the cock? And how about a spot of Regency* spice as well?

Flow freely, lovely wine and women, deign to smile!

Off with the brunettes, on with the blondes! What's your view, Daddy Dussardier?'

Dussardier made no reply. Everyone pressed him to speak out.

'Well,' he said blushing, 'personally I'd like to love the same woman all my life.'

He said this in such a way that for a moment no one spoke, some surprised by his genuine innocence, others perhaps recognizing their own secret longings.

Sénécal put his mug of beer down on the mantelshelf and dogmatically declared that since prostitution was tyrannical exploitation and marriage immoral, the best thing was to steer clear of women. Deslauriers used them to pass the time, that was all. Monsieur de Cisy stood very much in awe of them.

Having been brought up under the eyes of a pious grandmother, Cisy found the company of these young men as exciting as a brothel and as educational as any Sorbonne. They offered him plenty of instruction and he was proving a keen student, even trying to smoke, although invariably feeling sick every time. Frédéric showed him every consideration; he admired the colour of his neckties, his fur overcoat, and above all his slim boots which fitted him like a glove and were almost arrogant in their immaculate elegance; his carriage used to wait for him down in the street.

One snowy evening after he'd just left, Sénécal remarked that he was sorry for the coachman and then started declaiming against yellow gloves and the Jockey Club; he preferred a working man to any of these fine gentlemen.

'I work for my living at least! I'm a poor man!'

'That's pretty obvious,' rejoined Frédéric, finally losing patience.

The schoolmaster never forgave him for that remark.

However, when Regimbart mentioned knowing Sénécal slightly, Frédéric, keen to do a kindness to a friend of Arnoux's, invited him to their Saturday evening gatherings and the two patriots enjoyed meeting.

Yet they were different. Sénécal, who had an egg-shaped head, was interested only in systems, while Regimbart clung to facts, his main concern being the Rhine frontier.* He claimed to be an artillery expert and had his clothes made at the École polytechnique* outfitter.

On his first visit, he turned up his nose in scorn when he was offered cakes, saying cakes were for women; he didn't appear much more gracious on subsequent occasions, either. As soon as the conversation reached a higher level of ideas, he'd mutter: 'Oh, let's keep off Utopian dreams!' In matters artistic, although he was to be seen in artists' studios, where he obliged by giving fencing lessons, his views were far from sophisticated; he'd compare Monsieur Marrast's* style to Voltaire's and Mademoiselle Vatnaz to

Madame de Staël, because her 'Ode to Poland'* came 'straight from the heart'. In a word, Regimbart got on everybody's nerves, especially Deslauriers's, for the Citizen was a close friend of Arnoux's and the lawyer's clerk was eager to become a regular guest there in the hope of making useful contacts. 'When are you going to take me along with you?' he kept asking Frédéric. But Arnoux was snowed under with work or else away on some trip; anyway there wasn't any point, the dinner parties were coming to an end.

In an emergency Frédéric would have been ready to risk his life for his friend but, being anxious to show himself off to the best possible advantage, he kept careful watch over his language, his manners and his dress, to the point of never appearing at *L'Art industriel* unless he was immaculately gloved, and he was scared that with his shabby evening clothes, his counsel-for-the-prosecution approach and his bumptiousness, Deslauriers might not be to Madame Arnoux's liking, thereby undermining his own standing and lowering him in her estimation. He was quite prepared to accept the others but that particular person would have caused him far greater embarrassment. The clerk realized that he didn't want to keep his word and Frédéric's silence added insult to injury.

He would have dearly loved to exercise complete control over Frédéric's actions and see him develop in accordance with their youthful ideals; he was revolted by his inertia, which seemed to him a sort of insubordination and betrayal. Moreover, with Madame Arnoux permanently on his mind Frédéric kept constantly mentioning her husband, so Deslauriers hit on a diabolical 'gag' which consisted of repeating Arnoux's name scores of times a day, at the end of every sentence, like some sort of idiotic mannerism. Whenever a knock came on the door, he'd call out: 'Come in, Arnoux!' In the restaurant he'd order 'some Brie, just like Arnoux'; and in the night he'd pretend to be having nightmares and wake his friend up screaming: 'Arnoux! Arnoux!' Finally one day, at the end of his tether, Frédéric appealed to him miserably to 'leave me alone with your Arnoux!'.

'Never!' retorted the clerk.

Toujours lui! Lui partout! Ou brûlante ou glacée,
*L'image de l'Arnoux**

'Shut up!' yelled Frédéric, brandishing his fist.

He went on more calmly:

'You know very well it's a painful subject for me.'

'Oh, I'm sorry, my dear fellow,' replied Deslauriers with a deep bow. 'In future every consideration will be shown to the young lady's nervous condition. Once again, my apologies, my very deepest apologies!'

And nothing more was heard of that joke.

But one evening three weeks later, he said to him:

'Well, I saw Madame Arnoux this afternoon.'

'Where was that?'

'At the Law Courts with the solicitor Balandard. Brown hair, medium height, that's her, isn't it?'

Frédéric nodded, waiting for Deslauriers to go on; at the slightest hint of admiration, he'd have opened up his heart to him and been ready to love him like a brother. The other man still said nothing and eventually unable to restrain himself, he asked him in a casual voice what he thought of her.

Deslauriers thought her 'not bad; nothing special'.

'Ah, that's what you think,' said Frédéric.

August arrived, the time for his second examination. It was normally considered that a fortnight was long enough to swot it all up. Confident of his ability, Frédéric devoured at one go the first four books of the code of legal procedure, the first three books of the penal code, several sections of criminal procedure and part of the code of civil law, with Monsieur Poncelet's annotations. The night before the exam, Deslauriers made him revise the whole lot, which took him until the morning, and in order not to waste even the last few minutes, he continued to quiz him as they made their way on foot to the Sorbonne.

As several examinations were being held at the same time, there were a large number of people in the courtyard, including Hussonnet and Cisy; everybody came along to see a friend being examined. Slipping on the traditional dark gown and followed by a crowd of people, Frédéric went with three other students into a large hall lit by curtainless windows with benches lined up along the walls. In the centre stood a table covered in green baize and surrounded by leather-seated chairs. On one side of this table sat the examiners, all in red gowns with ermine hoods over their shoulders and round gold-braided caps on their heads. Being the last candidate but one Frédéric was badly placed. To the first question, on the difference between a contract and an agreement, Frédéric got his answer the wrong way round and the professor, a decent chap, said: 'Don't be nervous, young man, we're not going to eat you!' Then, after asking two easy questions and receiving rather fumbling answers, he moved on to the fourth candidate. Frédéric was demoralized by this poor start. Sitting opposite him with the general public, Deslauriers was making signs that all was not yet lost and the second time round, on criminal law, he gave reasonably good answers. But after the third round, on the question of sealed wills, as the examiner showed no reaction whatever, his anxiety increased, for although Hussonnet kept bringing his hands together as if clapping, Deslauriers was shrugging his shoulders. At last the moment arrived for him to answer on procedure! The question involved the opposition of a third party. The examining professor had been horrified to hear certain opinions expressed which were in disagreement with his own and asked him gruffly:

'Well, young man, is that your view? How can you reconcile the principle of Article 1351 of the Code with that extraordinary line of approach?'

Not having gone to bed the night before, Frédéric was suffering from a dreadful headache. Through a chink in the blinds a shaft of sunlight shone straight on to his face. He stood behind his chair shifting from foot to foot and tugging at his moustache.

'I'm still waiting,' said the man in the gold-braided cap.

And, irritated no doubt by Frédéric's gesture:

'You won't find the answer in your beard!'

This quip fetched a laugh from the spectators; gratified,

the professor relented. He asked him a couple more questions, on subpoenas and summary jurisdiction, and nodded his head approvingly. The public examination was over; Frédéric went back into the ante-room.

While the usher was removing his gown to slip it on to the next candidate without delay, his friends gathered round him and completed his bewilderment by offering conflicting views as to his performance. The result was soon announced loudly from the entrance to the examination hall: the third candidate was . . . 'referred'.

'Ploughed!' said Hussonnet. 'Come on, let's go!'

At the porter's lodge they met an excited and red-faced Martinon with a smile in his eyes and a triumphal halo: he'd just passed his finals with flying colours. In less than a fortnight he'd have his degree. His family knew a minister, he had the prospect of a 'fine career'.

'He's got you whacked, hasn't he?' commented Deslauriers.

There's nothing more mortifying than to see fools prosper when you yourself have failed. Frédéric replied crossly that he didn't give a damn. He had higher aspirations and, as Hussonnet was showing signs of leaving, he drew him aside:

'Not a word about this to them, of course!'

It was an easy secret to keep for Arnoux was due to leave for Germany next day.

When he came home that evening the clerk found a remarkable change in his friend; he was prancing round the room whistling. When Deslauriers expressed surprise at this change in mood Frédéric announced that he wasn't going home to his mother's but would spend the vacation working.

The news of Arnoux's departure had filled Frédéric with delight. Now he could call there any time he liked without fear of being disturbed during his visits. The absolute certainty of being safe would give him courage. At last he'd no longer have to keep his distance and be kept apart from *Her*! A bond more powerful than steel was holding him fast in Paris; an inner voice was bidding him stay.

There were obstacles. To overcome them he wrote to his mother: first, he confessed he'd failed—this was due to changes, unpredictable and unfair, in the syllabus; anyway, all the greatest lawyers—he quoted their names—had been no good at exams. All the same he intended to try again in November. So, with no time to lose, he wouldn't be coming home this summer; and could he please have an extra two hundred and fifty francs for private coaching (extremely helpful); all this embroidered with expressions of regret, commiseration, filial love and general claptrap.

Madame Moreau had been expecting him that very next day and was doubly distressed. She kept her son's set-back to herself and replied: 'Come all the same!' Frédéric stood firm. There was a quarrel. Nevertheless at the end of that week he did get his quarterly allowance and the extra for his coaching; with this sum he purchased a pair of pearl-grey trousers, a white felt hat, and a gold-topped riding switch.

Having acquired these accoutrements:

'Am I behaving like a commercial traveller?' he wondered.

And was thrown into a state of great perplexity.

To make up his mind whether or not to call on Madame Arnoux he decided to take the best of three tosses. Each time the omens were favourable. Fate had spoken. He took a cab to the rue de Choiseul.

He ran up the stairs and pulled the bell-cord; it didn't ring; he nearly collapsed. He gave the heavy red silk tassel an almighty tug; there was a loud peal which slowly died away. Silence fell. Frédéric felt scared.

He stuck his ear to the door; not a whisper. He put his eye to the keyhole; in the entrance hall he could see only the tops of two reeds sticking up amongst some artificial paper flowers against the wall. On the point of beating a retreat he decided to have one last try. This time he gave a very gentle tug. The door opened and there, scarlet in the face and with his hair dishevelled, stood Arnoux himself. He looked cross.

'Good God! What are you doing here? Come in!'

He didn't show him into the small drawing-room or his own room but into the dining-room where a bottle of champagne and two glasses were standing on the table.

He asked brusquely:

'Is there anything you want, my dear fellow?'

'Oh no, nothing, nothing at all,' stammered the young man, trying to think up a reason to explain his call.

Eventually he said he'd come to ask after him because Hussonnet had told him he'd gone to Germany.

'Quite untrue!' replied Arnoux. 'What a scatter-brain that young man is, always getting things wrong!'

To hide his confusion Frédéric started walking round the room. He kicked a chair and a sunshade lying on it fell on to the floor, snapping its ivory handle.

'Oh my goodness,' he exclaimed. 'I'm so sorry, I've broken Madame Arnoux's sunshade!'

The art dealer looked up at him with an odd smile. Seeing the opportunity to talk about her, Frédéric added hurriedly:

'Is there any chance of seeing her, perhaps?'

She'd gone to visit her sick mother.

He didn't dare ask how long she'd be away; he enquired what was her home town.

'Chartres! That surprises you, does it?'

'Surprise me? Of course not, why should it? I'm not surprised in the least.'

The conversation came to an abrupt halt.

Arnoux had rolled a cigarette and was walking round the table puffing at it. Frédéric was standing with his back to the stove, gazing at the walls, the whatnot and the floor; charming images flitted through his mind or rather before his eyes. Finally he took his leave.

A crumpled ball of newspaper was lying on the floor of the entrance hall. Arnoux picked it up and reached up on tiptoe to stuff it into the bell, in order, he said, to be able to continue his interrupted siesta. He shook hands:

'Will you tell the porter I'm not at home?'

He slammed the door behind him.

Frédéric made his way slowly downstairs. The failure of

70

this first try was discouraging for the likely success of any future attempt. Three months of boredom followed and since he had no work, his inactivity made him even more miserable.

He'd spend hours on his balcony, gazing down at the river flowing between its dull grey embankments, stained black with sewage in places; there was a washerwoman's floating platform moored against the bank where street urchins would occasionally muck about in the mud, giving their poodle a dip. When he'd finished looking at the stone bridge of Notre-Dame and the three suspension bridges on the left, he'd always turn away to gaze in the direction of the quai aux Ormes at a clump of old trees, similar to the lime trees growing by the wharfside at Montereau. Rising above a jumble of roofs in front of him were the Tour-Saint-Jacques, the Hôtel de Ville and the churches of Saint-Gervais, Saint-Louis and Saint-Paul; to the east, the Spirit of Liberty on top of the Bastille column shone like a large gold star, while to the west the massive blue dome of the Tuileries Palace stood out against the sky. Somewhere behind there, in the same direction, must be Madame Arnoux's house.

He would go back into his bedroom, lie down on his divan, and sink into a vague brown study in which writing projects, schemes for reorganizing his life and yearnings for the future were all jumbled together. In the end, to escape from himself, he'd get up and go out.

He'd wander aimlessly up to the Latin Quarter, normally so full of noise and bustle but deserted at this time of year, for the students had all gone home to their families. The stillness of the high walls of the various academic institutions made them seem longer and even grimmer than usual; there were all sorts of peaceful sounds: birds fluttering in cages, lathes whirring, a cobbler hammering; old-clothes-men would stand in the middle of the street casting a hopeful eye up towards every window, without success. In the back of a deserted café, the lady behind the bar would be seen yawning amidst her unemptied decanters of wine; the newspapers lay undisturbed on the reading room tables;

in the work-yards of the ironing women, linen was flapping about in the gusty wind. From time to time he'd stop to look into a bookshop window; a bus grazing the pavement as it came down the street would make him turn his head; and when he reached the Luxembourg Gardens he'd call a halt.

Occasionally the hope of finding something to distract his mind would take him up towards the boulevards. He'd emerge from the cool, damp smell of gloomy little lanes into vast squares, deserted and dazzlingly bright, with fine tall buildings casting jagged shadows along the edges of the cobbled streets. But then the carts and shops would begin again and he was bewildered by the crowds—particularly on Sundays, when an immense throng of people would flood over the asphalt amid clouds of dust and an unceasing din from the Bastille to the Madeleine; he was sickened by the sordid vulgarity of their faces, their inane remarks, the smug idiocy exuding from all these sweaty foreheads. However, the realization of his own superiority over such people did mitigate the strain of having to look at them.

Every day he went to *L'Art industriel*, and in order to find out when Madame Arnoux would be back, he enquired at great length after her mother. Arnoux's answer was invariably the same: 'the improvement was continuing and his wife and little girl would be back next week'. The longer her return was delayed, the more anxious Frédéric became, so much so that, touched by all this solicitude, Arnoux took him out to dinner half a dozen times.

During these long periods alone with him Frédéric came to realize that Arnoux was not very bright and there was a danger he might notice that Frédéric was less well-disposed towards him; here was a chance, then, to make some return for his kindness. Anxious to do things in style, he sold his entire new outfit to a second-hand clothes dealer for eighty-four francs and, adding a hundred more which he still had left over, he called at Arnoux's gallery to take him out to dinner. Regimbart was there. They all went off to the Trois-Frères-Provençaux.*

The Citizen began by removing his frock-coat and drew

72

up the menu himself, confident that the other two would defer to his expertise. But in spite of taking himself off to the kitchen to have a private word with the chef, and down to the cellar, where he knew the contents of every bin, and summoning the owner to tell him off, neither the food, the wines nor the service met with his approval! As each fresh course or each new bottle arrived, he'd take one nibble or one gulp, immediately drop his fork or push away his glass and, spreading his arms out over the table, exclaim that it was now impossible to get a decent meal in Paris! In the end, unable to think of anything more palatable he ordered haricot beans dressed in olive oil, 'nothing fancy', which just passed muster, though not entirely to his liking. Then he enquired from the waiter about previous waiters at the Provençaux: what had become of Antoine? And the one called Eugène? And Théodore who always used to serve downstairs? In those days the quality of the food was in a different class altogether and there were some first-growth Burgundies we'll never see the like of again!

Later on, there was a discussion about real estate in the suburbs, one of Arnoux's gilt-edged speculations. Meanwhile he wasn't getting any return on his capital. Since he was determined not to sell at a give-away price, Regimbart was to find a buyer for him; so, pencil in hand, the couple worked at their sums until dessert was over.

They repaired for coffee to a bar on the mezzanine floor in the passage du Saumon. He had to stand by and watch interminable games of billiards washed down with countless mugs of beer; there he stayed till midnight, not knowing why, out of cowardice or stupidity, vaguely hoping that something might happen to further his love.

When would he see her again? He was in despair. But one evening towards the end of November, Arnoux said to him:

'My wife came back yesterday, you know!'

Next day at five o'clock he was walking through her doorway.

He began by saying how glad he was to hear about her mother who'd been so ill.

73

'But she hasn't been ill! Who told you that?'

'Arnoux!'

She murmured 'Oh, I see!' under her breath and added that she'd been very worried at first, but that it was now all right.

She was sitting on the tapestry-covered wing-chair. He was on the settee holding his hat between his knees; conversation was desultory; she kept falling silent and he couldn't find a way to lead the subject round to his feelings. But as he was grumbling about having to study legal procedure and its various manoeuvres, she replied: 'Ah yes, I can well imagine . . . business . . .' and dropped her eyes, suddenly absorbed in her own train of thought; he longed to know these thoughts and indeed could think of nothing else. The shadows were gathering round them.

She stood up; she had some shopping to do; she came back wearing a velvet bonnet and a black cape trimmed with squirrel. He plucked up courage to ask if he might accompany her.

By now it was quite dark. It was also cold and the house-fronts were shrouded in an evil-smelling blanket of fog which Frédéric drew blissfully into his lungs, for through the soft layers of her clothing he could feel the shape of her arm and her hand, sheathed in a two-buttoned kid glove, her tiny hand that he was yearning to cover in kisses, was resting on his sleeve. It was slippery underfoot and they were both swaying slightly as they went along; he felt as if they were walking on air through clouds, lulled by the wind.

The bright lights of the boulevard brought him down to earth. This was his chance! Time was short. He gave himself until the rue Richelieu to declare his love. Then almost at once, she came to an abrupt halt in front of a china shop.

'Here we are. Thank you! It's next Thursday as usual, isn't it?'

The dinner parties started again; the more he saw Madame Arnoux the more lovesick he became.

Gazing at her unnerved him, like the scent of some

74

overpowering perfume, stirring him to the depths of his nature, affecting almost his whole way of feeling and opening up a new kind of life.

The prostitutes he'd see standing under the gas lights, singers trilling their flourishes, galloping horsewomen, housewives on foot, flighty little working girls at their windows, every single woman he saw reminded him, through similarity or stark contrast, of *Her*. He'd look at the cashmere shawls, the lace, the jewelled ear-rings displayed everywhere in the shops and imagine them draped round her hips, stitched on her bodice or glittering against her black hair. The flowers on the stalls opened their blooms for *Her* to choose as she went by; in the windows of shoe-shops, dainty satin slippers trimmed with swansdown seemed to be waiting for *Her* foot to slip them on; every street led to *Her* house and carriages were stationed in the squares merely in order to convey you to *Her* more quickly; Paris existed in relation to *Her* person and the humming of all the voices of that great city was like some vast orchestra surrounding *Her*.

When he went to the Jardin des Plantes, the sight of a palm tree would carry him away to distant lands. They'd be travelling together on a camel's back, under the canopies of elephants, in the cabin of a yacht cruising through blue archipelagos or side by side on two mules whose bells tinkled as they stumbled over broken columns hidden in the grass. Sometimes he would halt in front of old paintings in the Louvre, and as his mind reached back to embrace her even in centuries gone by, he would replace the figures in the picture by *Her*: with a hennin on her head, she'd be kneeling in prayer behind a lead-light window; in her castle in Flanders or the Castillas, she'd be sitting in starched ruff and whalebone bodice with immense puff-sleeves. Then she'd be walking down some splendid porphyry stairway, surrounded by senators, beneath a baldachin of ostrich feathers, in a brocaded gown. At other times he dreamed of her in yellow pantaloons, reclining on cushions in some harem; anything lovely, the twinkling

75

stars, certain tunes, the rhythm of a sentence, an outline, would bring his thoughts suddenly and subtly back to *Her*.

As for trying to make her his mistress, he felt sure that any attempt would be fruitless.

One evening Dittmer kissed her forehead when he arrived; Lovarias followed suit saying:

'It's a friend's privilege, isn't it?'

'It seems to me we're all friends here!' stammered Frédéric.

'But not all old friends!' she retorted.

This meant she was indirectly turning him down in advance.

Anyway, what could he do? Tell her he loved her? She'd doubtless show him the door or even indignantly ban him from the house altogether! And he'd prefer to endure anything rather than risk never seeing her again.

He felt envious of gifted pianists and battle-scarred warriors. He was longing to fall dangerously ill: that might attract her attention.

One thing which surprised him was that he didn't feel jealous of Arnoux and her innate modesty seemed so strong, relegating her sex to some shadowy secret background, that he could never picture her undressed.

However, he did have blissful dreams of living with her, of being on terms of intimate friendship, of running his hand leisurely over her hair or kneeling at her feet with his two arms round her waist, drinking in her soul through her eyes. But all that would have meant countering Fate and so, cursing his luck, accusing himself of cowardice yet unable to act, he'd pace round his room like a prisoner in his cell. He'd stay for hours without stirring, or else burst into tears; one day when he'd not had the strength to hold back his feelings, Deslauriers said to him:

'Good God, what on earth's wrong with you?'

He was just a bit on edge. Deslauriers didn't believe a word of it. Seeing him so unhappy revived his affection for Frédéric and he set about trying to comfort him. It was ludicrous for someone like him to let himself become so depressed! It was all very well for a boy but when you're older it's a waste of time.

'You're lowering yourself in my esteem! I want to see my Frédéric of old again! The same again, please, waiter! I liked that other fellow! Come on, you silly idiot, have a pipe of baccy! Snap out of it, you're making *me* depressed now!'

'You're quite right,' said Frédéric. 'I'm crazy!'

'Oh, I know what's on your mind, you old troubadour! A spot of heart trouble, eh? Own up! Aren't there enough fish in the sea, for Christ's sake? If you meet a woman who says: "No!" you console yourself with one who says: "Yes!" Would you like me to help you to get to know some of them? All you need do is to come along to the Alhambra!' (This was a recently opened dance-hall at the top of the Champs-Elysées, on too lavish a scale for the time, and which had to close down in its second season as a result.) 'They say it's fun, let's go and see. Bring your pals along— I'll even let you bring Regimbart!'

Frédéric didn't invite Regimbart and Deslauriers did without Sénécal. They took only Hussonnet and Cisy, together with Dussardier, and all five went in the same cab, which deposited them at the entrance to the Alhambra.

There were two long parallel galleries in the 'Moorish' style stretching out to left and right. The far end was closed off by the wall of a house and the fourth side, containing the restaurant, was a mock-Gothic cloister with stained glass windows. The band was sitting on a raised platform under a sort of Chinese roof; the space round was asphalted and in the distance there was a glittering ring of multi-coloured Venetian lanterns festooned on posts and lighting the area used for the quadrilles. Here and there were tiny jets of water squirting out of stone basins resting on pedestals. In the shrubberies, plaster casts of Hebe or Cupid could be seen with their paint still sticky; the many small paths of extremely yellow, meticulously raked, sand created an illusion of spaciousness.

Students were walking around with their lady loves; drapers' assistants were strutting about twirling their walking

sticks; schoolboys were smoking large Havanas; old bachelors were fondly combing their dyed beards; there were
Englishmen, Russians, South Americans and three Muslims
wearing their tarboush. Women of all sorts and descriptions—smart little tarts, saucy young working girls, or just
straight whores—had come along in the hope of picking up
some benevolent admirer, a sweetheart, a gold coin, or just
for the fun of dancing; and their sea-green, cherry-red, blue
or purple tunic dresses drifted and bobbed amongst the lilacs
and laburnums. Almost all the men were dressed in check
coats and some in white trousers despite the cool evening.
Gas jets were being lit.

Through his contacts with fashion magazines and the
little theatres, Hussonnet knew a lot of women, to whom
he kept throwing kisses, and from time to time he'd leave
his friends and go off to have a chat with them.

This made Deslauriers jealous. He brazenly went up to a
tall blonde wearing a pale yellow cotton frock. She gave
him a long, unfriendly look and turned on her heels,
remarking: 'I don't trust you, young fellow!'

He tried again with a large brunette who must have been
a trifle strange in the head because at his very first words,
she flared up and threatened to call the police if he
persisted. Deslauriers attempted to laugh it off; then,
discovering a little woman sitting all by herself under a gas
lamp, he invited her to join him in a quadrille.

Perched on the rostrum, the bandsmen were hurling
themselves around like monkeys, blowing and scraping
away with tremendous vim and vigour. The orchestra leader
stood woodenly beating time. People were crammed
together, thoroughly enjoying themselves; hat-strings had
come loose and were tangling with neckties, boots were
sliding under petticoats; the whole bunch were bouncing
up and down in time with the music; Deslauriers was
clasping his little woman tightly against him and carried
away by the mad fury of the cancan was threshing away in
the middle of the quadrilles like some giant puppet. Cisy
and Dussardier were continuing their stroll; the young
aristocrat kept scrutinizing the whores but, in spite of

Dussardier's urgings, didn't dare to speak to them; he had the idea that in such women's bedrooms there was always 'a man hidden in the wardrobe armed with a pistol who'd spring out and make you sign a cheque'.

They went back to Frédéric. Deslauriers had stopped dancing and they were wondering how to spend the rest of the evening when Hussonnet exclaimed:

'Good Lord! The Marquise d'Amäégui!'*

She was a pale-faced snub-nosed woman wearing long elbow-length mittens; her long black curls dangled down each side of her cheeks like dog's ears. Hussonnet said to her:

'We must organize a party at your place, an oriental frolic. Try and herborize a few of your girlfriends for these gallant Frenchmen. Well, what's holding you back? Expecting your hidalgo to turn up?'

The lady from Spain was looking down at her toes; being familiar with her friend's frugal habits, she was afraid she might find herself footing the bill. When she eventually blurted out: 'What about money?' Cisy produced five louis, everything he had on him, and they decided to go ahead. But Frédéric was no longer with them.

Thinking he recognized Arnoux's voice and catching a glimpse of a woman's hat, he'd made a bee-line for a nearby arbour.

Mademoiselle Vatnaz was sitting alone with Arnoux.

'Oh, I'm so sorry. Am I intruding?'

'Not in the least,' replied the art dealer.

From the last words of their conversation, Frédéric had gathered that Arnoux had hurried over to the Alhambra for an urgent business consultation with Mademoiselle Vatnaz; and Arnoux was probably not entirely convinced for he said to her nervously:

'Are you quite sure it's all right?'

'Of course it is! People like you! Oh, what a man!'

And she pouted her lips at him, thick red lips that seemed almost gorged with blood. But her eyes were superb, hazel with golden lights in their pupils, brimming over with intelligence, love, and sensuality, like lamps lighting up her rather sallow complexion and thin face. Arnoux seemed to enjoy being told off. He leaned over sideways towards her:

'You're a sweetie, give me a kiss!'

She took him by the ears and kissed his forehead.

At that moment the dancing stopped and the band leader was replaced by a good-looking young man, overweight and with a waxy complexion. His long black hair was dressed in a Christ-like style, he wore a sky-blue velvet waistcoat embroidered with gold palm leaves and looked as vain as a peacock and as stupid as a goose. He greeted the audience and launched into a comic song about a country bumpkin, describing in his own words his riotous visit to the capital. He was singing in a Normandy dialect and pretending to be drunk; the refrain:

> *Ah! j'ai t'y ri, j'ai t'y ri*
> *Dans ce gueusard de Paris!*

had everyone enthusiastically stamping their feet. Delmas, a 'mood' singer, was too expert a performer to let the applause die away; he quickly picked up a guitar and crooned a sentimental ballad entitled 'The Albanian Maiden's Brother'.

The words brought back to Frédéric those sung by the ragged man beside the paddle-box on the boat; without thinking his eyes fastened on the hem of the dress spread out in front of him. Each verse was followed by a long pause and the sighing of the wind in the trees seemed to him like the murmur of the waves.

With one hand Mademoiselle Vatnaz pushed aside the branches hiding the platform from her view and sat gazing at the singer with rapt attention, knitting her brows and dilating her nostrils, as if beside herself with joy.

'First rate!' said Arnoux. 'Now I understand why you came to the Alhambra this evening. You're fond of Delmas, my dear!'

She refused to admit anything.

'Aren't you coy!'

And pointing at Frédéric:

'If it's because of him, then you're mistaken. That young man is the soul of discretion!'

The others came into the arbour looking for their friend. Hussonnet introduced them. Arnoux passed round his cigars and offered them all a sorbet.

On seeing Dussardier, Mademoiselle Vatnaz had blushed. After a moment she stood up and held out her hand:

'Don't you remember me, Monsieur Auguste?'

'How do you come to know her?' asked Frédéric.

'We used to work for the same firm,' he replied.

Cisy was tugging his sleeve. They went off and hardly had he gone than Mademoiselle Vatnaz started to sing his praises; she even added that he had 'a heart of solid gold'.

The talk now turned to Delmas, who might well have a successful career in the theatre as a mime artist; a discussion ensued involving Shakespeare, Censorship, Style, the People, the takings at the Porte-Saint-Martin Theatre, Alexandre Dumas, Victor Hugo and Dumersan.* Arnoux had known a number of well-known actresses; the young men leaned forward to catch his words which were drowned in the din made by the band; and as soon as the quadrilles or polkas came to an end, everybody took the tables by storm. There was laughter, people called for waiters, beer and fizzy lemonade corks popped among the trees, women were cackling like hens; from time to time a couple of gentlemen would square up for a fight; a pickpocket was arrested.

Panting, red-faced and smiling, they rushed through like a whirlwind, dresses and coat-tails swirling; the trombones blared out more loudly than ever; the tempo speeded up; from behind the medieval castle there the crackle of fireworks; thunder flashes exploded; catherine wheels started twirling; for a minute the whole garden was lit up by the emerald-green glow of Bengal lights; and as the last rocket burst, the vast crowd gave a huge gasping sigh.

The throng slowly melted away. A cloud of gunpowder smoke was left hanging over the gardens. Frédéric and Deslauriers were picking their way through the mass of people when an odd sight brought them to halt: Martinon was gathering up his change at the left umbrella desk and he was accompanied by a woman in her fifties, superbly dressed, ugly, and of problematical social status.

'That young fellow,' said Deslauriers, 'has hidden depths. But where's Cisy got to?'

Dussardier pointed to the bar where they saw this scion of noble family sitting in front of a bowl of punch in the company of a pink hat.

At that moment Hussonnet, who'd been away for the last five minutes, reappeared with a girl clinging to his arm and addressing him loudly as 'Ducky'.

'Don't do that!' he was saying. 'Not in front of everyone! Why not call me Viscount! That gives you a wonderfully dashing image, all Louis XIII and floppy leather riding boots! Yes, you're right, chaps, it's an old flame! Isn't she nice?' He was taking her by the chin. 'So give greetings to these gentlemen! They're the scions of most noble families! I'm sharing their company, so they can make me an Ambassador!'

'What a crazy fellow you are!' sighed Mademoiselle Vatnaz.

She asked Dussardier to take her home.

Arnoux followed them with his eyes and turned to Frédéric.

'Do you fancy Vatnaz? And talking of that, you're a bit too secretive. I suspect you of keeping your love affairs to yourself!'

Frédéric had gone pale. He swore he'd got nothing to hide.

'But the fact is that no one's ever heard of you having a lady friend,' Arnoux went on.

Frédéric was tempted to mention some name or other; but this might get back to *Her* ears. He replied that in fact he hadn't got a steady girlfriend.

The art dealer was disapproving.

'Tonight was a golden opportunity! Why didn't you do like the others? They've all gone off with a woman.'

'Well, what about yourself?' retorted Frédéric, provoked by his persistence.

'It's not the same for me, young fella! I'm going back home to my wife!'

He hailed a cab and disappeared.

The two friends went off together on foot. An east wind was blowing. Neither of them spoke. Deslauriers was kicking himself for not having shone in front of a newspaper owner and Frédéric was relapsing into his depression. Finally he said that the Alhambra seemed to him cheap and stupid.

'Whose fault was that? If you hadn't gone off to talk to your Arnoux . . .'

'Rubbish! Anything I'd have done would have been completely futile!'

The lawyer had his own theories: to get something all you needed to do was to want it strongly enough.

'But earlier in the evening you yourself . . .'

'I didn't give a damn!' said Deslauriers, cutting short Frédéric's reminder. 'Do you think I'm going to get myself tangled up with women?'

And he launched into an onslaught on their pretentious-ness and general stupidity; in a word, he didn't like them.

'Oh, stop pretending!' said Frédéric.

Deslauriers made no reply. Then abruptly:

'Will you bet me a hundred francs that I don't make the first woman who comes along?'

'All right, it's on!'

The first one was a hideous beggar woman and then, just as they were beginning to fear that luck had deserted them, in the middle of the rue de Rivoli they spotted a tall young woman carrying a small cardboard box.

Deslauriers went up and accosted her under the arcade. She turned sharply away towards the Tuileries and quickly made off across the place du Carrousel, looking to left and right all the time. She ran to catch a cab; Deslauriers caught her up. He walked beside her, making extravagant gestures while he spoke. Eventually she accepted his arm and they went off along the quays. Then, when they were level with

83

the Châtelet, they walked up and down the pavement for a good twenty minutes or more, like two sailors on their watch. Now suddenly they crossed the Pont-des-Changes and the flower market to the quai Napoléon. Frédéric followed them in. His friend intimated that he'd be in the way and that what was needed was for him to follow his example.

'How much money have you got?'

'Two five-franc pieces.'

'That'll be enough! Good-night!'

Frédéric was taken aback, like someone witnessing a successful practical joke. 'He's having me on,' he thought. 'Suppose I go back up?' Perhaps Deslauriers would suspect him of grudging him his success. 'As if I didn't have a love of my own, a hundred times finer and stronger and more precious!'

He was being driven along by a sort of anger; he ended up outside Madame Arnoux's house.

None of the outside windows belonged to the part occupied by her.

Nevertheless he stood with his eyes fastened on the front of the building, as though believing the walls would open up if he gazed long enough. No doubt at this moment she'd be resting peacefully like a sleeping flower, with her wonderful black hair spread out over the lacy pillow, her lips half open, her head lying on her arm.

Then, all of a sudden, it was Arnoux's head which he could see. He fled.

He recalled Deslauriers' advice and was horrified. He wandered on through the streets.

Each time he saw someone coming towards him, he tried to pick out their features. Every so often, a shaft of light shining between his legs would cast a huge quarter circle across the cobble-stones and a man with a lantern would loom up out of the shadows carrying a basket on his back. Here and there iron chimney-pots clattered away in the wind. Distant sounds kept coming to mingle with the buzzing in his head while, dimly, he seemed to hear the refrain of the quadrilles carried on the air. The action of walking kept up his state of excitement. He found himself on the Pont-de-la-Concorde. Once more his thoughts went back to that night last winter when, having left her house for the first time, he'd been forced to stop because his heart was pounding so wildly with the hopes that had been aroused in it. And now these hopes had all been dashed.

Dark clouds were scudding across the moon. He gazed up at it, meditating on the immensity of space, the wretchedness of life, the emptiness of everything. Day broke. His teeth were chattering, his eyes full of tears; he asked himself: Why not put an end to it all? One leap would do it! The weight inside his forehead was sweeping him away, he could see his corpse floating on the water. Frédéric bent forward; the parapet was a trifle wide and sheer weariness stopped him from climbing over. Terror-stricken, he made his way back to the boulevards and slumped down on a bench. He was woken by the police, who were convinced he'd been out on a binge.

He set off once again. But as he felt very hungry and all the restaurants were closed, he had a bowl of soup in a bar in the Central Markets. After this, imagining it was still too early, he loafed around the Hôtel de Ville area until a quarter past eight.

Deslauriers had sent his little miss packing a long time ago and was sitting writing at the table in the middle of the room. At about four o'clock, Monsieur de Cisy came in.

Yesterday evening, thanks to Dussardier, he'd struck up an acquaintance with a lady and even taken her home in a cab, with her husband, to the door of her house, where she had suggested a further meeting, from which he'd just come. And she wasn't a notorious woman, either!

'What am I supposed to do about it?' asked Frédéric.

The young aristocrat launched into a long rigmarole: he talked about Mademoiselle Vatnaz, the Andalusian, and all the other women. Finally, after much beating about the bush, he came to the point: relying on his friend's discretion, he'd come to enlist his help in taking certain steps, after which he'd definitely look on himself as a man!

Frédéric didn't refuse and told Deslauriers about it, without revealing what part he'd personally have to play.

The lawyer's clerk expressed his opinion that he was now 'in better shape'. This compliance with his advice added to his good humour.

It was this good humour that had, at their very first meeting, seduced Mademoiselle Clémence Daviou, whose job was gold embroidery in a military outfitters; the gentlest creature you could ever meet, as slender as a willow, with a perpetually puzzled expression in her large blue eyes; the clerk took advantage of her innocence even to the extent of pretending that he had a decoration. When they were alone, he adorned his buttonhole with a red ribbon, but refrained from wearing it in public in order, so he said, not to humiliate his employer. Moreover, he kept her in her place, let her pamper him like a pasha, and thought it funny to refer to her as 'a member of the lower classes'. Every time they met, she'd bring him a posy of violets. It wasn't the sort of love that Frédéric would have liked for himself.

All the same, whenever they went out arm in arm for a meal in a private room at Pinson's or Barillot's, he did experience an odd pang of sadness; he didn't realize how hurt Deslauriers himself had felt every Thursday over the last year, each time he saw him cleaning his nails before going off to dine in the rue de Choiseul!

One evening, standing on his balcony having just seen the couple leave, he saw Hussonnet in the distance on the Pont-d'Arcole. The Bohemian signalled to him and when Frédéric had come down his five flights of stairs to meet him:

'Look, it's Madame Arnoux's name-day next Saturday, the 24th.'

'Is it? Surely she's called Marie?'

'Her second name's Angèle, but never mind! They're giving a party at their house in the country at Saint-Cloud. I've been asked to let you know. There's a carriage leaving the gallery at three o'clock. All right? Sorry to have fetched you down! I've got so many errands to run!'

Just as Frédéric was going back up to his rooms, the porter handed him a note:

'Monsieur and Madame Dambreuse request the honour of Monsieur Frédéric Moreau's company at dinner at their house on Saturday 24th. RSVP.'

'It's come too late,' he thought.

However he showed the letter to Deslauriers, who exclaimed:

'At last! But you don't seem too pleased? What's the matter?'

Frédéric hesitated and then told him of his other invitation on the same night.

'Do me the favour of sending the Arnoux packing, will you? Don't be such an idiot! If you're worried, I'll reply on your behalf.'

And the clerk wrote out an acceptance in the third person.

Never having seen high society except through the mirror of his own feverish ambitions, he imagined it as an artificial creation functioning with mathematical precision. Through a series of consequential reactions, a dinner party, a meeting with a man holding high office, or a pretty woman's smile could lead to stupendous results. Paris drawing-rooms were like those machines which take in raw material and give it back increased in value a hundred fold. He believed in diplomats under the spell of courtesans, rich marriages engineered by intrigue, convicts of genius, and Lady Luck submitting to the iron hand of Power. And he considered closer acquaintance with the Dambreuses so useful and argued his case so persuasively, that he put Frédéric in a quandary.

In any case, since it was Madame Arnoux's name-day, he'd have to give her a present. He naturally thought of a sunshade to replace the one damaged by his clumsiness and discovered one, a dove-grey, shot-silk marquise parasol with a tiny carved ivory handle, recently imported from China; but it cost one hundred and seventy-five francs and he hadn't a sou, was, indeed, living on credit from his next quarter's allowance. All the same, he coveted it; so, very reluctantly, he turned to Deslauriers for help.

Deslauriers replied that he hadn't got any money.

'I need it,' said Frédéric. 'I need it badly.

And when the clerk repeated his excuse, he lost his temper:

'Well, you might at least sometimes . . .'

'Sometimes what?'

'Oh, forget it!'

But the other man had taken the point. He took the appropriate amount out of his reserve fund and having counted it out, coin by coin:

'I shan't ask for an IOU because I'm sponging on you!'

Frédéric flung his arms round his neck, loudly protesting how fond he was of him. Deslauriers remained aloof. Then next day, noticing the sunshade lying on the piano, he said:

'So that's what you wanted it for!'

'I'll probably be having it sent,' replied Frédéric lamely.

Luck was on his side, for in the course of the evening he got a note on black-edged paper from Madame Dambreuse apologizing for having to postpone the pleasure of making his acquaintance, owing to the death of an uncle.

Two o'clock saw Frédéric already at Arnoux's office, but instead of waiting to give him a lift in his carriage, he'd gone off the previous day, unable to resist his passion for fresh air.

Every year, as soon as the first leaves appeared, he'd slip away in the morning for several days at a time, going for long country walks, drinking milk at farmhouses, flirting with the village girls, enquiring about the harvest, and bringing back lettuce plants in his handkerchief. Finally, realizing a long-cherished dream, he'd bought a house in the country.

While Frédéric was still talking to the assistant, Mademoiselle Vatnaz appeared; she was disappointed not to find Arnoux. Might he possibly be staying down there for another couple of days? The assistant advised her to go down and see him herself; she couldn't get away; or to write to him; she was afraid the letter might go astray.

Frédéric volunteered to deliver it himself. She quickly dashed off a note and asked him to be sure no one else was there when he handed it over.

Forty minutes later he was getting out of the carriage in Saint-Cloud.

The house stood a hundred yards below the bridge, half-way up the hill. The garden walls were concealed behind two rows of lime trees; a broad stretch of lawn led down to the water's edge. The entrance gate was open. Frédéric went through.

Arnoux was lying on the grass playing with a litter of kittens, an occupation which seemed to be absorbing his whole attention. Mademoiselle Vatnaz's letter brought him down to earth.

'Confound it! What a bore! She's quite right, I'll have to go back.'

Stuffing the note into his pocket, he took pleasure in showing Frédéric over the property. He showed him everything: the stables, the out-buildings, the kitchens. The drawing-room was on the right-hand side of the house and on the Paris side opened on to a verandah with a trellis covered in clematis. Suddenly, a voice overhead burst into a flourish: thinking no one was listening, Madame Arnoux was enjoying herself singing, practising scales, trills, arpeggios, long drawn-out notes that seemed to hover in the air and others which spilled out helter-skelter like drops from a waterfall. Her voice came through the shutters, piercing the deep silence and soaring up towards the blue sky.

It broke off abruptly as Monsieur and Madame Oudry, two neighbours, arrived.

Then she herself appeared at the end of the front terrace and as she came down the steps he caught a glimpse of her foot: she was wearing dainty openwork shoes of soft reddish-brown leather with three cross-straps forming a golden tracery on her stockings.

The guests arrived. Apart from a lawyer, Maître Lefaucheux, they were the usual Thursday night diners. Everyone had brought a present: Dittmer a Syrian stole, Rosenwald an album of love-songs, Burrieu a water-colour,

89

Sombaz a cartoon of himself, and Pellerin a charcoal sketch representing a sort of Dance of Death, weird and gruesome, and rather poorly drawn. Hussonnet hadn't bothered to bring anything.

Frédéric waited till last to offer his present.

She thanked him very much. He said:

'But it was really something I owed you! I was so annoyed . . .'

'What at?' she enquired. 'I don't quite understand . . .'

'Time to eat!' said Arnoux, gripping him firmly by the arm; then, in a low voice: 'You're not all that quick on the uptake, are you, young man?'

The dining-room, painted sea-green, couldn't have been more charming. At one end, a stone nymph was dipping her big toe into a shell-shaped basin. Through the open windows, the whole garden could be seen, with an old Scots pine which had lost three-quarters of its needles, standing on one side of the long lawn dotted with clumps of flowers sticking up here and there; beyond the river, the Bois-de-Boulogne, Neuilly, Sèvres and Meudon spread out in a broad semi-circle. In front of the entrance gate facing them, a sailing boat was tacking.

First they talked about that view, then about landscape in general, and as the discussion was getting under way, Arnoux gave his servant the order to have his American phaeton hitched up for half past nine. He'd been called back by a letter from his cashier.

'Would you like me to come back with you?' asked Madame Arnoux.

'Of course I should!' and making a grand flourish in her direction: 'You know full well, Madame, that it's impossible to live without you!'

They all said how lucky she was to have such a loving husband.

'Ah yes! You see there's someone else besides me!' she replied quietly, pointing to her little daughter.

The conversation now turned to painting and they mentioned a Ruysdael, for which Arnoux was expecting to get a considerable sum; Pellerin asked if it was true that the well-known London dealer Saul Mathias had been over last month and offered him twenty-three thousand francs for it.

'As true as I stand here!' and turning towards Frédéric he added: 'In fact that was the man I was showing round the Alhambra the other night, very unwillingly I promise you, because those English aren't much fun!'

Frédéric had suspicions that Mademoiselle Vatnaz's note was connected with some woman and had admired the masterly ease with which Arnoux had found a plausible pretext to get away, but this last, completely gratuitous, lie left him utterly flabbergasted.

The art dealer added with an innocent expression:

'Tell me, what was the name of your friend, the tall young man?'

'Deslauriers,' replied Frédéric curtly.

And to make up for the wrong he felt he'd done him, he stressed what a remarkably intelligent man he was.

'Is that so? But he didn't seem as nice as that other chap, the clerk in the firm of carriers.'

'Damn Dussardier!' thought Frédéric; she'd be imagining he went around with a common lot of people.

Now the question of the refurbishing of the capital came up and of the new development areas; old Oudry happened to mention the name of Dambreuse as one of the main speculators.

Here was his chance to show off: Frédéric said he knew him. But Pellerin launched into a diatribe against all grocers; he couldn't see any difference between selling candles and selling money. Then Rosenwald and Burrieu started chatting about porcelain; Arnoux discussed gardening with Madame Oudry; Sombaz, a humorist of the old school, was enjoying pulling her husband's leg by addressing him as Odry, like the actor, and insisting he must be descended from the dog-painter Oudry, because he could see the bump of animality on his forehead; he even tried to feel his skull but the other man demurred because of his wig; so dessert came to an end amid roars of laughter.

When they'd drunk their coffee, had a smoke under the

limes, and taken a few turns round the garden, they went for a walk down by the river.

The group stopped to watch a fisherman who was cleaning eels in a fish-tank. Mademoiselle Marthe wanted to look at them. He emptied out his tank on to the grass and the little girl, laughing and squealing with pleasure and fright, knelt down to pick them up. They all got away. Arnoux paid for them.

Next he suggested a boat trip.

One side of the sky was growing paler while on the other a broad band of orange was spreading out, with a deeper red over the crest of the hill which was now completely in shadow. Madame Arnoux was sitting on a boulder silhouetted against this fiery glow. The others continued their stroll; at the bottom of the slope, Hussonnet was playing ducks and drakes.

Arnoux came back towing an old rowing boat and, despite warnings to be careful, piled his guests into it. It started to sink; everyone had to scramble out.

In the drawing-room draped throughout in chintz, the candles in their crystal candelabra had already been lit. Old Madame Oudry was gently dozing off in an armchair and the rest were listening to a harangue by Maître Lefaucheux on legal luminaries at the Paris Bar. Madame Arnoux was standing by herself near the window. Frédéric went over to her.

They chatted about what was being discussed: she admired orators, he thought literary fame was better. But surely, she persisted, one must experience greater satisfaction stirring crowds of people directly, by your own efforts, seeing yourself inspiring them with your own feelings? Frédéric wasn't really attracted by that kind of success; he hadn't any ambition.

'Oh, but why not?' she said. 'You need to have at least some!'

They were standing close to each other in the window recess. In front of them the night was spread out like some vast dark veil speckled with silver. It was the first time they had exchanged anything but pure trivialities. He even discovered some of her likes and dislikes: certain scents upset her. She enjoyed reading books on history, she believed in dreams.

He broached the subject of relationships between the sexes. She felt sorry for victims of disastrous passions but repugnance for squalid deceivers; this integrity of mind matched the regular beauty of her features so perfectly that it seemed part of it.

Now and again she'd give a smile and her eyes would rest on him for a moment. He could feel them probing into his soul like sunbeams piercing through water to the very bottom; and he loved her with an absolute love, with no sort of ulterior motive or hope of return. Speechless with delight, carried away in a sort of ecstasy of gratitude, he longed to shower her forehead with kisses, while at the same time an inner impulse seemed to be projecting him upwards, out of himself. He felt a yearning to sacrifice himself, a need for instant dedication, all the stronger since there was no way in which he could satisfy them.

He stayed behind when the others left; so did Hussonnet: they were to go back to Paris with their host. While the American carriage waited at the foot of the terrace, Arnoux went into the garden to pick some roses. After tying them together with a piece of string, seeing that the stems were of unequal length, he fumbled in his pocket, which was crammed with odd bits of paper, took one out at random, wrapped the roses in it, secured the bunch with a thick pin and then, not without emotion, offered it to his wife.

'Here you are, my darling, and forgive me for having forgotten.'

She gave a tiny cry: the clumsily fastened pin had pricked her; she went up to her room. They waited nearly a quarter of an hour. Eventually she came out, picked up Marthe, and flung herself into the carriage.

'What about your roses?' said Arnoux.

'No, no, it's not worth the trouble!'

As Frédéric ran off to fetch them, she called after him:

'I don't want them!'

However, he came back with them almost immediately,

saying he'd just put them back into their wrapping, as he'd found them on the floor. She pushed them under the leather apron beside the seat and they set off.

Sitting close beside her, Frédéric noticed that she was trembling dreadfully. Then, after crossing the bridge, as Arnoux was taking the left turn:

'Not down there! You're going the wrong way! Go right!'

She seemed irritated; everything was upsetting her. Finally, when Marthe's eyes shut, she pulled the bunch of roses out and hurled it through the window, gripping Frédéric's arm and making a sign with her other hand never to mention the matter.

Then she pressed her handkerchief to her lips and sat without stirring.

Up on the box the other two were discussing printing and subscriptions. Arnoux was driving carelessly and lost his way in the middle of the Bois-de-Boulogne. They plunged into side-roads. The horses dropped to a walk; branches brushed against the hood. In the shadows, all that Frédéric could see of Madame Arnoux was her eyes. Marthe had stretched herself out on his lap and he was supporting her head.

'Is that tiring for you?' her mother enquired.

'Oh no, not a bit, really not!' Frédéric replied.

Clouds of dust were swirling gently around; they were driving through Auteuil; all the house-shutters were closed; now and again a street-lamp lit up the corner of a wall and then they'd plunge into darkness again. Once he saw she was crying.

A bad conscience? In need of something? Or what? This unknown distress seemed to concern him personally; there was now a new bond between them, a kind of conspiracy. As fondly as he could, he asked:

'Are you all right?'

'Oh, not too bad,' she replied.

The carriage continued on its way; the enervating scent of mock orange and honeysuckle drooping over garden fences was wafted into the night. His feet were covered under the many folds of her skirt. He seemed to be

94

communing with her whole person through this child's body lying between them. He bent over the little girl and, parting her pretty brown hair, kissed her softly on the forehead.

'What a kind man you are!' said Madame Arnoux.

'Why's that?'

'Because you're fond of children!'

'Not all of them!'

He said nothing more but stretched out his left hand in her direction letting it lie there, wide open, in the hope that she might do the same and that his would meet hers. Then he felt bashful and drew it back.

Soon they came to paved streets. The carriage started to go faster, the gas lamps were closer together; they were in Paris. In front of the Garde-Meuble* building Hussonnet jumped down from the box. Frédéric stayed inside the carriage until they'd driven into the courtyard and after getting out he lay in wait at the corner of the rue de Choiseul and saw Arnoux slowly walk up towards the boulevards.

The very next day he set to work with a vengeance.

He could see himself at the Assizes on a winter's evening; the defence pleas have all been made; this is when juries go pale, the expectant public are cramming the courtroom to overflowing and he, still on his feet after four hours, is summing up, piling proof on proof, sensing that with every phrase, every word, every gesture, the blade of the guillotine is being hoisted behind him; or at the dispatch box of the House, an orator on whose lips the salvation of an entire people depends, overwhelming his opponents with his invective, demolishing them with a crushing rejoinder, fulminating in a superbly modulated voice, ironic, full of pathos and passion, sublime. She'd be there with the rest of them, hiding her tears of elation under her veil; afterwards, they'd meet and what discouragement, slander or insult could ever hurt him if she were to say: 'Oh, aren't you wonderful!' as she lightly brushed her hands over his brow.

Stimulated by these visions of glittering prizes ripe for

the picking, his mind became sharper and stronger. He shut himself away in his room until August, when he passed his finals.

Deslauriers had again experienced considerable difficulty coaching him for his second exam at the end of December and his third in February; he was astounded by such keenness. All his previous hopes revived. Within ten years, Frédéric must become a Deputy, and a Minister within fifteen; why not? With the money he'd soon be inheriting, he could start a newspaper, as a beginning; afterwards, they'd see. As for himself, he still had ambitions for a chair in the Law Faculty; at his oral, the examiners of his doctoral thesis had congratulated him on a brilliant performance.

Frédéric got his own doctorate three weeks later, and before going off on holiday, he suggested a party to round off their Saturday night gatherings, with everyone bringing his own food and drink.

At the party he was in high spirits. Madame Arnoux was away on a visit to her mother in Chartres but he'd soon be seeing her again and at last go to bed with her.

Deslauriers had been elected a member of the Orsay Debating Society* that day and his speech had been warmly received. Normally abstemious, he got tipsy and over dessert exclaimed to Dussardier:

'You're an honest chap, once I'm rich I'll give you a job as my agent!'

Everybody was happy; Cisy was going to drop law, Martinon was all set to serve his probationary period in the provinces, where he'd been appointed Deputy Public Prosecutor, Pellerin was preparing to paint a large picture representing the 'Genius of the Revolution', next week Hussonnet was to read the draft of a play to the director of the Délassements and had no doubts as to the successful outcome.

'Everyone admits I'm good on dramatic structure and as for passion, well, I've knocked around enough to know all about that! And where wit's concerned, that happens to be my speciality!'

He did a somersault, landed on his hands, and walked round the table a few times with his legs in the air.

These boyish antics failed to cheer up Sénécal, recently sacked from his boarding school for thrashing a nobleman's son. As his plight grew more and more desperate he kept blaming the social order and inveighing against the rich; he poured out his woes to Regimbart who was becoming more and more disabused, depressed, and disgusted. The Citizen had now begun to turn his attention to budgetary matters, accusing the Guizot Mafia of squandering millions of francs in Algeria.

As he could never get to sleep without a prior call at the Alexandre Tavern, he slipped away smartly at eleven o'clock; while saying good-night to Hussonnet, Frédéric learned that Madame Arnoux must have returned the day before.

He went to the shipping line to change his ticket for that day and called at her house at about six o'clock that evening. The hall porter informed him that she'd put off her return till the following week. Frédéric dined by himself and then went for a stroll along the boulevards.

The clouds looked like elongated pink scarves hanging over the roof-tops; shops were beginning to roll up their awnings; water-carts were sprinkling the dust, and an unexpected coolness mingled with the various smells drifting out through the open doorways of the cafés in which tall bunches of flowers could be seen reflected in long wall mirrors amongst the silver and gilt. The crowds were sauntering along. Knots of men stood around chatting in the middle of the pavement; women went past, limp-eyed, with that camellia flesh-tint peculiar to the feminine complexion during the weary dog-days. Some mighty thing was overflowing and encircling the houses. Paris had never seemed so lovely and in the future, he could see nothing but an endless procession of years brimming over with love.

He stopped to look at the notice outside the Porte-Saint-Martin Theatre and, having nothing better to do, bought a ticket.

They were putting on an old-fashioned spectacular. The

audience was small. Up in the 'gods' the roof-lights appeared as tiny blue squares while the footlights formed one single yellow line. The scene represented a Peking slave market, with hand-bells, tom-toms, sultanesses, cone-shaped hats, and lots of puns. When the curtain came down, he went on a solitary stroll round the foyer, stopping to admire a large green landau outside the theatre on the boulevard, drawn by two greys held by a coachman in knee-breeches.

As he was returning to his seat, he saw a couple going into the first stage-box. The husband had a pale face with a fringe of grey beard, a rosette of the Legion of Honour, and the frigid demeanour usually attributed to diplomats.

His wife, a good twenty years younger, neither tall nor short, ugly nor pretty, was wearing her fair hair in ringlets, English-style; she had on a flat-bodiced dress and was carrying a large black lace fan. For people of this social class to come to a show of this type the only explanation could be chance, or the boring prospect of having to spend a whole evening in each other's company. The lady was chewing at her fan, her husband was yawning. Frédéric couldn't recall where he'd seen that face before.

During the next interval he came upon them in the corridor and, seeing his vague gesture of greeting, Monsieur Dambreuse recognized him and came over to speak, immediately offering his apologies for his unforgivable remissness. He was referring to the numerous visiting cards which Frédéric, following Deslauriers's advice, had left on them. However, he was somewhat confused as to dates, for he thought Frédéric was in the second year of his law studies. Then he expressed envy at Frédéric's being able to get away into the country. He could have done with a break himself, but business would be keeping him in Paris.

Madame Dambreuse was leaning on her husband's arm and gently nodding her head with a charming and witty expression on her face, far removed from her earlier glumness.

'All the same, there are some very pleasant distractions in Paris,' she said, taking up her husband's last words.

'What a stupid show this is, don't you think, Monsieur Moreau?' And they all three stood chatting about the theatre and new plays.

Accustomed to the posturings of middle-class provincial females, Frédéric had never before met such naturalness and ease of manner—a product of sophistication which the gullible interpret as a sign of instant affinity.

They'd be expecting him to call on them as soon as he was back in Paris. Monsieur Dambreuse asked him to convey his regards to old Roque.

When he got home, Frédéric made a point of telling Deslauriers how friendly the Dambreuses had been.

'Splendid!' the clerk replied. 'And don't let your Mama get round you! Come back straightaway!'

On the day after his return, when lunch was over, Madame Moreau took her son into the garden.

She said how pleased she was that he'd got a profession because they weren't as well off as people thought; farming wasn't very profitable, the tenants were reluctant to pay up; she'd even been forced to sell her carriage. She went on to explain their situation.

In her straitened circumstances after being widowed, she'd borrowed money from Monsieur Roque, an artful man; in spite of herself, she'd extended these loans and added to them. Then, out of the blue, he'd demanded payment and she'd accepted his conditions, selling him the Presles farm for a ludicrously low figure. Ten years later, her capital had been swallowed up in the failure of a Melun bank. Having a horror of mortgages and wanting to keep up appearances for the sake of her son's future, when old Roque again appeared on the scene, she'd listened to him once more. But now she'd paid off all her debts. In a word, they were left with an income of about ten thousand francs a year, two thousand three hundred of which belonged to him, and that represented his entire estate.

'It's not possible!' exclaimed Frédéric. She shook her head: it was all too possible.

But couldn't he expect something from his uncle?

Nothing was less certain.

They took a turn round the garden; neither said a word.

Finally she clasped him to her breast and in a voice shaken by sobs:

'Oh, my poor boy! How many dreams I've had to give up!'

He sat down on a bench in the shade of the big acacia.

Her advice was to go into the office of the solicitor, Monsieur Prouharam; he'd sell him his practice and if it did well, he could resell it and make a good match.

Frédéric wasn't listening. He was looking vacantly over the hedge into the garden opposite.

In it, all by herself, was a little girl about twelve years old, with red hair. She'd used rowan berries to make herself some ear-rings; her shoulders, left uncovered by her grey linen bodice, were tanned a golden brown; her white skirt was spotty with jam stains; her whole slender, wiry body possessed a youthful, untamed grace. Doubtless surprised at seeing a stranger, she had suddenly halted, still holding her watering can, and was watching him intently through her clear, blue-green eyes.

'That Monsieur Roque's daughter,' said his mother. 'He's just married his housekeeper and made her legitimate.'

CHAPTER VI

Dispossessed, ruined, and sunk without trace!

He remained sitting on the bench, cursing his unlucky stars. How he'd have loved to take it out on someone! And to add to his despair, he could feel a sort of odium of disgrace attached to him: he'd imagined his father's estate would one day amount to fifteen thousand francs a year and had hinted as much to the Arnoux. Now he'd be looked on as a boaster, an impostor, a guttersnipe who'd wormed his way into their confidence in the hope of some kind of advantage! How could he ever look Madame Arnoux in the face after that?

Anyway, with only three thousand a year, that would be completely impossible! He couldn't go on for ever living on a fourth floor, with the hall porter as his only servant, and turning up in shabby black gloves with grubby blue finger-tips, a greasy hat, and wearing the same frock-coat all the year round. No! No! Never! Yet without her, life was unbearable. A lot of men did manage on not much money, Deslauriers amongst others; and he thought how cowardly it was of him to attach such importance to trifles. Real poverty might well bring out all his talents; he was fired by the thought of so many great men working away in garrets. A noble spirit like Madame Arnoux would surely be touched by such a sight; her heart would be softened. This disaster was really a blessing in disguise; like an earthquake laying bare hidden treasures, it had opened his eyes to the secret abundance of his nature. But there was only one place in the world where he could bring such riches to fruition: Paris!—for in his mind Art, Knowledge and Love, those three faces of God, as Pellerin would have put it, were the exclusive purview of the capital.

That evening, he informed his mother he'd be going back there. Madame Moreau was surprised and outraged; it was absurd, it was madness! He'd do better to follow her advice and stay at home with her, in a local practice. Frédéric shrugged his shoulders: 'Really, Mama!' he felt insulted by such a suggestion.

The good lady tried another tack. Sobbing gently and in a voice full of motherly affection, she spoke of her loneli-ness, her old age, all the sacrifices she'd made. Now that she was in an even worse plight, he was going to desert her. She hinted at her early demise.

'My goodness, surely you can wait just a little while? It won't be all that long before you'll be a free man!'

These plaintive appeals were repeated a score of times a day for the next three weeks; at the same time he was being lured by home comforts; he was enjoying sleeping in a softer bed and having towels that weren't tattered. So, harassed and eventually defeated by the terrible force of gentle persuasion, Frédéric wearily allowed himself to be coaxed round to Maître Prouharam's office.

He proved unsuitable and incompetent. Up till now, he'd

been looked upon as an extremely talented young man, destined to become the leading light in the province. It was a public fiasco.

At first, he'd said to himself: 'I must let Madame Arnoux know', and for a whole week had toyed with the idea of writing her both long rhapsodic epistles and short notes, terse and sublime. He was held back by the fear of admitting his situation. Then he thought he'd do better to write to her husband. Arnoux was a man of the world, he'd understand. Finally, after a fortnight's humming and hawing:

'Oh, damn it all, I shan't be seeing her again, I'd better let them forget me! At least I'll not have gone down in her estimation! She'll merely think I'm dead and miss me . . . possibly.'

As extravagant solutions came easily to him, he swore never to go back to Paris and never even to enquire after Madame Arnoux.

All the same, he found himself pining even for the smelly gas jets and clattering buses. He'd turn over in his mind every word that had been spoken to him, recall the lilt of her voice, the light in her eyes; and since he saw himself as a dead man, he ended up doing precisely nothing.

He would get up very late and look out of his window at the wagoners' carts going by. The first six months were particularly agonizing.

Some days, however, he was filled with indignation towards himself. When this happened, he'd go out and walk through the meadows, half submerged by the winter floods of the Seine, and divided up by rows of poplars. Here and there a tiny bridge can be seen. He'd roam around till evening, kicking up the yellow leaves, filling his lungs with foggy air, jumping over ditches; his pulse would start to race and he'd be carried away by an urge to do something wild, become a trapper in North America, take service with some Eastern potentate, run away to sea. He poured out his heart in long letters to Deslauriers.

The latter, struggling to make his mark, viewed his friend's cowardly behaviour and endless jeremiads as stupid; their correspondence soon petered out almost completely. Frédéric had given all his furniture to Deslauriers, who had kept on his flat. His mother occasionally questioned him about this and one day, when he'd finally admitted making the gift and was being told off by his mother, he received a letter.

'What's the matter?' she asked. 'You're trembling all over!'

'Nothing's the matter,' he replied.

It was Deslauriers informing him that he'd taken Sénécal in and they'd been sharing the flat for the last fortnight. So Sénécal was now lording it amongst the articles bought from Arnoux! He'd be able to sell them, pass comment on them, make jokes about them! Frédéric was stung to the quick. He went up to his room. He wished he could die.

His mother called him downstairs. She wanted to consult him about some planting in the garden.

This garden was laid out like an English park and divided down the middle; half of it belonged to old Roque who had another one, for vegetables, down by the river. The two neighbours were on bad terms and took care not to be in the garden at the same time. Since Frédéric's return, however, the old man was to be seen there more often and was fulsomely polite to Madame Moreau's son. He commiserated with him at having to live in a small town. One day he told him that Monsieur Dambreuse had enquired after him. On another occasion he dwelt at length on the custom prevalent in Champagne of allowing titles to pass on through the female line.

'In those days you'd have been a lord because your mother was a de Fouvens. And people can say what they like, a handle to your name still means something, you know! After all,' he added with a sly look, 'it all depends on the Lord Chancellor!'

These aristocratic pretensions were strangely at odds with his personal appearance. He was short and his large brown frock-coat exaggerated the length of his body. When he took off his cap he revealed an almost feminine face with an extremely pointed nose; his tow-coloured hair looked like a wig; as he sidled along the street close to the wall, he'd bow very low to people he knew.

Till he was fifty he'd been content to have as housekeeper a woman from Lorraine, Catherine, the same age as himself and badly pock-marked. But in 1834 he brought back from Paris a lovely blonde with a sheep-like expression but who 'carried herself like a queen'. She was soon to be seen flaunting large ear-rings, and all was explained when a baby girl was born and registered under the name of Élisabeth-Olympe-Louise Roque.

Catherine had assumed jealousy would make her loathe the child; instead she loved her. She coddled and cosseted her in an attempt to supplant the mother and make her daughter dislike her, no difficult task for Madame Éléonore completely neglected the little girl, preferring to gossip with the tradesmen. No sooner was she married than she called on the Deputy Prefect, dropped her easy-going manner with the servants, and considered it 'good form' to be strict with her daughter. She sat in on her lessons; the tutor, an old local government official, was hopelessly incompetent. His pupil rebelled, got her face slapped, and went off to cry in Catherine's lap, where her conduct was invariably approved. Then the two women would quarrel; Monsieur Roque shut them up. He'd got married out of fondness for his daughter and didn't want her ill-treated.

Louise often wore a tattered white dress with frilly knickers; on grand occasions, she'd appear dressed like a princess; this was to bring those middle-class families down a peg or two for not allowing their own offspring to have anything to do with her because she was illegitimate.

She lived a lonely life, playing on her swing in the garden, chasing butterflies, and then suddenly stopping to look at the goldsmith beetles settling on the rose bushes. No doubt it was this kind of life which gave her an expression both bold and dreamy. She was also roughly the same height as Marthe and so, after only their second meeting, Frédéric said:

'Do you mind if I kiss you, Mademoiselle?'

'If you like!'

But they were separated by the paling fence.

'You'll have to climb on to it,' said Frédéric.

'No, you lift me up.'

He bent over the fence and picked her up by the arms, kissed her on both cheeks, and then set her down again on her own side; this manoeuvre was repeated on later occasions.

As soon as she heard him coming, she'd run up to meet him with no more shyness than a four-year-old or else hide behind a tree and yap like a dog to scare him.

One day when Madame Moreau was out, he took her up to his bedroom. She opened all his scent bottles, smeared brilliantine all over her hair, and then without the slightest embarrassment clambered up on to his bed and lay stretched out and very wide awake.

'I'm pretending we're married,' she said.

Next day he saw she was in tears. She admitted she was crying for her sins and when he enquired what they were, she lowered her eyes and replied:

'You're not to ask me anything more about it!'

Her First Communion was due soon; she'd been taken along to confession that morning.

The Communion service did little to improve her character; she sometimes flew into violent tantrums and Monsieur Frédéric would be called in to calm her down.

He often took her out on excursions. He'd walk along brooding while she picked poppies beside the wheat-fields, and when she saw him looking glummer than usual, she'd say something pleasant to cheer him up. In his lovelorn existence he clung to this friendship with a child; he'd draw funny faces for her, tell her stories, and started reading to her.

He began with the *Annales romantiques*, an anthology of prose and verse, very well known at the time. Then, so impressed by her intelligence that he forgot her age, he read her, one after the other, *Atala*, *Cinq-Mars* and the *Feuilles d'automne*.* But after he'd been reading her *Macbeth* in Letourneur's* prosy translation one evening, she woke up that night screaming: 'The spot! The spot!' Her teeth were chattering, she was trembling and staring horror-stricken at her right hand which she kept rubbing and saying: 'The spot's still there!' Finally the doctor was called and prescribed: 'No more excitement!'

The townspeople of Nogent saw in all this merely a sinister prognosis for her future morals. Some were saying 'that Moreau boy' had designs to put her on the stage later on.

Soon another event took place: Uncle Barthélemy came on a visit. Madame Moreau put him up in her own bedroom and even condescended to serve meat on Friday.

The old man made little effort to be affable. He was forever drawing comparisons between Le Havre and Nogent, whose air he found terribly stuffy, its bread of poor quality, its streets badly paved, its food far from good, and its inhabitants a lazy lot. 'Trade's very slack here!' He criticized his dead brother's extravagance, whereas he himself had amassed an income of twenty-seven thousand francs a year! He left at the end of a week and, poised on the footboard of his carriage, delivered himself of these hardly encouraging words:

'Well, I'm always glad to think you're comfortably off!'

'Not a penny for you there!' said Madame Moreau when she came back into the room.

He'd only come under pressure from his sister-in-law and throughout the week she'd been trying, perhaps too blatantly, to persuade him to reveal his intentions. She was sorry she'd done anything and sat tight-lipped in her armchair, looking at the floor. Frédéric sat opposite, watching her, and in exactly the same way as five years before, when he'd just come from Montereau, neither of them uttered a word. This coincidence struck him too and brought his mind back to Madame Arnoux.

At that moment the loud crack of a whip was heard under their window and a voice called up to him.

It was old Roque alone in his wagonette. He was off to spend the day at La Fortrelle, Monsieur Dambreuse's property, and amiably offering to take Frédéric along with him.

'There's no need of a special invitation when you're with me, never fear!'

Frédéric felt tempted to accept. But how could he explain why he'd settled in Nogent? And he hadn't any decent summer clothes; and what would his mother have to say? He declined.

From that time on, their neighbour proved less friendly. Louise was growing up: Madame Éléonore fell ill, dangerously ill; and the relationship lapsed, to the great relief of Madame Moreau who was afraid of the harmful effects such company might have on her son's future prospects.

She had dreams of buying him a clerkship to the court. Frédéric did not seem too opposed to the idea. These days, he accompanied her to Mass and played his hand of cards in the evening; he was becoming inured to provincial life, submerged by it, and even his love had taken on a kind of funereal placidity, a soporific charm. He'd poured so much of his distress into his letters, into his reading, into his country walks, scattering it broadcast, that it had almost dried up; his affection for Madame Arnoux had become so quiet and resigned that he looked on her as being dead and was surprised not to know where she was buried.

On 12 December 1845 at about nine o'clock in the morning, the cook brought up a letter to his room. The address was written in a large and unfamiliar hand; Frédéric was still feeling drowsy and in no hurry to open it. Finally he did.

JUSTICE OF THE PEACE
IIIrd District
LE HAVRE

Dear Sir,

Your uncle Monsieur Moreau having died intestate . . .

He was the heir!

As if fire had suddenly broken out in the next room, he shot out of bed barefoot, in his nightshirt; he ran his hand over his face, unable to believe his eyes, imagining that he was still dreaming, and to bring himself down to earth, he flung the window wide open.

Snow had fallen; the roof-tops were white; he even recognized in the backyard a wash-tub which had tripped him up the night before.

Three times he read the letter straight through: no doubt whatsoever? His uncle's entire estate! Twenty-seven thousand a year!—and the thought of seeing Madame Arnoux again almost drove him out of his mind with joy. In a kind of hallucination, he actually saw himself beside her, in her house, bringing her a present wrapped in tissue paper, while his tilbury stood waiting outside—no, a brougham would be better, a black one with a footman in brown livery; he could hear the horse pawing the ground and the clink of the curb mingling with the murmur of their kisses. And this scene would be repeated endlessly, day after day. He'd entertain at his place, in his own home; the dining-room would be in red leather, the boudoir in yellow silk, with divans galore; and just think of the mantelpieces! And the Chinese vases! And the rugs! All these images piled up so thick and fast that his head began to reel. Then he remembered his mother and went downstairs, still clutching his letter.

Madame Moreau tried to control her feelings and felt faint. Frédéric took her into his arms and kissed her forehead.

'Mother dear, now you can buy your carriage back, so don't be sad, cheer up and dry your tears!'

Ten minutes later the news was going the rounds, even in the remoter suburbs. Then Maître Benoist, Monsieur Gamblin, Monsieur Chambion and all their other friends came hurrying round. Frédéric slipped away for a minute to write to Deslauriers. More people called. The afternoon was taken up in congratulations. Meanwhile Monsieur Roque's wife was forgotten, although she was very low.

That evening, when they were alone together, Madame Moreau told her son she would advise him to set up as a lawyer in Troyes. Being better known in his own part of the world than elsewhere, he could more easily make a good match.

'Oh no, that's really too much!' exclaimed Frédéric.

Barely was happiness within his grasp than they wanted to take it away from him. He told her firmly that he intended to live in Paris.

'What would you do there?'

'Nothing!'

Surprised by his manner, Madame Moreau asked him what he wanted to become.

'A minister!' retorted Frédéric.

And he made it plain that he wasn't joking, that he intended to embark on a diplomatic career, that he felt drawn in that direction both by his training and by inclination. First of all he'd get into the Conseil d'État,* with the help of Monsieur Dambreuse.

'Do you know him then?'

'Certainly I do, through Monsieur Roque.'

'How odd,' said Madame Moreau.

He'd awakened old ambitious dreams in her own heart. She privately capitulated and never mentioned any of the others again.

Frédéric was anxious to be off like a shot but every seat on the stage-coach was booked for the next day and he had to possess his soul in patience until seven o'clock in the evening.

As they were sitting down to dinner, the church bell tolled three times and the maid came in to announce that Madame Éléonore had just passed away.

Her death, after all, was not a tragedy for anyone, even her daughter! The girl would be all the better off later on.

As the two houses were attached, they could hear much coming and going and a hubbub of voices; and the thought of this dead body so close at hand cast something of a funereal gloom over their parting. Two or three times Madame Moreau wiped away a tear. Frédéric had a heavy heart.

After dinner, he was intercepted by Catherine: Mademoiselle Louise wanted to see him urgently. She was waiting in the garden. He went out, stepped over the fence and headed for the Roque house, slightly bumping into some trees on the way. Lights were shining at a second-floor window; a shape loomed up in the darkness and a voice whispered:

'It's me.'

She seemed taller than usual, no doubt because of her black dress. At a loss for words, he merely took her by the hands and sighed:

'Poor Louise!'

She made no reply and for a long time stood peering into his face. Frédéric was afraid of missing his coach; he thought he could hear a rumbling in the distance and so decided to come to the point:

'Catherine said you had something . . .'

'Yes, there is. I wanted to tell you . . .'

She was addressing him far more formally than usual. Frédéric was surprised. Then, as she didn't go on:

'What was it you wanted to say to me?'

'Oh, I can't think . . . I've forgotten! Is it true you're going away?'

'Yes, in a few minutes' time.'

She repeated:

'Oh, only a few minutes? Is it for good? Shan't we be seeing each other any more?'

Her voice was shaken by sobs.

'Goodbye! Goodbye! Oh, do give me a kiss!'

And she flung herself into his arms.

PART TWO

CHAPTER I

He took his seat at the front of the stage-coach, and as it lurched forward with all five horses heaving together, he was swept away on a wave of elation. Like an architect designing a palace he drew up his plans for his future, full of things dainty and splendid, towering to the skies; and sunk in contemplation of such a rich array he lost all sense of the outside world.

At the bottom of Sourdun Hill, he realized where they were: they'd only done five kilometres, at best! He was indignant. He pulled down the window to watch the road and kept on asking the driver when, exactly, they'd be arriving. Then he calmed down and remained sitting in his corner with his eyes open.

The lamp hanging from the postilion's seat was shining on the shaft-horses' cruppers. Beyond them, he could just make out the other horses' manes tossing about like stormy, white-capped waves; their breath formed clouds of vapour on both sides of the team, their steel chains jangled, the windows were rattling in their frames, and the heavy coach went rumbling steadily on over the paving stones. From time to time, a solitary inn or else the wall of a barn loomed up out of the dark and as they passed through the villages, the fiery glow of a baker's oven would occasionally send the giant shadows of the horses eerily galloping along the house opposite. At the posting station, after they'd unhitched the horses, there was complete silence for a minute; then someone trampled round on top, under the canvas cover, while a woman stood in the doorway sheltering her candle with her hand. The driver sprang up on to the foot-board and they were off again.

At Momans a clock was striking a quarter past one.

'So it's already today!' he thought. 'Really today! It'll be any time now!'

But gradually his hopes and memories, Nogent and the rue de Choiseul, Madame Arnoux and his mother, all became jumbled up in his head.

He was woken up by the clatter of planks; they were crossing the Charenton* bridge: it was Paris! One of his fellow travellers removed his cap, the other one his head-scarf, and they both put on hats and began to chat. The first one, a florid, burly man wearing a velvet frock-coat, was a merchant; the other man was coming to the capital to consult a doctor; Frédéric was in such a state of blissful emotion that, on an impulse, he apologized to him, fearing he might have disturbed him in the night.

The coach drove straight on, no doubt because the quayside terminus was flooded out. They found themselves back in the country again. In the distance he could see tall smoking chimneys. Then they turned into Ivry. They drove along a street and all of a sudden, there was a glimpse of the Panthéon.

Bulging out across the desolate plain, with its vaguely dilapidated look, were the enclosure walls of the Paris fortifications stretching out horizontally; the muddy foot-paths beside the road were lined with branchless trees protected by wooden palings bristling with nails. Chemical factories alternated with timber-yards. Tall, half-open gate-ways which looked like farm entrances offered revolting glimpses of filthy courtyards with dirty puddles in the middle. Between their first-floor windows, long, dark red taverns displayed two crossed billiard cues set in a round wreath of plaited flowers. Here and there were plaster hovels, half-completed and abandoned. Eventually, only a double row of houses was left; from time to time a giant tin cigar stood out against the bare shop-fronts of tobacconists; midwives were represented by a sign showing a matronly figure dandling a babe-in-arms in a lace-trimmed quilt; corner walls were covered by tattered posters flapping like rags in the wind; men in smocks were on their way to work, together with brewers' drays, laundresses' vans and butch-ers' carts. It was cold and drizzling, the sky was drab; but for him, through the mist, two eyes were gleaming more brightly than any sun.

At the toll-gate, they were held up for a long time because the way was blocked by country people, wagoners, and a flock of sheep. The guard had his cape thrown back and was pacing up and down in front of his sentry box to keep warm. The toll-keeper clambered up to the top deck. There was a loud blast on a cornet and off they went at a brisk trot down the boulevard, with swingle-trees rattling and traces flying. The lash of the long whip cracked in the damp air, the driver shouted: 'Mind your backs!', the crossing sweeper stood back, and pedestrians leapt to one side; the windows were splattered with mud, they kept meeting tip-carts and buses. At last the railings of the Jardin-des-Plantes stretched out ahead.

At the bridges, the Seine, a dirty yellow, was almost up to the roadway; cool air drifted up from it and Frédéric took a deep breath to fill his lungs with that tangy old Paris air and its heady atmosphere of love and intellectual stimulus. His first glimpse of a cab made his heart melt, and he even loved the straw-covered entrances of wine-shops, the grocers' assistants shaking their coffee-roasters, even the shoe-blacks with their little boxes. Women were scuttling along under their umbrellas; he leant forward to examine their faces: some chance might have brought Madame Arnoux out of doors.

The shops were racing past, the crowds were growing thicker, the noise louder. After the quai Saint-Bernard, the quai de la Tournelle, and the quai Montebello, they came to the quai Napoléon; he tried to pick out the windows of his lodging; they were a long way off. Then they crossed the Seine again by the Pont-Neuf and drove along as far as the Louvre; then they took the rue Saint-Honoré, the rue Croix-des-Petits-Champs and the rue Bouloi to the rue Coq-Héron, where they went into the courtyard of the hotel.

To savour his pleasure, Frédéric took as long as possible in dressing and even made his way on foot up to the boulevard Montmartre; he kept smiling at the thought that he'd soon be seeing that beloved name on the marble plate; he looked up: no shop-window, no pictures, nothing!

He rushed round to the rue de Choiseul. There were no Monsieur and Madame Arnoux living there and a neighbour was acting as door-keeper; Frédéric waited for him to appear and when he eventually did so, he turned out to be not the same man as before. He didn't know their address.

Frédéric went off to a café and over lunch consulted the Business Directory. Out of three hundred Arnoux, there wasn't one single Jacques! Where could they be living? Pellerin would be sure to know. He took a cab to his studio at the very top of the Faubourg-Poissonnière. Since there was no bell or knocker, he banged on the door with his fist; he called and shouted. The only reply was hollow silence.

Then he thought of Hussonnet. But how could he lay hands on a man like that? He'd once gone back with him to his girlfriend's house in the rue de Fleurus. When he got to the rue de Fleurus, Frédéric realized he didn't know the girl's name.

He tried police headquarters and wandered about upstairs and down from one office to another; the information desk was just closing; he was told to come back again next day.

Then he called on all the art dealers he could find, to discover if any of them knew Arnoux. Monsieur Arnoux was no longer in the business.

In the end, harassed and depressed and sick at heart, he returned to his hotel and went to bed. Just as he was stretching out under the sheets, a thought struck him; he jumped for joy.

'Regimbart! What an idiot not to have thought of that before!'

By seven next morning he was waiting in the rue Notre-Dame-des-Victoires outside the door of a liquor shop where Regimbart was in the habit of imbibing white wine. It wasn't yet open. He went for a stroll round the district and returned half an hour later: Regimbart had left that very minute. Frédéric dashed out into the street. He even thought he caught sight of his hat in the distance; a hearse and mourning carriages blocked his path. By the time the way was clear, the apparition had vanished.

Fortunately, he remembered that the Citizen used to lunch every day at eleven o'clock on the dot at a cheap little restaurant in the place Gaillon. He'd have to be patient; and after strolling interminably from the Bourse to the Madeleine and from the Madeleine to the Gymnase Theatre, at eleven o'clock sharp Frédéric went into the restaurant in the place Gaillon, certain of finding his quarry.

'Don't know 'im!' snapped the owner superciliously.

When Frédéric persisted, he repeated:

'I have ceased to know him, my dear sir!' looking haughtily down his nose and with much wagging of his head, to indicate some dark secret. However, at their last meeting the Citizen had mentioned an Alexandre's Tavern. Gulping down a brioche, Frédéric jumped into another cab and enquired of the driver if there were not a certain Alexandre's Café, somewhere up by Sainte-Geneviève. The cabby drove him up to an establishment of that name in the rue des Francs-Bourgeois, and when he asked: 'Monsieur Regimbart, please?' the proprietor answered with an extremely ingratiating smile:

'We haven't seen him yet, sir', casting a knowing glance at his wife sitting behind the bar. And with a quick look at the clock:

'But I hope we'll be seeing him in about ten minutes time, fifteen at the outside—newspapers for the gent, Célestin, look sharp! What would the gentleman like to drink?'

Although feeling in no need of a drink, Frédéric downed a glass of rum, then a glass of kirsch, then one of curaçao, then various types of punch, hot and cold. He read the morning *Le Siècle** from the first page to the last and then through again; he scrutinized the cartoon in *Le Charivari*;* including the texture of the paper; in the end he knew the advertisements by heart. From time to time, boots clumped on the pavement: it must be him!—and a figure would appear in the window-frame; but they always passed on. To relieve his boredom Frédéric kept changing his seat: he went to sit at the far end, then over to the left, after that the right; and he remained sitting in the middle of a bench-seat along the wall with his arms sprawled out sideways. But a cat delicately picking its way along the velvet back made him start by suddenly leaping down to lick up the syrupy drops on the tray; the child of the house, an insufferable brat of four, was playing with his rattle on the steps of the bar. His mother, a small sickly-looking woman with rotten teeth, wore a stupid smile on her face. What the devil was Regimbart doing? Frédéric continued to wait, with death in his soul.

The rain was pelting down like hail on the hood of the cab. Through the gap in the muslin curtains, he could see the poor horse standing motionless between the shafts, stiller than one made of wood. The gutter had overflowed into the roadway and the water was streaming between two spokes of the wheels while the cabby, half asleep, was sheltering under his apron. However, fearing his fare might try to slip away, every so often he'd poke his nose in at the doorway, dripping like a seal; and if looks could kill, the clock from which Frédéric hardly took his eyes would have been smashed into smithereens. But the hands continued to move. The worthy Alexandre kept walking up and down, repeating:

'He'll be along, never fear. He'll be here soon!' maintaining a constant flow of conversation to divert him, talking politics, and even obligingly offering him a game of dominoes.

Eventually, at half past four, having been there since twelve o'clock, Frédéric sprang to his feet declaring he'd wait no longer.

'I just can't understand it!' said the café proprietor with an innocent expression. 'It's the first time Monsieur Ledoux hasn't turned up!'

'Did you say Ledoux?'

'Of course, sir!'

'But I asked for Regimbart!' exclaimed Frédéric.

'Oh, pardon me, sir, you must be mistaken! That's right, my dear, isn't it? The gentleman did say Ledoux?'

And calling out to the waiter:

'You heard him too, didn't you, Célestin?'

Doubtless to pay off an old score with his employer, the waiter merely smiled.

Exasperated at having wasted his time, Frédéric drove up towards the boulevards, furious with Regimbart, while still imploring him to appear, like some *deus ex machina*, and grimly determined to dig him out of his wine-cellar, however remote. The cab was getting on his nerves and he paid it off; his mind was growing confused and then all of a sudden the name of every café he'd ever heard mentioned by that cretin flashed into his head, like the hundreds of separate items of a firework display: Café Gascard, Café Frimbert, Café Halbout, the Bordeaux, the Havre and the Havana Taverns, the Boeuf-à-la-Mode, the Brasserie Allemande, Mother Morel's, and he drove round to the lot, one after the other. But in one of them Regimbart had just left, in another, he was 'on his way—maybe', in a third, he'd not been seen for six months; somewhere else, he'd ordered a leg of lamb, yesterday, for next Saturday. Finally, as he was going through the door of Vauthier's Winebar, Frédéric ran into the waiter.

'Do you know Monsieur Regimbart?'

'Do I know him, sir! I've just had the pleasure of serving him, he's upstairs at this very moment, finishing his dinner!'

The owner of the establishment himself came up, with his napkin under his arm.

'Were you asking for Monsieur Regimbart, sir? He left here only a moment ago!'

Frédéric swore loudly; but the bar owner assured him he'd find him at Bouttevilain's, never fear.

'Take my word for it! He left a bit earlier than usual because he's meeting some people on business. But you can be certain to find him, sir, at Bouttevilain's, 92, rue Saint-Martin, second staircase on the left at the rear of the courtyard, on the mezzanine, right-hand door!'

And at last, through the pipe smoke, he sighted him at the back of the room beyond the bar, sitting by himself behind the billiard table with his chin sunk on his chest meditating in front of a mug of beer.

'So there you are! I've been looking for you for ages!'

Quite unmoved, Regimbart held out a couple of fingers for him to shake and reeled off a few trite comments on the opening of the parliamentary session, as if he'd seen him only yesterday.

Frédéric cut him short to ask as casually as he could:

'How's Arnoux?'

Regimbart was in no hurry to reply; he was rolling his drink round his mouth.

'Not too bad!'

'And where's he living now?'

'In the rue Paradis-Poissonnière, of course!' replied the Citizen in surprise.

'What number?'

'Good Lord, man, number 37. What a queer fellow you are!'

Frédéric got to his feet.

'Off so soon?'

'Yes, I've forgotten something I've got to do.'

Frédéric left the bar to go off to Arnoux's, cosily floating along on warm air, with the complete effortlessness of dreams.

Soon he found himself on a second floor standing outside a door with the bell ringing; a maid appeared; a second door opened; Madame Arnoux was sitting beside the fire-place; Arnoux rushed forward and embraced him. She had a little boy about three years old on her lap; her daughter, now as tall as her mother, was standing at the other side of the fire.

'Let me introduce this young gentleman to you,' said Arnoux, taking hold of his son under the armpits.

For a few minutes he amused himself by throwing him high in the air and catching him at arms' length, while his mother kept exclaiming:

'My goodness, you'll kill him! Please don't do that!'

But Arnoux swore there was no danger and made no

attempt to stop, even encouraging the little boy: 'Upsy-daisy, laddikins!'*

Then he asked Frédéric why he'd been so long without writing, what on earth he'd been up to down in the country, and what had brought him back.

'As for me, my dear fellow, I'm in the ceramics industry now, pottery and all that. But let's talk about yourself!'

Frédéric pleaded a protracted law suit and his mother's health, with particular emphasis on this last fact to create a favourable impression. In a word, he was going to settle in Paris, for good this time; he kept quiet about his legacy; it might have damaged his past reputation.

Like the furnishings, the curtains were of dark red woollen damask; a couple of pillows lay touching on a bolster; a kettle was simmering on the coals; the apartment was bathed in the subdued light of a shaded lamp standing on the edge of the chest of drawers. Madame Arnoux was wearing a slate-blue merino dressing-gown. She was gazing into the embers with her hand resting on the little boy's shoulder and undoing the string of his vest with the other while the little mite whimpered and scratched his head like Monsieur Alexandre junior.

Frédéric had been expecting to be thrown into raptures of delight but in unfamiliar surroundings, passions wither and decay, and seeing Madame Arnoux in circumstances different from those in which he had first known her, she seemed to him diminished, somehow vaguely degraded, in fact to be no longer the same woman. He was shocked at feeling so unmoved. He asked after his friends, including Pellerin.

'I don't see much of him,' replied Arnoux.

She added:

'We don't entertain as much as in the old days.'

Was this a warning not to expect an invitation? However, Arnoux continued to exude friendliness; he complained that Frédéric should have just dropped in for dinner, to take pot-luck, and went on to explain why he'd changed his business.

'What can one do in decadent times like ours? Great art

has gone out of fashion! Anyway, art can find a place everywhere. You know what a lover of beauty I am! I must show you round my factory one of these days.'

And he insisted on showing him some of his products then and there; they were stored in the mezzanine.

The floor was littered with dishes, soup tureens, plates and bowls. Large floor tiles representing mythological subjects in the Renaissance style, for bathrooms and dressing-rooms, were stacked against the wall while down the middle, double rows of shelves reaching to the ceiling were crammed with wine-coolers, flowerpots, candelabra, small plant-stands and large polychrome statuettes depicting a blackamoor or a Pompadour shepherdess. Frédéric was cold, hungry and bored by Arnoux's displays.

He made tracks for the Café Anglais and had a splendid supper, saying to himself meanwhile:

'What an idiot I was to be so depressed in Nogent! She had a job to recognize me! She's nothing but a middle-class housewife!'

In a sudden outburst of healthy energy, he determined to pursue his own aims without consideration for anyone else. His heart was as hard as the table under his elbows. From now on, he could throw himself into society without any qualms. The Dambreuses came into his mind: he could make use of them; then he remembered Deslauriers.

'Well, can't be helped!' But he did send a note by messenger arranging to lunch together next day at the Palais-Royal.

Luck had been less kind to him.

For his post-graduate examination he had submitted a thesis on 'Probate and the Validity of Wills', in which he'd argued that testamentary capacity should be strictly limited, and as his cross-questioner at the *viva* had led him on to talk nonsense, he had done so at great length while the examiners had remained inscrutable. Then, as bad luck would have it, Prescription* had turned up as the topic for exposition. Deslauriers had launched into quite outrageous theories: old claims were to be given no more weight than new ones; why should an owner be denied his property merely on the grounds that he can't furnish proof of title until thirty-one years have elapsed? It amounted to giving the heir of a thief the same security as an honest man. Any extension of this right would sanction every kind of injustice; it would be a tyrannical abuse of power. He even went so far as to exclaim:

'Let's abolish it and then the Franks will no longer oppress the Gauls, the English the Irish, the Yanks the Red Indians, the Turks the Arabs,* the whites the blacks, Poland* . . .'

The chief examiner had cut him short:

'All right, all right! Your political beliefs are no concern of ours, you may submit yourself for re-examination at a later date, sir!'

Deslauriers had declined to try again* but the bee in his bonnet over that unfortunate twentieth section of the third book of the Civil Code had taken on monstrous proportions and he was working on a *magnum opus* on 'Positive and Negative Prescription considered as the basis of Civil and Natural Law' and had become lost in the study of Dunod, Rogerius, Balbus, Merlin, Vazeille, Savigny, Troplong and other important jurists. In order to have more free time to devote to this, he'd given up his job as chief clerk and was earning his living by private tutoring and writing other men's theses. Meanwhile, at the Debating Society, his virulent opinions were arousing so much alarm among the conservatives, all confirmed Guizot admirers, that in certain circles he had achieved a sort of notoriety, not unmixed with personal distrust.

He arrived wearing a voluminous greatcoat lined with red flannel, similar to the one worn by Sénécal in the old days.

Concerned at their effect on the numerous passers-by, they cut short their demonstrations of affection and linking arms with tears of pleasure in their eyes they went off giggling all the way to Véfour's.* Then, as soon as they were by themselves, Deslauriers exclaimed:

'Well, it's going to be the good life for us from now on, isn't it!'

Frédéric disliked this prompt take-over of his new prosperity. His friend seemed too pleased by their joint good fortune and not appreciative enough of his alone.

Deslauriers now told him about his set-back and then little by little about his work and his way of life, talking philosophically about himself and sourly about everybody else. He was full of disgust; there wasn't one single holder of high office who wasn't either a fool or a knave. He flared up at a waiter over a dirty glass and when Frédéric expostulated:

'D'you think I'm going to worry my head about trash like that, who get up to six or eight thousand a year, who have the vote, and can perhaps even become Deputies?* Not on your life!'

Then, with a mischievous look:

'Oh, I'm forgetting I'm talking to a capitalist, a Mondor, because you are a Mondor* now!'

And coming back again to the question of inheritance, he expressed his view that collateral succession was unfair in essence, though he was glad Frédéric had benefited from it, and one of these fine days, in the coming Revolution, it would be abolished.

'Oh, you think so, do you?' said Frédéric.

'You can bet your boots on it,' retorted the other man. 'Things can't go on like this! It causes too much suffering. Think of the appalling situation of someone like Sénécal . . .'

'Off we go again with Sénécal!' thought Frédéric.

'Anyway, what news? Are you still in love with Madame Arnoux? It's all over, isn't it?'

At a loss for a reply, Frédéric closed his eyes and looked down.

With regard to Arnoux himself, Deslauriers told him that his paper was now owned by Hussonnet, who'd transformed it; it was now called *L'Art*, a literary foundation and joint stock company, with paid-up capital of forty thousand francs in hundred-franc shares; every shareholder had the right to have articles in it because '"the company aims at making known the first works of young authors, in order to spare writers of talent, perhaps even of genius, the sad plight which can overtake . . ." and so on and so forth, you can recognize the usual humbug!' All the same, something could be done, such as improving the quality of the paper and then, while still keeping the same editors and promising not to drop the serials, springing a political journal on to the subscribers. It wouldn't need a lot of extra working capital. 'Well, how about it? Would you like to have a go?'

While not rejecting the suggestion out of hand, Frédéric would have to straighten out his affairs first.

'But if you should be needing anything . . .'

'Thanks, old chap!' said Deslauriers.

Afterwards, resting their elbows on the plush-covered window-sill, they looked out on to the garden, puffing away at their excellent cigars. The sun was shining, the air was soft, flocks of birds fluttered round, preparing to land, the bronze and marble statues, washed by the rain, were gleaming, nurse maids in aprons were sitting on chairs, chatting, and they could hear children's laughter blending with the constant gentle splashing of the fountain.

Deslauriers's bitterness had made Frédéric uncomfortable, but under the influence of the wine circulating through his veins, with the light shining full into his eyes, in a drowsy torpor, he could feel only a sense of immense well-being and a shiver of sensuous delight, like a plant soaking up warmth and moisture. Deslauriers was gazing vacantly into space. He drew a deep breath and started to speak:

'Ah, how much more glamorous it was when Camille Desmoulins would have been standing over there, urging the people on to the Bastille! In those days you were really alive, you could make your mark and prove your strength. Mere lawyers were ordering generals about and barefoot beggars were trampling on kings, while nowadays . . .'

He paused and then suddenly:

'Never mind! The future's full of possibilities!'

And he tapped out the charge on the window-pane as he declaimed the lines from Barthélemy:

That terrible Assembly which, forty years on,
Still stirs your mind, will return,
Fearless colossus marching with forceful stride* . . .

I've forgotten the rest! But it's getting late, shall we go?'
And he continued to expound his doctrines in the street.

Frédéric wasn't listening; he was looking into the shop-windows for materials and furniture for his new lodgings. Perhaps it was the thought of Madame Arnoux which brought him to a halt in front of a second-hand dealer, where three faience plates were on display; they were decorated with yellow arabesques in a metal lustre and priced at a hundred francs each. He asked for them to be put on one side for him.

'If I were you I'd buy lots of silver,' said Deslauriers, whose modest family background had left him with a weakness for display.

As soon as he was alone, Frédéric went round to the renowned Pomadère and ordered three pairs of trousers, two coats, five waistcoats, and one fur coat; then on to a boot-maker, a shirt-maker, and a hatter, giving instructions that they were to be as quick as possible.

Three days later, on his return from Le Havre, he found his complete outfit delivered at his flat; eager to make the most of them he determined to pay a call on the Dambreuses straightaway; but it was too early, only just eight o'clock.

'Why not go round to the other ones?' he said to himself.

Arnoux was alone, shaving in front of a mirror. He suggested taking him somewhere amusing and when Frédéric mentioned Monsieur Dambreuse:

'Well now, that's splendid, you'll be meeting some of his friends there! Do come, it'll be fun!'

As Frédéric was politely declining, Madame Arnoux recognized his voice and wished him good evening through the partition: her daughter was rather poorly and she was not feeling well herself; he could hear a spoon tinkle against a glass and all the rustling of things being gently moved associated with sick-rooms. Then Arnoux disappeared to say goodbye to his wife. He was reeling off a whole string of reasons:

'You know how important it is! I've got to go, people are expecting me, they need me there!'

'Off you go then, my dear! Have a good time!'

Arnoux hailed a cab.

'Palais-Royal, Galerie Montpensier!'

And collapsing on to the cushions:

'I'm all in, my dear boy! It's killing me!'

And leaning forward, in a confidential whisper:

'I'm trying to discover the copper-red of the Chinese!'

And he went into the secrets of glazing and firing.

When they reached Chevet's he was handed a large hamper, which he had loaded into the cab. Then he selected some grapes, some pineapples and various exotic delicacies 'for his poor dear wife' and asked for them to be delivered the following morning.

Then they went to a theatrical costumier's; it was a fancy dress ball they were going to. Arnoux chose blue velvet breeches, a jacket to match and a wig of red hair; Frédéric took a domino; then they went down the rue de Laval to a house where the second floor was ablaze with coloured lanterns.

From the foot of the stairs they could hear the sound of violins. 'Where on earth are we?' enquired Frédéric.

'Don't be scared, she's a good sort!'

The door was opened by a footman and they went into the entrance hall where chairs were piled with cloaks, shawls and greatcoats. A young woman dressed as a Louis XV dragoon was just going through: she was Mademoiselle Rose-Annette Bron, the lady of the house.

'Well?' said Arnoux.

'It's all arranged,' she replied.

'Oh, thanks, you're an angel!'

And went to give her a kiss.

'Mind out, you idiot, you'll mess up my make-up!'

Arnoux introduced Frédéric.

'Put it there, Monsieur Frédéric, you're very welcome!'

She pulled aside the door-curtain behind her and announced dramatically:

'Our good friend and scullion Arnoux and a princely companion!'

Frédéric was dazzled by the lights; at first all he could see was silk and velvet, bare shoulders, and a medley of colours swaying to the sound of an orchestra hidden away in a mass of greenery, surrounded by walls hung in yellow silk with a few pastel portraits here and there and Louis XVI crystal torch-lights. In the corners, tall lamps with frosted glass globes looking like snowballs towered over console tables bearing baskets of flowers while straight ahead, through a second smaller room, a third one offered a glimpse of a bed with wreathed columns and a Venetian mirror at its head.

The dancing stopped and Arnoux made his entry amidst a burst of clapping and screams of delight, carrying his hamper on his head. 'Mind the chandelier!' Frédéric looked up at the ceiling: it was an antique Meissen chandelier which used to adorn the gallery of *L'Art industriel*; the memory of those bygone days passed through his mind but an infantryman in undress uniform with that half-witted look traditionally associated with conscripts barred his way with arms outstretched in surprise, and in spite of the frightful black, ultra-spiky moustache disfiguring his face, he recognized his old friend Hussonnet. The Bohemian addressed him as 'Colonel!' and deluged him with compliments in a half-Alsatian, half-pidgin sort of gibberish. Frédéric felt intimidated by all these people and was at a loss for a reply. A violin-bow tapped on a music-stand and the men and women lined up to dance. There were about sixty people present, the women dressed mainly as village maidens or duchesses, the men, almost all middle-aged, as navvies, stevedores or sailors.

Frédéric stood with his back to the wall and watched the quadrille.

Madame Rosanette, wearing a green coat, a pair of stockinette breeches and soft leather boots with gilt spurs, was dancing with an old buck dressed in the long purple silk gown of a Venetian doge. The couple facing them consisted of an Albanian, weighed down with yataghans, and a blue-eyed Swiss miss, milk-white and as plump as a partridge, in a short-sleeved blouse and red bodice. To set off her hair, which came down almost to her calves, a tall blonde who had walk-on parts at the Opéra, had got herself up as a Native Woman: over her brown tights she was wearing merely a leather loincloth, some glass bead bangles and a tinsel diadem with a tall spray of peacock feathers on top. Facing her was a Pritchard floating in a grotesquely loose tail-coat and beating time to the music on a snuff-box, with his elbow. A little Watteau Shepherd Boy, all blue and silver like a moonlit night, was tapping his crook against the thyrsus of a Bacchante wearing a crown of grapes, buskins tied with gold ribbons and a leopard skin hanging down her left side. Across the room, a Polish Woman in a short reddish-orange velvet jacket was tossing her gauze petticoat about and revealing pearl-grey silk stockings emerging from pink bootees trimmed with white fur. She was smiling at a paunchy 40-year-old man disguised as a Choirboy who was prancing wildly about, lifting his surplice up with one hand while he held his clerical headgear on with the other. But the star, the queen of the ball, was the dancer Mademoiselle Loulou, well known in the dance-halls. Being in funds at the moment, she was wearing a deep lace collar over her plain black velvet jacket, and her wide flame-coloured silk trousers, skin-tight over her buttocks and drawn in by a cashmere sash at the waist, had tiny real white camellias stitched on all down the seams. Her pale, slightly puffy face with its upturned nose seemed even saucier under her tousled wig, with a man's grey felt hat cocked over her right ear, and at every leap she made, her dancing shoes with their diamond buckles nearly kicked the nose of the dancer next to her, a tall medieval Baron, loaded down in his suit of armour. There was also an Angel holding a golden sword in her hand and with two swans-down wings on her back, reeling from side to side, constantly losing her partner Louis XIV, completely at sea in the figures, and wrecking the quadrille.

Gazing at all these people, Frédéric felt ill at ease and forsaken; the thought of Madame Arnoux was still running through his head and it seemed to him that he was taking part in some evil conspiracy to do her wrong.

When the quadrille came to an end, Madame Rosanette came up to him. She was panting slightly and under her chin her gorget, as smooth and gleaming as a mirror, was heaving gently up and down.

'So you're not dancing, Monsieur?' she said.

Frédéric explained that, unfortunately, he didn't know how to.

'Really? Even with me? Quite sure?'

And poised on one hip with her other knee drawn back, she stroked the mother-of-pearl pommel of her sword with her left hand and gazed at him for a minute with a half-mocking, half-pleading expression. Finally she said: 'In that case, good-night!', spun round on the tip of her toe, and disappeared.

Annoyed with himself and not knowing what to do, Frédéric started to wander round amongst the dancers.

He went into the boudoir, upholstered in pale blue silk embroidered with bunches of wild flowers; in a gilt-wood circle on the ceiling, Cupids were frolicking on a fleecy coverlet of clouds set against an azure sky. He was dazzled by such elegance which, a generation later, would be mere frippery for the Rosanettes of this world. He admired everything: the artificial Morning Glory adorning the mirror surround, the curtains at the fireplace, the Turkish divan and, in a recess, a sort of pink canopy with white muslin at the top. The black bedroom furniture was brass-inlaid, and on a dais covered in swansdown stood the large tester bed decorated with ostrich plumes. The pin-cushions were studded with jewel-headed pins; rings were lying scattered about on trays, and in the dim glow of a Bohemian crystal chandelier hanging on three chains, there was a dull gleam of silver caskets and gold-framed lockets. Through a tiny, half-open, door you could see a conservatory extending the whole width of a terrace with an aviary at the end.

It really was an attractive sort of society. In a sudden

burst of youthful revolt, he swore to enjoy it. His diffidence melted away and, going back to the entrance to the drawing-room, where more people had gathered—by now the whole scene was a sort of brilliant, dust-laden pandemonium—he stood watching the quadrilles, his eyes half-closed in order to see better, his nostrils wide-open to the soft fragrances of women, as penetrating as an all-embracing kiss.

But nearby, on the other side of the doorway, he caught sight of Pellerin—a Pellerin dressed in full evening dress with his left hand resting in the breast of his coat and holding in his right, in addition to his hat, a tattered white glove.

'Good Lord, we've not seen you for ages! Where the devil have you been? Making a trip? Italy perhaps? Rather old hat, Italy, don't you think? Not quite as super as they say, eh? Never mind, bring some of your sketches round one day, won't you?'

And without waiting for a reply, the artist started talking about himself. He'd made a lot of progress, now that he'd finally recognized the stupidity of *Line*: one ought not to bother so much about the *Beauty* and *Unity* of a work as about the *Diversity* and *Character* of things.

'Because since everything is to be found in Nature, everything is a legitimate subject, everything's *plastic*. You see, the only thing needed is to strike the *right note*. And I've discovered the secret!' Digging him in the ribs with his elbow, he repeated several times: 'I've discovered the secret, you see. Just take a look at that little woman with the sphinx-like hair-style over there, dancing with the Russian Postilion, it's tidy, it's sharp, cut-and-dried, nothing but plane surfaces and crude tones: indigo-blue under the eyes, a spot of vermilion on the cheeks, sepia on the temples: bang, bang!' And he slashed the brush strokes in the air with his thumb. 'Whereas that big woman over there, for instance,' he went on, pointing to a Fishwife in a cherry-coloured dress, with a gold cross round her neck and a lawn fichu tied behind her back, 'nothing but curves, flared nostrils matching the wings of her bonnet, lips turned up at the corners, sagging chin, she's all fat, melting and abundant, quiet and sunny, a genuine Rubens. Yet they're both perfect. So where's your *Typical Woman*?' He was warming to his theme. 'What is a *Beautiful Woman*? What is *Beauty*? Ah, you're going to say, Beauty is . . .' Frédéric cut him short to enquire who the Clown was, with the goat-like profile, busily blessing the dancers in the fourth figure of the quadrille.

'A complete nonentity! A widower with three sons whom he lets run around with the seats out of their breeches while he spends his days at the club and goes to bed with the skivvy . . .'

'And what about the one got up as a Bailiff standing over there in the window recess, talking to the Pompadour Marquise?'

'The Pompadour is Madame Vandoel who used to be an actress at the Gymnase Theatre. She's the mistress of the Doge, the Comte de Palazot. They've been together now for twenty years, no one can quite understand why. What lovely eyes that woman used to have! The fellow beside her goes by the name of Captain d'Herbigny, one of the old guard, whose only assets are his decoration and his pension. He acts as uncle, to chaperone aspiring young tarts at official gatherings, arranges duels, and is a great diner-out.'

'A shady character?' said Frédéric.

'Not at all, straight as a die!'

'Oh!'

The artist mentioned a few other names and then, catching sight of a man wearing a flowing black serge gown, like Molière's doctors, but open all the way down the front, to display his many watch-charms:

'And that figure there is Doctor Des Rogis; he's furious at not being famous, has written a book of medical pornography, has a weakness for boot-licking in high society, and is very discreet. The ladies adore him. He and his wife— that's the skinny Lady of the Manor in the grey dress—lug each other around to every public occasion and a few others as well. Although they haven't a bean, they hold a regular "at home"—arty little tea parties where people recite poetry. Look out!'

The doctor was making his way towards them and the three stood chatting at the entrance to the drawing-room, forming a group that was then joined by Hussonnet, followed by the Native Woman's lover, a young poet displaying his extremely modest physical endowments below his short Francis I cape; and finally by a witty young man disguised as a disreputable-looking Turk; but his gold-braided jacket had travelled so many a mile on the back of itinerant extractors of teeth, his wide, creased trousers were such a faded red, his turban, rolled up like an eel in mustard sauce, was so seedy, in a word, his whole get-up was so brilliantly squalid, that the ladies couldn't hide their feelings of disgust. The doctor consoled him by lavishly praising his mistress, the Stevedore. The Turk was a banker's son.

Between dances, Rosanette kept making her way towards an armchair beside the fireplace in which a well-fed little old gentleman was sitting, dressed in a dark red coat with gold buttons. Despite his sunken cheeks sagging over his high white neck-cloth, his hair, still fair and naturally frizzy like a poodle's, gave him quite a sprightly air.

Bending over his face, she listened to him, and then brought him a glass of cordial. Nothing could have been daintier than her hands showing through the lace of her sleeves, which were protruding from the cuffs of her green tunic. Having taken his drink, the old gentleman kissed her hands.

'But that's Arnoux's neighbour, Monsieur Oudry!'

'Moved on!' said Pellerin with a laugh.

'What do you mean?'

A Postilion of Longjumeau* clasped her round the waist; a waltz was striking up. At this the women sitting on the sofas along the walls all rose to their feet, one by one, with great alacrity, and their skirts and shawls and head-dresses all began to swirl around.

They swirled past Frédéric so closely that he could see the tiny beads on their foreheads, and as this giddy spinning motion quickened and fell into a rhythm, he was gripped by a kind of intoxication and all these equally dazzling women gyrating in front of his eyes, each with her own special fascination, brought other thoughts surging into his mind. The Polish Woman, relaxed and langorous, aroused in him a desire to clasp her in his arms as they sped together, in a sledge, over some snow-bedecked plain. Beneath the waltzing feet of the Swiss Girl, dancing with her body erect and eyes cast down, there opened up vistas of quiet delight, in a chalet, beside a lake. Then, suddenly, the raven-haired Bacchante, flinging back her head, gave him a vision of voracious caresses, in oleander groves, under stormy skies, to the confused drumming of tabors. Struggling to keep up with the music, the Fishwife burst into breathless laughter and he longed to go tippling with her at the Porcherons,* foraging with both hands under her fichu, as in days of yore. But the agile limbs and earnest expression of the Stevedore, whose nimble toes were skimming over the floor, seemed to conceal all the sophistication of modern love, with its scientific accuracy and birdlike volatility. Rosanette was whirling round with one hand resting on her hip; her bob-wig bounced up and down on her collar, spraying orris powder in all directions; and each time she spun round, she nearly caught Frédéric with the points of her gold spurs.

As the last chord of the waltz was subsiding, Mademoiselle Vatnaz appeared. She was wearing an Algerian handkerchief on her hair, a large number of piastres on her forehead, and a kind of long, black cashmere jacket over a pale silver lamé skirt; her eyes were rimmed with kohl and she was holding a Basque drum.

She was followed by a tall young man in the traditional Dante costume; this was—and she now made no secret of it—the former Alhambra singer who, born Auguste Delamare, had first taken the name of Anténor Dellamarre, then Delmas, then Belmar and finally Delmar, modifying and improving his name to match his growing fame, for he had left the cheap dance-halls for the theatre and recently made a resounding début at the Ambigu in *Gaspardo le Pêcheur*.*

At the sight of him, Hussonnet's face darkened. Ever since his own play had been rejected, he'd taken a strong dislike to actors. You couldn't imagine the vanity of those gentlemen, and that one in particular! 'Just look how he's showing off!'

After a perfunctory greeting to Rosanette, Delmar had taken up his stance with his back to the fireplace, hand on heart, left foot placed forward, gazing heavenwards with his crown of gilded laurels resting on his hood, striving to achieve a soulful, poetic look to charm the ladies. People were beginning to come over from all parts of the room to form a large circle round him.

Meanwhile Mademoiselle Vatnaz, after giving Rosanette a long hug, came up to Hussonnet to ask him to cast an eye over the style of an educational work she was hoping to get published, *A Young Ladies' Garland, a literary and moral miscellany*. The writer promised to see what he could do. Next, she asked him if he couldn't give her friend a little publicity in one of the papers to which he contributed and even, later on, find him a part—a request which made Hussonnet forget to help himself to a glass of punch.

This punch was an Arnoux concoction and he was offering it round with a satisfied look, followed by the Doge's lackey with an empty tray.

When he came to Monsieur Oudry, Rosanette stopped him:

'Well, how about that little bit of business?'

He blushed slightly and then, turning to the old fellow:

'Our friend here told me you'd be kind enough to . . .'

'But of course, my dear chap! Anything to oblige a neighbour!'

Monsieur Dambreuse's name was mentioned but as they were conversing in an undertone Frédéric could hear only vaguely what they were saying, so he moved across to the other side of the fireplace, where Rosanette and Delmar were chatting together.

This showman was a vulgar-looking fellow and, like stage scenery, was better viewed from a distance, having coarse hands, big feet and a heavy jowl. He was busily running down the most celebrated stage performers of the day, pouring scorn on poets and continually harping on 'my

133

voice, my physique, my gifts'; he was fond of interlarding his remarks with words he hardly understood himself, such as 'morbidezza, analogous, homogeneity'.

Rosanette was giving little approving nods as she listened. Under her make-up, admiration was bringing colour to her cheeks and a kind of glazed, sloppy look was spreading across her pale eyes, of indeterminate hue. How could she find that sort of man attractive? Frédéric inwardly urged himself to despise him even more, perhaps in order to suppress the kind of envy he was feeling towards him.

Mademoiselle Vatnaz had now joined Arnoux and in between peals of laughter, she kept glancing towards her friend, whom Monsieur Oudry was watching like a hawk.

Then Arnoux and Vatnaz disappeared; the old fellow went over and whispered something to Rosanette.

'Oh, all right then, it's agreed. Just leave me alone!'

She asked Frédéric to see if Monsieur Arnoux was in the kitchen.

The floor was covered with a small army of half-empty glasses, and the casseroles and saucepans, the fish-kettle and frying-pans were all quivering and sizzling. Arnoux was in command, ordering the kitchen staff about with the utmost familiarity, whisking the *rémoulade*, tasting the other sauces and larking about with the maid.

'Right you are,' he said. 'Go and warn her I'm starting to serve.'

The dancing had stopped, the ladies had just gone back to their seats, and the men were strolling around. In the middle of the room, one of the window curtains was billowing out and, despite everyone's warnings, the Sphinx was cooling off her clammy arms in the draught. Where could Rosanette have gone? Frédéric went off in search of her, even trying the boudoir and bedroom. A few people had slipped away there, either to be alone or in couples. The shadows were full of whispers. There was stifled laughter from behind handkerchiefs, and in the dark he could sense the swishing of fans held breast-high, like the fluttering wings of some wounded bird, soft and slow.

He went into the conservatory and there, on the canvas

couch beside the fountain, lying on his stomach under a broad-leaved caladium, was Delmar; sitting beside him and running her hand through his hair was Rosanette; they were gazing into each other's eyes. At the same moment, Arnoux came in at the other end through the aviary. Delmar shot to his feet and, without bothering to look backwards, made an unconcerned exit, even pausing by the doorway to pick an hibiscus flower which he put in his buttonhole. Rosanette bent her head; Frédéric could see her from the side and realized she was crying.

'Goodness me, what's the matter?' enquired Arnoux.

She shrugged and made no reply.

'Is it because of him?' he said.

Putting her arms round his neck and kissing him, slowly:

'You know I'll always love you, my pet. Let's forget about it and go and have some supper!'

The walls of the supper-room were completely covered in pieces of antique faience; it was lit by a blazing forty-candle brass chandelier, which made the gigantic turbot directly underneath, surrounded by dishes of fruit and hors-d'oeuvres and in the centre of a table-cloth bordered by platefuls of bisque, appear even whiter. With a rustling of clothes the women gathered up their skirts, sleeves and stoles and sat down, cheek by jowl; the men settled for the corners. Pellerin and Oudry were put close to Rosanette; Arnoux sat opposite. Palazot had just left with his mistress.

'Enjoy your trip!' she said. 'And now let's get down to it!'

And the Choirboy, who was a wag, ceremoniously crossed himself and started to say grace.

The ladies were shocked, especially the Fishwife, who had a daughter whom she was anxious to bring up properly. And Arnoux 'didn't like that sort of thing either'; religion deserved respect.

A German cuckoo clock chimed two o'clock, sparking off a large assortment of witticisms regarding that bird, followed by an assortment of puns, boasts, anecdotes, bets, lies claiming to be true, unlikely assertions, a hubbub of voices which soon turned into scattered private conversations. Wines were circulating, dish followed dish; the doctor was carving. An orange and a cork were flung across the room; people left their seats to talk to other people. Rosanette kept turning round to look at Delmar, standing motionless behind her; Pellerin was gabbling away and Monsieur Oudry had a smile on his face. Almost unaided, Mademoiselle Vatnaz polished off the heaped-up pile of crayfish, cracking the shells between her greedy teeth. Perched on the piano stool, the only place where her wings allowed her to sit, the Angel was placidly munching away without a pause.

'What an appetite!' the Choirboy said wonderingly. 'What an appetite!'

The Sphinx was drinking brandy, shouting at the top of her voice and flinging herself about like a madwoman. Suddenly her cheeks bulged and, unable to hold back the gush of blood, she stuffed her handkerchief to her mouth and then threw it under the table.

Frédéric had seen her.

'Oh, it's nothing!'

And when he urged her to go home and take care of herself, she replied slowly:

'What's the point? It's no worse than anything else! Life's not very funny!'

An icy shiver of distress ran down his spine, as if he'd just caught a glimpse of whole worlds of wretchedness and despair, a charcoal heater beside a truckle bed, corpses in the morgue dressed in their leather aprons, with the tap running cold water over their hair.

Meanwhile Hussonnet had squatted down at the Native Woman's feet, taking off Grassot* and croaking:

'Oh, be not cruel, Celuta!* This little family celebration is charming! Intoxicate us with delight, O lovely ladies! Let us sport and frolic!'

And he began kissing them on their shoulders. His prickly moustache made them jump; next he hit on the idea of breaking a plate by gently tapping it against his head. Others followed suit; bits of pottery began flying all round the room like slates in a gale and the Stevedore shouted:

'Off you go, me hearties! It won't cost a penny! The gent wot makes 'em is letting us have 'em free, gratis and for nuffink!'

All eyes turned on Arnoux who replied:

'Oh no, only as per invoice, if you don't mind!'

He was no doubt keen to appear not to be, or to have stopped being, Rosanette's lover.

Two angry voices suddenly rang out.

'Idiot!'

'Blackguard!'

'I'm at your disposal!'

'Anytime you like!'

The Knight in Armour was quarrelling with the Russian Postilion; the latter had commented that armour made courage unnecessary and the former had taken offence. They wanted to fight, everyone was trying to intervene, and the Captain was endeavouring to make himself heard above all the din.

'Gentlemen, will you please just listen to me for a moment! I've got experience in this sort of thing!'

Rosanette tapped her glass with a knife to obtain silence and addressed first the Knight, who'd kept his helmet on, and then the Postilion, who was wearing a bearskin hat:

'First of all, take off that pot of yours, it's making me feel hot and you there, take off your wolf's head. Will you do what I tell you, for God's sake! Don't you recognize my epaulettes! I'm your Marshal!'

They did as they were told; everybody clapped and shouted:

'Long live the Marshal! Long live the Marshal!'

She took a bottle of champagne standing on the stove and held it high in the air, to pour into the outstretched glasses. As the table was so wide, all the guests and specially the women went round to her side, standing on tiptoe and on the staves of the chairs, momentarily forming a pyramid of bare shoulders, lunging arms, slanting bodies, and head-dresses and the whole group was covered in a long, glittering spray as Arnoux and the Clown each uncorked a bottle and spurted it over everyone's face from the corners of the room. The door of the aviary had been left open and the tiny scared birds invaded the room, fluttering round the chandelier, crashing into the window-panes and against the furniture; some of them perched on people's heads, looking like large flowers in the middle of their hair.

The band had left. They dragged the piano out of the hall into the drawing-room, Vatnaz sat down at it, and to the accompaniment of the Choirboy's Basque drum, launched into a wild country dance, hitting the keys like a horse stamping its hooves and lurching to and fro in time with the music. The Marshal carried Frédéric off, Husson-net turned a cartwheel, the Stevedore was twisting and jerking like a clown, while the Clown pretended to be an orang-utan and the Native Woman held her arms out sideways and imitated the pitching and tossing of a ship. In the end, everyone stopped, exhausted. Somebody opened a window.

Daylight streamed in and the cool of the morning. There was an exclamation of surprise and then silence. The yellow candlelight was flickering and now and again a sconce would shatter; the floor was strewn with ribbons, flowers and pearls; the side-tables were sticky with spilt punch and cordial; the hangings were stained, the costumes crumpled and covered in dust; the women's hair hung down in strands over their shoulders; and under their make-up, smudged with sweat, their complexions were ghastly pale, their eyelids red and bleary.

The Marshal, bright-eyed and pink-cheeked, looked as fresh as if she'd come straight out of her bath. She flung away her wig and her hair tumbled down all round her like a mane, leaving only her breeches visible and producing a comical and charming effect.

The Sphinx's teeth were chattering and she needed a stole, which Rosanette ran off to fetch from her bedroom;

as the other woman was going after her, she quickly closed the door in her face.

The young Turk commented that nobody had seen Monsieur Oudry leave. They were all too tired to take up this mischievous remark.

People were muffling themselves up in cloaks and capes as they waited for their carriages. The Angel was still sitting at the supper table, eating sardine and butter paste; the Fishwife was on a chair beside her, smoking cigarettes and giving her tips on life.

The cabs finally arrived and the guests departed. Being a correspondent for a provincial paper, Hussonnet had to read fifty-three newspapers before lunch; the Native Woman had a rehearsal at the theatre, Pellerin had a model coming, and the Choirboy had three appointments. The Angel was now overtaken by the first symptoms of a stomach upset and had to be carried out to her cab by the Knight in Armour.

'Mind your wings!' the Stevedore yelled out of the window.

On the landing Mademoiselle Vatnaz said to Rosanette:

'Bye-bye, my dear! A really wonderful party!'

Bending forward she whispered:

'And hang on to him!'

'Until something better turns up,' replied the Marshal, slowly turning away.

Frédéric and Arnoux left together, as they'd come. The former art dealer looked so depressed that Frédéric thought he couldn't be feeling well.

'Not feeling well? Of course I am!'

He was scowling and gnawing at his moustache. Frédéric asked him if he'd got any business worries.

'None whatsoever!'

Then, out of the blue:

'You used to know old Oudry, didn't you?'

Adding venomously:

'He's stinking rich, the crafty old bastard!'

Then he mentioned that a large firing was due to be

carried out at his factory that day. He wanted to be there; the train was leaving in one hour's time.

'But I must go and kiss my wife goodbye.'

'His wife!' thought Frédéric to himself.

And he went to bed with an excruciating ache in the back of his head, and drank a decanter of water to relieve his thirst.

He'd developed another thirst: a thirst for women, for luxury, for everything connected with life in Paris. He felt rather dazed, like someone coming ashore after a sea voyage; and as he dropped off to sleep, an hallucinating vision of the Stevedore's hips and the Polish Woman's calves swam to and fro in front of his eyes. Then two large black eyes, which hadn't been at the dance, loomed up like bright fluttering butterflies, flickering and blazing like torches, soaring up to the cornice and swooping down to meet his lips. He tried desperately to identify them, without success. And now his dreams took over: he was harnessed beside Arnoux in the shafts of a cab and the Marshal was astride him ripping him open with her gold spurs.

CHAPTER II

Frédéric found a small townhouse on the corner of the rue Rumford* and at one swoop bought himself the brougham, the horse, the furniture and two flower-stands, which he got at Arnoux's, to put each side of his drawing-room door. There was a bedroom beyond and then a den, where he thought of putting up Deslauriers. But how could he arrange for *Her*, his future mistress, to visit him? A friend's presence would prove embarrassing. He knocked down a partition to enlarge his drawing-room and turned the den into a smoking-room.

He had endless projects for work and bought his favourite poets, travel books, atlases and dictionaries; he kept urging on his workmen, dashed round from shop to shop, and in his eagerness to gloat over his purchases, never bothered to haggle over prices.

From the accounts of his various suppliers, Frédéric

realized that he'd soon have to pay bills amounting to about forty thousand francs, not including death duties, which would be over thirty-seven thousand, and as the money was in landed property, he wrote off to his solicitor in Le Havre telling him to dispose of part of it, to enable him to clear his debts and have some cash in hand. Then, keen to get to know, at long last, that vague, indefinable will-o'-the-wisp, 'society', he wrote to the Dambreuses enquiring if he might call on them. Madame Dambreuse replied inviting him for the following day.

It was her 'at home' day. There were carriages standing in the courtyard. Two flunkeys hurried out from the glass porch and a third was waiting at the top of the steps to lead him into the house.

Frédéric went through an entrance hall, another room, and then a large drawing-room with high windows and a monumental mantelpiece, on which stood a globe-shaped clock and a pair of porcelain vases of monstrous proportions from which two clusters of sconces were sprouting like two golden bushes. On the wall were paintings in the style of Ribera; the tapestry door-curtains were heavy and majestic and the furniture—the tables, consoles and armchairs—all in Empire style, had something so imposing and diplomatic about them that, in spite of himself, Frédéric had to smile.

Finally he reached an apartment, oval in shape, panelled in rosewood, crammed with exquisite pieces of furniture, and lit by one single plate-glass window looking out on to a garden. Madame Dambreuse was sitting beside the fire with a dozen people grouped round her. She showed no surprise at not having seen him for so long and with a friendly nod invited him to sit down.

As he came in, they were singing the praises of the eloquent sermons of Father Coeur.* Then, in reference to a theft committed by a footman, they bemoaned the immorality of servants. There was an endless stream of gossip: that old Sommery woman had a cold, Mademoiselle Turvisot was getting married, the Montcharrons wouldn't be back in town before the end of February, nor would the Bretancourts, people were staying on in the country later these days. The opulence of the surroundings seemed to emphasize the futility of the conversation; but what was being said was less stupid than the pointless, desultory and dreary way in which it was being spoken. Yet there were men present who had great experience of life, a former minister, the incumbent of a large parish, two or three senior government officials; they were confining their remarks to the weariest of platitudes. Some of them looked like tired old dowagers, others like shady horse-dealers; and there were old men with wives young enough to be their grand-daughters.

Madame Dambreuse was greeting all of them graciously. If there was talk of illness, she'd knit her brows sympathetically, and any mention of balls or parties would make her face light up. She herself was shortly going to be deprived of such pleasures, as she'd be taking one of her husband's nieces under her wing, an orphan about to leave her convent school. People were impressed: a mother couldn't have been more devoted.

Frédéric sat scrutinizing her. The waxy skin of her face seemed taut, youthful, but lifeless, like *glacé* fruit, but her hair, hanging in ringlets in the English style, was finer than silk, her sparkling blue eyes had a glint, her every gesture was elegant. She was sitting on a settee at the far end of the room and fondling the tassels of a Japanese fan, no doubt to show off her long slender hands, a trifle thin, with upturned fingertips. She was wearing a grey, watered-silk dress with a high, somewhat puritanical, neckline.

Frédéric enquired whether she wouldn't be going to La Fortrelle that year. She'd no idea. He could well understand that, of course: she must find Nogent deadly dull. More and more guests were arriving. There was a constant swish of dresses on the rugs, the ladies, perched precariously on their chairs, would give a nervous laugh or two, utter a few words, and after five minutes leave with their daughters. Soon the conversation became impossible to follow but as Frédéric was taking his leave, Madame Dambreuse said to him: 'Now remember Monsieur Moreau, every Wednesday', atoning by this single sentence for her previous indifference.

He felt happy. All the same, once in the street, he took a deep breath, and with a need to find a less rarefied atmosphere, he remembered he owed the Marshal a call.

The entrance hall door was open. Two tiny Maltese lap-dogs came scampering in. A voice called out:

'Delphine! Delphine! Is that you, Félix?'

He remained standing where he was; the dogs went on yapping. Eventually Rosanette appeared in a sort of frilly muslin dressing-gown, wearing Turkish slippers on her bare feet.

'Oh, do excuse me, I thought it was my hairdresser. Shan't be a sec!'

He was left to his own devices in the dining-room.

The Venetian blinds were closed. As Frédéric was casting his eye around and remembering the hullaballoo of the other night, he noticed a man's hat, a battered, greasy, and revolting old felt hat, lying on the table in the middle. Whose could it be? It seemed to be flaunting its unstitched crown and proclaiming: 'Why should I worry? After all, I'm the master here!'

The Marshal reappeared. She seized hold of him, opened the conservatory door, propelled him through it, closed it again (meanwhile other doors were being opened and closed), and led him through the kitchen into her dressing-room.

It was obviously the most used room in the house, in a way its real spiritual centre. The walls, armchairs and an immense sprung divan were covered in a broad-leafed pattern chintz; a pair of large blue stoneware wash-basins were standing, some distance apart, on a white marble-topped dressing-table; above this ran wide glass shelves cluttered with flasks, brushes, combs, sticks of cosmetics and boxes of face-powder; the fire was reflected in a tall cheval-glass, a sheet was dangling over the edge of a bath-tub, and the air was thick with the scent of almond cream and friar's balsam.

'Sorry about the mess. I'm going out to dinner tonight.'

And she spun round on her heels, nearly crushing one of her dogs underfoot. Frédéric remarked how charming they were. She picked them both up and holding their black muzzles up towards him:

'Good doggies, now give gentleman a nice smile and a little kiss!'

A man in a grubby frock-coat with a fur collar suddenly materialized.

'Félix, you pet! You'll get your money next Sunday, never fear!'

The man started dressing her hair and giving her news of her friends: Madame de Rochegune, Madame de Saint-Florentin, Madame Lombard, all titled ladies, like those at Madame Dambreuse's. Then he talked theatre: there was a gala performance at the Ambigu that evening.

'Are you going?'

'Good heavens no! I'm staying at home.'

Delphine appeared, and was told off for going out without asking. The other woman swore she'd come 'straight from the market'.

'All right, just show me your list! Excuse me, won't you?'

And Rosanette read the shopping list to herself, commenting on every item. It had been added up wrongly.

'You owe me twenty centimes!'

Delphine handed them over and after sending her away:

'Jesus, what a trial these people are!'

Frédéric was shocked by these recriminations, which reminded him all too vividly of the others and suggested an unfortunate parallel between the two households.

Delphine came back and whispered something into the Marshal's ear.

'No, I don't want to see her!'

Delphine came back again.

'She won't go away, madam.'

At that moment the door was pushed open by an elderly lady dressed in black. Frédéric didn't see or hear what transpired as Rosanette hurried out to meet her in the bedroom.

When she came back, she looked flushed and sat down on one of the armchairs without saying a word. A tear fell

144

on her cheek; then turning towards the young man, in a gentle voice:

'What's your first name?'

'Frédéric.'

'Ah, Federico! You don't mind if I call you that?'

And there was a beguiling, almost tender look in her eyes. Then she gave a sudden cry of joy as she saw Mademoiselle Vatnaz.

The artistic lady had no time to spare as she was due to take charge of her restaurant at six o'clock sharp; she was panting exhaustedly.

First of all she took a watch-chain and a piece of paper out of her large shopping basket, then various other purchases.

'I must tell you that they've got some really magnificent suede gloves at eighteen francs in the rue Joubert! Your dyer wants another week. As for the lace for the pillows, I said we'd look in again. Bugneaux's got the deposit. I think that's the lot? That makes one hundred and eighty-four francs you owe me.'

Rosanette took ten twenty-franc pieces out of a drawer. Neither of them had any change; Frédéric offered to help.

'I'll let you have them back later,' said Vatnaz, stuffing the fifteen francs into her bag. 'But you're a naughty man, I don't like you any more, you didn't dance with me once the other night! Oh my dear, I've found a shop on the quai Voltaire selling a frame made of really heavenly stuffed humming birds! If I were you I'd make myself a present of it! Here, what do you think of this?'

And she produced an old offcut of pink silk which she'd bought in the Temple, to make a medieval doublet for Delmar.

'He did come today, didn't he?'

'No!'

'That's queer!'

And a moment later:

'What are you doing tonight?'

'Going to Alphonsine's,' replied Rosanette—her third version of how she intended to spend the evening.

Mademoiselle Vatnaz went on:

'And what news of the Old Man of the Mountain?'

But with a sharp look the Marshal warned her to drop that subject, and she showed Frédéric out through the entrance hall, enquiring if he'd be seeing Arnoux in the near future.

'Do tell him to come round—not in front of his wife, of course!'

At the top of the stairs, an umbrella was leaning against the wall, next to a pair of clogs.

'Vatnaz's galoshes,' explained Rosanette. 'What a foot, eh? A tough customer, that little pal of mine.'

And in a melodramatic tone, trilling the last word:

'Not to be *trrusted*!'

Encouraged by what seemed like a confidential remark, Frédéric tried to kiss her on the neck. She said calmly:

'Oh, please don't mind me! There's no charge!'

Frédéric took himself off feeling very cheerful, having no doubt that the Marshal would soon fall into his arms. One desire led to another and despite the sort of grudge he still bore Madame Arnoux, he felt the need to go and see her.

In any case, he had to go there to deliver Rosanette's message.

'But probably,' he thought, as it was just striking six, 'Arnoux will be home by now.'

He put off his call until next day.

She was sitting in the same attitude as before, sewing a child's smock. Her little boy was playing with a set of wooden zoo animals; Marthe was sitting writing nearby.

He began by complimenting her on her children and she replied without any display of maternal drooling.

The room was quiet and peaceful. It was a bright sunny day outside and light was reflected on the corners of the furniture; Madame Arnoux was sitting near the window and a ray of sun was shining on the kiss-curls on the nape of her neck, bathing her amber skin in a flood of golden light. He said:

'I can see one young lady who really has grown up in the last three years! Do you remember that time in the carriage,

Mademoiselle, when you fell asleep in my lap?' Marthe didn't remember. 'It was one evening driving back from Saint-Cloud.'

A look of extraordinary sadness came into Madame Arnoux's eyes. Was she trying to tell him not to mention this private memory of theirs?

Her wonderful dark eyes with their dazzling white schlerotic coat were moving softly under their rather heavy lids, and in the depths of their pupils lay an infinite kindness. Once again, more strongly than ever before, his heart was flooded with immense love, and as he gazed on her he could feel his mind growing numb. He shook it off: he must make the most of himself—but how could he set about it? He puzzled his brains and came up with nothing better than money. He started to talk about the weather: it wasn't as cold as in Le Havre.

'Is that where you've been?'

'Yes—family business, a legacy.'

'Oh, I'm so glad,' she replied, with such a genuinely delighted expression that he felt as touched as if he'd just been granted a great favour.

She enquired what he intended to do; a man must have some occupation. He remembered his earlier lie and said he hoped to get into the Conseil d'État, thanks to the parliamentary Deputy Monsieur Dambreuse.

'Perhaps you know him?'

'Only by name.'

Then in a low voice:

'He took you to that dance the other night, didn't he?'

Frédéric made no reply.

'That's what I wanted to know. Thank you.'

Then she asked a few discreet questions about his family and his life in the provinces. It was very nice of him not to have forgotten them after he'd been away for so long.

'But I could hardly have forgotten, could I?' he said. 'Did you ever doubt I would?'

Madame Arnoux stood up.

'I think you're genuinely fond of us. Goodbye . . . for now.'

147

She looked him straight in the eyes and shook him firmly by the hand. Wasn't this a commitment, a promise? Frédéric was overcome with joy and had difficulty in restraining himself from singing; he felt the need to share his happiness with someone, to perform some act of charity. He looked around to see if there was anybody needing help. There was no poor wretch in sight at the moment; his generous impulse petered out; and he was never one to go out searching for that kind of opportunity.

Then he thought of his friends, first Hussonnet and then Pellerin. The lowly status of Dussardier obviously warranted special consideration; as for Cisy, he was looking forward to showing him some of his affluence. He wrote off to all four, inviting them to a house-warming party the following Sunday at eleven o'clock sharp, telling Deslauriers to bring Sénécal along.

The latter had just been given the sack as junior assistant from his third school, this time for having opposed prize-giving as élitist. He was now employed in a machinery factory and had left Deslauriers's flat six months ago.

Their parting had been painless: in recent times Sénécal had been receiving visits from men in smocks, patriots all,* all workers and splendid fellows, but whose company the lawyer found tiresome. Moreover, certain of his friend's ideas, however excellent for militants, were not to his liking, although his own ambition prevented him from saying so. He was keen to remain on good terms with Sénécal, so as to guide him in the right direction, eagerly anticipating a great upheaval, in which he was confidently expecting to make his mark and carve out a little niche for himself.

Sénécal's aspirations were less selfish. Every evening after work, he'd clamber back up to his garret and seek justification for his dreams in books. He'd annotated Rousseau's *Social Contract*.* His head was stuffed with ideas from the *Revue indépendante*.* He knew the works of Mably, Morelly, Fourier, Saint-Simon, Comte, Cabet, Louis Blanc,* all that bunch of ponderous socialist writers who insisted on reducing mankind to a barrack-room existence, sweated labour in shop or factory and finding relaxation in bawdy-houses. With this hotch-potch, he'd worked out his ideal of a democracy full of virtuous qualities, a blend of share-cropping peasants and factory workers, a sort of American Sparta, in which the individual would exist purely to serve a Society more omnipotent, absolute, infallible and divine than the Dalai Lama or Nebuchadnezzar. He was quite certain that his ideas were likely to be realized in the near future and ferociously attacked anything which he saw as standing in their way, arguing with Euclidean rigour and all the conviction of an Inquisitor. He was shocked by titles, decorations or crests, especially by liveries, and even by over-illustrious reputations; every day, his reading and his own tribulations went to reinforce his basic hatred of any kind of distinction or superiority.

'What obligation do I have to be civil to that capitalist? If he wanted me, he could come and call on me himself!'

Deslauriers prevailed on him to come along.

They discovered their friend in his bedroom. Blinds, reversible curtains, the Venetian mirror, nothing had been forgotten. Frédéric was lolling in a wing-chair, wearing a velvet jacket and smoking Turkish cigarettes.

Sénécal scowled like a Puritan taken along to an orgy. Deslauriers took it all in at a glance and gave a low bow:

'My liege, pray accept my homage!'

Dussardier flung his arms round his neck:

'So now you're rich? Good for you, dammit, good for you!'

Cisy appeared with a black ribbon round his hat. At his grandmother's death he'd come into a sizeable fortune and was less interested in having a good time than in being 'distinguished', different from everyone else, in a word, 'having style', as he put it.

But it was twelve noon and everybody was yawning; Frédéric was expecting someone else. At the mention of Arnoux's name, Pellerin pulled a face. Ever since he'd deserted the arts, he'd looked on him as a renegade.

'How about starting without him? What do you think?'

They all agreed.

The door was opened by a servant in gaiters, revealing the dining-room, with its high oak plinth picked out in gold-leaf and its two sideboards loaded with plates and dishes. The bottles of wine were warming up on the stove; beside the oysters they noticed the glint and gleam of brand-new cutlery; the milky tint of the delicately engraved glasses struck a pleasing, rather subdued, note; and the table was hidden under quantities of game and fruit, an extraordinary array of all kinds of things. Such hospitality was lost on Sénécal.

First he asked for home-made bread, as crusty as possible, and took the opportunity of dragging in the Buzançais murders* and the food crisis.

Nothing like that would have occurred if agriculture had been better protected, if everything weren't being sacrificed to competitiveness, anarchy, the disastrous doctrine of free enterprise! That's how the new plutocracy is being created, worse than the old feudal aristocracy. But people had better look out, in the end the workers will get fed up and get their own back against the capitalists, either by bloody evictions or by ransacking their grand mansions.

In a flash, Frédéric had a sudden vision of a gang of bare-armed men bursting into Madame Dambreuse's large drawing-room and smashing the mirrors with their pikes.

Sénécal wasn't finished: by reason of their low wages, the workers were worse off than the helots of ancient Greece, negroes or pariahs, particularly if they had children.

'Are they to be forced to get rid of them by suffocating them, as recommended by an English doctor, whose name I forget, a follower of Malthus.'*

And turning to Cisy:

'Are we going to be reduced to taking the infamous advice of Malthus?'

Being ignorant of Malthus's infamous advice and indeed of his very existence, Cisy replied that, after all, many poor wretches were receiving assistance and the upper classes . . .

'Aha, the upper classes!' sneered the socialist. 'Firstly, there's no such thing, true nobility comes from the heart!

We don't want charity, d'you understand? We want equality, a fair share of the goods produced by labour.'

What he was asking for was the possibility for workers to become capitalists and for privates to become colonels. The trade guilds, by limiting the number of apprentices, had at least prevented the labour market from becoming cluttered up and fostered the feeling of brotherhood by their festivals and banners.

Speaking as a poet, Hussonnet was sorry to see banners go, as was Pellerin; this was an idea he'd picked up while listening to Phalansterians in the Café Dagneaux. He was sure Fourier was a great man.

'Oh, come on!' said Deslauriers. 'An old fool who sees the fall of empires as a sign of divine vengeance! It's like that fellow Saint-Simon and his "church", with his hatred of the French Revolution. A bunch of humbugs who'd like to foist a new kind of Catholicism on us!'

No doubt for information, or else to create a good impression, Monsieur de Cisy enquired mildly:

'So those two learned gentlemen don't share Voltaire's views?'

'Don't talk to me about Voltaire!' said Sénécal.

'Really? But I thought . . .'

'No, never! He didn't love the People!'

The conversation lapsed into current events: the Spanish marriages,* the Rochefort frauds,* the new chapter at Saint-Denis,* which would lead to a doubling of the rates. In Sénécal's view people were already paying more than enough, goodness knows!

'And why, for heaven's sake? To build palatial monkey-houses at the Zoo, to help the General Staff organize dazzling parades in Paris squares or to maintain medieval etiquette with the flunkeys at Versailles!'

'I read in *La Mode*',* said Cisy, 'that at the Saint Ferdinand's Day Ball at the Tuileries, they were all dressed up as if for a public dance-hall.'

The socialist shrugged his shoulders in disgust: 'Isn't it pitiful!'

'And then there's the gallery at Versailles!' exclaimed

151

Pellerin. 'Let me tell you something, those idiots have cut a piece off a Delacroix and stuck a bit on a Gros!* In the Louvre, they've restored and scratched about and messed up all the pictures so badly that in ten years' time, there'll be not one left! As for the catalogue, a German has written a whole book about all the mistakes in it! Honestly, foreigners are just making fun of us!'

'Yes, we're the laughing stock of Europe!' agreed Sénécal.

'It's all because Art is subservient to the Crown!'

'Until everybody gets the vote . . .'

'Now, just a second!'—for the artist had had his works refused for every one of the official Salons for the last twenty years and was furious with representatives of Power—'Look, I'm not asking for anything but to be left alone! It's just that Parliament ought to legislate in the interests of Art. They should establish a Chair of Aesthetics and if its holder's a working artist as well as an academic, I hope he could succeed in uniting the general public. Wouldn't it be a good idea, Hussonnet, to slip a word on the subject into your paper?'

'Do you imagine newspapers are free? Do you imagine we're free ourselves?' said Deslauriers heatedly. 'When you realize that there may be as many as twenty-eight forms to fill up before you can put a small boat on the river, I feel like going off to live amongst cannibals! The government is swallowing us all up! They own everything, the law, philosophy, the arts, the very air we breathe! France is on its death-bed, helpless under the jackboot of the police and the cassock of the clerics!'

The budding Mirabeau was pouring out his anger in a flood of invective and finally, springing to his feet, with flashing eyes and his hand on his hip:

'I drink to the complete destruction of the existing order, that is, everything that goes under the name of Privilege, Monopoly, Regulations, Hierarchy, Authority, and the State!'—his voice rose to a scream—'which I would like to smash like this!'—and he hurled his fine long-stemmed wine-glass down on to the table where it splintered into a thousand pieces.

Everybody clapped, Dussardier louder than anyone.

Any kind of injustice made him see red. He was concerned about Barbès;* he was the sort of man who'd fling himself under a carriage to rescue a fallen horse. His whole learning was limited to two works: one called *The Crimes of Kings*, the other *The Secrets of the Vatican*. He'd been listening delightedly, open-mouthed, to the lawyer. Now, unable to restrain himself:

'What I blame Louis-Philippe for is letting down the Poles!'

'Wait a minute,' said Hussonnet. 'In the first place, there's no such thing as Poland. It was invented by Lafayette!* Generally speaking, the Poles are all to be found in the suburb of Saint-Marceau, the genuine ones all drowned with Poniatowski.'* In short, 'he no longer believed all that rot, he'd got over all that!' It was like sea monsters, the Revocation of the Edict of Nantes, and that 'stale old joke, Saint Bartholemew's Day'!*

While not defending the Poles, Sénécal took the journalist up on those last few words: the Popes had been maligned; after all, they did stand up for the masses; and he described the League* as 'the dawn of democracy, a great egalitarian movement against Protestant individualism'.

Frédéric was a trifle surprised at these ideas, while Cisy probably found them boring, because he brought the conversation round to the tableaux being performed at the Gymnase, which were attracting large audiences at the time.

Sénécal thought they were deplorable. Spectacular shows like that were corrupting the daughters of the proletariat; afterwards, you'd see them flaunting themselves in all sorts of finery. This was why he approved of the Bavarian student who'd abused Lola Montez.* Like Rousseau, he thought more highly of a charcoal burner's wife than a king's mistress.

'You're a prize idiot,' Hussonnet said crushingly and he took Rosanette's side and started defending such ladies.

Then, as he was talking about her ball and Arnoux's costume:

'Aren't people suggesting he's in trouble?' asked Pellerin.

The art dealer had just had a lawsuit over his building land in Belleville and he was at the moment involved in a china clay company in Lower Brittany, in association with a bunch of similar humbugs.

Dussardier had more information on him, because his employer, Monsieur Moussinot, had been making enquiries about Arnoux from the banker Lefebvre who'd told him that in view of the way he kept asking for an extension of credit, he didn't think he was a very sound business proposition.

After dessert they adjourned to the drawing-room— Louis XVI and hung in yellow damask, like the Marshal's.

Pellerin criticized Frédéric for not having gone for neo-classical; Sénécal struck matches on the wall; at this stage, Deslauriers made no comment but in the library he remarked that it was 'a girls' library'. Most contemporary men of letters were represented but it proved impossible to talk about their works, because Hussonnet immediately launched into personal anecdotes concerning them, criticizing their appearance, their morals and their clothes while singing the praises of tenth-rate hacks and disparaging writers of quality, as well, of course, as bemoaning modern decadence. The simplest little folk-song had more poetry in it than the entire output of the nineteenth-century lyric poets; Balzac was overrated, Byron sunk without trace, Hugo hadn't the foggiest notion of drama, and so on and so forth.

'Why', Sénécal wanted to know, 'haven't you got any examples of our worker poets?'

And Monsieur de Cisy, who dabbled in literature, was surprised to see on Frédéric's table 'not one of those new "physiologies",* such as the *Physiology of the Smoker*, *The Physiology of the Angler* or *The Physiology of the Toll-Keeper*?'

They irritated him so much that he was tempted to take them by the shoulders and chuck them out. 'I'm being a silly fool!' Drawing Dussardier on one side, he asked him if there was anything he could do for him.

The nice young fellow was touched; but with his cashier's job he didn't need anything.

Next, he invited Deslauriers into his bedroom and taking two thousand francs out of his secretaire:

'Here, old chap, slip that into your pocket. It's the last of my old debts.'

'But what about the paper?' said the lawyer. 'I've spoken about it to Hussonnet, you know.'

And when Frédéric replied that 'he was a little low on ready cash at the moment', the other man gave a sour smile.

After liqueurs they drank beer and after the beer, punch. They relit their pipes. Eventually, at five o'clock, they all left, and as they were walking along side by side, Dussardier broke the silence by remarking that Frédéric had 'done them proud'. They all agreed.

Hussonnet commented that his lunch had been a bit too rich; Sénécal criticized the flashiness of the furnishings; Cisy was of the same opinion: there was a complete lack of 'style'.

'I don't think it would've hurt him to commission a picture from me,' said Pellerin.

Deslauriers fingered the banknotes in his pocket and said nothing.

Frédéric was left alone. As he thought of his friends, he could feel a deep, dark gulf yawning between himself and them. He'd offered them his hand, in a genuine spirit of friendship, and they'd failed to respond.

He remembered Pellerin's and Dussardier's remarks about Arnoux. No doubt it was just ill-natured gossip, a cock-and-bull story? And he had a vision of Madame Arnoux ruined, in tears, and forced to sell up her furniture. The thought tortured him all that night and next day he called on her.

Not knowing exactly how to pass on his information, Frédéric began by asking if Arnoux still had his building land in Belleville.

'Yes, he's still got it.'

'He's joined in a china clay venture in Lower Brittany, hasn't he?'

'That's right.'

'His factory's doing well, isn't it?'

'I imagine so.'

And seeing him hesitating:

'What's the matter? You're frightening me!'

He told her he'd been carrying over his debts. She lowered her eyes and said:

'I suspected as much!'

In order to maximize his speculation, Arnoux had refused to sell, was using the land as security to borrow heavily and, being unable to find any purchaser, had thought he could recoup his losses by setting up a factory. The outlay had turned out to be greater than he'd anticipated. That was all she knew; he was evasive and kept repeating that things were going 'swimmingly'.

Frédéric endeavoured to reassure her. Perhaps it was merely a passing embarrassment. In any case, should he hear anything, he'd let her know.

'Oh, please do, won't you?' she said, clasping her hands together, pleadingly, in a charming gesture.

So he could be of help to her! He was making his way into her life, into her heart!

Arnoux appeared.

'Now isn't that nice of you to come and take me out to dinner!'

Frédéric was speechless.

After a few casual remarks, Arnoux warned his wife he'd be home very late, as he'd be seeing Oudry.

'At his house?'

'Yes, of course, at his house.'

Going downstairs he confessed that as the Marshal happened to be free, they were off to have a little jollification at the Moulin-Rouge; and as he always needed someone to confide his secrets to, he prevailed on Frédéric to give him a lift right to the door.

Instead of going in, he paced to and fro on the pavement,

gazing up at the second-floor windows. Suddenly the curtains were pulled apart.

'Splendid! Old Oudry's gone. Good-night!'

So she was being kept by old Oudry? Frédéric didn't know what to think.

From that day onwards, Arnoux was even friendlier; he'd invite him to dinner in his mistress's flat and before long Frédéric had become a regular caller at both houses.

He found Rosanette's amusing. People would drop in there of an evening, after the theatre or on their way from their club; there'd be a cup of tea, a game of lotto; on Sundays there'd be charades. Rosanette was more exuberant, more ingenious and funnier than any of the others, as when she scuttled around on all fours or stuck a man's night-cap on her head. She'd stand at the window decked out in a sort of leather cowboy hat, watching the passers-by; she smoked chibouques and she could yodel. To while away her afternoons, she'd cut flowers out of a piece of chintz to stick on her window-pane, plaster make-up on her little dogs, burn joss-sticks in her bedroom or tell her own fortune. Incapable of resisting any impulse, she'd fall for some knick-knack she'd seen, lose sleep over it, dash out and buy it, and then swap it for something similar; she'd botch up her dress materials, lose her jewellery, squander her money, and give the dress off her back for a stage-box. She often used to ask Frédéric to explain some word she'd come across, without waiting for him to reply, for she'd skip from one idea to another, asking endless questions. Outbursts of gaiety would be followed by childish tantrums; or else she'd sit brooding on the floor with her head down and both hands clasped round her knees, more inert than a torpid snake. She would get dressed in front of him with complete disregard, slowly pulling on her silk stockings and then splashing water all over her face and throwing herself back in her chair like some shivering river nymph. Her white, laughing teeth and sparkling eyes, her beauty and her gaiety, dazzled Frédéric and set his nerves tingling.

He'd almost always find Madame Arnoux teaching her little boy his letters or standing behind Marthe as she practised her scales on the piano; while she was sewing, he felt very happy when he could sometimes pick up her scissors. Her every movement spoke of immense, quiet dignity; her tiny hands seemed made to distribute alms or to wipe away his tears; her voice, naturally rather low-pitched, was full of gentle inflexions like a softly fluttering breeze.

She had no deep feeling for literature but did express her views with a charming simplicity and insight. She liked travel, the rustling of wind in the forest, and walking bare-headed in the rain. Frédéric would listen delightedly to all these things, scenting a foretaste of her surrender.

His continual visits to these two houses made, as it were, two kinds of music in his life: one wild and playful and amusing, the other solemn and almost religious; and as they were both vibrating in unison, they expanded and gradually blended, so that if Madame Arnoux so much as brushed him with her finger, immediately his desire would conjure up the other woman, if only because his chances of success in that direction were less remote; in Rosanette's company, if something happened to touch his heart, he at once remembered his True Love.

This confusion sprang from similarities between the two households. One of the chests formerly to be seen in the Boulevard Montmartre now adorned Rosanette's dining-room and the other one, Madame Arnoux's drawing-room. The dinner services of both were identical and even the same velvet smoking cap would be lying on the armchair; while a host of small gifts, screens, boxes and fans would shuttle backwards and forwards between wife and mistress because Arnoux had no scruples in taking away something he'd given one of them and presenting it to the other.

The Marshal used to laugh with Frédéric over Arnoux's naughty ways. After dinner one day, she took him into the hall and showed him a bag of cakes in his overcoat pocket which he'd just purloined from the table, presumably as a treat for his two children. Some of his little tricks bordered on the criminal. He felt in duty bound to diddle the Customs; he'd never think of paying for a seat at the theatre and always felt he had the right to slip into the stalls when his ticket was for the pit; he thought it a tremendous joke to tell people how, instead of fifty centimes, he had the habit of dropping a trouser button into the saucer to tip the attendant at the bathing establishment; and nothing of all this prevented the Marshal from loving him.

One day, however, as they were talking about him:

'Oh, he's really getting on my nerves! I've had enough! Ah well, it can't be helped, I'll have to find another man!'

Frédéric suggested that the 'other man' had already been found and that he was called Monsieur Oudry.

'Well, what's that got to do with it?' said Rosanette.

And in a tearful voice:

'After all, it's not as if I ask him for very much and the brute still won't do it! He just won't! Of course, there's never any shortage of promises!'

He'd even promised her a quarter share in the famous china clay company and no profit had been forthcoming; nor had the cashmere shawl he'd been dangling before her eyes these last six months.

Frédéric immediately thought of giving her one himself. Arnoux might take it as a rebuke and be offended.

Yet he was kind-hearted, even his wife said so. But so crazy! Instead of inviting people to dinner at home every day, he'd now taken to entertaining his acquaintances in restaurants. He'd buy completely useless articles, gold chains, clocks, household equipment; Madame Arnoux even showed Frédéric an enormous quantity of kettles, chafing dishes and samovars stored away in the passageway. Finally, one day she confessed to being worried: Arnoux had made her sign an IOU payable to Monsieur Dambreuse.

Meanwhile, in a vague attempt to keep faith with himself, Frédéric had not relinquished his literary projects. As a result of his conversations with Pellerin, he wanted to write a history of aesthetics and then, through the indirect influence of Deslauriers and Hussonnet, to dramatize different periods of the French Revolution, as well as composing a major comedy. As he was working, the face of one or

159

other of the two women would pass through his mind; he'd struggle against the urge to see her and quickly give in; and he was sadder whenever he came away from Madame Arnoux.

One morning when he was brooding beside the fire, Deslauriers came in. Sénécal's inflammatory remarks had worried his employer and he was once more penniless.

'What am I supposed to do about it?' asked Frédéric.

'Nothing. I know you've not got any money but would it really be too much of a chore for you to find him a job, either through Monsieur Dambreuse or Arnoux?'

The latter was bound to be needing technicians in his factory. Frédéric had a flash of inspiration: Sénécal could keep him informed when the husband was going to be away, act as messenger and help him in the thousand and one matters that might arise. Such good offices are quite normal amongst men. What's more, he'd find ways and means of making use of him without his realizing it. Chance was offering him an ally; this was a good omen and he must snap it up, so in a casual voice, he replied that he'd see about it.

He did so at once. Arnoux was taking a great deal of trouble over his factory. He was trying to reproduce the copper-red of the Chinese but his colours kept being burnt up during the firing. In order to prevent his pottery from developing cracks, he mixed lime in with the clay but most of the pieces broke up, the enamel on the unfired clay boiled, and his larger tiles warped; blaming these failures on his inadequate equipment, he was intending to install new crushing mills and different drying pans. Frédéric remembered something of all this and so he got in touch to tell him he'd discovered an extremely clever man capable of finding the secret of this famous red. At this, Arnoux pricked up his ears but after listening to what Frédéric had to say, replied that he didn't need anybody.

Frédéric stressed Sénécal's amazing abilities: a first-rate mathematician, an engineer, a chemist and an accountant, all rolled into one.

The pottery manufacturer agreed to see him.

The pair squabbled over the salary; Frédéric intervened and, by the end of the week, had managed to persuade them to come to an agreement.

However, since the factory was at Creil,* Sénécal wasn't going to be of any help to him. The realization of this elementary fact came as a nasty blow to his morale.

He reckoned that the further Arnoux drifted away from his wife, the better his own chances would be, and launched a sustained campaign in favour of Rosanette, pointing out how poorly he'd treated her, telling him of her recent vague threats, and even mentioning the cashmere shawl, making no secret of the fact that she considered him mean.

Stung by this accusation and uneasy as well, Arnoux presented Rosanette with her cashmere, while telling her off for complaining to Frédéric; when she retorted that she'd reminded him of his promise dozens of times, he claimed he'd forgotten because 'he'd been so busy.'

Frédéric called round next day. Although it was two o'clock, the Marshal was still in bed; installed at a little table at her side, Delmar was polishing off a slice of liver pâté. As soon as she saw him, she called out: 'I've got it! I've got it!' and then, taking hold of his ears, kissed him on the forehead and thanked him profusely, calling him 'darling' and even getting him to sit down on her bed. Her pretty eyes were sparkling and loving, her lips moist and smiling; her sleeveless night-dress exposed her shapely round arms and through the cambric, he could feel at times the firm curves of her body. During all this, Delmar's eyes were almost popping out of his head.

'But really, my dear, really!'

It was just the same on later occasions: as soon as Frédéric came in, she'd stand on a cushion so that he could kiss her properly, call him her 'sweetie darling', put a flower in his buttonhole and straighten his necktie. These delicate attentions were more marked when Delmar was there.

Was she making up to him? Frédéric thought she must be. And as for deceiving a friend, in his place Arnoux would certainly not have worried! He surely had the right not to show any scruples where his mistress was concerned, when he'd always been so scrupulous about his wife, for he did think he had been, or rather, he'd have liked to persuade himself that he had been, to justify his arrant cowardice. However, he thought he was being stupid and decided to have a go at the Marshal head on.

So one afternoon, when she was bending over her chest of drawers, he went up behind her and made such an unambiguous gesture that she shot upright, red in the face. He immediately did it again; she burst into tears, saying that because she was down on her luck wasn't any reason to treat her like dirt.

He made further attempts. She adopted another tactic and always made fun of him. He thought he'd be clever and give her tit-for-tat, only more so. But he used to appear too cheerful to be taken seriously and they were such good pals that they were inhibited from expressing any deeper feelings. Finally one day, she replied that she didn't want another woman's left-overs.

'What other woman?'

'You know! Go and see Madame Arnoux!'

In fact, Frédéric often did talk about Madame Arnoux and Arnoux had a similar obsession as well; she was tired of hearing about this woman's wonderful qualities all the time and her allegation against Frédéric was a way of getting her own back.

Frédéric didn't forgive her for that remark.

What's more, he was beginning to find her terribly irritating. Sometimes she'd pose as a woman of the world and laugh at love in a sneering way that made Frédéric itch to smack her face. A quarter of an hour later, love was the only thing worth living for and she's clasp her hands in front of her as if hugging someone and murmur: 'Oh, it's so wonderful, it's so wonderful!' with half-closed eyes as though almost swooning in ecstasy. It was impossible to understand her, to know, for instance, whether she loved Arnoux, for while making fun of him, she'd still seem jealous. It was the same with the Vatnaz woman, whom she'd sometimes describe as a bitch and at others as her best friend. Indeed her whole person, even the way her hair was caught up at the back, contained something which defied description, a sort of challenge, so his desire for her was mainly the pleasure of taming her, showing her who was boss.

What could he do? She'd often send him packing quite unceremoniously, whispering: 'I'm busy, see you tonight!' as she darted through the room; or else she'd be surrounded by a dozen people and once they were alone, there'd be so many interruptions that it was unbelievable. He used to invite her to dinner; she always declined; once she did accept and failed to turn up.

Suddenly he hit on a Macchiavellian scheme.

Having been told by Dussardier of Pellerin's grumbles against him, he commissioned him to paint a life-size portrait of the Marshal, which would obviously require a large number of sittings; he wouldn't miss a single one of them, so the painter's notorious unpunctuality would allow them to have a great deal of time to themselves. He therefore suggested to Rosanette that she have her picture painted so as to be able to offer her likeness to her dear Arnoux. She jumped at the chance; she could already see herself in the Grand Salon in the place of honour, with the crowd gazing at her and the newspapers writing about it, thus 'launching her on her career'.

Pellerin couldn't wait to begin: this portrait would be a masterpiece and reveal him as a genius.

He ran over in his mind all the portraits by old masters which he knew and finally settled on a Titian, with a few ornamental touches in the style of Veronese. So, he wouldn't use any artificial shadow but bring the flesh tints together into one unified tone by means of a strong natural light, to add glitter to the various trappings.

'Suppose I put her in a silk dress with an Arab burnous?' he thought. 'No, burnouses are common as dirt! Perhaps if I dressed her in blue velvet against a grey background, with strong colours? We could also give her a white lace collar, with a black fan and a scarlet curtain behind?'

And every day he looked further afield, broadening his conception and thinking how wonderful it was.

When Rosanette arrived at his studio with Frédéric, for her first sitting, his heart gave a leap. He stood her on a sort of dais in the middle of the room; then, grumbling about the light and how he missed his old studio, he first of all made her lean forward with her elbows resting on a pedestal and then sit down in an armchair, while he stood back, before moving in to flick the folds of her dress into place, peering at her through half-closed eyes, and consulting Frédéric with a word here and there.

'No, I don't think so, after all!' he exclaimed. 'I'll go back to my first idea. You're a Venetian and that's flat!'

She'd have a flame-red velvet gown with a jewelled silver and gold girdle and the wide sleeves, lined in ermine, would set off her bare arms, which would be touching the balustrade of a staircase rising up behind. To her left, there'd be a column reaching to the top of the canvas, where it would join up with architectural features to form an arch. Down below, you'd be vaguely able to pick out clumps of almost black orange trees, providing a contrast with the blue sky streaked with white clouds. On a rug covering the balustrade, there'd be a silver dish containing a bunch of flowers, an amber rosary, and an old ivory casket, slightly yellowed, spilling over with gold sequins, some of which would even be scattered on the floor, forming a series of bright splashes of colour to lead the eye towards the tip of her foot, for she'd be standing on the next-to-bottom step, in a natural pose, and in full light.

He fetched a crate used for carrying pictures and placed it on the dais to form a step; then, using a stool to represent the balustrade, he laid out his 'props', his jumper, a shield, a tin of sardines, a bundle of quills and a knife, and throwing a handful of coins on the floor in front of her, he arranged her in her pose.

'Imagine those things as treasure, wonderful gifts! Head a bit to the right! Perfect! Now don't move! That stately attitude suits your type of beauty.'

She was wearing a tartan dress, carrying a large muff and trying hard not to laugh.

'As for your hair, we'll weave a string of pearls into that, it always looks good with red hair!'

The Marshal protested that she hadn't got red hair.

'Don't worry! Artist's red is not the same as your run-of-the-mill middle-class red!'

He began to sketch in the masses and so obsessed was he by the great Renaissance masters that he couldn't stop talking about them; for an hour he dreamed out loud of the magnificent lives of these geniuses, of their fame and splendour, of triumphant entries into cities and torchlight galas amongst half-naked women, divinely beautiful.

'You were made to live in times like those! A creature of your quality would have been worthy of a prince!'

Rosanette thought these compliments very nice. They fixed a date for the next sitting. Frédéric undertook to provide the accessories.

As she was rather dazed from the heat of the stove they went back on foot via the rue du Bac and came to the Pont-Royal.

The weather was superb, keen and fine. The sun was setting; in the distance some of the window-panes of the houses on the Cité gleamed like sheets of gold, while behind, on the right, the towers of Notre-Dame stood out black against the blue sky bathed in a soft grey haze on the horizon. The wind was gusty; Rosanette announced she was hungry and they went into the English Cake Shop.

Young wives were standing with their children eating at the marble buffet covered with plates of little cakes under glass covers. Rosanette demolished two cream tarts. The icing sugar gave her a moustache at the corners of her mouth. From time to time, she'd pull her handkerchief out of her muff to wipe it away; under her green silk hood, her face looked like a rose blooming amid its leaves.

They set off again; in the rue de la Paix, she stopped in front of a jeweller's to look at a bracelet; Frédéric wanted to give it to her as a present.

'No,' she said. 'Keep your money.'

Frédéric was hurt.

'What's wrong with my pet? Is he sad?'

And as the conversation resumed, Frédéric, as always, brought it round to his love for her.

'You know very well it's impossible!'

'Why?'

'Oh, just because . . .'

They were going along side by side; she was leaning on his arm and the flounces of her dress were flapping against his legs. Then he recalled one winter's evening at dusk when Madame Arnoux was similarly walking beside him on that selfsame pavement; and he grew so absorbed in this recollection that he no longer noticed Rosanette and stopped thinking of her.

She was staring vaguely ahead, dragging on his arm like some listless child. It was that time of day when people were returning from their drive and carriages were trotting briskly by on the dry cobble-stones. She heaved a sigh, perhaps recalling Pellerin's flattering words.

'Oh, aren't some women lucky! I'm meant for a rich man, definitely!'

'But you've got one!' he retorted caustically, for Monsieur Oudry was reputed to be a millionaire three times over.

She asked for nothing better than to get rid of him.

'What's stopping you?'

And he launched into a bitter, mocking attack on this aged money-grubber with his wig, pointing out that such a relationship was degrading and she ought to break it off.

'Yes,' replied the Marshal, as if talking to herself. 'I expect that's what I'll do eventually.'

Frédéric was impressed by such self-sacrifice. She was walking more slowly now and he thought she must be tired. She continued to insist on not taking a cab and when they reached her door, she kissed her fingertips to him and sent him away.

When he arrived home he was in a black mood.

Hussonnet and Deslauriers were waiting for him.

The Bohemian was sitting at his table drawing funny faces, while the lawyer was drowsing on his divan in his muddy boots.

'So there you are at last!' he exclaimed. 'But how savage you look! Is it safe to talk to you?'

He was becoming less popular as a coach because he kept cramming his pupils with theories not in line with the examiners'. He had taken on two or three briefs, lost the cases, and each new set-back had made him keener to realize his old dream: a paper where he could display his abilities, settle old scores, get his ideas and his resentment off his chest. Fame and fortune would follow, naturally. It was with this hope in mind that he had prevailed on the Bohemian to come along. Hussonnet ran a news-sheet.

At the moment he was having it printed on pink paper; he'd invent false reports, make up picture puzzles, try to spark off controversies, and even (in spite of the premises) organize concerts! The annual subscription 'entitles a member to an orchestra stall seat in one of the top Paris theatres; in addition, the editorial staff undertake to provide visiting foreign tourists with all relevant information, artistic or otherwise'. But the printer was uttering threats, the landlord was owed a quarter's rent; all sorts of problems kept cropping up and but for the lawyer's daily exhortations to buck up, Hussonnet would have let *L'Art* go under. He'd been brought along to add weight to Deslauriers's appeal.

'We've come to see you about the paper,' he said.

'Good Lord, so you're still thinking about that!' replied Frédéric, his mind on other things.

'Of course I am!'

And once again he went over his plan. By supplying Stock Exchange reports, they'd establish connections with financial circles and this would enable them to raise the hundred thousand francs required as surety bond. But for the news-sheet to be transformed into a political newspaper, you first needed a wide readership and that would involve a certain capital outlay for paper, printing and staff costs; in a word, fifteen thousand francs.

'I haven't got that amount of ready cash,' said Frédéric.

'And what about us!' countered Deslauriers, folding his arms.

Frédéric was offended by this gesture. He retorted:

'Is that any fault of mine?'

'Oh, that's wonderful! They've got firewood in their grates, truffles on their table, a cosy bed, a library, a carriage, all the creature comforts! And others are shivering in garrets, buying one-franc meals, toiling like slaves and up to their necks in poverty! Well, is that any fault of theirs?'

And he kept repeating these last words in an ironical voice, in the best Ciceronian legal tradition. Frédéric was trying to interrupt the flow.

'And of course, I do realize that certain . . . aristocratic needs have to be met, because I expect some woman . . .'

'And supposing that is the case, aren't I free . . .?'

'Oh yes, of course you're free!'

There was a pause.

'Very convenient things, promises!'

'But I'm not taking them back, for heaven's sake!' exclaimed Frédéric.

The lawyer went on:

'At school, people make promises: they'll set up a phalanstery, they'll copy Balzac's *Les Treize*!* Then they meet later on and it's: "Good-night, old chap, and don't forget to shut the door behind you!" Because the one who could help the other man sits on everything he's got and wants it all for himself!'

'What do you mean by that?'

'Oh yes, you haven't even introduced us to the Dambreuses!'

Frédéric looked at him: with his shabby frock-coat, his tarnished spectacles and pasty face the lawyer looked such a typical fatuous pedant that he was unable to repress a scornful smile; Deslauriers saw it and his face flushed.

He'd already put on his hat to go. Very worried, Hussonnet was looking at him beseechingly, trying to soften his heart, and just as Frédéric was turning away:

'Come on, old man! Be my Maecenas! Support the arts!'

Frédéric suddenly caved in; seizing a sheet of paper, he scribbled a few lines and passed it over to him. The Bohemian's face lit up and, handing it to Deslauriers:

'Render your apologies, my lord!'

It was an urgent request from their friend to his solicitor, asking him to send fifteen thousand francs as soon as possible.

'Ah, that's the old friend I used to know!' said Deslauriers.

''Swounds!' exclaimed Hussonnet, 'You're a fine fellow! You've earned yourself a niche in the Hall of Useful Men!'

The lawyer went on:

'You'll not be the loser by it! It's a gilt-edged investment!'

''Steeth!' exclaimed Hussonnet. 'I'll put my head on the block if 'tis not so!'

And he proceeded to reel off such a string of idiotic remarks and make such fabulous promises (which he may indeed have believed himself) that Frédéric didn't know whether he was poking fun at them or himself.

That evening he got a letter from his mother.

In a slightly teasing tone, she expressed some surprise that he wasn't a Minister yet. Then she talked of her health and told him that Monsieur Roque and she were now on calling terms. 'Since he's been a widower, I thought there was nothing to stop me inviting him. Louise is greatly changed for the better.' And in a postscript: 'You haven't mentioned your grand acquaintance, Monsieur Dambreuse; if I were you, I'd cultivate it.'

Why not indeed? His intellectual aspirations had gone up in smoke and his financial situation, he realized, was not all that strong; once he'd paid off his debts and handed over the promised sum to the other two, his income would be reduced by four thousand francs, at least! What's more, he was feeling the need to break away from his present way of life and find something stable to hang on to. So next day during dinner at Madame Arnoux's, he said his mother was badgering him to adopt some profession.

'But I thought,' she said, 'that Monsieur Dambreuse was going to get you into the Conseil d'État? That would be perfect for you.'

So *She* wanted it. He obeyed.

As when they'd first met, the banker was sitting at his

desk and motioned to him to wait for a moment; a gentleman with his back to the door was discussing an important matter with him, concerning coal and involving a merger of various companies.

A pair of portraits, of General Foy* and Louis-Philippe, were hanging one on each side of the mirror; in front of the panelling there were filing shelves reaching up to the ceiling; there were six rush-bottomed chairs. Monsieur Dambreuse didn't need any grander rooms for his business; it was like those gloomy kitchens which turn out superb banquets. Frédéric noted particularly two massive strong-boxes standing in the corners. He wondered how many millions of francs they might contain. The banker went over to one to open it and its steel lid swung back to reveal nothing but lots of blue paper notebooks.

Finally the person went out, passing Frédéric. It was old Oudry. They both blushed as they greeted each other, which seemed to surprise Monsieur Dambreuse. In any case, he proved most helpful. Nothing would be easier than to recommend his young friend to the Lord Chancellor. They'd be only too glad to take him on; and his friendly welcome ended with an invitation to an evening party which he was giving in a few days' time.

Just as Frédéric was getting into his brougham to go to the party, a note arrived from the Marshal:

'My dear, I've followed your advice. I've just sent my Sioux packing. From tomorrow evening, I'll be a Free Woman! Now call me a coward!'

That was all. But it was an invitation to slip into the vacancy. He gave an exclamation, tucked the note into his pocket, and drove off. The street was guarded by two armed mounted policemen. Chinese lanterns were festooned over the double carriage gates and in the courtyard flunkeys were calling the carriages up to the foot of the entrance steps under the glass canopy. Then, in the entrance hall, the noise suddenly subsided.

The stair-well was full of tall shrubs. The walls shimmered in the white satiny light of porcelain globes. Frédéric ran up the stairs. An usher bellowed his name; Monsieur

Dambreuse held out his hand; Madame Dambreuse appeared almost immediately.

She had on a mauve dress trimmed with lace; her ringlets were more luxuriant than usual; she wasn't wearing a single jewel.

She complained of not seeing him more often and managed to say a brief word or two. But guests were arriving; their greeting consisted either of a sideways jerk of their body, a bow that bent them double, or a nod. Then a married couple, a family, came through, and everyone spread out into the already packed drawing-room.

In the middle under the chandelier stood a huge circular ottoman with a plantstand rising out of its centre whose flowers curled down like feathers over the heads of the women sitting round it; others were occupying armchairs arranged in two straight lines, divided symmetrically by the reddish-orange velvet window curtains and the tall door-bays with gilded lintels.

Across the room, the throng of men standing around, hat in hand, formed a compact black mass, dotted here and there by the red ribbons in their buttonholes, and made all the darker by contrast with their monotonous white bow-ties. Apart from a few whipper-snappers with incipient beards, they all seemed bored; a few dandies rocked glumly to and fro on their heels. There were large numbers of grey heads and wigs and the odd bald pate, glistening; their faces, bright scarlet or very pale, all looked prodigiously tired and careworn—the guests were all either politicians or business men. A sprinkling of distinguished scholars, a few judges and two or three eminent doctors had been invited as well; and the host was modestly disclaiming the compliments on his hospitality and any reference to his wealth.

An assiduous army of flunkeys in heavily gold-braided livery were in attendance. The large candelabra were like great bunches of fire blossoming against the hangings; they were duplicated in the mirrors; and at the end of the dining-room, which was trellised in jasmine, the supper table looked like some jeweller's display or the high altar of a cathedral, with its array of dishes, covers, silver and silver-gilt knives, forks and spoons, in the scintillating cross-fire of iridescent cut-glass. The three other drawing-rooms were chock-a-block with precious objects: landscapes by famous painters on the walls; pieces of ivory and china along the tables; Chinese curios on the consoles; lacquer screens extending in front of the windows; clumps of camellias rearing up in the fireplaces, while in the distance there came a soft throb of music, like the hum of bees.

They weren't playing many quadrilles and from the unenthusiastic way the dancers were shuffling round, they seemed to be finding it a chore.

Frédéric overheard such remarks as:

'Were you at the last charity do at the Hôtel-Lambert?'*

'No, I was not!'

'It's going to get terribly hot later on.'

'Yes, absolutely stifling!'

'Do you know who composed this polka?'

'Goodness me, I've no idea, Madame!'

And behind him, tucked away in a window recess, three old fops were whispering smut to each other; elsewhere people were discussing railways or free trade; a sportsman was telling a story about some shooting party; a Legitimist and an Orléanist were having an argument.

Sauntering from group to group, he reached the card-room where, in a circle of earnest-looking players, he recognized Martinon, 'now practising at the Bar in the capital'.

His large waxen face fitted snugly into the fringe of his beard, a miracle of neatly trimmed black hair, and to maintain a happy balance between the elegance required of his youth and the proper dignity of his profession, he had one thumb hooked in his armpit, in imitation of the young smart set, and an arm inserted into the front of his waistcoat, like a Guizot supporter. Although he was wearing ultra-shiny patent leather dancing pumps, he'd shaved his temples to give himself a lofty intellectual brow.

He made a few aloof remarks and then turned back to his little group. A landowner was saying:

'They're the sort of people who dream of turning society upside down!'

'They want the organization of labour! Can you imagine!' another man added.

'Is that surprising', a third man asked, 'when we find Monsieur de Genoude backing *Le Siècle*?'*

'And even some conservatives labelling themselves progressives! And what are they trying to bring about? A republic! As if a republic were possible in France!'

Everyone asserted that a republic was not possible in France.

'Anyway', remarked one man in a loud voice, 'people are showing too great an interest in the Revolution. Books and all sorts of bunkum are being published on the subject!'

'Quite apart from the fact', said Martinon, 'that there are perhaps more serious topics worth studying.'

A man from a ministry started taking certain scandalous theatrical productions to task:

'For instance, that new drama *La Reine Margot** really does go too far! Why on earth tell us about the Valois? It all shows up royalty in an unfavourable light! It's the same with the Press! Say what you like, the September Laws were too soft! As for me I'd like to see courts martial to muzzle the journalists! At the slightest sign of insubordination, haul 'em up before the military tribunal! And let 'em have it!'

'Steady on now, sir, steady on!' said a professor. 'Don't let us endanger all those precious rights we won in 1830. We mustn't undermine any form of our freedom. The answer would rather be to decentralize, to distribute the surplus urban population round the countryside.'

'But the countryside is a sink of iniquity!' a Catholic exclaimed. 'Religion must be strengthened!'

Martinon was quick to agree.

'Yes, certainly, it is a restraining influence.'

The whole root of the evil was this modern urge to rise above your station, to live in luxury.

'All the same', objected an industrialist, 'luxury boosts

173

trade. And I approve the Duc de Nemours* for insisting on knee-breeches at his evening receptions.'

'Monsieur Thiers went in trousers. You know that witty remark* of his?'

'Yes, delightful. But he's turning into a demagogue and the speech he made on incompatibility can't have failed to have some influence on that assassination attempt in April '46.'*

'Fiddlesticks!'

'Oh yes!'

The circle was forced to make way for a footman carrying a tray into the card-room.

The tables were lit by green-shaded candles and covered in rows of cards and gold coins. Frédéric paused at one of them, lost the three hundred francs he'd brought with him, swung on his heels, and discovered that he was standing in the doorway of the boudoir in which Madame Dambreuse was now installed.

It was full of women sitting side by side on backless seats; their waists emerged from the long folds of their petticoats billowing like waves around them; their breasts on display in low-cut dresses; almost all of them had a posy of violets in their hand. The dull colour of their gloves set off the white flesh of their arms; various trimmings and pendants dangled over their shoulders and now and then certain wobblings and quivers suggested that their dresses were about to slip down. But their decorous expressions belied the outrageousness of their clothes; a number of them indeed showed an almost cow-like placidity; such a gathering of half-naked women conjured up thoughts of a harem—and a less genteel comparison flashed through the young man's mind. Many different types of beauty were in fact represented: English women, whose profile came straight out of a keepsake; an Italian, whose dark eyes flashed like a Vesuvius; three sisters from Normandy dressed all in blue, as fresh as apple trees in April; a tall red-head with an amethyst necklace; and the white sparkle of sprays of diamonds in their hair, the precious stones glittering on their bosoms and the soft glow of pearls framing their faces blended with the gleam of gold rings, the lacework, the powder, the plumes, the scarlet of tiny mouths, and the lustrous sheen of teeth. The dome-shaped ceiling made the room seem like an elegant fruit basket full of fragrant air wafted by the fluttering fans.

Frédéric stood behind them gazing through his monocle and finding fault with more than one pair of shoulders; thinking of the Marshal helped to repress his temptation or to console him for being tempted.

Meanwhile he was looking at Madame Dambreuse and finding her attractive, in spite of her rather large mouth and her overly wide nostrils. But she had a special charm all her own. Her ringlets hinted at a sort of wistful, dreamy passion, while her forehead, the colour of agate, looked as if it had lots of things hidden inside and warned you she was the boss.

She'd set her husband's niece down beside her: a rather plain girl. From time to time she'd turn to welcome incoming guests; and as the buzz of female voices grew louder, it sounded like birds cackling.

They discussed the Tunisian delegates and their costumes. One lady had attended the last admission to the Academy; another mentioned Molière's *Dom Juan*, recently produced at the Comédie-Française. But Madame Dambreuse threw a glance towards her niece and put her finger to her lips, with an involuntary smile which belied her prudishness.

Suddenly Martinon appeared in the doorway opposite. She stood up. He offered her his arm. To watch the progress of these flirtatious manoevres, Frédéric made his way between the card-tables and caught up with them in the large drawing-room. Madame Dambreuse immediately left her companion and began to talk to him in a very friendly manner.

She could understand why he didn't play cards or dance.

'When you're young, you're unhappy!' And then casting her eye round the room full of dancers:

'And anyway, all this isn't much fun! At least for certain types of people.'

She kept stopping in front of the row of armchairs, dropping a few affable remarks here and there, while old men with double-sided spectacles came up to pay court to her. She introduced Frédéric to some of them. Monsieur Dambreuse tapped him gently on the elbow and led him out on to the terrace.

He'd spoken to the Minister. It wasn't an easy matter. Recruitment to the Conseil was by examination. In an inexplicable burst of confidence, Frédéric replied that he was familiar with the subjects required.

In view of Monsieur Roque's high opinion of his ability, the financier was not surprised.

This name reminded Frédéric of little Louise and he saw his house and bedroom; he recalled similar nights when he'd stayed at his window listening to the passing wagoners. The memory of his unhappiness brought his mind back to Madame Arnoux and, still walking along the terrace, he fell silent; the sound of the dancing was dying down; carriages were beginning to leave.

'Why are you so keen on the Conseil d'État?' enquired Monsieur Dambreuse.

And adopting a liberalistic tone, he explained that, frankly, public service was a dead-end—he knew something about that! Business was better. Frédéric pointed out how hard it was to learn the way it worked.

'Nonsense! It wouldn't take any time at all to put you on the right track.'

Was he looking to take him on as a business associate?

In a flash the young man could see himself becoming immensely wealthy.

'Let's go back in,' said the banker. 'You will stay to supper, won't you?'

It was three o'clock; people were going. In the dining-room a supper table had been laid for a few close friends.

Monsieur Dambreuse caught sight of Martinon; he went up to his wife and whispered:

'Did you invite him?'

'Yes, certainly!' she retorted sharply.

The niece was no longer to be seen. There was a good

deal of drinking, raucous laughter and coarse jokes, at which no one blinked an eyelid; everybody was in that state of euphoria that follows a prolonged period of restraint. Only Martinon didn't unbend; but while refusing to take any champagne—it was not 'good form'— he did show himself amiable and extremely polite; when Monsieur Dambreuse, who was narrow-chested, complained of difficulty in breathing, he asked several times after his health; and then he'd turn his watery blue eyes on to his wife.

She questioned Frédéric as to which girls he'd found attractive. He hadn't noticed any of them and in any case preferred women of thirty.

'That's probably not such a bad idea!' she replied.

Then, as everybody was putting on coats and furs, she said to him:

'Come and see me one of these mornings. We'll have a little chat.'

Downstairs, Martinon lit a cigar and as he sucked away at it, he looked so heavy-jowled that Frédéric couldn't help blurting out:

'My goodness, you've got a funny-shaped head, haven't you?'

'It's turned a few in its time,' retorted the young barrister, half smugly and half crossly.

As he was going to bed Frédéric ran over the evening's events. First, his clothes—he'd examined himself in the mirror a number of times—left nothing to be desired, from the cut of his coat to the bow on his patent leather pumps; he'd spoken to men of importance, had viewed rich women at close quarters; Monsieur Dambreuse had proved most helpful and his wife even inviting. One by one he weighed up her slightest words, the way she'd looked at him, a thousand and one things that defied analysis but must mean something. It'd be absolutely staggering to have a mistress like that! And yet, why not? He was certainly as good as anybody else. Perhaps she wasn't all that choosy? Then he recalled Martinon; and he dropped off to sleep smiling with pity at the poor chap.

The thought of the Marshal woke him up; the words in

her note: 'From tomorrow evening I'll be a Free Woman' were surely an invitation to him to call that very day? He waited till nine o'clock and then hurried round to her place.

Someone was going upstairs ahead of him and shut the door in his face. He tugged at the bell; Delphine came to the door and assured him that madam wasn't at home.

Frédéric stood his ground and pleaded with her. He'd something of the utmost importance to tell her, just a couple of words. In the end, he clinched his argument with a five-franc piece and the maid left him by himself in the entrance hall.

Rosanette appeared, half undressed, with her hair down. From the far side of the room she shook her head and waved her arms to indicate that she wasn't free.

Slowly Frédéric made his way downstairs; this last whim of hers outdid all the rest. He couldn't understand it.

Outside the porter's lodge, he was stopped by Mademoiselle Vatnaz.

'Did she let you in?'

'No!'

'They sent you away?'

'How did you know?'

'It's obvious. But come on, I can't breathe, let's go!'

Gasping for breath, she led him out into the street. He could feel her skinny arm trembling against his. Suddenly she burst out:

'Oh the rotten beast!'

'Who d'you mean?'

'Him, of course! Who else? Delmar!'

'Are you quite sure?' asked Frédéric, humiliated by her disclosure.

'I tell you I followed him here!' exclaimed Vatnaz. 'I saw him go in! Now do you understand? I should have expected it, of course, I was stupid enough to take him there. And heavens above, if you only knew! I took him in, fed him, clothed him! And all those things I did for him in the newspapers! I was like a mother to him!' And then with a sneer: 'The truth is, that fine gentleman needs velvet gowns! Just playing the market, of course! And her! To think that when I first met her, she was making underwear! Without my help she'd have ended up in the gutter a dozen times or more! But I'm going to make sure she does end up there! Oh yes, I'm going to see she kicks the bucket in a public hospital! I'll take the lid off everything!'

And in a wild outburst of rage, she poured out the whole squalid story, like someone emptying a pail of slops.

'She's been to bed with Jumillac, Flacourt, young Allard, Bertinaux, Saint-Valéry—the pock-marked one, no, it was the other one, it doesn't really matter, they're brothers. And when she was hard up, I looked after everything. And what did I get out of it all? She's incredibly stingy! And you must admit that it was sheer kindness on my part to have anything to do with her because, after all, we belong to different worlds, I'm not a tart, am I? I don't sell my body, do I? Not to mention that she's as thick as they come! She spells category with two Ts! Actually that makes a pair of them, they're a perfect match, even if he does call himself an artist and think himself a genius! But good God, if he'd had an ounce of intelligence, he wouldn't have played a dirty trick like that, you don't leave an exceptional woman for a slut! Oh, I don't give a damn, really! He's losing his looks! I loathe and detest him and let me tell you, if I met him I'd spit in his face!' She spat. 'Yes, that's what I think of him now! And how about Arnoux? Isn't it horrible? He's forgiven her so many times! You can't imagine the sacrifices he's made for her! She ought to be kising his feet! Oh, he's so kind and generous!'

Frédéric was delighted to hear her abusing Delmar; having come down on Arnoux's side, he saw Rosanette's betrayal as unnatural and unfair. In his sympathy for the old maid's plight, he was beginning to feel rather sorry for him. All of a sudden they were standing outside his door; unnoticed by him, Mademoiselle Vatnaz had led him down the Faubourg Poissonnière.

'Here we are,' she said. 'I don't want to go up but there's nothing to stop you, is there?'

'What for?'

'Why, to tell him everything, of course!'

The scales suddenly fell from his eyes. Frédéric realized the hateful part he was being urged to play.

'Well?' she insisted.

He looked up at the second floor. Madame Arnoux's lamp was burning; there was indeed nothing to stop him from going up.

'I'll wait down here for you. Up you go!'

Her bullying tone finally destroyed any sympathy he still felt. He said:

'I'll be some time. You'd better go. I'll come and see you tomorrow.'

'No! No!' Vatnaz stamped her foot. 'Get hold of him now. Take him round there and he can catch them red-handed.'

'But Delmar will have left.'

She looked down.

'Yes, I suppose he will?'

She remained standing in the street, amongst the carriages, not saying a word. Then, glaring at him like a wild cat:

'I can trust you, can't I? We've made a sacred pact, haven't we? I'll see you tomorrow!'

As he went along the passage, Frédéric could hear two voices arguing. Madame Arnoux was saying:

'Don't lie! Do stop lying!'

He went in. There was a hush.

Arnoux was pacing up and down and his wife was sitting in the little chair beside the fire, as pale as a sheet and with a set look in her eyes. Frédéric made a move to leave. Glad to be rescued, Arnoux grasped his hand.

'I'm afraid that . . .' began Frédéric.

'Don't go,' Arnoux whispered in his ear.

Madame Arnoux said:

'You must bear with us, Monsieur Moreau. It's one of those things that sometimes arise between husband and wife.'

'It's because somebody puts them there!' said Arnoux breezily. 'Women get such queer ideas into their heads. Now this one here isn't a bad sort, in fact she's quite the

180

opposite. Well, she's spent a whole hour plaguing me with a load of rubbish!'

'What I said was true!' retorted Madame Arnoux impatiently. 'You did buy it!'

'Me?'

'Yes, you! From the Persian!'

'The cashmere!' thought Frédéric to himself.

He felt scared and guilty.

She added quickly: 'Last month, Saturday the 14th.'

'Well, on that particular day I was in Creil. So you see!'

'No, you weren't, because we dined at the Bertins' on the 14th.'

'The 14th? Arnoux looked up at the ceiling as if expecting to find the date written there.

'And the assistant who sold it to you had fair hair!'

'How can I remember the assistant?'

'Anyway, he wrote down the address you gave him, 18, rue de Laval!'

'How do you know that?' Arnoux asked, completely taken aback.

She shrugged.

'Quite simply. I went to have my cashmere repaired and the head of the department told me they'd just sent an identical one to Madame Arnoux.'

'Can I help it if there's a Madame Arnoux in the same street?'

'Ah, but not a Jacques Arnoux!' she retorted.

Still protesting his innocence, he began to shift his ground. It was a complete misunderstanding, a sheer coincidence, one of those incomprehensible things that do happen. People shouldn't be condemned on mere suspicion, on the flimsiest of evidence; and he quoted the example of the unfortunate Lesurques.*

'Anyway, I'm telling you you're mistaken! Do you want me to swear it on my word of honour?'

'There's no point!'

'Why not?'

She looked him straight in the eyes and then, without a

181

word, reached out, picked up the silver casket on the mantelshelf, and handed him an opened bill.

Arnoux blushed to the roots of his hair and his drawn face became puffy.

'Well?'

'But', he said slowly, 'what does that prove?'

'Ah!' she answered with a strange note of mingled irony and distress in her voice. 'Ah, what indeed?'

Arnoux was still holding the piece of paper in his hand, staring at it and turning it over as if expecting it to provide the key to some great mystery.

'But of course, now it's all coming back to me,' he said eventually. 'Someone asked me to do it—you must know all about it, don't you?' he added, addressing Frédéric, who remained silent. 'I was asked to do it by . . . by . . . old Oudry.'

'And who was it for?'

'His mistress.'

'For your mistress!' exclaimed Madame Arnoux bounding to her feet.

'I swear . . .'

'Don't go on! I know everything!'

'So I'm being spied on, am I?'

She replied coldly:

'I suppose that offends your sense of decency?'

'When people start losing their temper,' replied Arnoux, looking round for his hat, 'and there's no chance of rational discussion . . .'

Then, with a deep sigh:

'Never get married, dear boy, believe me, never!'

And he made himself scarce; he needed a breath of fresh air.

Deep silence fell. Everything seemed suddenly more still. The Carcel lamp was casting a white patch of light on the ceiling; the dark corners of the room seemed draped in layers of black muslin; the ticking of the clock mingled with the crackling of the fire.

Madame Arnoux had sat down again in the armchair at the other side of the fireplace; she was shivering and biting her lips; her two hands flew to her face, a sob broke from her lips; she was crying.

He sat down on the little chair and in the soft, coaxing voice used with invalids:

'You must know that I sympathize . . .'

She made no reply but, pursuing her own train of thought out loud:

'I give him all the freedom he wants. He had no need to lie!'

It was probably a result of the sort of life he led, he hadn't really given it much thought . . . Perhaps in more important matters . . .

'What do you consider more important than that?'

'Oh, nothing!'

Frédéric acquiesced with a deferential smile. All the same Arnoux did have his good points. He was very fond of his children.

'Yes, and he's doing his best to ruin them!'

That was because he was too easy-going; and after all, he wasn't a bad sort . . .

'What does that mean, not a bad sort?'

He continued to defend him in the vaguest possible terms yet, while feeling sorry for her, in his heart of hearts he was pleased, in fact overjoyed: if she wanted to get her own back or needed a shoulder to cry on, she'd look to him. His hopes soared and his love grew stronger.

Never had she seemed so captivating, so utterly lovely. From time to time she caught her breath and her breast heaved; her eyes were set as if contemplating some inner truth and her lips half-open as if about to reveal her most private feelings. Now and again she pressed her handkerchief to her mouth; how he longed to be that tiny square of cambric soaked in her tears! In spite of himself, he kept casting a glance at the divan standing at the back of the alcove and imagining her head lying on the pillow; and he could see it all so clearly that he could scarcely resist the impulse to seize her in his arms.

She was calmer now; slumped in her chair, she closed her eyes. He went over and leaned over her, gazing greedily at her face. There was a thud of boots in the passage; it was the other man. He heard him shut the door of his bedroom. Frédéric made a sign to ask if he should go and see him.

She nodded and this tacit exchange of their thoughts was a kind of consent, a prelude to adultery.

Arnoux was unbuttoning his frock-coat and preparing to go to bed.

'Well, how is she?'

'Oh, she's better,' said Frédéric. 'She'll get over it.'

But Arnoux was upset.

'You don't know her! She's in such a state of nerves. That idiot of a shop assistant! That's what comes of being too kind! If only I hadn't given Rosanette that blasted shawl!'

'You mustn't be sorry about that! She's tremendously grateful to you!'

'Do you really think so?'

Frédéric was in no doubt about it. The proof was that she'd just sent old Oudry packing.

'Oh, the poor little darling!'

And Arnoux felt so touched that he wanted to rush round and see her straightaway.

'There's no point, I've just come from there myself. She's a bit out of sorts.'

'That's all the more reason!'

He was quickly slipping on his frock-coat again and had picked up his candle. Cursing himself for his stupidity, Frédéric pointed out that in all decency, he'd have to spend the rest of the evening with his wife. He couldn't leave her all alone, it would be really too bad!

'Honestly, it just wouldn't be right! There's no urgency about Rosanette. You can go tomorrow. Surely you can do that for my sake?'

Arnoux put down his candle and gave him a hug:

'What a kind-hearted chap you are!'

CHAPTER III

Now Frédéric's calvary began. He became the hanger-on in the house.

If someone wasn't well, he'd call three times a day to enquire after their health; he'd go round to the piano-tuner's, think up endless ways of being helpful, look pleased even when Marthe was in one of her sulky moods or when Eugène wiped his grubby paws all over his face. He dined with Monsieur and Madame Arnoux, who'd sit facing each other without exchanging a word; or else Arnoux would infuriate his wife by his preposterous remarks. When the meal was over, he'd have a game with his little boy in his bedroom, playing hide-and-seek behind the furniture or crawling about on all-fours, giving him a piggy-back, like Henri IV.* Finally, he'd go off and she would launch into her constant subject of complaint: Arnoux.

It wasn't his misconduct that riled her. But her pride seemed to have been hurt and she couldn't conceal the revulsion she felt for this unprincipled, tasteless and dishonest man.

'Or perhaps he's just out of his mind!' she'd say.

Frédéric would try cleverly to draw her out and soon got to know her whole life.

Her middle-class parents had lived in modest circumstances in Chartres. One day while sketching beside the river (at that time he fancied himself as a painter) Arnoux had caught sight of her coming out of church and asked to marry her; as he was well-off, there was no hesitation. Moreover he was wildly in love with her. She added:

'And in fact, he still does love me, in his way!'

During the early months of their marriage they'd travelled in Italy.

Despite his enthusiasm for the landscape and the artistic treasures, Arnoux had done nothing but moan about the wine and had amused himself organizing picnics with some English people. After successfully selling a few pictures, he'd been encouraged to go into art dealing. Then he'd taken a sudden fancy to a ceramics factory. Now he was being lured into other speculative ventures and becoming more and more vulgar and falling into coarse and extravagant habits. It wasn't so much his morals as all his activities which she blamed. He couldn't possibly change now; her predicament seemed inescapable.

Frédéric complained that his life had been similarly blighted.

But he was very young; why should he give up hope? And she would give him advice: 'Settle down to some work! Get married!' His reply was a bitter smile, for instead of admitting the real reason for being depressed, he pretended it was something else; he'd put on a sort of Antony* act of a man 'thwarted by fate'—an expression, in fact, not all that far from his own opinion.

For certain men, the stronger their desire, the less capable they are of taking action; they lack self-confidence and are fearful of giving offence; moreover, like a virtuous woman, deep affection goes through life with downcast eyes, afraid of being recognized.

Although—perhaps because—he now knew Madame Arnoux better, he was more cowardly than ever. Every morning he'd promise himself to be more enterprising and then be overcome by bashfulness; and he hadn't any precedent to guide him, because this woman was unlike other women. In his dreams he'd placed her above ordinary humanity; in comparison with her, his own importance here on earth was less than the sprigs of silk left behind by her scissors.

Then he'd think up grotesque plans, such as taking her by surprise in the night, using false keys and drugs; anything seemed easier than having to face her disdain.

In any case, the children, the two maids, the layout of the rooms, were insurmountable obstacles. So he decided to carry her off for himself, alone; they'd leave together and live far, far away, in complete isolation; he even tried to imagine which lake would be blue enough, which beach adequately balmy; was it to be Spain, Switzerland or

186

somewhere in the East? And he'd carefully look out for days when she seemed more irritated to tell her that she must break away, find some means or other, that separation was the only solution he could see. But her love for her children would never allow her to take such an extreme step. These high principles increased his respect.

He would spend his afternoons going over in his mind the previous day's visit and looking forward to the next one that evening. Whenever he wasn't dining with them, at about nine o'clock Frédéric would station himself at the corner of their street and as soon as Arnoux had closed the front door behind him, he would quickly go upstairs and ask the maid innocently:

'Is the master in?'

Then he'd pretend to be surprised when he wasn't.

Arnoux used often to come back unexpectedly and then Frédéric would be taken along to a little café in the rue Sainte-Anne, now a regular haunt of Regimbart's.

The Citizen would start by voicing fresh grievances against the Crown. Then they'd chat, hurling friendly abuse at each other, for Arnoux thought Regimbart had a first-class mind and was distressed to see such talent going to waste; he'd taunt him with his laziness, while the Citizen, although admiring Arnoux's great kindness of heart and imagination, considered him definitely too immoral and as a result showed him no mercy; he refused even to go to dinner in his house because 'formality got on his nerves'.

Sometimes, just as they were about to leave, Arnoux would suddenly feel peckish: he 'must have' an omelette or a few boiled potatoes; and as the food was never available on the spot, Arnoux arranged for it to be sent out for. They'd wait. Regimbart stayed on and in the end would accept something to eat, not without grumbling.

He was, however, depressed and would sit for hours in front of a half-empty glass. The stars were not guiding things in accordance with his ideas. He was becoming a hypochondriac, wouldn't even read the papers, and bellowed with rage at the mere mention of England. Once he shouted at an incompetent waiter:

'Haven't we been insulted enough by bloody foreigners?'

Apart from these outbursts, he would sit tight-lipped hatching some 'foolproof scheme to blow up the whole caboodle!'.

While he was immersed in such thoughts Arnoux, looking a trifle drunk, monotonously reeled off incredible tales of exploits where he always came out on top, thanks to his effortless resourcefulness; and no doubt because of basic similarities, Frédéric would somehow feel quite strongly drawn towards him, a weakness which he found annoying. Shouldn't he, really, hate him?

Arnoux would bemoan his wife's attitude, her stubbornness and her unfair prejudices. She hadn't always been like that.

'If I were you,' Frédéric would say, 'I'd make her an allowance and live by myself.'

Arnoux made no reply and then, a moment later, he'd start singing her praises: she was kind, devoted, intelligent, high-principled; he'd proceed to describe her physical attributes in great detail, like those foolhardy people who show off their valuables in hotels.

The even tenor of his life was upset by a catastrophic event.

He had joined the board of directors of a china clay company and, blindly believing all that he was told, had signed misleading reports and approved, without checking, annual statements drawn up by a fraudulent manager. The company had collapsed and, being legally responsible, Arnoux was sentenced, together with other members of the board, to pay damages. This represented a personal loss of roughly thirty thousand francs, the amount having been increased because of aggravating circumstances.

Frédéric read about this in a newspaper and rushed round to the rue Paradis.

He was shown into Madame Arnoux's bedroom. It was breakfast time. A small table standing beside the fire was cluttered with bowls of white coffee. There were slippers scattered over the carpet and pieces of clothing lying about on the armchairs. Arnoux, wearing his underpants and a woollen jacket, looked red-eyed and dishevelled; little Eugène had mumps and was snivelling as he nibbled his bread and butter; his sister was eating quietly; Madame Arnoux, slightly paler than usual, was serving the three of them.

'Ah well!' said Arnoux with a deep sigh. 'So you've heard the news.' And as Frédéric made a gesture of commiseration: 'So there we are! I'm being punished for having such a trusting nature!'

He said no more and despondently pushed his breakfast away. His wife looked up at the ceiling and shrugged her shoulders. He ran his hand over his forehead.

'After all, I'm not the guilty one, there's nothing I need blame myself for. It's unfortunate but never mind, we'll pull through!'

And he responded, indeed, to his wife's appeal and took a bite of brioche.

That evening, Arnoux tried to persuade his wife to have dinner with him, all by themselves, in a private room at the Maison d'Or. Madame Arnoux failed to appreciate the real tenderness behind this offer and even felt offended at being treated like a tart—which, coming from Arnoux, was in fact a sign of affection. So, being bored, he went off to the Marshal's to forget his worries.

Up till now, Arnoux had been able to get away with a good deal thanks to his good nature. His appearance in court had branded him as a man of dubious reputation. His house was boycotted.

Frédéric felt in honour bound to continue to call on them all the more. He took a box at the Italian Opera and invited them along every week. However, they'd reached that stage when the mutual concessions forced on ill-matched couples have so battered and exhausted them that life together has become intolerable. Madame Arnoux had difficulty in restraining her outbursts, while her husband was becoming more and more dejected. The sight of these two unhappy people made Frédéric sad.

As Frédéric was in the other man's confidence, she had asked him to keep up to date with the state of her husband's

189

business affairs. But he felt ashamed and embarrassed to be eating his dinners while having designs on his wife. Nevertheless, he did continue to visit them on the excuse that he must stand up for her and the opportunity might arise to help her.

He'd called on Monsieur Dambreuse a week after the dance. The financier had offered him a couple of dozen shares in his coal-mining venture; Frédéric hadn't gone back. Deslauriers continued to write to him; he didn't reply. Pellerin had invited him to come round to see the portrait but Frédéric kept on putting him off. However, he did agree to Cisy's pressing request to be introduced to Rosanette.

She greeted him very amiably though without throwing her arms round his neck as on earlier occasions. His companion was pleased to be admitted into the presence of a fallen woman, and, above all, an actor: Delmar was there.

An historical drama in which he had played the part of a village yokel, who gives Louis XIV a thorough telling off and prophesies the French Revolution, had brought him so much into the public eye that the same role was being created for him over and over again: his function was to jeer at monarchs of all nations. As an English brewer, he hurled abuse at Charles I, as a student in Salamanca, he thundered against Philip II, and as a fond father, he denounced Madame de Pompadour. This was his finest hour! Little boys would wait for him at the stage-door and his biography, on sale during the intervals, depicted him as caring for his aged mother, reading the Gospels, succouring the sick and poor, in a word as a Saint Vincent de Paul with a touch of Brutus and Mirabeau thrown in. People referred to him as 'Our Delmar'! He had a mission; he was turning into Jesus Christ.

Rosanette had been fascinated by all this and, not being of a mercenary nature, had got rid of old Oudry without a second thought.

Arnoux knew her nature and had taken advantage of it to keep her at little cost to himself over a long period; then the old chap had come along and all three had been careful not to have a show-down. In the belief that she'd sent the other man packing purely on his account, Arnoux had increased his subsidy; but although she was living less extravagantly, in some mysterious way her requests for funds were becoming more frequent; she'd even reached the point of selling her cashmere, being anxious, so she said, to clear off her debts; he was besotted by her and kept on forking out, while she continued to exploit him unmercifully. The result was that his house was being bombarded with bills and summonses. Frédéric felt that the storm was about to break.

One day when he called on Madame Arnoux, she was not at home; the master was working down in the warehouse.

In fact, Arnoux, surrounded by large porcelain vases, was in the process of trying to 'con' some newly-weds, a young middle-class couple up from the country. He was talking about 'turning' and 'throwing', of 'glaze' and 'crackled'; not wishing to appear complete ignoramuses, the others were nodding their heads and paying up.

When they had gone, he said he'd had a little squabble with his wife that morning. In order to forestall any remarks on the subject of his spending, he'd informed her that the Marshal was no longer his mistress.

'In fact, I told her she was yours.'

Frédéric was furious but realizing that recriminations might give the game away, he stammered:

'That was wrong of you, very wrong indeed!'

'What's it matter?' retorted Arnoux. 'What's disgraceful about being taken for her lover? After all, I am! Wouldn't you be delighted to be?'

Had she said something? Was this an insinuation? Frédéric said hurriedly:

'Yes, of course, you're right!'

'Well then?'

'Yes, I agree, it's quite unimportant.'

Arnoux went on:

'Why have you stopped coming round there?'

Frédéric promised that he would be doing so.

'Oh, I was forgetting! When you're talking to my wife

about Rosanette, you might just let slip a few words . . . I don't quite know how but you'll hit on something . . . just a word or two to convince her that you *are* her lover. You will do that for me, won't you?'

The young man was content to give a non-committal look; any aspersion of that sort would wreck his chances. He called on her that very evening and gave her his word that Arnoux's allegations weren't true.

'Honestly?'

He seemed sincere and after taking a deep breath, she said with a lovely smile: 'I believe you'; then she lowered her eyes and without looking at him added:

'Anyway, you're not beholden to anyone, are you?'

So she hadn't the faintest idea and despised him, since she didn't think him capable of loving her so much that he couldn't love anyone else!

Overlooking his attempts with the other woman, Frédéric found her tolerant attitude insulting.

Later, she asked him to call on 'that woman' occasionally to see how the land lay.

At this point, Arnoux came in and five minutes later tried to take him along to Rosanette's.

The situation was becoming unbearable.

His attention was diverted from it by a letter from his solicitor promising to let him have the fifteen thousand francs by the following day; and to make amends for his cavalier treatment of Deslauriers, he went round straight-away to tell him the good news.

The lawyer lived in the rue des Trois-Maries, on the fifth floor overlooking the courtyard. The main decoration of his office, a tiny cold room with a tiled floor and drab grey wallpaper, was the prize he'd received for his doctorate, a gold medal set in an ebony frame propped up against the mirror. In the glass-fronted mahogany bookcase there were about a hundred volumes. The centre of the room was occupied by a leather-topped desk. Four old green plush armchairs stood in the corners and wood-chips were blazing in the fireplace, where he always kept a log handy to put on when the doorbell rang. It was his consulting hour; he was wearing a white tie.

The announcement of the fifteen thousand francs, which he'd doubtless given up for lost, brought a sardonic smile of pleasure to his lips.

'Well done, old chap, that's great!'

He flung some wood on to the fire, sat down again, and immediately started to talk about the newspaper. The first thing to do was to ditch Hussonnet.

'I'm fed up with that idiot! As for standing up for a cause, the best thing is not to have one, that's the fairest and most effective way!'

Frédéric looked surprised.

'But of course it is! The time has come to treat Politics scientifically. The old guard were just getting going in the eighteenth century when along came Rousseau and the literary fraternity with all sorts of poetic and philanthropic humbug—to the great joy of the Papists—a natural alliance, incidentally, because, as I can prove, all modern reformers believe in Revelation. But if you celebrate Masses for Poland, if instead of the God of the Dominicans, who was a thug, you take the God of the Romantics, who's an interior decorator, in a word, if your conception of the Absolute is no broader than that of your forefathers, then any republican system will always contain an element of Monarchy and your Phrygian bonnet* will never be anything but a priest's skull cap! The only difference will be to replace torture by solitary confinement, sacrilege by "offences against religion" and the Holy Alliance by the Concert of Europe and in this splendid New Order, so greatly admired, made up of Louis XIV rubble, a few Voltairean ruins, with a splash of Imperial whitewash on top and some scraps of the British constitution, we'll be seeing town councils trying to bully the mayor, county councils doing ditto to the Prefect, Parliament to the king, the Press to the government, and the bureaucrats to all and sundry; but all those good souls go into raptures over the Civil Code* which was drawn up, whatever you may say, in a mean and despotic spirit, because instead of doing their proper job which is to codify common law, the legislators set themselves up as Lycurguses* to mould society. Why does the law impose restrictions on the father of a family when making a will? Why does it interfere in forced sales of personal estates? Why does it punish vagrancy as a crime, when it oughtn't even to be a misdemeanour? And that's not the end of it either! I know the lot! and so I'm going to write a little novel entitled *The History of the Idea of Justice* and won't it be funny! But I'm absolutely parched! How about you?'

He leaned out of the window and shouted to the porter to go and fetch some grog from the tavern.

'So, summing up, I can see three parties, no, three groups, and I'm not interested in any of them: the "haves", the "used to haves" and those trying hard to have. But they're all agreed on making a ridiculous fetish of Authority! For instance, Mably recommends that philosophers should be prevented from publishing their doctrines; Monsieur Wronsky,* a geometrician, describes censorship—I quote—as "judicious restriction of unbridled speculation"; Father Enfantin* glorifies the Hapsburgs for having "reached out across the Alps with a heavy hand to curb Italy"; Pierre Leroux* wants to force you to listen to a speech and Louis Blanc* favours state religion: that shows the frantic urge to *govern* of this bunch of helots! But though they're constantly appealing to principles, not one of their constitutions is legitimate! After all, *principle* means *origin* and one always has to go back to a revolution, to an act of violence, a short-lived phenomenon. And so the principle underlying ours is national sovereignty involving parliamentary institutions, although Parliament refuses to admit it! But why should the sovereignty of the people be more sacred than the divine right of kings? They're both fictions! So that's enough metaphysics and phantasms! You don't need dogma to keep the streets clean! People will say I'm trying to overturn society! So what? Where's the harm in that? The truth is, society's a mess!'

Frédéric could have taken him up on a good many points but as these ideas of his were so different from Sénécal's, he felt very tolerant. He merely retorted that a system like that would make them widely hated.

'Quite the opposite! As we'll promise every party to hate the one next to it, they'll all have confidence in us. *You* must get down to work, too, and produce some transcendental criticism!'

They'd have to attack all accepted ideas, the Academy, the École normale,* the Comédie-Française, anything resembling an institution. That's how they could give their magazine a body of doctrine. Then once it was well established, they'd suddenly turn it into a daily; then they'd start attacking personalities.

'And you can be sure of one thing: people will respect us!'

Deslauriers was in striking distance of achieving an old dream of his: to become an editor-in-chief, that is to say, to have the indescribable satisfaction of ordering people about, carving up their articles, commissioning some and rejecting others. Behind his spectacles, his eyes were glinting, and as he kept tossing off one glass of grog after another without thinking, he was becoming increasingly elated.

'You'll have to give a weekly dinner party. It's absolutely essential, even if it costs the earth! People will be keen to come, it'll be leverage for you and a centre for others and by controlling public opinion from both ends, literature and politics, in less than six months, you'll be cock of the roost in Paris, you'll see!'

As he listened, Frédéric could feel himself growing younger, like a man being taken out into the fresh air after long confinement in his bedroom. The enthusiasm was infectious.

'Yes, I've been lazy and stupid, you're quite right!'

'Splendid!' exclaimed Deslauriers. 'That's like my old Frédéric!'

And brandishing his fist under his chin:

'Ah, you had me worried! Never mind, I love you all the same!'

Full of emotion, they stood gazing at each other ready to fall into each other's arms.

A woman's bonnet poked through the entrance hall doorway.

'What are you doing here?' asked Deslauriers.

It was his girlfriend Clémence.

She replied that as she'd been passing, she hadn't been able to resist coming up to see him; and she put some cakes on the table, for them to have a little treat together.

'Mind my papers!' snapped the lawyer. 'And that makes the third time I've told you not to call on me during my consulting hours!'

She tried to give him a kiss.

'That's enough of that! Off you go! Buzz off!'

He pushed her away. She gave a big sob.

'God, you really are a bore!'

'But I love you!'

'I don't want people to love me, I want people to do what I want!'

This cruel remark put a stop to her tears. She went over to the window and stood motionless, pressing her forehead against the glass.

Deslauriers was finding her silence and attitude irritating.

'When you've finished, just order your carriage, will you?'

She swung round.

'You're turning me out?'

'Right first time!'

She stared at him through her big blue eyes, no doubt making a final plea, drew the ends of her tartan shawl across her chest, still waiting, and then, after a minute, left the room.

'You ought to call her back,' said Frédéric.

'You're joking!'

And as he had to go out, Deslauriers went into his kitchen, which was also his dressing-room. On the tiled floor, next to a pair of boots, were the remains of a frugal meal and in the corner a mattress rolled up in a blanket.

'That'll prove to you that I don't have many duchesses calling on me. Oh, it's easy to do without them, you know, and without the other ones, too. The ones who don't cost

you anything take up your time. Time is money and I'm
not a rich man! And then they're all so stupid! Have you
ever managed to talk to a woman?'

At the corner of the Pont-Neuf they parted.

'So it's agreed, you'll bring the stuff along tomorrow as
soon as you get it?'

'Right!' said Frédéric.

On waking up next morning, Frédéric received through
the post his bankers' draft for fifteen thousand francs.

For him this scrap of paper represented fifteen large
bagfuls of silver, and he said to himself that with that sum
he could, first of all, hang on to his carriage for another
three years instead of selling it, as he would have to do; or
else buy himself two wonderful suits of damascene armour
which he'd noticed on the quai Voltaire, as well as lots of
other things—paintings, books, and God knows how many
bunches of flowers and presents for Madame Arnoux. In a
word, any of those things would have been more attractive
than risking—losing?—so much money in that newspaper.
Deslauriers seemed to him bumptious and yesterday's
callous behaviour had dampened his sympathy for him. In
the midst of all this soul-searching, he was amazed to see
Arnoux come into his room. He slumped down on his bed
like a man completely crushed.

'What on earth's the matter?'

'I'm scuppered!'

He'd borrowed eighteen thousand francs from a man
called Vanneroy and now had to pay him back, in the
solicitor Maître Bauminet's office in the rue Sainte-Anne,
that very day.

'It's a disaster completely out of the blue! After all, to
keep him happy, I'd let him have a mortgage. But he's
threatening to foreclose if it's not paid by this afternoon!'

'So?'

'So it's very simple. He'll foreclose on my home. As soon
as the first notice goes up, I'm a ruined man, that's the sum
and substance of it! If only I could find someone to lend me
the blasted money, he could take over from Vanneroy and

I'd be all right! I suppose you don't happen to have it, do you?'

The bankers' draft was on his bedside table. Frédéric hastily covered it with a book lying beside it as he replied:

'Me? Good Lord no, my dear Arnoux!'

But it hurt him to have to refuse Arnoux.

'You can't find anyone who might be able to . . .?'

'There's no one! And to think that in a week's time I'll be getting some repayments myself! I'm owed something like . . . fifty thousand by the end of this month!'

'Couldn't you ask any of your debtors to let you have something in advance?'

'I ask you!'

'But don't you have any securities or promissory notes?'

'Not a bean!'

'So what are you going to do?'

'That's exactly what I'm wondering myself!'

He paced up and down the room in silence.

'God knows it's not for me, it's for my children, my poor wife!'

Then, stressing every phrase:

'Well . . . I must be strong . . . I shall pack up . . . and go away . . . and try to make a fresh start . . . somewhere or other . . . I can't think where . . .'

'But you can't do that!'

Arnoux replied calmly:

'How can I possibly go on living in Paris after all this?'

There was a long pause.

'When would you repay the money . . .?' began Frédéric.

Not that he'd got any, far from it! But there was nothing to stop him from going round to see some friends, making some enquiries . . . And he rang for his servant in order to get dressed, while Arnoux thanked him.

'You need eighteen thousand francs, don't you?'

'Oh, I'd be satisfied with sixteen . . . I can certainly get two thousand five hundred or three thousand for my silver, assuming Vanneroy gives me till tomorrow. And you can tell the lender, even promise him, that he'll be repaid in a week's time, perhaps even in five or six days. Anyway, the mortgage will provide a surety. So you realize there'll be absolutely no risk.'

Frédéric assured him that he did realize this and that he'd be off straightaway.

He stayed at home cursing Deslauriers, because he wanted to keep his word and still help Arnoux.

'Suppose I were to approach Monsieur Dambreuse? But what excuse could I find to ask him for money? On the contrary I'm supposed to be letting him have some for his coal-mining shares . . . Oh, he can go to hell with his shares! I don't owe him anything for them!'

And Frédéric congratulated himself on his independence, as if he'd refused to do Monsieur Dambreuse a favour.

'Well now,' he went on, 'since I'm making a loss there, because I could turn that fifteen thousand into a hundred thousand, it does sometimes happen on the Stock Exchange . . . since I'm letting one of them down, aren't I free to do as I like? Anyway, what if Deslauriers does have to wait? No, that's bad, I must get going!'

He looked at his clock.

'Oh, there's no hurry, the bank's open till five!'

And at half past four, when he'd drawn the money:

'There's not much point, I wouldn't be able to find him now! I'll see him later this evening'—thereby allowing himself time to go back on his decision; once we've let casuistry in, it'll never go away entirely, like the after-taste of a cheap liqueur.

He went for a walk along the boulevards and dined by himself in a restaurant. Then, to take his mind off his problem, he watched one act at the Vaudeville Theatre. But he felt uncomfortable, as if he were carrying stolen bank-notes about on him. He wouldn't have been sorry to lose them.

When he got home he found a note:

'What news?
My wife joins with me in hoping . . . etc . . .
Yours . . .'

And his initials.

His wife! *She*'s asking me!

At that moment Arnoux appeared to discover if he'd managed to lay hands on the much-needed money.

'Here you are, here it is!' said Frédéric.

And twenty-four hours later, in reply to Deslauriers:

'I haven't got anything yet.'

The lawyer called again three days in a row. He kept urging him to write to his solicitor. He even volunteered to make the trip to Le Havre.

'No, don't worry, I'll go myself.'

At the end of the week, Frédéric timidly asked for his fifteen thousand francs; our good friend put him off till the next day and then the day after. Frédéric was scared to go out before dark, for fear of running into Deslauriers.

One evening, at the corner of the Madeleine, a man bumped into him.

It was Deslauriers.

'I'm just on my way to pick it up,' he said.

So Deslauriers went along with him to the door of a house in the Faubourg-Poissonnière.

'Wait for me here.'

He waited. Eventually, forty-three minutes later, Frédéric came out with Arnoux. He made him a sign to be patient a little while longer. Arm in arm, the ceramics dealer and his companion walked up the rue Hauteville and turned into the rue Chabrol.

It was a dark night with a warm gusty wind; Arnoux was sauntering along talking about the Galeries-du-Commerce, a series of arcades aimed at linking the boulevard Saint-Denis with the Châtelet, a marvellous speculative venture in which he was keen to participate; and from time to time, he'd stop outside shop-windows to take a look at the faces of the girls working there, before continuing his disquisition.

Frédéric could hear Deslauriers's footsteps dogging him like stabs of conscience. But bashfulness and a fear that it would be fruitless were making him reluctant to put his question. The other man was coming up from behind. He decided to take the plunge.

Arnoux airily explained that he was not in a position to repay the fifteen thousand francs, at this moment of time, as he'd not succeeded in recovering the money owing to him.

'You're not in actual need of them, I imagine?'

At that moment, Deslauriers came up to Frédéric and drew him on one side.

'Out with it, be honest, have you got the money or not?'

'Well, no, I haven't,' replied Frédéric. 'I've lost it.'

'Oh yes, and how did you do that, pray?'

'At cards!'

Without replying, Deslauriers made a deep bow and went off. Arnoux had taken advantage of the delay to light up a cigar in a tobacconist's. He came back and asked who the young man was.

'Nobody—just a friend.'

Three minutes later, outside Rosanette's door:

'Come on up,' said Arnoux, 'she'll be glad to see you. How unsociable you are these days!'

He was standing under the light of a street-lamp opposite and with his jaunty air and his cigar stuck between his white teeth there was something insufferable about him.

'Oh, by the way, my solicitor called on yours this morning to transfer the mortgage. My wife reminded me about it.'

'A very efficient woman!' said Frédéric mechanically.

'Yes indeed!'

And once again Arnoux began singing her praises. Intelligent, affectionate, a good housekeeper, she was incomparable; and in a low voice, with a leer:

'And you ought to see her undressed!'

'I'm going!' said Frédéric.

Arnoux gave a start.

'Good Lord, why?'

And with his hand half-outstretched he stood gazing at him, quite taken aback by the anger on Frédéric's face.

'I'm off, goodbye!' replied Frédéric brusquely.

Devastated and heart-broken, he set off headlong down the rue de Bréda like a dislodged stone, raging against Arnoux and vowing he'd never see him again, nor her either. Instead of the break-up which he'd been hoping for, here was this other man now utterly devoted to her, from the hair on her head to the depths of her soul. The man's vulgarity was appalling. So the fellow had got everything! He could see him again, standing outside that tart's doorway, and his mortification about the break-up was compounded by rage over his powerlessness. What's more, Arnoux's honesty in offering a security for his loan was humiliating; he'd have liked to wring his neck; and over and above his resentment, his conscience was troubled by the spectre of his cowardly treatment of his friend. His tears were choking him.

Deslauriers was swearing out loud as he plunged headlong down the rue des Martyrs. His scheme had now assumed lofty proportions in his eyes, like an obelisk which had been knocked down. He considered he'd been robbed, and terribly wronged. His friendship was now dead and done with and this thought delighted him: that was some consolation! He hated the rich and felt sympathetic towards Sénécal's ideas. He promised himself he'd adopt them.

Meanwhile, comfortably ensconced in an armchair by the fire with Rosanette on his knee, Arnoux was relishing the aroma of his cup of tea.

Frédéric stopped visiting them and in order to distract his mind from his disastrous passion, he determined to write a *History of the Renaissance*, which was the first subject that came into his head. He piled his table high with a random assortment of humanists, philosophers and poets; he went to the Print Room and looked at Raimondi's* engravings; he made an effort to understand Macchiavelli. Gradually the soothing effect of work restored his peace of mind. By immersing himself in the personality of others, he forgot his own, which is perhaps the only way not to suffer from it.

One day, as he was quietly making notes, the door was opened and his man announced Madame Arnoux.

It really was her! By herself? No, she was holding little Eugène's hand and he was followed by his nanny in a white apron. She sat down and gave a cough.

'You haven't been to see us for such a long time.'

As Frédéric was unable to think up an excuse, she went on:

'It's because you're so tactful!'

'Tactful?'

'Because of what you did for Arnoux!'

Frédéric made a gesture, meaning: 'I don't give a damn about him, I did it for your sake!'

She sent her son off with his nanny to play in the drawing-room. They enquired briefly about each other's health. The conversation lapsed.

She was wearing a dress of a rich brown, the colour of Spanish wine, and a black velvet coat trimmed with marten; the fur invited thoughts of being stroked and her long sleek hair parted in the middle was asking to be kissed. But something was making her uneasy; she looked towards the door.

'Isn't it a little stuffy in here?'

He realized the meaning of her wary look.

'Oh, the door's only pushed to!'

'Ah yes, so I see!'

And she gave a smile, as if to say: 'I'm not scared!'

He immediately asked why she'd come.

'My husband', she replied painfully, 'wanted me to come because he didn't dare approach you himself.'

'Why not?'

'You do know Monsieur Dambreuse, don't you?'

'A little.'

'Ah, a little!'

She stopped.

'Never mind. Please go on.'

She told him that yesterday, Arnoux had been unable to meet four promissory notes of one thousand francs each, payable to the banker, which he'd got her to sign. She couldn't forgive herself for having jeopardized her children's future; but anything was better than disgrace and if Monsieur Dambreuse stopped his proceedings, he'd soon be paid, quite certainly: she was going to sell a small property she owned in Chartres.

'Poor woman!' muttered Frédéric to himself. Then:

'I'll go and see. You can rely on me!'

'Oh, thank you!'

She stood up to go.

'Oh, there's no need to go yet!'

She remained standing, examining his panoply of Mongol arrows hanging from the ceiling, his bookcase, his bindings, all his writing materials; she picked up the bronze bowl containing his quill pens; her heels shifted to various parts of the carpet. She had visited Frédéric a number of times, but always with Arnoux. Now they were on their own, in his own house; it was an extraordinary happening, almost like an unexpected amorous adventure.

She asked to see his little garden; he offered her his arm to show her round his estate, a thirty-foot plot shut in by the walls of houses, with ornamental shrubs in the corners and a flowerbed in the middle.

It was early April; the lilacs were already coming into leaf, a breath of pure air was swirling around, tiny birds were chirping and their song chimed in with the clanging of a coach-builder's forge in the distance.

Frédéric went to fetch a fire-shovel and while they strolled round, side by side, the little boy made sand heaps on the path.

Madame Arnoux didn't expect him to turn out very original but he did have an affectionate nature. His sister, on the other hand, showed a lack of feeling that sometimes hurt her.

'She'll change!' said Frédéric. 'While there's life there's hope!'

'While there's life there's hope,' she echoed.

Somehow this mechanical repetition of his words seemed encouraging; he picked a rose, the only one in the garden.

'Do you remember a certain bunch of flowers one night, in the carriage?'

She blushed slightly; then, with a look of amused tolerance:

'Ah, I was very young in those days!'

204

'And will the same thing happen to this rose?' asked Frédéric in a low voice.

She twirled the stalk between her fingers like the thread of a spinning wheel and replied:

'No, this one I'll keep!'

She made a sign to the nursemaid to pick the little boy up; then standing in the doorway outside in the street, she sniffed the rose, tilting her head sideways over her shoulder with a glance as gentle as a kiss.

When he went back into his study, he gazed at the armchair in which she'd been sitting and all the objects she'd touched. Some part of her was still breathing around him, her presence still lingered like the soft touch of a hand.

His heart swelled with an immense tenderness.

When he called on Monsieur Dambreuse at eleven o'clock next morning, he was shown into the dining-room where the banker was sitting at lunch opposite his wife. Next to her sat his niece and on the other side her governess, an Englishwoman, badly pock-marked.

Monsieur Dambreuse invited his young friend to sit down with them and when he declined:

'Well now, please tell me what I can do for you.'

As casually as possible, Frédéric explained that he'd come with a request from a certain Arnoux.

'Aha! The one-time art dealer,' said the banker, with a gentle chuckle which bared his gums. 'Oudry used to back him. They've fallen out since then.'

And he began to go through his correspondence and the newspapers lying beside him on the table.

There were two servants waiting at table, gliding noiselessly over the parquet flooring; and the height of the ceiling, the three tapestry door-curtains, the pair of white marble fountains, the gleaming hot-plates, the array of hors-d'oeuvres and even the crisply folded table-napkins formed a contrast in Frédéric's mind with that other meal at Arnoux's. He couldn't pluck up courage to disturb Monsieur Dambreuse.

Madame Dambreuse noticed his embarrassment.

'Do you see our friend Martinon occasionally?'

'He's coming tonight,' the niece put in quickly.

'Are you quite certain of that?' her aunt said, giving her a long hard look.

Then, as one of the footmen whispered something in her ear:

'Your dressmaker's here, my girl . . . Miss John!'

The governess obediently took herself off with her charge.

Distracted by the scraping of chairs, Monsieur Dambreuse asked what was the matter.

'It's Madame Regimbart.'

'Ah, Regimbart! I know that name, I've seen his signature somewhere.'

Frédéric finally broached the subject of his errand; Arnoux's was a worthy case; he was even going to sell a house belonging to his wife in order to meet his commitments.

'They say she's very pretty,' remarked Madame Dambreuse.

The banker added in a friendly tone:

'Are you a particularly close friend of theirs?'

Without giving a direct answer, Frédéric said he would be extremely obliged if he could take into account . . .

'Well, since that's what you'd like, all right, we'll wait! There's no rush! How about coming down to my office?'

Lunch was over. With an odd smile on her face, half ironical and half polite, Madame Dambreuse gave him a slight bow. Frédéric had no time to ponder over it, because as soon as they were by themselves, Monsieur Dambreuse said:

'You didn't come to collect your shares.'

And without waiting for any excuse:

'That's quite all right! It's only fair for you to know a bit more about the business.'

He offered him a cigarette and began.

The Consortium of French Coal-mining Companies had now been set up and needed only the statutory order of approval. In itself the merger would reduce labour and

206

maintenance costs and maximize profits. What was more, the company was planning an innovation, namely to involve the workers themselves in the operation. They would be provided with housing and hygienic living conditions and the company would undertake to supply its staff with everything at cost price.

'And they will be the gainers, my dear Monsieur Moreau; this represents real progress! It's a splendid reply to the fuss being made by some republicans! On our board'—he held out a prospectus—'we have a peer, a distinguished scientist from the Academy, a former senior army officer from the Royal Engineers, well-known names, which will inspire confidence in cautious investors and attract the support of the ones with intelligence.' The company would be able to rely on orders from the State and, later on, from the railways, the steam-fired navy, the metallurgical industry, gas companies, domestic cookers. 'In this way we shall be providing heat and light and gain access to the most modest households. But you'll want to know how we can guarantee a market? That will be thanks to possessing exclusive rights and these we shall be granted, my dear fellow! That will be our concern! As for me, I'm an out-and-out protectionist! Our country first and foremost!' He'd been made chairman but he wouldn't have time to attend to certain details, such as writing up reports! 'I haven't kept up with my reading, I've forgotten all my Greek! I'd need someone who could put my ideas down on paper.' And abruptly: 'Would you like to be that someone? With the title of company secretary?'

Frédéric didn't know what to say.

'Well, what's your difficulty?'

His job would be merely to write the annual report to the shareholders, he'd be in daily contact with the workforce, he'd naturally become extremely popular with them, and this would enable him later to move on to the town council, to become a member of the Chamber of Deputies.

Frédéric could feel a buzzing in his ears. What was behind this kind offer? He thanked Monsieur Dambreuse profusely.

However, the banker went on, it was important that he should not be dependent on anybody and the best way to ensure this was to take up a few shares, 'a superb investment, incidentally, because your holding would guarantee your position and your position would guarantee your holding'.

'How much would that come to, roughly?' enquired Frédéric.

'Well, it'd be up to you, of course. I'd think between forty and sixty thousand.'

For Monsieur Dambreuse this was a mere flea-bite and Frédéric was so impressed by his prestige that he decided on the spot to sell off a farm. He'd accept. Monsieur Dambreuse would be fixing a day to meet and finalize the arrangement.

'So I can tell Jacques Arnoux?'

'Whatever you like! Poor chap! Anything you like!'

Frédéric wrote to tell the Arnoux that their minds could be at rest and sent the letter by messenger who got the reply:

'Splendid!'

But his help deserved more than that. He expected a call or at least a letter. No one called. There was no letter.

Had they forgotten or was it deliberate? Since Madame Arnoux had called round once, what was preventing her from calling again? Was her vague hint or confession merely a stratagem prompted by self-interest? 'Had they set out to make a fool of me? Is she in the plot?' Despite his strong desire to find out, a sort of bashfulness held him back.

One morning three weeks after their interview, Monsieur Dambreuse wrote to say he would like to see him, that very day, in an hour's time.

On the way there, he was again plagued by thoughts of the Arnoux and, being unable to think of any reason for their behaviour, he was overcome by a feeling of dread, a kind of grim presentiment. To ease his mind he called a cab and drove to the rue Paradis.

Arnoux was away on a trip.

'Madame Arnoux?'

'In the country, at the factory.'

'When will the master be back?'

'Tomorrow for certain!'

He'd find her alone; now was the time! He could hear a voice inside him commanding him loudly: 'Go on!'

But what about Dambreuse? 'Ah well, it can't be helped! I'll have to tell him I wasn't well.' He rushed off to catch a train and then, sitting in the carriage: 'Perhaps I was wrong? What does it matter, damn it!'

The flat green landscape stretched out all around; the train rumbled along; the little station buildings slipped by like stage sets and the engine spewed out great puffs of smoke, always on the same side; they billowed in the air for a while before dispersing.

Alone in his compartment Frédéric gazed idly out on this view, bored, and sunk in that gentle torpor that comes over you after being too impetuous. But here were hoists and warehouses. It was Creil.

Built on the slopes of two low hills, one bare, the other wooded on top, the town with its church tower, its houses of various shapes and sizes, and its stone bridge, seemed to him a cheerful, discreet and friendly sort of place. A large flat-bottomed boat was moving downstream in the choppy water whipped up by the wind; there was a wayside cross at the foot of which hens were pecking about in some straw; a woman went by carrying damp washing on her head.

Crossing the bridge, he found himself on an island with a ruined abbey on the right. The wheel of a water mill was turning; the mill itself spanned the whole of the second branch of the Oise over which the factory projected. Frédéric was much impressed by the size of the building. His respect for Arnoux increased.

He went in. The woman on the gate shouted to him to come back:

'Where's your permit?'

'What permit?'

'To visit the factory.'

Frédéric answered gruffly that he'd come to see Monsieur Arnoux.

'Who's he?'

'He's the head, the boss, the owner, of course!'

'No sir, this factory belongs to Messrs. Leboeuf and Milliet.'

No doubt the woman was having him on. There were some workmen coming through the gate; he went up to a couple of them and they told him the same.

Frédéric stumbled his way out like a drunk, so bewildered that on the Pont-de-la-Boucherie, a man smoking his pipe asked him if he needed help. He knew Arnoux's factory; it was at Montataire.

Frédéric enquired about a carriage. You could get one only at the station. He walked back there. In front of the luggage office there was one solitary broken-down barouche drawn by an old nag whose harness was coming to pieces and hanging down between the shafts.

A little street urchin volunteered to go and find 'old Pilon'. He came back ten minutes later: old Pilon was having lunch. Frédéric had had enough; he set off on foot. The level-crossing was closed and he had to wait for two trains to go through. At last he marched off into the countryside.

It was green and monotonous, like some vast billiard table. Heaps of iron slag lined both sides of the road like regular ballast. A little further on, he came to a cluster of smoking factory chimneys. In front, on a small mound, stood a little turreted mansion with a square church tower. Below there were long walls winding their way unevenly between trees; the village houses themselves lay spread out at the very bottom.

They were single-storied, with three drystone steps leading up to them. From time to time the tinkle of a grocer's shop-bell could be heard. Clumping feet were struggling through deep layers of black mud; a light drizzle was falling, etching the pale blue horizon with hundreds of lines.

Frédéric kept to the middle of the cobbled street; then on the left, at the entrance to a narrow lane, he came on a high wooden arch bearing the inscription, in gilt lettering: CERAMICS.

Arnoux had not chosen the proximity to Creil by accident: by locating his factory as close as possible to the other one, long established and reputable, he was creating confusion in the minds of the public and thereby enhancing his own prospects.

The main building stood on the very edge of a river running through meadows. The owner's residence stood in a garden and was distinguished by a terrace adorned with four vases of spiky cacti. Heaps of white clay were drying out in hangars; there were other heaps out in the open; and in the middle of the yard stood Sénécal, wearing his inevitable blue greatcoat with the red lining.

The former assistant teacher held out a chilly hand.

'You've come to see the boss, have you? He's away.'

Taken by surprise Frédéric replied stupidly:

'I know,' but quickly recovering added:

'It's something which concerns Madame Arnoux. Is she available?'

'Oh, I haven't seen her these last three days,' replied Sénécal.

He proceeded to recite a whole litany of complaints. When he'd accepted the owner's conditions he'd been expecting to stay in Paris, not to be tucked away in the country, separated from his friends and deprived of newspapers. But never mind, he could put up with that! But Arnoux seemed quite unaware of his qualities. What's more, he was blinkered and reactionary, a complete ignoramus! Instead of artistic innovations, he'd have done better to introduce gas and coal firing. The fellow was *going under*; Sénécal stressed the words. In short, he didn't like the sort of work he was being expected to do and he all but demanded Frédéric to speak up on his behalf for a rise in salary.

'Don't worry!' the other man replied.

He met no one on the stairs. On the first floor he poked his head into an empty room: it was the drawing-room. He called out, very loudly: presumably the cook had gone out and the maid as well; finally, on the second floor, he pushed open a door. Madame Arnoux was alone, standing in front of her wardrobe mirror. Her dressing-gown was half open, its belt dangling down beside her hips. The whole of one side of her hair rippled in a dark wave over her right shoulder; her arms were lifted to support her chignon with one hand while she thrust a hairpin into it with the other. She gave a cry and vanished.

She returned properly dressed. Her figure, her eyes, the rustle of her dress, everything about her held Frédéric spellbound. He could barely restrain himself from covering her with kisses.

'You must forgive me,' she said, 'but I couldn't . . .'

Daringly, he interrupted:

'But . . . you looked very nice . . . a moment ago.'

No doubt she found the compliment a trifle crude, because she flushed. He was afraid he might have offended her. She went on:

'What happy chance brings you here?'

Frédéric didn't know what to say, so to give himself time to collect his thoughts, he gave a snigger.

'If I told you would you believe me?'

'Why shouldn't I?'

Frédéric explained how he'd had a dreadful dream the other night.

'I dreamt you were seriously ill, on the point of dying.'

'Oh, neither my husband or I are ever ill!'

'I was only dreaming about you,' he said.

She looked him calmly in the eyes.

'Dreams don't always come true.'

Frédéric stammered, trying to find words, and finally launched into a rhetorical discourse on twin souls: there was a power capable of overcoming space and establishing a relationship between two people which would make them aware of their feelings and bring them together.

She was listening with her head down and smiling her lovely smile. He watched her delightedly out of the corner of his eye, finding it easier to pour out his love with the help of banalities. She suggested showing him round the factory and, when she insisted, he agreed.

As an amusing introduction, she showed him a sort of museum decorating the staircase. The specimens hanging on the walls or standing on shelves bore witness to Arnoux's successive trials and enthusiasms. After attempting to rediscover the copper-red of the Chinese, he'd wanted to produce majolica, faience, Etruscan, oriental and finally more modern developments. So there was a series of large vases covered in mandarins, bronze lustre bowls, pots with Arabic characters in relief, Renaissance-style ewers and large plates with two dainty, shadowy, human figures, like red chalk sketches. Now he was producing letters for shop-signs and wine-labels; but since his mind was incapable of reaching the peaks of high art and not philistine enough to aim purely at profit, he was falling between two stools and heading for disaster. As they were looking at these things, Marthe went by.

'Don't you recognize this gentleman?' asked her mother.

'Of course I do,' she replied, holding out her hand, while her clear girlish gaze seemed to be wondering suspiciously: 'What's he doing here?' as she continued on her way upstairs, glancing back over her shoulder.

Madame Arnoux now took Frédéric down into the yard and very carefully explained how the clay was crushed, washed and sifted.

'The important thing is preparing the paste.'

She showed him into a large room full of vats, in which a vertical axle with horizontal arms was rotating. Frédéric was growing annoyed with himself for not having flatly refused her suggestion earlier on.

'These are the puggers,' she said.

He thought the word sounded ludicrous and almost indecent on her lips.

Broad belts whirred across the ceiling and twirled over drums; everything was in an exasperating, mathematical, state of constant agitation.

They went out and passed by a dilapidated hut, once a gardener's tool-shed.

'It's not fit for use now,' she said.

'Happiness might find a home there,' he replied. His voice was trembling.

The clatter of the steam-pump drowned his words and they went on into the roughing-in room.

Men were sitting at a narrow table, placing lumps of clay on a potter's wheel, and as they scraped out the inside with their left hand, they gently smoothed the surface, so that you could see the vases rising up like flowers.

Madame Arnoux got them to bring out the moulds used for the more elaborate pieces.

In another room they were working on bands, grooves and raised lines, while on the floor above they were obliterating the joins and filling in any little holes left by previous operations.

There were rows of pots everywhere, on gratings, in corners, down the middle of corridors.

Frédéric was getting bored.

'Are you feeling tired?' she asked.

Afraid that the tour might be brought to an abrupt conclusion, Frédéric pretended that far from being tired, he was very keen to go on. He even said how sorry he was not to have gone into the industry himself.

She seemed surprised.

'Of course! I'd have been able to see more of you!'

Seeing that he was trying to gaze into her eyes Madame Arnoux turned away and picked up from a pier-table some balls of clay left over from unsuccessful attempts at repairs, squeezed them into a flat cake and pressed her hand down on to it.

'May I have that?' asked Frédéric.

'My goodness, what a child you are!'

He was about to reply when Sénécal came in.

Before he was through the door, the deputy manager had spotted a breach in the regulations. The workshop had to be swept out every week and as it was Saturday and the workers had done nothing about it, Sénécal informed them that they would have to stay on an hour later.

'You've only yourselves to blame!'

They bent over their work without a murmur but their heavy breathing left little doubt as to their anger. In any case, they were not easy to handle, for they had all been sacked from the big factory. The republican ruled them with a rod of iron. Being a theoretician, he saw men in the mass and was ruthless towards individuals.

His presence embarrassed Frédéric and he asked Madame Arnoux in a whisper whether they could see the kilns; but just as she was explaining the use of the crucibles, Sénécal pushed his way between them and, without being invited, took over the demonstration, expounding at length on the various kinds of fuel, the firing, the pyroscopes, the kiln hearths, the slips, lustres and metals with an ostentatious display of chemical terms, chloride, sulphur, borax and carbonates. Frédéric couldn't understand a word and kept turning to look at Madame Arnoux.

'You're not listening,' she said, 'even though Monsieur Sénécal is being very clear. He knows much more about all this than I do.'

Flattered by her praise, Sénécal suggested going to see how the colours were applied. Frédéric cast an anxious look at Madame Arnoux. She showed no reaction, no doubt not wanting to be left alone with him nor yet to leave him. He offered her his arm.

'No, thank you very much! The stairs are too narrow.'

When they had reached the top, Sénécal opened the door of a very large room full of women.

They were busy with paint brushes, small bottles, shells and sheets of glass. Along the cornice were rows of engraved plates; tiny scraps of paper floated about in the air; a cast-iron stove threw out a sickening heat which mingled with the smell of turpentine.

The women workers were all squalidly dressed, with one notable exception, who was wearing a headscarf and long ear-rings. Slim but well-covered, she had the big dark eyes and fleshy lips of a black woman. Her ample bosom pressed hard against her shift which was held in at the waist by the cord of her skirt; one elbow rested on the bench while her other arm dangled down at her side; she was staring vacantly out at the landscape. On the table beside her were a few scraps of cold meat and a wine-bottle. In the interests of hygiene and to avoid contaminating the product, it was forbidden to eat in the workshop. Either from a sense of duty or else through sheer bossiness, Sénécal pointed to a framed notice and called out across the room:

'Hi, you there, the lass from Bordeaux! Just read me Article 9 out loud!'

'Well, so what?'

'So what, young woman? You'll be docked three francs from your pay, that's what!'

She stared him insolently in the face.

'Do you think I care? As soon as the boss gets back, he'll let me off! I don't give a damn for you, little man!'

Strutting up and down with his hands behind his back like a master supervising a bunch of schoolboys:

'Article 13, insubordinate behaviour, ten francs!'

The woman from Bordeaux went back to her job. Madame Arnoux had remained discreetly silent but she was frowning. Frédéric said in an undertone:

'Well, for a democrat, you're pretty strict!'

The other retorted peremptorily:

'Democracy doesn't mean unbridled licence for individuals. It means equal status for everyone under the law, fair shares of work and discipline!'

'You're leaving out common humanity!' said Frédéric.

Madame Arnoux slipped her arm into his; perhaps offended by this tacit approval, Sénécal took himself off.

Frédéric was enormously relieved. All that morning he'd been looking for a chance to make his feelings known and now he had it. Furthermore, Madame Arnoux's spontaneous gesture seemed to him to contain a promise; and so he asked if they might go up to her room, on the pretext of wanting to warm his feet. But having sat down beside her, he started to feel embarrassed: he lacked an opening gambit. The thought of Sénécal came to his rescue.

'What an absolutely stupid punishment,' he said.

'You have to be strict sometimes,' replied Madame Arnoux.

'You say that, when you're so kind-hearted yourself? No, that's wrong, you do sometimes like to make people unhappy!'

'I'm not very good at riddles, young man!'

More than her words, the stern look in her eyes brought him up short. He was determined to keep on trying. A volume of Musset was lying on the chest of drawers. He thumbed over a few pages and started to talk about love, with all its delights and depths of despair.

For Madame Arnoux, all that sort of thing was criminal or bogus.

Hurt by this rebuff, the young man countered by quoting the evidence of cases of suicide reported in the papers; he enthused over such literary figures as Phèdre, Dido, Romeo and Desgrieux.* He was giving himself away.

The fire in the hearth had gone out; rain was lashing against the window-panes. Madame Arnoux sat with both hands on the arms of her chair, quite still; her bonnet-tabs dangled down like the head-bands of a sphinx; her clear-cut profile stood out pale against the surrounding shadow.

He longed to fling himself at her feet. He didn't dare.

Moreover he was held back by a sort of religious awe. This dress merging into the shadows seemed to him prodigious, never-ending, quite impossible to lift and, for that very reason, his desire grew stronger than ever. Yet the fear of going too far, or else not going far enough, completely paralysed his power to make up his mind.

'If she doesn't like me,' he thought, 'then let her turn me out! If she does, then she must show me some encouragement!'

He said with a sigh:

'So you don't admit a man's love for a . . . woman?'

Madame Arnoux replied:

'If she's free to marry, then you marry her. If she's not, you leave her and go away.'

'So happiness doesn't exist?'

'Oh yes, it does! But it won't be found in a life full of lies or anxiety or remorse!'

'What does that matter, if the reward is such bliss?'

'It's too high a price!'

He tried irony:

'So virtue's just cowardice?'

'Call it rather clear-sightedness. Even for those women who might forget their duty or their religion, common sense is enough. Selfishness is a good basis for decent behaviour.'

'You produce all these middle-class formulas!'

'Oh, I don't claim to be anyone very grand!'

At that moment her little boy came running in.

'Are you ready for dinner, Mummy?'

'Yes, in a second.'

Frédéric stood up and at the same time Marthe appeared. He couldn't tear himself away. With a pleading look:

'So those women you were talking about must have very hard hearts!'

'No, but when necessary they do have very deaf ears!'

And she stood there in the doorway with her two children at her side. Wtihout saying a word, he bowed; silently, she did the same.

His first feeling was one of stupefaction. He was crushed by the way in which she'd shown him the futility of his hopes. He felt lost, like a man who's fallen into a chasm and knows that he's doomed and that no one will come to his rescue.

However, he kept on walking, blindly, at random, stumbling over boulders. He lost his way. The sound of clogs nearby came to his ears; it was the workers leaving the foundry. Then he recognized where he was.

On the skyline, there was a line of lights traced by the railway lamps. He arrived just as the train was leaving, found himself being pushed into a compartment, and fell asleep.

An hour later, on the boulevards, the liveliness of Paris by night suddenly made his trip seem already part of a distant past. He tried to be strong and relieved his feelings by heaping the most insulting abuse on Madame Arnoux:

'She's a stupid idiot, a silly bitch, let's forget her!'

When he got home he found an eight-page letter in his study written on glossy blue paper, with the initials R. A.

She began by mildly complaining:

'What's up with you, my dear? I'm bored!'

But the handwriting was so dreadful that Frédéric was about to throw the whole thing into the wastepaper basket when his eyes caught the PS:

'I'm relying on you to take me to the races tomorrow!'

What did this invitation mean? Was it another of the Marshal's tricks? But you don't make a fool out of the same man twice without some reason; his curiosity was aroused and he read the letter through carefully.

He was able to decipher: 'Misunderstanding . . . on the wrong track . . . disillusioned . . . poor helpless children that we are . . . like two rivers flowing into each other . . . ,' and so on.

This wasn't at all the lorette's normal style. What had brought about the change?

He continued to hold the sheets of paper in his hand for a long time; they smelt of lilies and in the shape of the letters and the uneven spacing of the lines there was something which reminded him of the disorder of her clothes and disturbed him.

'Why not go?' he said to himself. 'But supposing Madame Arnoux gets to hear about it? Oh, why bother! All the better if she does and it makes her jealous! I'll get some of my own back!'

CHAPTER IV

The Marshal was ready and waiting.

'This *is* nice of you!' She gave him an affectionate glance; she had pretty eyes, full of fun.

After tying her cape, she sat down on her divan and remained silent.

'Shall we be off?' asked Frédéric.

She looked at the clock.

'Not until half past one,' as if she'd privately decided to wait till then before making up her mind.

Then, as the clock struck:

'Right you are, andiamo, caro mio!'

219

She gave one last twist to her hair and issued her instructions to Delphine.

'Will Madame be having dinner at home?'

'Why should we? We'll go out to dinner together some-where, the Café Anglais, wherever you like!'

'Yes, let's do that!'

Her tiny dogs were yapping round her.

'We can take them with us, can't we?'

Frédéric carried them out to the carriage himself. It was a hired berline, with two post-horses and a postilion; he'd put his own manservant on the back seat. The Marshal seemed gratified by so much attentiveness; then, as soon as she'd taken her seat, she asked him whether he'd called on Arnoux recently.

'Not for a month,' Frédéric replied.

'I met him myself a couple of days ago. He'd even have come along today but he's in all sorts of trouble, another lawsuit, I'm not exactly sure. What a funny man!'

'Yes, very funny!'

He added offhandedly:

'By the way, do you still see anything of . . . what did you call him? . . . that ex-singer . . . Delmar?'

She answered abruptly:

'No, that's all over!'

So they'd definitely parted. Frédéric's hopes rose.

They drove at walking pace through the Bréda district; it was Sunday, the streets were deserted and householders' faces could be seen at their windows. The carriage speeded up; at the clatter of wheels, the passers-by turned their heads; the open leather hood was bright and gleaming, the servant stuck out his chest and the two lap-dogs lying side by side on the cushions looked like two ermine muffs. Frédéric was swaying gently to the movement of the spring-braces. The Marshal was looking left and right and smiling.

Her straw hat was trimmed with black lace; it had a lustrous sheen. The hood of her burnous floated in the wind and she was shading herself from the sun under a pagoda parasol of lilac satin.

'What adorable little fingers!' said Frédéric gently taking

hold of her other hand, the left one, which was adorned by a gold curb-chain bracelet. 'I say, that's nice! Where did you get it?'

'Oh, I've had it for ages!' said the Marshal.

The young man raised no objection to this hypocritical reply, preferring to 'seize the opportunity', and still holding her wrist, he pressed his lips between her glove and her cuff.

'Do stop, people'll see us!'

'Good Lord, what does that matter?'

After the place de la Concorde, they followed the quai de la Conférence and the quai de Billy; there was a cedar in a garden; Rosanette thought Lebanon was in China. She laughed at her own ignorance and asked Frédéric to give her some geography lessons. Then, leaving the Trocadéro on their right, they crossed the Pont-d'Iéna and finally came to a halt in the middle of the Champ-de-Mars beside the other carriages already parked in the Hippodrome.

The public was swarming over the grassy slopes. There were spectators on the balcony of the École militaire while the two buildings outside the paddock, the two grandstands inside the enclosure, and a third one in front of the royal enclosure were packed with a smartly dressed crowd whose deferential attitude showed their respect for this recently introduced sport. The race-going public, more exclusive in those days, was less vulgar in appearance: it was the age of trouser-straps, velvet collars and white gloves. The ladies were in gaily coloured, high-waisted dresses and as they sat on the tiers of seats in the stands, they looked like great banks of flowers speckled with black by the dark clothes of the men. But every eye was turned towards the celebrated Algerian Bou-Maza,* sitting impassively between two staff officers in one of the private stands. The Jockey Club stand was occupied exclusively by solemn-looking gentlemen.

The keener fans had taken up their positions down below, next to the track, which was cordoned off by ropes strung between two rows of posts; in the immense oval thus created coconut vendors twirled their rattles while other men were selling race-cards or hawking cigars; a confused babble arose all around; the municipal police were walking up and down in the crowd; a bell hanging from a post covered in numbers rang and five horses appeared. People streamed back into the stands.

Meanwhile large clouds were swirling low over the elms opposite. Rosanette was afraid it might rain.

'I've brought some brollies,' said Frédéric, 'and everything else we need to pass the time', he added, lifting the boot and revealing a hamper full of things to eat and drink.

'What a wonderful man you are! We're set to understand each other!'

'And we're going to get to understand each other even better, aren't we?'

'Could be!' she replied blushing.

The jockeys in their silk jackets were reining their horses in with both hands, trying to get them in line. Someone let fall a red flag, the five jockeys crouched over their horses' manes, and they were off! At first they formed a compact mass but this soon stretched out and split up; half-way round the first bend, the jockey in the yellow jacket nearly came off; for a while Filly and Tibi struggled for the lead; then Tom Thumb took up the running; but Clubstick, left at the start, overhauled them and was first past the post, two lengths ahead of Sir Charles; it was an upset; people yelled; the wooden booths shuddered under the stamping feet.

'What fun!' said the Marshal. 'Darling, I love you!'

Frédéric now felt certain he was home and dry; Rosanette's last words confirmed it.

A hundred yards away a lady appeared in a victoria; she kept sticking her head out of the window and then drawing it back. She repeated this manoeuvre several times; Frédéric couldn't see her face properly. He had a sudden suspicion that it was Madame Arnoux. That couldn't be possible! What would she be doing here? On the pretext of taking a turn round the paddock, he got out of the carriage.

'That's not very gallant of you!' said Rosanette.

He ignored her remark and went off. The victoria swung round and started to trot away.

At that very moment Frédéric was buttonholed by Cisy.

'Hello, my dear fellow, how are things with you? Husson-net's over there. Did you hear what I was saying?'

Frédéric was endeavouring to slip away and catch up with the victoria.

The Marshal was beckoning to him to come back. Cisy caught sight of her and insisted on going over to have a word.

Ever since he had gone out of mourning for his grand-mother, Cisy had been realizing his dream of 'having style'. Tartan waistcoat, bum-freezer, large tassels on his shoes, entrance ticket stuck in his hat-band—nothing had been neglected in order to be, in his own words, 'smart', the smartness of a dashing, rabid anglophile. He began by running down the Champ-de-Mars, a thoroughly lousy racecourse, and proceeded to talk about the racing at Chantilly and the 'rattling good time' you could have there, swore he was capable of downing a dozen glasses of 'champers' in the time it took to strike midnight, invited the Marshal to 'have a little flutter' and gently fondled the lap-dogs; resting his other elbow on the carriage window ledge, he straddled his legs, arched his back, sucked at the top of his riding switch, and kept up an uninterrupted flow of drivel. Frédéric was standing beside him, fuming, and still trying to discover what had become of the victoria.

The bell rang again and Cisy took himself off, to the great pleasure of Rosanette, who found him a bore, so she said.

The second race was nothing special, nor was the third, except for a jockey being carried off on a stretcher. The fourth, with eight horses competing for the Prix de la Ville, was more interesting.

The spectators in the stands had climbed on to their seats. Standing up in their carriages, the others followed the race through their binoculars. As they swooped past the crowds lining the edge of the course, the jockeys looked like red, yellow, white and blue spots. From a distance they didn't seem to be moving particularly fast; at the far end of the Champ-de-Mars they even seemed to be slowing down and somehow sliding along, their horses' bellies brushing the ground with their legs straight out and not bending. But when they raced back at full speed, they became larger; the ground trembled as they sliced through the air, stones were flung up; the wind forced its way into the jockeys' tunics, which flapped like sails in a stiff breeze; the riders lashed the animals with their riding whips to urge them on to the finishing post. The numbers were taken down, another was hoisted in their place; applause greeted the winning horse as it limped, stiff-jointed, covered in sweat and with drooping head, back into the paddock, while its rider sat in the saddle clutching his chest, seemingly at his last gasp.

The start of the final race was delayed by a protest. The bored crowd was starting to disperse. Down at the foot of the stands, groups of men were standing chatting; their talk was not for tender ears and, shocked at having to rub shoulders with tarts, some of the society ladies left.

There were also well-known dance-hall performers, actresses from the little theatres, and it wasn't the prettiest ones who were being most fêted. Old Georgine Aubert, horribly painted up, whom one satirist had dubbed the 'Louis XI of tarts', was lying stretched out in her long barouche, wearing a sable tippet as if it was mid-winter, and every so often emitting a raucous cackle. Having achieved notoriety through her lawsuits, Madame de Remoussot was enthroned in state on the box of a break surrounded by a cluster of Americans; and Thérèse Bachelu, looking as always like a Gothic virgin, was occupying with her flounces the whole of the inside of a 'snail',* whose dashboard had been replaced by a long box of flowers. All these celebrities made the Marshal feel jealous and to draw attention to herself she began to wave her arms about and talk very loudly.

Recognizing her, some of the gentlemen riders bowed and raised their hats. She acknowledged their greetings and told Frédéric their names. They were all counts, viscounts, dukes and marquises; and he swelled with pride for all their eyes expressed a certain admiration for his conquest.

Cisy looked equally happy in the circle of elderly men surrounding him. They were talking patronizingly behind their neckties as if making fun of him; finally, he gave a hasty handshake to the oldest of them and walked over to the Marshal.

With a great display of gluttony, she was attacking a slice of *foie gras*. Frédéric was dutifully following suit, with a bottle of wine on his lap.

The victoria reappeared; it *was* Madame Arnoux. She went deathly pale.

'Give me some bubbly!' said Rosanette.

And holding her full glass up as high as she could, she shouted:

'Good health to all you respectable married women! Especially to the one whose hubby looks after me so nicely! Olé!'

There was a burst of laughter all around; the victoria disappeared. Frédéric was tugging at her dress, on the point of losing his temper; but Cisy now came up. Striking the same attitude as before and cockier than ever, he asked Rosanette if she'd come and have dinner with him that evening.

'Out of the question!' she answered. 'The two of us are going on to the Café Anglais now.'

Cisy went off looking a trifle disconsolate. Frédéric pretended not to have heard anything and said nothing.

While Cisy had been talking at the right-hand window, Hussonnet had come up on the other side and, hearing the mention of the Café Anglais:

'That's not a bad little place! How about going there for a bite?'

'If you feel like it,' replied Frédéric, slumped in a corner of the berline and watching the victoria disappear, with the dreadful feeling that something irreparable had just occurred and that he'd forfeited the great love of his life. And the other sort of love, the slap-and-tickle, was sitting there beside him! He felt weary and in a turmoil of conflicting desires, incapable of knowing what he now wanted, desperately unhappy and wishing he were dead.

He was brought back to reality by the sound of loud voices and footsteps: some young ragamuffins had just climbed over the ropes to come and look at the stands. People were leaving. A few drops of rain fell. The crush of traffic grew worse. Hussonnet had been lost.

'Ah well, it can't be helped!' said Frédéric.

'Nicer to be on our own?' the Marshal added, placing her hand on top of his.

At that moment, with a glitter of brass and steel, a superb landau swept by drawn by four horses and driven, Daumont-style, by two outriders in gold-braided velvet jackets. Madame Dambreuse was sitting beside her husband, with Martinon facing them; all three had a look of astonishment on their faces.

'They've recognized me!' said Frédéric to himself.

Rosanette wanted to stop in order to watch the procession of carriages better. Madame Arnoux might well be coming back. He called out to the postilion:

'Come along, get going!'

And the berline drove off rapidly in the direction of the Champs-Elysées amidst all the other carriages, the barouches, britzskas, wursts, tandems, tilburies, dog-carts, leather-curtained delivery vans full of workers out on the spree singing at the tops of their voices, demi-fortunes* cautiously driven by the head of the family himself. In some victorias crammed with passengers, a youngster could be seen sitting on the floor amongst all the feet, dangling his legs out at the side. Dozing dowagers were being carried along in their large cloth-upholstered broughams or a magnificent high-stepper would trot by drawing a gig as smart and simple as a dandy in evening dress. It was starting to pour. Umbrellas, sunshades and raincoats were being produced; people were hailing each other from afar: 'G'd evening!' 'Everything fine?', 'Yes!', 'No!', 'See you anon!', and faces were flitting by like a magic lantern show. In a sort of daze from watching all these wheels constantly spinning, Frédéric and Rosanette had stopped talking.

Every so often the carriages pressed on too fast and were

forced to pull up several lines abreast; being close together, people could examine each other. Behind carriage doors bearing coats of arms, titled eyes would look casually down on the crowd; envious glances glared out of the depths of public cabs; the stiff-necked and haughty faced sneering smiles; admiring idiots gawped open-mouthed; and here and there a pedestrian would leap backwards to avoid a galloping horseman who was managing to extricate himself from amongst the carriages. Then the whole lot set off again; the coachmen slackened their reins and lowered their long whips; the horses would shake their curbs, scattering froth all around, and their damp cruppers and harnesses steamed in the haze pierced by the setting sun. It shot a reddish shaft of light through the Arc-de-Triomphe, head-high, glinting on the wheel-hubs, the door handles, the tips of the shafts and the saddle-rings; and on each side of the vast avenue that seemed like some great river in which pieces of clothing, horses' manes and human heads were bobbing up and down, the trees shimmering with rain formed two tall green walls. In the sky, the occasional patches of blue were satin-soft.

And Frédéric's mind went back to those now far-off days when he used to envy the unutterable bliss of someone sitting in one such carriage beside one such woman. He was such a man and he was none the happier.

The rain had stopped. The passers-by who'd taken shelter under the arcade of the Garde-Meuble were moving on. In the rue Royale people were making their way up towards the boulevards. In front of the Ministry of Foreign Affairs, sightseers were queueing on the steps.

By the Chinese Baths potholes in the street forced the berline to slow down. A man in a light brown overcoat was walking along the edge of the pavement. A muddy shower of water spurted out from under the carriage springs and spattered his back. The man swung round with a snarl. Frédéric went pale as he recognized Deslauriers.

When they reached the Café Anglais, Frédéric paid off the carriage and Rosanette left him to settle up with the postilion while she went on ahead.

He caught up with her on the staircase, where she was chatting with a gentleman. Frédéric took her by the arm but half-way along the corridor she was stopped by another of her grand acquaintances.

'You go on,' she said. 'One sec and I'm all yours!'

He went into the private room by himself. Through the two open windows, people could be seen at the casements of the houses opposite; parts of the drying asphalt had the shimmer of watered silk and the room was filled with the scent of the magnolia at the edge of the balcony. The fragrance and the cool air relaxed his nerves; he flopped down on to the red divan underneath the mirror.

The Marshal came in and kissed him on the forehead.

'My poor pet's got something on his mind, hasn't he?'

'Perhaps I have,' replied Frédéric.

'Don't worry, you're not the only one!' meaning: 'Let's both forget about it and enjoy ourselves now we're here together!'

She put a petal between her lips and offered it to him to nibble. The gracefulness of this gesture, with its suggestion of gentle sensuality, made his heart melt.

'Why are you so unkind to me?' he asked; he was thinking of Madame Arnoux.

'What, me unkind?'

With both hands on his shoulders she stood looking at him through half-closed eyes.

His fine principles and his resentment were swept away in abject surrender.

Pulling her down on to his lap he said:

'Because you won't love me!'

She didn't resist; he'd put both arms round her waist; her silk dress was shimmering; his excitement grew.

'Where are they?' enquired Hussonnet's voice outside in the passage.

The Marshal sprang to her feet and made for the other end of the room, turning her back on the door.

She asked for some oysters; they sat down at the table.

Hussonnet was not funny. Writing as he did every day

on every sort of subject, reading lots of newspapers, listening to a lot of discussion and tossing off paradoxes in order to dazzle other people, he'd lost his sense of reality and was blinded by his own feeble fireworks. His previously light-hearted existence had turned sour and he lived in a permanent state of unrest; unable to accept his own futility, he'd become grumpy and sarcastic. Talking of the new ballet, Ozäi,* he launched a violent attack, first on dancing in general, then on the Opéra itself, and from there on the Italian Opera, now replaced by a troupe of Spanish actors 'as if we weren't fed up to the teeth with the two Castiles!'. Frédéric's romantic affection for Spain was shocked and to change the subject, he asked about the Collège de France from which Edgar Quinet and Mickiewicz* had just been banned. But Hussonnet was an admirer of Monsieur de Maistre* and expressed support for Authority and Spirituality. At the same time he questioned the most undisputed facts, poured scorn on history, and raised doubts on matters nobody would think of querying, even exclaiming, when geometry was mentioned: 'What utter tripe that is!' He interspersed all this with imitations of actors, his favourite being Sainville.*

These preposterous antics were driving Frédéric to distraction; he shuffled his feet impatiently under the table and his boot caught one of the dogs.

They both set up a fiendish yapping.

'Why not get somebody to take them home?' exclaimed Frédéric.

Rosanette didn't trust anyone.

He turned to the Bohemian:

'How about it, Hussonnet? Be a good chap!'

'Oh yes, my dear, that'd be terribly sweet!'

Hussonnet left without further urging.

What would be his reward for being so obliging? Frédéric didn't bother to think. He was even beginning to find their twosome quite delightful when a waiter came in.

'There's someone asking for you, Madame.'

'What? Someone else?'

'I'm afraid I'll have to go and see,' said Rosanette.

She'd excited him, he'd got to have her. Leaving him like this seemed like letting him down, almost an insult. What was she up to? Wasn't she satisfied with being rude to Madame Arnoux? and as for *Her*, it served her right, anyway! How he loathed all women! His tears were choking him, for his love had been spurned and his lust was being frustrated.

The Marshal came back with Cisy:

'I've asked this gentleman to join us. That was right, wasn't it?'

'Of course, of course!' With an agonized smile Frédéric invited the young viscount to sit down.

The Marshal started going through the menu, stopping at the unfamiliar names.

'How about a rabbit *turban à la Richelieu* and some Orléans pudding to follow?'

'Oh no, not Orléans pudding!' exclaimed Cisy, who was a Legitimist and imagined he was being witty.

'Would you rather have turbot *Chambord*?' she went on.

This pandering to Cisy outraged Frédéric.

The Marshal opted for a plain fillet steak, crayfish, truffles, fresh pineapple and vanilla water ice.

'After that, we'll see. It'll do to begin with. Oh, I forgot, I'd like some sausage, not a garlic one!'

And she persisted in calling the waiter 'young man', tapped her knife on her glass, and tossed the crumb of her bread up at the ceiling. She suggested drinking some Burgundy straightaway.

'People don't drink that at the beginning of a meal,' said Frédéric.

Sometimes you did, according to the viscount.

'Oh no, never!'

'But I assure you some people do!'

'So you see!'

And the look she gave him as she made this remark meant: 'He's a rich man, so just listen to what he says!'

In the meantime, the door kept opening and shutting, the waiters were bawling and in the room next door someone was pounding out a waltz on a dreadful piano.

Then the question of racing brought up the subject of riding and the two rival systems. Cisy was a supporter of Baucher, Frédéric of the Comte d'Aure.*

Rosanette gave a shrug.

'Oh, drop it, for heaven's sake! He knows more about it than you, you know!'

Elbow on table, she was biting into a pomegranate; the candles in the candelabra in front of her flickered in the draught; this white light gave her skin a pearly glow, turning her eyelids pink and making her eyeballs gleam; the redness of the fruit blended with the scarlet of her lips, her thin nostrils were twitching, and her whole person had a sort of insolent, drunken, abandoned air that exasperated Frédéric and gave him a wild longing to possess her.

Then she calmly asked who owned the big landau with the dark red livery.

'Countess Dambreuse,' replied Cisy.

'They've got a lot of money, haven't they?'

'Yes, indeed, although Madame Dambreuse was only plain Mademoiselle Boutron, the daughter of a Prefect and not very well off.'

Her husband on the other hand was due to come into a number of legacies which Cisy proceeded to list; as a frequent guest in their house, he knew all about them.

Determined to be unpleasant, Frédéric insisted on contradicting him: Madame Dambreuse had been a *de* Boutron and he could vouch for her blue blood.

'Never mind that, I'd still like to have her landau,' said the Marshal, lolling back in her armchair.

The sleeve of her dress slipped back and revealed a bracelet set with three opals on her left wrist.

Frédéric caught sight of it.

'Goodness me! Surely that . . .'

They all three stared at each other and blushed. The door opened discreetly a few inches and the brim of a hat appeared, followed by a side-view of Hussonnet's face.

'Excuse me if I'm disturbing the love-birds!'

He stopped short, surprised at seeing Cisy and that he'd taken his seat.

They had another place laid and as he was very hungry, he grabbed an assortment of left-overs at random, some meat from a dish, fruit from a basket, drinking with one hand while he served himself with the other and described his recent errand: the two dogs had been safely delivered. Nothing to report. He'd found the cook with a soldier—this was untrue and invented purely for effect.

The Marshal took her cape down from the hook. Frédéric hurriedly rang the bell, calling to the waiter outside:

'Get a carriage!'

'I've got mine here,' said the viscount.

'But I . . .'

'Well?'

They both stood glaring at each other, pale-faced and with hands trembling.

Finally, the Marshal took Cisy's arm and pointing to the Bohemian, still sitting at the table:

'Do keep an eye on him, he's going to choke himself! I shouldn't like his self-sacrifice on behalf of my two tykes to lead to his death!'

The door swung to behind them.

'Well?' said Hussonnet.

'Well what?'

'I thought . . .'

'What did you think?'

'Weren't you going to . . .'

He completed his sentence with a gesture.

'Of course I wasn't! Not on your life!'

Hussonnet didn't press the point.

In inviting himself to dinner, he had a purpose in mind. His paper, no longer called *L'Art* but *Le Flambard* with the slogan: 'Gunners, stand to!', was in the doldrums and he was keen to turn it into a weekly, on his own, without Deslauriers's collaboration. He talked about his earlier scheme and explained his new plan.

No doubt Frédéric did not really understand; he replied non-committally. Hussonnet gathered up a handful of cigars from the table, said: ''Night, old chap!' and departed.

Frédéric asked for his bill. It was a long one; and as the

waiter stood with his napkin under his arm waiting for the money, another waiter, a pallid individual with a vague resemblance to Martinon, came in and said:

'Beg pardon, sir, the cashier forgot to put the cab on the bill.'

'What cab?'

'The one the gent took earlier on for the little dogs.'

The waiter pulled a long face as if commiserating with the hapless young man. Frédéric felt like punching his nose. He handed back his twenty francs change as a tip.

'Thank you, your honour!' said the waiter with the napkin, making a low bow.

Frédéric spent the whole of the next day chewing over his humiliation and anger. He blamed himself for not slapping Cisy's face. As for the Marshal, he swore he'd never see her again; there were bags of women just as beautiful and since, in order to get women like that, you needed money, he'd play the Stock Exchange with the proceeds of the sale of his farm, he'd get rich and crush the Marshal and all the others under the weight of his opulence. By the evening he was surprised not to have thought once about Madame Arnoux.

'Good job too! What's the point?'

Next day Pellerin called on him at eight o'clock in the morning. He began by admiring the furniture and making other complimentary remarks. Then abruptly:

'You were at the races on Sunday, weren't you?'

'Yes, unfortunately!'

The painter launched into a violent attack on the anatomy of English horses and spoke approvingly of Géricault's and those on the Parthenon. 'Was Rosanette with you?' And he craftily started to sing her praises.

Frédéric's cool reaction nonplussed him. He didn't know how to bring up the question of the portrait.

At first, he had intended to paint a Titian. Gradually, however, he had been lured on by the model's varied colouring and had begun to work freely, piling on brushstrokes and highlights by the dozen. In the beginning Rosanette had been delighted; then her assignations with

Delmar had interrupted the sittings, leaving time for Pellerin to be dazzled by his own work. But his admiration had cooled and he wondered whether his painting was grand enough. He'd gone back to look at the Titians, realized the size of the gap between them and, recognizing his mistake, had started to rework his outlines more simply. Then he'd tried to subdue and blend the tones of the face and the background by softening them; the head had become more solid, the shadows stronger. Finally, the Marshal had come back and had even been impertinent enough to raise objections. The artist had naturally persevered and, though initially infuriated by her stupidity, had admitted she might be right. Then his soul-searching had begun, anguished misgivings which give you stomach cramp, sleepless nights and self-disgust. He'd had the courage to do some retouching but his heart wasn't in the work and he had the feeling that he'd bungled it.

To Frédéric he merely complained at having been turned down for the Salon* and then reproached him for not coming to have a look at the Marshal's portrait.

'She can go to hell!'

Encouraged by this remark:

'Would you believe, the silly bitch now doesn't want it?'

He omitted to mention that he'd asked her a thousand gold francs for it; and the Marshal, more or less unconcerned about who was going to foot the bill and preferring to extract more immediate benefits out of Arnoux, hadn't even mentioned it to him.

'How about Arnoux?' asked Frédéric.

She'd suggested trying him. The ex-art dealer didn't want anything to do with the portrait.

'He claims it's hers.'

'Yes, that's right, so it is.'

'What do you mean? It's she who's sent me to see you about it!' retorted Pellerin.

Had he been convinced that the work was outstanding he might perhaps not have considered turning it into cash. However, money—large amounts of it—would confound

234

the critics and strengthen his own position. Wanting to get rid of him, Frédéric politely asked him his figure.

He was outraged at its exorbitance.

'No, definitely not!'

'But you are her lover and it was you who gave me the commission!'

'Excuse me, I was just the go-between!'

'But I can't have it left on my hands!'

The artist was beginning to lose his temper.

'I must confess I didn't think you were so mercenary!'

'Or you so stingy! Good-day to you!'

Barely had he left than in came Sénécal.

Taken aback, Frédéric stirred uneasily.

'What's the matter?'

Sénécal told him.

'About nine o'clock last Saturday, Madame Arnoux got a letter calling her back to Paris and as there happened to be no one about to go into Creil to fetch a carriage, she wanted me to. I refused because it's not my job. She went off and came back on Sunday night. Yesterday Arnoux turned up unexpectedly at the factory in the morning. That girl from Bordeaux complained to him. I've no idea what the situation is between them but he let her off her fine in front of everybody. We exchanged a few heated words. The long and the short of it is that he paid me off and here I am!'

And stressing each word, he added:

'Anyway I've no regrets, I did my duty. All the same, it's your fault.'

'What do you mean?' exclaimed Frédéric, scared that Sénécal might have found out his secret.

But he hadn't, for he went on:

'I mean that but for you I might have got a better job.'

Frédéric suddenly felt rather guilty.

'What can I do to help you now?'

Sénécal wanted some kind of employment, a settled job.

'That won't be a problem for you, you know so many people, including Monsieur Dambreuse, according to what Deslauriers says.'

This reminder of Deslauriers was disagreeable for his

friend. And he wasn't particularly keen to call on the Dambreuses again since their encounter at the Champ-de-Mars.

'I don't know them well enough to recommend anyone to them.'

The democrat took the rebuff stoically and after a short pause:

'I'm positive all this comes from the Bordeaux woman and from your Madame Arnoux as well.'

This *your* extinguished what little goodwill Frédéric still felt. However, being kind-hearted, he reached for the key of his bureau.

Sénécal forestalled him:

'No thanks!'

Then, forgetting his own troubles, he talked about the affairs of their country—the lavish king's birthday honours list, the cabinet reshuffles, the Drouillard and Bénier* affairs, two current scandals,—denounced the middle classes, and predicted a revolution.

A Japanese kris* hanging on the wall caught his eye. He took it down, handled it and then with a look of disgust flung it on to the settee.

'Goodbye, I must be going, I've got to go to Notre-Dame-de-Lorette.'

'What on earth for?'

'There's a memorial service for Godefroi Cavaignac* today. Ah, there's a man who died with his boots on! But things aren't over yet! . . . Who knows?'

Resolutely he thrust out his hand:

'This may be the last time we ever meet! Goodbye!'

This 'Goodbye' which he twice repeated, his knitted brow as he gazed at the kris, his resignation and, above all, his solemn look, set Frédéric thinking, though not for long.

That same week, his solicitor in Le Havre sent him the proceeds of the sale of his farm, one hundred and seventy-four thousand francs. He split it, investing half in government bonds and handing over the rest to a broker to play the stock market.

He started eating in fashionable little restaurants, frequently went to the theatre, and was trying hard to relax and enjoy himself when he got a letter from Hussonnet telling him with great glee that the Marshal had kicked Cisy out the day after the races. Frédéric was pleased to hear this but didn't attempt to find out why Hussonnet had told him about it.

As chance would have it, he met Cisy three days later. The viscount put a brave face on it and even invited him out to dinner for the following Wednesday.

On the morning of that day, Frédéric received an official communication informing him that Monsieur Charles Jean Baptiste Oudry had, by court order, acquired possession of property located in Belleville and that he was prepared to pay the purchase price of two hundred and twenty-three thousand francs. The document went on to point out that since the mortgage on the property exceeded the purchase price, Frédéric's claim on the property was no longer valid.

The whole trouble stemmed from the failure to re-register the mortgage by the due date. Arnoux had undertaken to do so and then forgotten. Frédéric flew into a rage but when he'd cooled down:

'What the hell? If it might save his skin, good luck to him! It's not the end of the world for me, so let's forget it!'

But while going through papers on his desk, he came across Hussonnet's letter and saw a PS which he'd previously missed. The Bohemian was asking for just five thousand francs, no more, no less, to get his project going.

'He's a pest!'

He wrote a curt note bluntly refusing. After this he dressed to go to the Maison d'Or.

Cisy introduced his other guests, beginning with the most respectable-looking, a large white-haired gentleman.

'The Marquis des Aulnays, my godfather.' Then: 'Monsieur Anselme de Forchambeaux', a slightly built, fair-haired young man, already balding; and pointing to an unpretentious-looking forty-year-old: 'My cousin Joseph Boffreu; and this is my old tutor Monsieur Vezou'; this last man was a cross between a theology student and a carter, with bushy whiskers and a long frock-coat fastened by a single bottom button, producing a shawl-collar effect.

Cisy was still expecting someone else, a Baron de Comaing, 'who may possibly be coming but it's not quite sure'. He kept going out to take a look; he seemed anxious. In the end, at eight o'clock, they all went into a large, magnificently lit room, far too large for the number of guests. Cisy had chosen it deliberately; he liked show.

A silver-gilt epergne laden with fruit and flowers occupied the centre of the table, which was covered with silver dishes, in the old French style; round the edge were small dishes of spiced and salted titbits; jugs of chilled rosé were placed at regular intervals; five glasses of different sizes stood in front of every seat, together with objects whose function was not immediately obvious, an arsenal of ingenious eating implements; and for the first course alone there was sturgeon's cheeks doused in champagne, a York ham cooked in Tokay, thrushes in cheese sauce, roast quails, cream-sauce vols-au-vent, sautéd red-legged partridge, and at either end of this display, dishes of finely sliced truffle potatoes. The enormous room with its red damask hangings was lit by a chandelier and various candelabra. Four waiters in full dress were standing behind the Morocco leather armchairs. The guests exclaimed admiringly, especially the tutor.

'My word, how absolutely superb! Our honourable host really has surpassed himself!'

'This?' said Cisy. 'Oh, come now!'

And having taken his first spoonful:

'Well, my dear des Aulnays, have you been to see *Père et portier** at the Palais-Royal yet?'

'You know very well I haven't got the time!' retorted the marquis.

His mornings were taken up by a forestry course, his evenings at the Farmers' Club, and every afternoon by visits to look at firms manufacturing agricultural equipment. Spending as he did three-quarters of the year in Saintonge,* he took advantage of his trips to the capital to widen his knowledge; his broad-brimmed hat lying on a pier-table was crammed with pamphlets.

Seeing Monsieur de Forchambeaux refusing wine, Cisy said:

'For heaven's sake man, drink up! You're being very spineless for your last bachelor meal!'

Everyone leaned forward to congratulate him.

'And I'm sure the lucky young lady is extremely charming!'

'She is indeed!' exclaimed Cisy. 'All the same, he's making a mistake! Marriage is stupid!'

'You're not thinking what you're saying, my dear boy,' said Monsieur des Aulnays and his eyes became moist at the thought of his dead wife.

And Forchambeaux chanted with a grin:

'They'll get you yet! They'll get you yet!'

Cisy protested. He preferred having a good time, being a 'man about town'. He wanted to learn the savate,* visit the low grog-shops in the Cité, like Prince Rodolphe in the *Mystères de Paris*.* He pulled a clay pipe out of his pocket; he was drinking too much, bullying the waiters and, to prove his sophistication, continually criticizing the food. He even sent the truffles back to the kitchen and the tutor, who adored them, said sycophantically:

'They're not a patch on your grandmother's "floating islands"!'

Then he turned again towards his neighbour, the farming expert, who found many advantages in living in the country, if only because he could bring up his daughters with simple tastes. The tutor enthusiastically approved, being anxious to curry favour, because he imagined he might have influence over his pupil, with whom he was secretly hoping to get a job as steward.

Frédéric had come with a strong feeling of grievance against Cisy but was disarmed by his silliness. All the same, his gestures, his face, his whole person kept reminding him of the dinner at the Café Anglais and he was beginning to grate on his nerves; he was also listening to the unflattering comments about him being whispered by the cousin Joseph, a stockbroker and an affable young man, far from wealthy, who was fond of shooting. Cisy jokingly several times called him 'a thief'; then suddenly:

'Ah, here comes the baron!'

In came a well set-up young man of thirty, somewhat brusque in manner, with a springy stride, his hat cocked over one ear and a flower in his buttonhole. He was the viscount's Ideal Man. In his delight at having captured him and stimulated by his presence, he even tried to produce a pun: as the grouse was being passed round, he said:

'Well, we certainly can't grouse about the baron!'

He then proceeded to ply Monsieur de Comaing with questions concerning people quite unknown to his guests and then, as though struck by a sudden idea:

'Oh, by the way, did you think of me?'

The other man shrugged:

'You're not old enough, my lad! Not a hope!'

Cisy had asked him to get him into his club. No doubt wanting to soothe his wounded pride, the baron added:

'Oh, I was forgetting! Many congratulations on your bet, my dear chap!'

'What bet?'

'The one you made at the races that you'd go back to that young woman's place that very night!'

Frédéric felt as if he'd been slashed by a whip. Cisy's look of discomfiture immediately soothed his feelings.

In fact, the Marshal had been extremely embarrassed next morning when her first lover Arnoux, her man, had turned up that very day. They had both made it very plain to the viscount that he was 'in the way' and had unceremoniously shown him the door.

Cisy seemed not to have heard. The baron went on:

'What's dear old Rosie up to these days? . . . Are her legs still as nice as ever?', thereby proving that they were very closely acquainted.

This discovery annoyed Frédéric.

'No need to blush,' the baron went on. 'She's a first-rate proposition!'

Cisy clicked his tongue.

'Pooh! Not as hot as all that!'

'Really?'

'Yes, honestly. In the first place, as far as I'm concerned, she's not all that wonderful and in the second place, women like her can be picked up all over the place because, let's face it, she's for sale!'

'Not to everybody!' Frédéric interposed sharply.

'He thinks he's different from everyone else!' replied Cisy. 'What a joke!'

A titter ran round the table.

His heart was beating so fast that he could scarcely breathe. He gulped down two glasses of water in quick succession.

The baron had pleasant memories of Rosanette, all the same.

'Is she still with that man Arnoux?'

'I've no idea,' replied Cisy. 'I don't know the gentleman!'

All the same, he did suggest he was a bit of a crook.

'Steady on!' exclaimed Frédéric.

'But there's no doubt about it. He's even been hauled up before the courts.'

'That's not true!'

Frédéric sprang to Arnoux's defence, vouching for his honesty with facts and figures made up as he went along, and even beginning to believe what he was saying himself. Still smarting with resentment and tipsy into the bargain, the viscount persisted in his assertions until Frédéric said to him solemnly:

'Are you trying to offend me, sir?'

He glared at him with eyes as glowing as his cigar.

'No, not in the least! I'm even ready to concede that he has one very good thing in his favour—his wife!'

'So you know her, do you?'

'Of course I do! Everybody knows old Sophie Arnoux!'*

'What did you say?'

Cisy, who had got to his feet, spluttered:

'Everybody knows old Sophie!'

'Don't you dare say that! She's not the sort of woman you associate with!'

'No, thank God!'

Frédéric flung his plate at his face.

241

It shot across the table, smashed a fruit dish, hit the epergne, shattered into three pieces and struck the viscount in the stomach.

Everyone sprang forward to restrain him. He was shouting and struggling in a sort of frenzy; Monsieur des Aulnays kept saying:

'Calm down! Calm down! Really, dear boy!'

'But this is dreadful!' the tutor was crying.

Forchambeaux, who'd gone as livid as the plums, was trembling; Joseph was laughing his head off; the waiters were sponging up the wine and picking the broken glass and other things up from the floor; and the baron went over to close the window, because the uproar could be heard in the street above the noise of the traffic.

Since at the moment when the plate was thrown, they'd all been talking at once it proved impossible to ascertain the exact cause of the offence, whether it was Arnoux, his wife, Rosanette or someone else. The only certainty was Frédéric's incredibly uncouth behaviour, for which he categorically refused to offer the slightest apology.

Aided by the cousin, the tutor and even Forchambeaux, Monsieur des Aulnays attempted to calm him down. Meanwhile the baron was comforting Cisy who was in tears, suffering from nervous reaction. Frédéric, on the other hand, was growing increasingly irritated and they would all have been there till the early hours had the baron not put an end to the matter by saying:

'The viscount will arrange for his seconds to call on you tomorrow, Monsieur Moreau.'

'What time?'

'Will twelve noon suit you?'

'Perfectly!'

Once outside, Frédéric took a deep breath; he'd been holding his feelings pent-up far too long and now at least they had found release. He felt proud, manly, an exhilarating flow of inner strength. He'd need two seconds. The first person who came to his mind was Regimbart and he promptly made his way to a tavern in the rue Saint-Denis. The front was closed down but a light could be seen through a pane of glass above the door. It opened and, ducking under the shutters, he went in.

The room was lit by a tallow candle on the edge of the bar which was deserted. The stools had been up-ended on the tables and in the corner, next to the kitchen, the owner and his wife were having supper with their waiter. Regimbart was sitting with his hat on sharing their meal and even crowding the waiter, who was forced to turn sideways each time he took a bite. Frédéric briefly explained what had happened and appealed for his help. The Citizen rolled his eyes and seemed at first to be pondering. Without replying, he walked up and down the room several times before finally saying:

'All right, I'll be glad to!'

And when he heard that the opponent was a viscount, his face lit up with a murderous grin.

'Don't worry, we'll soon settle his hash. But first things first: it'll be swords.'

'But do I have the right . . .?' Frédéric objected.

'I'm telling you, we're going for swords,' the Citizen retorted curtly. 'Do you know how to shoot?'

'A bit . . .'

'Ah, a bit! That's what they all say! And yet they're all keen to have a go! Now just listen to me: stay back, keep your distance, circle round and keep on disengaging, it's quite within the rules! Tire him out! And then lunge at him, hard! And above all, don't try to be too clever, none of La Fougère's* tricks! No, just a simple one-two and disengage! Here, watch me! You turn your wrist, like turning a key in a lock. Vauthier, just hand me your stick! Ah, this'll do.'

He picked up the pole used to light the gas, bent his right arm, curved his left one upwards, and began lunging at the partition. He was stamping his foot, working himself into a state of excitement and even pretending to be having problems, as he shouted: 'You're there, are you? Are you there?'; his enormous figure was silhouetted on the wall and his hat seemed to be touching the ceiling. Every so often the landlord said: 'Well done! Very good!' and his wife was also admiring him, rather uneasily, while Théodore, an old soldier and a great fan of Regimbart's in any case, sat transfixed with awe.

Early next morning, Frédéric hurried round to Dussardier's shop. After going through a series of rooms filled with lengths of cloth, on shelves or spread out over tables, and a few mushroom-shaped wooden stands draped with shawls, he finally caught sight of him standing in a sort of wire cage writing at a desk and surrounded by account books. The nice young fellow immediately dropped his work and came along with Frédéric.

Cisy's seconds arrived before noon. Frédéric thought it proper not to be present.

The baron and Joseph declared they'd be satisfied with the most perfunctory of apologies. But on the principle of never giving an inch and anxious to defend Arnoux's reputation—Frédéric hadn't mentioned anything else—Regimbart insisted that it was up to the viscount to apologize. Monsieur de Comaing was appalled at such effrontery. The Citizen refused to budge. Since reconciliation was thus out of the question, they would have to fight.

Other problems arose, for choice of weapons lay, technically, with the offended party, Cisy. Regimbart, however, maintained that by issuing the challenge, Cisy was now the offender. His seconds protested strongly that a slap in the face was surely the most blatant insult. The Citizen started hair-splitting: a blow wasn't a slap. In the end, it was decided to get the advice of the military and the four seconds set off to find a barracks somewhere and consult some officers.

They stopped at the one on the quai d'Orsay and Monsieur de Comaing went up to a couple of captains to explain the issue.

With Regimbart putting in his oar, the bewildered officers hadn't the faintest idea what it was all about. They advised the gentlemen to draw up a detailed statement and they would then give their final verdict.

The four men repaired to a café. For greater secrecy, they designated Cisy as H and Frédéric as K.

They then trooped back to the barracks. The two captains had gone out. On their return, they confirmed that the choice of weapons obviously lay with Monsieur H. All four now went back to Cisy's place. Regimbart and Dussardier waited outside on the pavement.

When the viscount heard the decision, he was so upset that they had to repeat it to him several times; and when the baron named Regimbart's demands, he muttered: 'Well, then?', being not too reluctant, for his part, to accept them. Then he collapsed into an armchair and declared he wasn't going to fight.

'What's that?' exploded Monsieur de Comaing.

Cisy started babbling incoherently. He wanted to fight with a blunderbuss, at point-blank range, with only one pistol.

'Or else you can put some arsenic in a glass and draw lots to decide who drinks it. They do that sometimes, I read about it somewhere!'

Quick-tempered by nature, the baron said roughly:

'These gentlemen are waiting for your reply. This is getting beyond a joke! What are you going to choose? Make up your mind! Is it swords?'

The viscount nodded agreement and the encounter was fixed for seven o'clock sharp next day at the Porte-Maillot.

Dussardier had to get back to work, so Regimbart went off to warn Frédéric.

He'd been left without any news all day and his patience had reached breaking point.

'That's fine!' he exclaimed.

The Citizen was pleased at his reaction.

'Just imagine, they wanted us to apologize! They weren't hoping for much, one word would have been enough. But I sent them off with a flea in their ear! That was the right thing to do, don't you agree?"

'I suppose so,' said Frédéric, thinking to himself he'd have done better to pick a different second.

Then, when he was alone, he said to himself several times:

'I'm going to fight a duel! My goodness, I'm going to fight a duel! Isn't that odd!'

He was walking up and down in his bedroom; as he passed in front of his mirror, he noticed that he looked pale.

'I wonder if I'm scared?'

He was suddenly thrown into a dreadful panic at the thought of being afraid during the duel.

'But supposing I'm killed? That's what happened to my father! Yes, I'm going to be killed!'

And suddenly he saw his mother dressed in black; incoherent images kept flashing through his mind. He was exasperated at his own cowardice. He was swept up in a wild burst of bravery. He was lusting for blood. He could have tackled a whole battalion. When this rush of blood had died down, he was delighted to feel himself no longer vulnerable. He went off to the Opéra where they were giving a ballet. He listened to the music, scrutinized the ballerinas and drank a glass of punch during the interval. But when he got home, the sight of his study and his furniture, which he might be seeing for the last time, made him feel faint.

He went down into his garden. The stars were bright and as he gazed up at them, the thought that he was fighting for a woman made him feel grander and nobler. He went to bed at peace with the world.

Not so Cisy. After the baron had gone, Joseph tried to cheer him up and when the viscount failed to respond:

'Look here, old man, if you want to let the whole thing drop, I'll go along and let them know.'

Cisy didn't have the guts to say: 'Go ahead', but he was annoyed with his cousin for not doing so on his own initiative.

He'd have liked Frédéric to die of apoplexy during the night, or rioters suddenly to put up barricades to block access to the Bois-de-Boulogne, or for something to prevent one of the seconds from turning up, because without seconds the duel couldn't take place. He longed to take a fast train to anywhere. He was sorry he didn't know some sort of medicine which would make him seem dead, without actually putting his life in danger. He even reached the stage of wanting to fall ill, very ill.

He tried to get in touch with Monsieur des Aulnays for help and advice, but this kindly man had gone back to Saintonge on receiving a telegram that one of his daughters wasn't well. To Cisy this seemed an ill omen. Fortunately his tutor Monsieur Vezou came round. He confessed his misgivings.

'What can be done, for heaven's sake? What can be done?'

'Well, if I were you, my dear count, I'd hire some thug to give him a good hiding.'

'He'd always find out who arranged it,' replied Cisy.

He kept making little moaning sounds.

'And do we really have the right to fight a duel?'

'It's a relic of a barbarous age. What can one do?'

The tutor invited himself to dinner, purely to oblige his pupil; his charge ate nothing and after the meal felt the need for a stroll.

Passing by a church, he said:

'Shall we go in for a second, just to look?'

Vezou was happy to agree and even offered him the holy water.

It was May; the altar was covered in flowers, voices were pealing, the organ was booming; but he found it impossible to pray, for any religious ritual reminded him of funerals; he could almost hear the chanting of the 'De profundis'.

'Let's go, I'm not feeling very well!'

They spent the whole night playing cards. To guard against bad luck, the viscount made every effort to lose and Monsieur Vezou was very happy to aid and abet him. Finally, in the early hours, Cisy slumped down over the baize, completely exhausted, and fell into a troubled sleep.

However, if courage means trying to overcome your weakness, the viscount showed courage; his vanity warned him that any backing down now would disgrace him, so when his seconds came to fetch him, he did his best to pull

247

himself together. Monsieur de Comaing complimented him on looking so well.

But during the drive, the swaying of the cab and the heat of the morning sun unnerved him. His energy had evaporated. He couldn't even make out where he was.

The baron enjoyed adding to his distress by talking about the 'corpse' and the way to smuggle it back into town. Joseph played up to him; they both considered it a ludicrous affair and were convinced it would be settled amicably.

Cisy's head was sunk on his chest; he now gingerly raised it and pointed out that they hadn't brought a doctor along.

'There's no point,' said the baron.

'So there's no danger?'

Joseph replied in solemn tones:

'We sincerely hope not!'

A hush fell in the cab.

At ten minutes past seven they arrived at the Porte-Maillot. Frédéric was there with his seconds, all three dressed in black. Instead of a necktie, Regimbart had a military horsehair collar and was carrying the sort of long violin case reserved for such occasions. They exchanged frigid greetings. Then they all struck out into the Bois-de-Boulogne along the route de Madrid looking for a suitable spot.

Regimbart said to Frédéric, who was walking between Dussardier and himself:

'Got the wind up a bit, have we? Well, if there's something you need, say the word, I know what it's like! It's only natural to feel afraid!'

Then in an undertone:

'No smoking, if softens you up!'

Frédéric tossed away his cigar, which had been giving him some trouble, and strode on firmly. The viscount was walking behind, leaning on his seconds' arms.

They met a few passers-by. The sky was blue; the odd rabbit could be heard scampering away. At a bend in the track, a woman in a headscarf was chatting to a man in a smock, while in the main avenue, grooms in linen jackets were exercising their horses. Cisy was recalling those happy days when, with his monocle in his eye, he'd canter along beside carriage doors on his chestnut; these memories increased his distress; he was suffering from a burning, unendurable thirst; the droning of flies mingled with the pounding of his arteries; his feet kept sinking into the sand; he felt as if he'd been walking since the beginning of time.

The seconds kept peering both sides of the road, without stopping. They debated whether to go on to the Croix-Catelan or to the foot of the walls of Bagatelle.* In the end, they turned off to the right and stopped amongst some pines where the trees were arranged in staggered rows.

They picked an area with equally level ground for each party and marked out the places for them to stand. Regimbart opened his case. Inside were four charming hollow-ground swords with filigree handles lying on padded red leather. Through the leaves, a ray of sun fell on them and they seemed to Cisy like silver vipers in a pool of blood.

The Citizen showed that they were of equal length; he picked a third one for himself to part the opponents if necessary. Monsieur de Comaing was carrying a stick. A hush fell. They all looked at each other; every face seemed grim or apprehensive. Frédéric had removed his frock-coat and waistcoat. Joseph helped his cousin to do the same; when his necktie was undone a religious medal could be seen round his neck. Regimbart gave a pitying smile.

In order to allow Frédéric a little further time for reflection, Monsieur de Comaing raised a quibble. He insisted on the right to wear a glove and to seize hold of an opponent's sword with the left hand. Regimbart agreed; he was keen to get on with it. Finally, the baron turned to Frédéric:

'It's up to you, sir! There's never any disgrace in acknowledging you're in the wrong!'

Dussardier nodded his approval. The Citizen became indignant.

'Do you think we're here to shell peas, damn it? . . . On guard!'

The adversaries stood facing each other, with their seconds on either side. He gave the signal.

'Go!'

Cisy went as white as a sheet. The point of his sword was quivering like the tip of a riding whip. His head jerked back, his arms swung outwards and he fell flat on his back in a faint. Joseph raised him up and shook him violently, pushing a bottle of smelling salts under his nose. The viscount opened his eyes and made a sudden leap for his sword, like a man possessed. Frédéric had kept his raised and was standing watchfully, waiting for the attack.

There was a sound of galloping and a voice shouting: 'Stop! Stop!' as the hood of a cab smashed its way through the branches. A man was leaning out of the window waving a handkerchief and still calling: 'Stop! Stop!'

Thinking it was the police, Monsieur de Comaing raised his stick:

'That's that, gentlemen! The viscount's bleeding!'

'Am I?' said Cissy.

In fact, in his tumble he'd grazed his left thumb.

'But that was when he fell!' the Citizen observed.

The baron affected not to hear.

Arnoux had jumped out of the cabriolet.

'I'm too late! Oh no, thank God!'

He'd clasped Frédéric in his arms and was showering him with kisses.

'Oh, I know the reason. You wanted to stand up for your old friend! Oh, that's wonderful, really wonderful. I'll never forget it! Oh, what a good, kind man you are! My dear boy!'

He was gazing at him, positively blubbering and grinning with joy. The baron turned to Joseph.

'I think we may be in the way at this little family celebration. It's over and done with, isn't it, gentlemen? Viscount, put your arm in a sling. Here, take my scarf.' Then, with a peremptory wave of his hand: 'Come now, no hard feelings! Do the right thing!'

The two opponents exchanged a limp handshake. The viscount, Monsieur de Comaing and Joseph disappeared while Frédéric and his friends went off in the other direction.

As they weren't far from the Restaurant de Madrid, Arnoux suggested a glass of beer there.

'We could even have breakfast,' said Regimbart.

But Dussardier couldn't spare the time, so they confined themselves to a drink in the garden. All four were in that state of elation that comes from a happy ending. The Citizen was, however, annoyed that the duel had been scotched at the eleventh hour.

When he'd heard about the affair from one of Regimbart's cronies, a certain Compain, Arnoux had been extremely touched and impulsively rushed off to prevent it, in the belief, in fact, that he was the cause. He asked Frédéric to tell him the details. Frédéric was also touched by this proof of affection and was reluctant to add to his illusions:

'No, don't let's talk about it!'

Arnoux thought this discretion showed great delicacy of feeling. Then, volatile as ever, he changed the subject:

'What news, Citizen?'

And they started to talk bank-drafts and date-lines. For greater secrecy, they even retreated to hold a whispered conversation at another table.

Frédéric managed to pick out phrases such as: 'You'll underwrite it for me . . .', 'Yes, but of course you must . . .', 'In the end I settled for three hundred . . .', 'My word, that's a damned good commission!' In short it was obvious that Arnoux was involved in a large number of shady deals with the Citizen.

Frédéric thought of reminding him about the fifteen thousand francs. But his action that morning had put any rebuke, however gentle, out of the question. Anyway, he felt tired. The place wasn't appropriate. He'd put it off to some later date.

Sitting in the shade of a privet, Arnoux was puffing away very cheerfully at his cigar. He looked up at the doors of the private rooms, all opening on to the garden, and remarked that he'd been there a good deal in the old days.

'Not by yourself, I daresay?' the Citizen said.

'What do you think!'

'What an old goat you are! And a married man too!'

'Well, what about you?' retorted Arnoux; and with an indulgent smile: 'I'll even bet any money that old rogue's got a room tucked away somewhere to entertain little girlies in!'

The other man merely arched his eyebrows to admit the soft impeachment. Then our two gentlemen went on to discuss their tastes: Arnoux now liked 'em young, little working-class girls; Regimbart couldn't abide 'stuck-up' women; he favoured the 'no-nonsense' variety. The conclusion drawn by the ceramics manufacturer was that it was wrong to take women seriously.

'And yet he loves his wife,' reflected Frédéric as he made his way home. He considered him a blackguard and felt resentment towards him over the duel, as if he'd just risked his life on his account.

But he was grateful to Dussardier for supporting him so loyally and before long, with his encouragement, the clerk was coming round to see him every day.

Frédéric lent him books: Thiers, Dulaure, Barante, Lamartine's *Les Girondins*.* The nice young man would listen to him with rapt attention and accepted his views unquestioningly.

One evening he arrived full of dismay.

On the boulevard that morning, a man had run full tilt into him, recognized him as a friend of Sénécal's, and said: 'They've just nabbed him! I'm off.'

It was quite true. Dussardier had spent the whole day making enquiries. Sénécal was under lock and key, charged with attempted assassination.

Sénécal had been born in Lyons the son of a foreman; he'd been taught at secondary school by one of Chalier's* former supporters and on arriving in Paris had immediately joined the Société des Familles.* The police had their eye on him and his habits were well known. He'd played an active part in the May 1839 riots, since when he'd lain low; he'd become increasingly fanatical and as a passionate admirer of Alibaud,* he combined his personal grudge against society with the people's dislike of monarchy; every morning he'd wake up hoping for a revolution that would change the face of the world in the space of a couple of weeks, or a month. Finally, in disgust at the flabbiness of his fellow members, infuriated by the delays in the realization of his dreams, and in despair at the state of the country, he'd become involved in the incendiary bomb plot, using his skills as a chemist, and had been caught red-handed in possession of gunpowder, which he was intending to try out in Montmartre in a final attempt to set up a republic.

Dussardier had an equally strong affection for republicanism which, in his eyes, stood for liberation and universal happiness. In 1834, in front of a grocer's in the rue Transnonain*—he was fifteen at the time—he'd seen soldiers with bayonets red with blood and hair sticking to their rifle-butts; ever since, he'd felt bitter resentment against government as the embodiment of Injustice. He made little distinction between murderers and policemen; a police spy was the sort of man who'd kill his father. In his simplistic view, Power was responsible for all evil and he loathed it with a permanent, deep-seated, heartfelt and carefully cultivated hatred. He'd been dazzled by Sénécal's impassioned harangues. What did it matter whether or not he was guilty of trying to commit a horrible crime? He was the victim of Authority and must be helped.

'The Peers will certainly condemn him and then he'll be taken away in a police van like a convict and shut up on the Mont-Saint-Michel where the government lets them die! Austen went mad! Steuben committed suicide! To get Barbès into his cell, they had to drag him along by his legs and hair! They trampled all over his body and his head banged against every step on the stairs! It's obscene! They're swine!'

He was pacing round the room like a man distraught, choking with sobs.

'But we ought to do something! Let's work something out, I can't think properly myself! How about trying to rescue him? While they're taking him to the Luxembourg, we could overpower his escort in the corridor! A dozen determined men can always get through anywhere!'

There was a feverish gleam in his eye that sent a shudder down Frédéric's back.

Sénécal now seemed a greater man than he'd thought. He recalled all that he'd suffered, his spartan way of life, and without sharing Dussardier's enthusiasms, he did feel for him the sort of admiration that anyone arouses who's sacrificing his life for a cause. He said to himself that, had he helped Sénécal, the man wouldn't be where he was now. The two friends searched long and hard to find some way of rescuing him.

It proved impossible for them to get in touch with him, so Frédéric set about gathering information as to his fate from newspapers and for three weeks spent a good deal of time in public reading rooms.

One day he came across several copies of *Le Flambard*. Its leading article was invariably devoted to tearing some famous man or other to pieces. Then came the gossip column and society news. Next, they poked fun at the Opéra, Carpentras,* fish-farming and people condemned to death, if there were any. The sinking of a passenger steamer was a year-long source of amusement. The third column contained an art section in the form of advice or anecdotes and provided tailors' advertisements, reports of parties and auction sales, book reviews; a collection of verse would be treated in the same vein as a pair of boots. The only serious part of the magazine was criticism of the little theatres, in which two or three managers were constantly hounded and the interests of Art were invoked on behalf of the stage sets of the Funambules or the female leads at the Délassements.

Frédéric was just about to toss it all away when his eye was caught by an article headed 'A pullet and three roosters'. It was a sprightly account of his duel, with spicy undertones. He had no difficulty in recognizing himself, for he was humorously referred to throughout as 'the young man from Sens (who failed to acquire any sense at school)'. He was even represented as a miserable country bumpkin, a dim nonentity trying to rub shoulders with his betters. The viscount was given the hero's role, first of all at the supper, when he forced his attentions on Frédéric, then with the bet, since he got the girl, and finally in the duel, where he behaved like a true aristocrat. Frédéric's courage wasn't directly impugned but it was hinted that a third party, the girl's patron himself, had interceded in the nick of time. The sting came in the tail, hinting at further unpleasantness:

'What's the secret of their great affection? It's puzzling! And in the words of Don Basilio,*who the devil's fooling whom?'

There was absolutely no doubt that Hussonnet was getting his own back because Frédéric had declined to let him have those five thousand francs.

What could he do? If he demanded satisfaction, the Bohemian would protest his innocence. The best thing was to take it lying down and say nothing. After all, nobody read *Le Flambard*.

As he left the reading room, he saw a number of people gathered outside an art gallery. They were gazing at the portrait of a woman with these words written underneath in black: 'Mademoiselle Rose-Annette Bron, the property of Monsieur Frédéric Moreau, of Nogent'.

It was definitely her—more or less—seen from the front with her breasts exposed and hair hanging loose; in her hands she was holding a red velvet purse while, behind her, a peacock was poking its beak forward over her shoulder and fanning out its immense tail-feathers against a wall.

Pellerin was exhibiting the portrait to force Frédéric to pay up, fully convinced that he was famous and that all Paris society would take this daub to their hearts and rally round him.

Was it a conspiracy? Were the painter and the reporter working hand in glove?

His duel had failed to protect him. He was becoming a figure of fun; everybody was laughing at him.

Three days later, at the end of June, the *Nord* shares jumped fifteen francs and as he'd bought two thousand of them the month before, he found himself thirty thousand francs better off. This lucky break restored his confidence. He said to himself that he didn't need anyone, that all his troubles stemmed from shyness and vacillation. He should have been tough with the Marshal from the start, refused Hussonnet point-blank, and not become involved with Pellerin; so to prove how little he cared, he went to one of Madame Dambreuse's regular evening parties.

Martinon was standing in the middle of the entrance hall, having just arrived; he looked round:

'Good Lord, what are you doing here?' He seemed surprised and almost put out.

'Paying a call. Shouldn't I be?'

And Frédéric proceeded into the drawing-room, wondering why Martinon had greeted him like that.

Despite the corner lamps, the light was dim, for the tall, wide-open windows formed three parallel black squares of shadow. Under the pictures in the gaps between them were plant-stands reaching head-high and at the far end was a mirror reflecting a silver teapot and a samovar. There was a gentle buzz of voices. Dancing pumps moved over the carpet, squeaking.

He had an impression of black tail-coats, then a round table lit by a lamp under a large shade, seven or eight women in summer dresses and just beyond, in a rocking chair, Madame Dambreuse wearing a lilac taffeta gown whose slashed sleeves were frothy with puffs of muslin; the subdued tone of the material matched her hair. She was leaning slightly backwards with the tip of her foot resting on a cushion, a delicate and serene work of art, a pedigree hothouse flower.

Monsieur Dambreuse was walking up and down the room with a white-haired old gentleman. Here and there a few of the men were talking, perched on the edges of small divans; the rest were standing in a circle in the middle. Their conversation was about votes, amendments, amendments to amendments, Monsieur Grandin's speech and Monsieur Benoist's reply. The centre party really was going too far! The centre left should have been more mindful of its origins! The government had suffered a set-back. It was reassuring that there wasn't an immediate succession in view. In a word, the situation was identical to that obtaining in 1834.

These things bored Frédéric, so he joined the ladies. Martinon was standing close by with his hat under his arm, three-quarters face, and suitably posed to look like a piece of Sèvres. He picked up a copy of the *Revue des deux mondes* lying on the table between an *Imitation of Christ* and a copy of Gotha's *Almanach*, volunteered some patronizing criticism of an eminent poet, announced that he was attending the Saint Francis Xavier lectures,*complained of having a sore throat and swallowed a couple of lozenges, meanwhile talking about music and being generally jaunty. Monsieur Dambreuse's niece was embroidering a pair of cuffs for herself and watching him surreptitiously through her pale blue eyes; the snub-nosed governess Miss John had dropped her tapestry work; they both seemed to be exclaiming inwardly:

'Isn't he handsome!'

Madame Dambreuse turned towards him:

'Do fetch my fan from that pier-table over there! No, that's not the one, that one over there!'

She stood up and as he was coming back, they met face to face in the middle of the drawing-room; she uttered a few sharp words, no doubt to tell him off, judging by her arrogant expression. Martinon forced a smile and went over to the earnest group of men. Madame Dambreuse returned to her seat and leaning over sideways said to Frédéric:

'I met someone who mentioned you a couple of days ago—a Monsieur de Cisy. You know him, don't you?'

'Oh yes . . . just slightly.'

Suddenly Madame Dambreuse exclaimed:

'Oh, Duchess, how very nice!' and went over to the door to meet a little old lady wearing a light-brown taffeta dress and a lace bonnet with long tabs. As the daughter of a companion in exile of the future Charles X and widow of an imperial marshal who had been made a peer in 1830, she had a foot in both the old and the new royal families and could be instrumental in obtaining many things. The men standing talking moved to one side and then continued their discussion.

They were now dealing with the question of poverty, whose ravages, in the view of these gentlemen, were grossly exaggerated.

'All the same', Martinon objected, 'we must admit that extreme poverty does exist. But the cure doesn't depend either on science or on the government. It's purely a matter for the individual. When the lower classes are ready to give up their vices, they'll no longer be needy. So the people must become more moral, and then they'll no longer be so poor!'

According to Monsieur Dambreuse, nothing good would be achieved without an unlimited supply of capital. So the only possible course was to place Progress, 'as indeed the Saint-Simonians had said—goodness me, didn't they have some good ideas, honour where honour's due—to place Progress in the hands of those capable of increasing the public wealth!' By degrees they moved on to the development of heavy industry, railways and coal-mining. Monsieur Dambreuse whispered to Frédéric:

'You didn't come and see me about that little matter of ours.'

Frédéric pleaded ill health but, feeling that his explanation was a bit lame:

'And I needed the cash, too!'

'To buy a carriage?' interposed Madame Dambreuse who was passing by with a cup of tea; and she looked back at him for a moment over her shoulder.

The innuendo was obvious: she thought he was Rosanette's lover. It even seemed to Frédéric that the ladies in the background all had their eyes on him and were whispering amongst themselves. To discover what they were thinking, he moved over towards them.

On the other side of the table Martinon was standing beside Cécile, thumbing through an album of lithographs representing Spanish costumes. He was reading the subtitles aloud: 'A woman from Seville'; 'a gardener from

Valencia'; 'an Andalusian picador'; and once, going down to the bottom of the page, he went on in the same breath:

'Jacques Arnoux, publisher—a friend of yours, isn't he?'

'That's right,' said Frédéric, nettled by his manner. Madame Dambreuse added:

'Yes, you came here one morning . . . about a house, I think it was? One belonging to his wife.' (Meaning: 'She's your mistress.')

He blushed to the roots of his hair; and coming up at that very moment, Monsieur Dambreuse added:

'You even gave the impression that you were greatly interested in them.'

These last words completed Frédéric's discomfiture. His confusion, which he felt must be obvious, was about to confirm everybody's suspicions when Monsieur Dambreuse added:

'You're not doing any business with him, I imagine?'

He shook his head vigorously to deny any such suggestion, failing to realise that the financier was offering him advice.

He'd have liked to leave but was held back by the fear of seeming cowardly. A footman was gathering up cups of tea; Madame Dambreuse was chatting with a diplomat wearing a blue coat; facing one another with their heads together, two girls were showing each other a ring; other girls, sitting in armchairs in a semi-circle, were gently swivelling their pale faces framed in fair or dark hair from side to side; no one in fact was paying him the slightest attention. He beat a retreat in a series of long zigzags across the room and had nearly reached the door when, as he was passing by a console table, he noticed a folded newspaper lying on top, between a Chinese vase and the panelling. He eased it towards him and read the words: *Le Flambard*.

Who'd brought that along? It could only have been Cisy! Anyway, what did it matter? They'd believe the article, perhaps by now they all actually *did* believe it. Why this persecution? He felt blanketed in an ironical silence, as if lost in a desert. Now Martinon spoke to him:

'Talking of Arnoux, I read the name of one of his

employees, Sénécal, in the list of people detained in connection with that incendiary bomb business. Is that the one we know?'

'Yes, it is,' replied Frédéric.

Martinon exclaimed very loudly:

'What, that's our Sénécal?'

He was questioned about the conspiracy: being at the Bar, he must have some inside knowledge.

He confessed he didn't have any. In any case, he hardly knew the person concerned, having met him on only a couple of occasions, and, to put it bluntly, considered him a pretty shady character. Frédéric protested indignantly.

'Not a bit of it! He's a very decent young fellow!'

'Decent young fellows don't get into plots, sir!' said a landowner.

Most of the men there had served under at least four governments and would have sold their country or mankind to protect their wealth, get themselves out of financial difficulties or other trouble, or even through sheer lack of principle, a deep inborn respect for force. They all declared that political crimes were unforgivable! It was easier to excuse those brought about by dire necessity! And inevitably out trotted the example of the bread-winner stealing the proverbial crust from the proverbial baker.

One senior civil servant even exclaimed:

'If I heard that my own brother was conspiring, sir, I'd denounce him to the police!'

Frédéric pointed out the right to resist oppression and, recalling a few of Deslauriers's comments, quoted Desolmes, Blackstone, the English Bill of Rights and Article 2 of the Constitution of 1791.* Indeed, it was by virtue of that right that Napoleon had been deposed. It had been recognized in 1830 and was the first article of the Charter.

'What's more, when a sovereign doesn't honour his contract, justice itself requires him to be overthrown!'

'But that's appalling!' exclaimed the wife of a Prefect.

Vaguely horrified, none of the other women said anything, as if they could already hear the bullets whistling past their ears. Madame Dambreuse sat rocking in her chair, listening with a smile on her face.

An industrialist and one-time carbonaro* tried to convince him that the d'Orléans were a fine family; there were, of course, certain abuses.

'Well then?'

'But they mustn't be mentioned, my dear sir! If you only knew all the harm caused to industry through all this bleating by the opposition!'

'I don't give a damn for business!' retorted Frédéric.

These corrupt old men exasperated him and, carried away by that recklessness that sometimes overtakes the most timorous, he launched into an attack on financiers, Deputies, the government, the king, stood up for the Arabs,*and talked a great deal of nonsense. There was some ironic encouragement: 'Good for you!'; 'Let 'em have it!' while others muttered: 'God, what a hothead!' In the end, he thought it was time to go. As he was taking his leave, Monsieur Dambreuse referred to the job of company secretary:

'Nothing's been definitely decided yet, but don't be too long making up your mind.'

And Madame Dambreuse:

'I hope we'll see you again soon!'

Frédéric took these remarks as a sarcastic parting shot. He was determined never to set foot in that house again or have any further dealings with such people. Not realizing society's almost unlimited capacity for indifference, he thought he'd offended them! He felt particularly indignant towards those women, not one of whom had supported him even tacitly. He resented them for having failed to be roused by him. As for Madame Dambreuse, he saw in her a blend of sweet and sour which made it impossible to enclose her in a formula. Had she got a lover? Who would it be? Was it the diplomat or someone else? Could it be Martinon? Quite out of the question! Yet, somehow, he felt jealous of him and a mysterious ill will towards her.

As usual Dussardier had called round to see him that evening and was waiting for him. Frédéric's heart was bursting; he poured out all his woes and though they were vague and difficult to understand, the kind-hearted young clerk felt sorry for him. Frédéric even complained of being lonely, so Dussardier suggested, rather hesitantly, calling to see Deslauriers.

As soon as he heard this name, Frédéric was seized by a great longing to meet him again. He was feeling an urgent need for intellectual company and Dussardier was a poor substitute. He told the latter to see what he could do.

Deslauriers, too, had been feeling a gap in his life since their quarrel and had no hesitation in responding to their friendly overtures.

They fell into each other's arms but avoided any mention of personal matters. Frédéric appreciated Deslauriers's tact and the next day, as a sort of compensation, told him how he'd lost the fifteen thousand francs, without explaining that they'd originally been intended for him. However, the lawyer realized the truth and was so completely placated by this bit of bad luck of Frédéric's, which confirmed his anti-Arnoux prejudice, that he made no further mention of the famous promise.

Frédéric misinterpreted this silence and thought he'd forgotten it. A few days later he asked him if there was any way to recover the money.

They could look into the previous mortgage, take Arnoux to law on the grounds of fraudulent misrepresentation, start expropriation proceedings against his wife . . .

'Oh no, not against her!' exclaimed Frédéric, and when questioned by his friend, confessed the truth. Deslauriers was convinced he wasn't telling the whole truth, no doubt for reasons of discretion, and this lack of trust hurt his feelings.

All the same, they were as close as they'd ever been and even enjoyed being together so much that they began to find Dussardier's company irksome. On the pretext of having other commitments, they gradually managed to drop him. There are men whose only role in life is to act as go-betweens; you use them as a bridge and then move on, leaving them behind.

Frédéric had no secrets from his old friend. He told him all about the coal-mining venture and Monsieur Dambreuse's offer. It set the lawyer thinking.

'That's odd! For a job like that you need someone with a pretty good knowledge of law!'

'But you'll be able to help me out,' said Frédéric.

'Yees . . . well . . . of course I shall!'

That same week he showed him a letter from his mother.

She accused herself of misjudging Monsieur Roque, who'd offered a satisfactory explanation of his behaviour. Then she talked about Frédéric's financial situation and the possibility, later on, of his marriage to Louise.

'That mightn't be so stupid,' said Deslauriers.

Frédéric vigorously rejected the idea and anyway, old Roque was an old rogue. The lawyer said that was immaterial.

At the end of July the *Nord* shares mysteriously slumped. Frédéric had held on to his and at one blow lost sixty thousand francs. His income was considerably reduced. He'd have to cut down his expenditure, find a job, or else make a good marriage.

Deslauriers reminded him of Mademoiselle Roque. In any event there was nothing to prevent him from going down to see the lie of the land himself. Frédéric was a bit tired and being with his mother in the country would buck him up. Frédéric went.

The sight of the streets of Nogent under moonlight brought back old memories; he had that anxious feeling of coming back after a long journey.

His mother was still surrounded by the same old cronies: Messieurs Gamblin, Heudras and Chambrion, the Lebruns, 'those Auger girls'; and, in addition, old Roque, while, sitting at a card-table opposite Madame Moreau, was Mademoiselle Louise. She was a young woman now. As she stood up she gave a cry. Everyone bustled around; she remained standing quite still; the four silver candelabra on the table made her face seem paler. When she resumed her game, her hand was trembling. Frédéric, whose pride had received a nasty jolt, was immensely flattered. He said to himself: 'Ah, *you* will love me!' and to make up for all the slights he'd suffered in the capital, he began to play the part of the Parisian man-about-town, talked about the latest news from the theatre world, offered a few items of society gossip, which he'd picked up in the little scandal sheets; in a word, he set out to dazzle his fellow townsmen.

Next day, Madame Moreau dwelt on Louise's excellent qualities and then gave a list of the woods and farmland she'd be coming into later. Monsieur Roque was extremely well-off.

He had acquired his wealth through his investments on Monsieur Dambreuse's behalf, for by lending money to people offering sound security on mortgages, he was able to ask for extra interest or commission and with his ever-watchful eye there was no capital risk. In any case, old Roque never hesitated to foreclose; he'd then buy back the mortgaged property, at a cut price, and as Monsieur Dambreuse saw that he was recovering his outlay, he considered his business affairs were being well run.

However, since such financial manipulation was hardly strictly legal, Monsieur Dambreuse could be open to pressure from his agent and he was in no position to refuse him anything. It was as a result of such pressure that he'd been so friendly towards Frédéric.

In fact, old Roque nourished a long-standing ambition: he wanted his daughter to end up a countess, and in order to achieve this without risking her happiness, Frédéric was the only young man he knew.

Through Monsieur Dambreuse's influence, Frédéric could be granted his grandfather's title, as Madame Moreau was the daughter of a Comte de Fouvens and, moreover, related to the Lavernades and the d'Étrignys, old families in the Champagne. As for the Moreaus, an inscription in Gothic lettering in the vicinity of the mills at Villeneuve-l'Archevêque mentioned a Jacob Moreau as having rebuilt them in 1596; and the tomb of his son Pierre, first equerry at the court of Louis XIV, could be seen in the Saint-Nicholas chapel.

Monsieur Roque, the son of a former footman, was

fascinated by all these titles. If a count's coronet weren't forthcoming, he'd be happy to accept something else in its place: when Monsieur Dambreuse was elevated to the peerage, Frédéric might become a Deputy, able to help him in his business transactions, to obtain concessions for him and access to suppliers of various goods. He liked the young man personally. In short, he wanted him as a son-in-law because he'd long been set on it and the idea was growing on him every day.

He'd now become a churchgoer and won Madame Moreau's support, largely through the lure of a title. However, she'd been careful not to give her unconditional agreement.

So, one week later, without any firm commitment having been entered into, Frédéric was looked on as Mademoiselle Louise's 'intended'; and the crafty old Roque would sometimes leave the young couple alone together.

CHAPTER V

When he left Frédéric, Deslauriers had taken away with him a copy of the document giving him power of attorney but after making his way up his five flights of stairs, sitting in his leather chair, all alone in the middle of his dismal office, the sight of the official paper filled him with nausea.

He was fed up with it all, with his six-franc meal tickets, with catching buses, with his wretched poverty and his struggles. Picking up some of the papers gathering dust on his desk, he noticed some others lying beside them: the prospectuses of the coal-mining company, listing the mines with details of their reserves, which Frédéric had left with him for his opinion.

A thought struck him: why not go round to Monsieur Dambreuse and ask for the job of company secretary? He'd be required to purchase a certain number of shares, of course. Realizing the folly of his scheme, he said to himself:

'No, it wouldn't be right!'

He started to think of ways to recover the fifteen thousand francs. Such a sum was a flea-bite for Frédéric! But what an edge it would have given him! The thought of Frédéric's money made him angry.

'It's pitiful to see how he spends it! He's completely selfish. Oh, to hell with his fifteen thousand!'

Why had he lent them? Because he was soft on Madame Arnoux! She was his mistress, there was no doubt about that. 'That's another thing money's useful for!' A wave of resentment swept over him.

Then he thought about Frédéric himself. He'd always had a sort of feminine appeal for him and it wasn't long before he found himself admiring him for having brought off a conquest which he recognized as being beyond his own powers.

But wasn't determination the chief factor in any undertaking? And since with determination you can achieve anything . . .

'Ah, that really would be fun!'

All the same, a dirty trick like that made him feel ashamed. Then, a moment later:

'Damn it all, what is there to be scared of?'

Through hearing so much about Madame Arnoux, he had finally created an extraordinary image of her in his mind. Such undeviating devotion had become a sort of irritating problem for him and its rather theatrical earnestness had grown tiresome. Moreover, the society woman (or one whom he thought of as such) was in his eyes a dazzling symbol, the epitome of a thousand and one arcane delights. Being poor himself, he had a yearning for luxury in its most conspicuous form.

'After all, why worry if she does get annoyed? He's behaved far too badly towards me for me to bother about him? There's no proof she's his mistress! He's denied it himself! So I'm free to do what I want!'

He was obsessed by the desire to try his luck; it would be a trial of strength which he looked forward to; so, suddenly, one day he polished his boots himself, bought himself some white gloves and set out, putting himself into his friend's place, and almost into his skin, by a strange

266

mental process which was a mixture of vengeance, sympathy, imitation and daring.

He gave his name as Doctor Deslauriers.

Madame Arnoux was at a loss, since she'd not asked for any medical assistance.

'Oh, do please forgive me! I'm a doctor of law. I've come on Monsieur Moreau's behalf.'

The name seemed to fluster her.

'All the better!' thought the former lawyer's clerk. 'If she was glad to have him, she'll have me!', spurring himself on by the widespread belief that it's easier to supplant a lover than a husband.

He'd had the pleasure of meeting her once already, at the Law Courts; he even recalled the date. Madame Arnoux was surprised at his good memory. He went on, in an oily voice:

'You were already in some difficulty over your financial affairs.'

She made no reply; it must be true.

He started to talk about one thing and another: her apartment, the factory; and catching sight of some inset portraits along the edge of the mirror:

'Ah, family portraits, I imagine?'

He noticed an old lady, Madame Arnoux's mother:

'She looks a fine old lady, a typical southerner.' And when she pointed out that her mother came from Chartres:

'Ah, Chartres! What a pretty little place!'

He praised its cathedral and its pies; then he reverted to the portrait, discovered similarities with Madame Arnoux, throwing in a few oblique compliments by the way.

She showed no offence. His self-assurance rose and he remarked that he'd known Arnoux for a long time.

'What a nice chap he is! But he does land himself in awkward situations. Take that mortgage for instance, one can't imagine a more thoughtless . . .'

'Oh yes, I know,' she said with a shrug.

This involuntary admission of her low opinion of her husband encouraged Deslauriers to go on:

'That china clay business of his, you may not know this,

but it was very nearly a disaster and even his reputation . . .'

Her frown brought him up short.

He took refuge in generalizations and expressed pity for those unfortunate wives whose husbands squander their wealth.

'But it's all *his* money! I've got nothing of my own!'

Never mind! One could never tell . . . A person of experience might be able to help. He offered his unconditional co-operation and made much of his own excellent qualities. He kept peering at her; his spectacles were glinting.

She could feel her mind going vaguely numb; then suddenly:

'Please, could we come to the point?'

He produced the papers.

'Here's Frédéric's power of attorney. With a document like that in the hands of a bailiff, and an order to pay, it's as easy as falling off a log. Within a day . . .'

She wasn't reacting; he tried another tack.

'Anyway, as far as I'm concerned, I can't see why he's so keen on claiming this money, he's got absolutely no need for it!'

'What do you mean? Monsieur Moreau was good enough to . . .'

'Oh yes, I quite agree!'

And Deslauriers began by praising him, before gently proceeding to run him down; he was forgetful, self-centred and mean with his money.

'I thought he was a friend of yours?'

'That doesn't make me blind to his shortcomings. For instance, he has very little understanding . . . how can I put it . . . for the sympathy . . .'

Madame Arnoux was leafing through the thick file and cut him short, to enquire the meaning of a word.

He bent over her shoulder, so close that he brushed her cheek. She blushed; this blush electrified him; greedily he kissed her hand.

'Doctor Deslauriers! What are you doing?'

She backed against the wall, with an angry look in her large black eyes that riveted him to the spot.

'You must listen! I love you!'

She burst into a shrill peal of laughter, so heart-breakingly cruel that in his anger he could have strangled her; he restrained himself and, like a beaten man pleading for quarter:

'Ah no, you've got me wrong. I'm not like him, I'd never . . .'

'Who are you talking about?'

'Frédéric.'

'I've already told you that Monsieur Moreau doesn't greatly concern me!'

'Oh, I'm sorry, so sorry, but . . .'

And sarcastically he drawled:

'As a matter of fact I did think that you were sufficiently interested in him to be glad to learn . . .'

She went as pale as a ghost. Deslauriers went on:

'That he's getting married.'

'Married?'

'In four weeks' time at the latest, to Mademoiselle Roque, the daughter of Monsieur Dambreuse's agent. He's even gone down specially to Nogent to see about it.'

Her hand flew to her heart as if she'd been struck in the chest; but she immediately tugged the bell-pull. Deslauriers didn't wait to be shown the door; when she turned round, he'd vanished.

She could scarcely breathe. She went over to the window to recover.

On the pavement opposite a man in shirt-sleeves was nailing down a crate. Cabs were driving by. She pulled the window closed and went back to her chair. The tall houses opposite shut out the sun; the light in the room was cold. Her children had gone out and indoors nothing was stirring. She felt completely forsaken.

'He's going to get married! Is that possible?'

She was shaken by a nervous trembling.

'What's the matter with me? Am I in love with him?'

Then abruptly:

'Yes, I am! I love him!'

She seemed to be sinking into a bottomless pit. The clock struck three. She heard the chimes die away and remained sitting on the edge of her chair, with a vacant stare and a fixed smile still on her face.

On that same afternoon, at the selfsame moment, Frédéric and Mademoiselle Louise were strolling round the garden owned by Monsieur Roque on the tip of the island. Old Catherine was keeping a wary eye on them in the distance. As they walked along side by side, Frédéric was saying:

'Do you remember how I used to take you for walks in the country?'

'Weren't you kind to me! You used to help me to make sand pies, fill my watering can and push me on my swing.'

'What's happened to all those dolls of yours, all named after queens or duchesses?'

'Do you know, I've no idea!'

'And your pug Moricaud?'

'He got drowned, poor pet!'

'And that Don Quixote with the illustrations we coloured in together?'

'Oh, I've still got that!'

He reminded her of her First Communion and how nice she'd looked at Vespers with her white veil and her long candle, while the little girls all processed round the chancel and the bell was ringing.

This reminder didn't seem to appeal to Mademoiselle Roque very much and she could find nothing to say in reply. Then a minute later:

'Who's the naughty man who didn't let me have any news of himself at all?'

Frédéric pleaded hard work.

'What work do you do then?'

Embarrassed by the question, he eventually replied that he was a student of politics.

'Oh, I see!'

And without pursuing the matter further:

'Well, that gives you something to do but how about me?'

She told him of her dreary existence with nobody to meet, no amusements, nothing at all to entertain her. She would have liked to take up riding.

'The priest says it is not a nice thing for a girl to do! Isn't being nice silly? In the old days people let me do what I liked and now I can't do a thing!'

'But your father's very fond of you!'

'Yes, but . . .'

She gave a sigh, meaning: 'That's not enough to make me happy!'

There was silence. The only sound they could hear was the crunch of sand under their feet and the rippling of the waterfall, for upstream from Nogent the Seine splits into two and one of the branches cataracts over the mill-wheels and joins the main river lower down. Coming from the direction of the bridges, you can see on the right a grassy bank with a white house on top, while on the left there are broad meadows studded with poplars; the skyline opposite is cut off by a bend in the river. Large insects darted across its still surface; clumps of reeds and rushes were dotted unevenly along its banks; all sorts of vegetation were flourishing together, haphazardly: lanky green plants and drooping yellow clusters, golden bachelors' buttons, cats' tails and purplish love-lies-bleeding. One backwater was carpeted with water-lilies; on the river side of the garden, the only protection was a line of old oak trees in which wolf-traps were concealed.

Further back was the kitchen garden, enclosed by four walls with slate copings and showing brown patches of newly dug earth. The cloches on the narrow melon beds glittered in the sun; artichokes, green beans, spinach, carrots and tomatoes alternated with each other, leading up to an asparagus bed looking like a tiny feathery forest.

Under the Directoire the whole area had been what used to be called a 'folly'. Since that time, the trees had grown huge. The hornbeams and other trees were tangled with clematis, the avenues were moss-covered, brambles were rampant everywhere. Among the weeds were fragments of crumbling statuary. As you walked along, odd bits of wire would snatch at you. All that remained of the gazebo was two ground-floor rooms with peeling blue wallpaper. At the front was a pergola, with a vine growing over a wooden trellis supported on brick pillars.

They went under it together and as Frédéric looked sideways to talk to Louise, he could observe the play of the sun and shade in the dappled light cast by the leaves.

Her hair was held in a bun by a pin with a glass knob meant to imitate an emerald and, despite being in mourning, her childish bad taste had led her to wear straw slippers with pink satin bows, no doubt some vulgar rubbish picked up at a fair.

He noticed them and offered sardonic compliments.

'Don't make fun of me!' she replied.

Then, looking him all over from his grey felt hat down to his silk socks:

'Aren't you smart!'

Then she asked him to tell her some books she ought to read. He mentioned a number of titles.

'Aren't you clever!'

While still only a child, she had fallen for him, as children do, with a love both as pure as religion and violent as hunger. He was her playmate, her big brother and her master, he had charmed her mind, set her heart on fire and all unwittingly aroused a deep, secret and lasting ferment of excitement. His departure had sparked off a tragic crisis and her despair had been compounded by her mother's death. His absence had led her to idealize him; he'd come back surrounded by a sort of halo and she made no attempt to hide her delight.

For the first time in his life, Frédéric was feeling loved and this novel pleasure, even if only a moderately agreeable feeling, was making him, so to speak, swell inwardly; he spread out his arms and flung back his head.

A large cloud was passing over.

'That's on its way to Paris,' said Louise. 'You'd like to be following it, wouldn't you?'

'Me? Why?'

'Who knows?'

And peering at him closely:

'Perhaps you've got . . .' (she was groping for a word) 'some sort of attachment there.'

'What do you mean? No, I've not got any attachment anywhere!'

'Honestly?'

'Yes, honestly!'

In less than a year she'd undergone a transformation which astonished Frédéric. For a minute neither spoke. Then:

'We ought to use first names like we used to. Shall we?'

'No!'

'Why not?'

'Because . . .'

He persisted. She looked down and said:

'I don't dare!'

They'd reached the end of the garden, down by the water's edge. Boyishly Frédéric started playing ducks and drakes. She told him to sit down. He obeyed and then, looking at the weir:

'It's like the Niagara Falls!'

He started to talk about distant countries and long expeditions. She found the prospect of embarking on them exciting. She'd never be afraid of lions or hurricanes.

As they sat talking side by side, they picked up handfuls of sand and let them trickle through their fingers; the warm breeze from the plains wafted fragrant gusts of lavender over them, mingled with the smell of tar from a boat behind the lock. The sun was sparkling on the sluice; the greenish slabs of the low wall over which the water poured were masked by a kind of continuously unfolding veil of silvery gossamer; at the bottom a long fringe of foam kept splashing up in tiny spurts; and all this water was bubbling and swirling in countless cross-currents before merging into one single, flat, limpid pool.

Louise murmured how much she envied fish.

'It must be wonderful to be able to twist and turn in the

273

water as much as you like and feel yourself being stroked all over!'

She was giving little squirms of delight.

A voice called:

'Where are you?'

'There's your maid calling you,' said Frédéric.

'Oh, all right, all right!'

Louise made no sign of moving.

'She'll be cross.'

'I don't care! And anyway . . .' Mademoiselle Roque made a gesture suggesting that, where the maid was concerned, she held the whip hand.

However, she did get to her feet but then complained of having a headache. As they were going past a huge shed containing bundles of firewood:

'How about going into the cote?'

He pretended not to understand the local word and even teased her over her accent. Slowly the corners of her mouth began to droop; biting her lips she walked away from him to sulk.

Frédéric came after her and promised he hadn't wanted to hurt her feelings and was very fond of her.

'Are you really?' she exclaimed; a smile lit up the whole of her rather freckled face.

She was so fresh, so forthright, so young; he found this irresistible. He said:

'Why should I be lying to you? Do you doubt my word, eh?' and slipped his left arm round her waist. A soft cooing sound like a dove's came from her lips; her head fell backwards and she went limp; he had to hold her up to prevent her falling. But he had no need to call on any scruples or sense of honour; the sight of this pure young girl offering herself had given him a nasty shock. Gently he helped her take a few steps but refrained from making any more affectionate remarks, and to keep the conversation on a mundane level, started talking about various members of Nogent society.

Suddenly she pushed him away and said bitterly:

'You'd never have the courage to take me away from here, Frédéric!'

He stood stock-still, bewildered. She burst into tears and nestled her head against his chest.

'How can I live without you?'

He endeavoured to calm her down. She placed both hands on his shoulders to look him squarely in the face, with her green, tear-laden eyes glaring almost savagely into his own:

'Do you want me as your wife?'

'Well . . .' replied Frédéric, not knowing quite what to say, 'well . . . really . . . there's nothing I'd like more . . .'

At that moment Monsieur Roque's head popped up from behind a lilac.

He took his 'young friend' away for a couple of days on a little trip round the neighbourhood, showing him his properties. When Frédéric got back he found three letters waiting for him at his mother's.

The first was from Monsieur Dambreuse inviting him to dinner for the previous Tuesday. What was behind all this affability? Was his indiscreet behaviour going to be overlooked?

The second one came from Rosanette. It thanked him for having risked his life for her; at first Frédéric couldn't understand what she was getting at and then, after a good deal of beating about the bush, she implored him (appealing to his friendship and relying on his tact and discretion), on bended knees (her expression) and as casually as if she was asking for a slice of bread, to let her have a paltry sum, just five hundred francs, to see her through an emergency. On the spot Frédéric decided to give them to her.

The third letter, from Deslauriers, talked about the power of attorney. It was long and involved: the lawyer hadn't yet decided what action to take. He advised him to stay put: 'no sense in coming back'; he even stressed this point in a very odd manner.

Frédéric was completely perplexed and decided to go back to Paris; he found this attempt to dictate his actions obnoxious.

In any case, he was beginning to feel homesick for the boulevards; and his mother was being so persistent, too.

Monsieur Roque prowled around all the time and Mademoiselle Louise was so much in love with him that he couldn't
delay making his intentions clear much longer. He needed
time to think, he'd size the matter up better from a distance.

He concocted a story to justify his trip and left, telling
everybody—and even believing himself—that he wouldn't
be away long.

CHAPTER VI

His return to Paris gave him no pleasure whatsoever; on
this late August evening the boulevard seemed deserted,
any passers-by had sour looks, the asphalt tar-boilers all
around were giving off fumes and many of the houses were
completely shuttered up. He went to his house; his curtains
were covered in dust; as he ate his dinner he felt strangely
forlorn; and it was then that he thought of Mademoiselle
Roque.

Marriage didn't seem now so outrageous an idea. They'd
travel, go to Italy, the East! And he saw her standing on a
hillock, surveying the landscape, or else leaning on his arm,
in an art gallery in Florence, stopping to look at the
pictures. What a real pleasure it would be to see this sweet
little creature opening up to the wonders of Art and Nature!
Once she'd broken with her environment, it wouldn't take
long for her to become a charming companion for him. And
Monsieur Roque's wealth had its attractions, too. All the
same, he did feel this sort of motive was a sign of weakness,
degrading.

But whatever happened, on one thing he was quite
determined: he'd change his way of life, stop squandering
his affection in futile passions. He even wondered whether
to carry out the errand given him by Louise to buy from
Jacques Arnoux two large polychrome statuettes of blackamoors, like the ones in the Prefecture in Troyes. She knew
the manufacturer's mark and didn't want anyone else's.
Frédéric was scared that if he went back *there* he'd relapse
into his old love.

He spent the whole evening worrying about all this.

Then, just as he was about to go to bed, a woman came into his room.

'It's me,' said Mademoiselle Vatnaz cheerfully. 'I've got a message frm Rosanette.'

So they'd made it up?

'Good heavens, yes! I'm an easy-going sort of person, you know! Anyway, that poor girl . . . oh, it'd take too long to tell you!'

To cut a long story short, the Marshal wanted to see him and was waiting for an answer to a letter which had made its way from Paris to Nogent. Mademoiselle Vatnaz didn't know what was in it. Frédéric enquired after the Marshal.

She was now with a very rich man, a Russian prince, Tzernoukov, who'd seen her at the Champ-de-Mars races last summer.

'They've got three carriages, a saddle horse, livery, a smart English-style groom, a country house, a box at the Italian Opera and lots of other things as well. That's how things go, my dear!'

Vatnaz herself seemed more sprightly and happier, as if she too had benefited from Rosanette's changed fortunes. She took off her gloves and examined the furniture and various knick-knacks in the room, pricing them as accurately as any second-hand dealer. If he'd consulted her, he'd have got them cheaper. She complimented him on his good taste.

'Oh, that's pretty, that's really nice! You're the only person who could have thought of that!'

Then, noticing a door by the bedside table in the recess:

'Ah, that's where you spirit away your little lady loves, eh?'

And she gave him a friendly chuck under the chin. The touch of her long hands, thin but soft, made him jump. She had lace edging round her wrists and gold braid, like a hussar, on the bodice of her green dress. The brim of her black tulle hat drooped over her face, half concealing her forehead; underneath, her eyes were gleaming; her hair, parted in the middle, gave off a penetrating scent of patchouli; the Carcel lamp on the table lit up her face from below, like stage footlights, making her jaw jut out; and all of a sudden Frédéric felt a great wave of lust, a fierce animal desire, for this ugly woman and the sinuous panther-like curves of her figure.

She took three slips of paper from her purse and said in a bland voice:

'You'll take these off me, won't you?'

They were three tickets for a benefit performance on behalf of Delmar.

'What, for him?'

'Certainly!'

Without further comment, Mademoiselle Vatnaz added that she adored him more than ever. To her mind, the actor ranked without doubt amongst the 'greatest stars of the age'. And he didn't play just any particular character but the very genius of France, the People! He had a *humanitarian* soul; he understood 'the sacred priesthood of Art'. To cut short these panegyrics, Frédéric handed over the money for the three tickets.

'No need to mention this when you go . . . My goodness, it's late, I must dash! Oh, I was forgetting the address; it's 14, rue Grange-Batelière.'

And as she was going out:

'Farewell, you beloved man!'

'Beloved? Who by!' Frédéric wondered to himself. 'What an odd person!'

And he recalled that one day Dussardier had said of her:

'Oh, she's not much to write home about!' as if hinting at something a trifle shady in her past.

Next day he called on the Marshal. She was living in a newly built house with awnings overhanging the street. On the wall of every landing there was a mirror and rustic plant-stands stood in front of the windows; a canvas carpet went all the way up the steps. Indoors, it was refreshingly cool.

The door was opened by a footman in a red waistcoat. In the entrance hall a woman and two men, no doubt tradesmen, were sitting on a bench, waiting, as though in some ministerial ante-room. Through the half-closed door of the dining-room on the left he caught a glimpse of empty bottles standing on sideboards and table-napkins dangling over chair-backs; there was a long gallery extending parallel, with an espalier of roses supported on gold-painted posts. In the courtyard below, two bare-armed stable lads were polishing a landau. You could hear them talking from above, together with the occasional clink of a curry comb knocking against a stone.

The footman came back: 'Madam would see the gentleman now'; and he led Frédéric through a second large room, then a spacious dining-room hung with yellow brocatelle, in which rope mouldings ran up from the corners to the centre of the ceiling and seemed to be carried through by the ornamental cable-styled foliage of the candelabra. There must have been a party the night before; the console tables were still covered in cigar ash.

Finally, he was shown into a sort of boudoir dimly lit by stained glass windows. The wooden lintel was carved in a trefoil pattern; behind a hand-rail there stood a divan consisting of three purple mattresses on which lay a hubble-bubble. Above the fireplace, instead of a mirror there was a mantelpiece shaped like a pyramid, containing a miscellaneous assortment of curios on each tier: old silver watches, Bohemian crystal dice-boxes, jewelled clasps, jade buttons, enamels, Chinese porcelain figurines, a tiny Byzantine Virgin with a silver-gilt hood; and with the bluish carpet, the glimmer of mother-of-pearl stools and the tawny reddish-brown of the leather-covered walls, everything blended into a golden half-light. The air was thick with the scent of large bunches of flowers in bronze vases standing on small pedestals in the corners.

Rosanette appeared. She was wearing a pink satin jacket with white cashmere pantaloons, a necklace made from piastres and a red skull cap encircled by a sprig of jasmine.

Frédéric gave a start of surprise and then proffered the bank draft, saying that he'd brought 'the necessary'.

She looked at him dumbfounded and seeing himself left standing there with the piece of paper in his hand:

'Well, aren't you going to take it?'

She took it and tossed it on to the divan:

'It's very kind of you!'

The money was going towards the purchase of a piece of land in Bellevue, which she was buying in annual instalments. Her offhand manner offended Frédéric. Ah well, all the better! It settled old scores.

'Do sit down,' she said. 'No, here, closer.' Then, in a solemn voice: 'First of all, Frédéric, I have to thank you for having risked your life!'

'Oh, it wasn't anything at all!'

'What do you mean, it was wonderful of you!'

The Marshal's gratitude was embarrassing, for she must be imagining he'd fought purely on Arnoux's behalf, since the latter was suffering under the same misapprehension and would certainly have been unable to resist telling her about it.

'Perhaps she's having me on?' thought Frédéric.

There being nothing further for him to do, Frédéric stood up, explaining that he had to meet someone.

'Oh, please don't go yet!'

He sat down again and complimented her on her clothes. She replied dejectedly:

'It's the prince who wants me to look like this! And I have to smoke gadgets like this,' she added pointing to the hubble-bubble. 'Suppose we have a go? Would you like a try?'

The contrivance had to be lit and when the tombac* proved reluctant, she started stamping her feet impatiently. Then she subsided into lethargy and lay quite still on the divan with a cushion under her armpit, her body slightly twisted, one knee bent and the other leg straight. The long red Moroccan leather snake lying in rings on the carpet was coiled round her arm. She was gripping the amber mouthpiece between her lips and blinking at Frédéric through the smoke spiralling round her. As she breathed in, the water gurgled and from time to time she muttered:

'The poor pet! The poor darling!'

He was trying to find an agreeable topic of conversation

and remembered Vatnaz. He remarked that he thought she looked very smart.

'And well she might!' retorted the Marshal. 'She's jolly lucky to have me, that girl!'

She didn't enlarge on the subject; the atmosphere was very strained.

Both of them had the uneasy feeling that there was some obstacle separating them. The truth was that this duel, which Rosanette was imagining as fought on her behalf, had flattered her self-esteem and she'd been greatly surprised that he hadn't come along to claim his reward on the spot; she'd therefore invented the loan of five hundred francs to force him to call on her. Why wasn't Frédéric asking for a little love in return? It did show an amazing delicacy of feeling! In a sudden burst of affection, she blurted:

'Won't you come and stay with us at the seaside?'

'Who's us?'

'Me and my pet! I'll pass you off as my cousin, like they do in those old comedies.'

'You really are too kind!'

'Or else you could find somewhere to stay nearby.'

The thought of hiding from a rich man was humiliating.

'No, it's out of the question!'

'Ah well, please yourself!'

Rosanette turned her head away with a tear in her eye. Frédéric noticed it and to show some interest in her, remarked that he was glad to see her well set up at last.

She shrugged her shoulders. Why wasn't she happy? Was it perhaps because nobody loved her?

'Oh, people always love me!'

And added:

'It depends what sort of love.'

She complained of being 'stifling hot' and undid her jacket; under her silk slip, the lower part of her body was bare and as she threw him a sideways glance over her shoulder, she looked like a slave-girl, tantalizing him.

That the viscount, Monsieur de Comaing or some other man might suddenly appear would never have entered the head of anyone less calculatingly selfish than Frédéric. But he'd been led up the garden path by those selfsame eyes too often to want to be caught out yet again in a humiliating situation.

She asked about his connections and his pastimes; she even went so far as to enquire into his business affairs and offered to lend him money should he need it.

This was the last straw. He picked up his hat.

'Well, there we are, my dear Rosanette. Have a nice time at the seaside. I'll see you sometime.'

She stared at him wide-eyed and then, curtly:

'Goodbye!'

He went out through the yellow drawing-room and the second ante-room. On the table, between a bowl full of visiting cards and an inkstand, there was an engraved silver casket. It was Madame Arnoux's. His heart melted and at the same time he felt a sort of shock of sacrilege. He longed to pick it up and open it. Then, afraid of being observed, he left.

Frédéric held fast to his principles: he didn't go back to the Arnouxs'. He gave his man the necessary instructions and sent him round to buy the two blackamoors, which were sent off to Nogent in a crate that very evening. Next day, on his way to call on Deslauriers, at the corner of the boulevard and the rue Vivienne, he ran straight into Madame Arnoux.

Their first reaction was to draw back; then the same smile came to the lips of both of them and they went up to each other. For a minute neither spoke.

She was bathed in sunlight; and her oval face, her arched eyebrows, her black lace stole clinging to her shoulders, her dove-grey shot-silk dress, the posy of violets in the corner of her poke-bonnet, everything about her seemed extraordinary and magnificent; her wonderful dark eyes had an infinite, velvety softness; desperately, he snatched at the first words that came into his head and stammered:

'How's Arnoux?'

'Well, thank you!'

'And the children?'

'They're very well.'

'Ah . . . ah . . . what wonderful weather we're having, aren't we?'

'Yes, isn't it superb.'

'Are you going shopping?'

'Yes.'

And with a gentle bend of the head:

'Goodbye!'

She hadn't offered to shake hands, hadn't uttered one friendly word, hadn't even invited him to call on her. What did it matter? He wouldn't have exchanged this meeting for the most glamorous love affair in the world, and as he went on his way her charm still continued to weave its spell.

Deslauriers was surprised to see him but hid his annoyance; he hadn't abandoned all hope of success with Madame Arnoux and his letter advising his friend to stay on in Nogent was intended to give him a freer hand in his campaign.

He did explain, however, that he'd been to see her to find out whether their marriage contract stipulated joint ownership, in which case it would have been possible to proceed against the wife; 'and didn't she look put out when I told her about your marriage!'

'I say, that was going a bit far!'

'I had to do it to prove that you needed your capital! And no one who wasn't greatly interested would have almost fainted like she did!'

'Really?' exclaimed Frédéric.

'Aha, you've given yourself away, old man, come on, own up!'

Madame Arnoux's fond lover was swept by a gust of cowardice.

'Oh no! . . . I promise you! . . . Honestly! . . .'

These limp denials left no doubt in Deslauriers's mind; he offered his congratulations and asked for the 'details'. Frédéric didn't give any and even resisted the temptation to invent some.

As for the mortgage, he told him not to do anything for the moment. Deslauriers thought he was wrong and told him so most emphatically. The lawyer was, moreover, gloomier, more spiteful, and more irritable than ever. If his luck didn't change, in a year's time at most he'd be on a boat to America or else blow his brains out. In fact, he seemed so frantically opposed to everything and such an out-and-out radical that Frédéric couldn't help exclaiming:

'You're just like Sénécal!'

At this Deslauriers told him that he'd been released from the Sainte-Pélagie prison, no doubt because the preliminary inquiry had found insufficient evidence to put him on trial.

To celebrate his release, Dussardier was intending to give a party with a bowl of punch and invited Frédéric to 'drop in', with the warning that Hussonnet, who'd been very kind to Sénécal, would also be there.

In fact, *Le Flambard* had recently incorporated a commercial agency with a prospectus announcing a 'Wine-producers' Trading Bank—Advertising Agency—Investigation and Debt-collecting Service, etc.'. But the Bohemian had been afraid that his business activities might prejudice his literary reputation and had taken on the former maths master to look after the accounts. It wasn't much of a job but without it, Sénécal would have starved. Not wishing to hurt the feelings of a nice chap like Dussardier, Frédéric accepted.

Three days beforehand, Dussardier, with his own hands, polished the quarry tiles of his garret, beat the dust out of his easy chair and wiped down his mantelshelf, on which an alabaster clock sat under a glass globe between a stalactite and a coconut shell. As his two candlesticks and single taper-stick were inadequate, he borrowed two sconces from his porter and these five lights were set out on a chest of drawers spread with three napkins to provide a worthier setting for the macaroons, the biscuits, a cake and a dozen bottles of beer. Opposite the yellow-papered wall stood a mahogany bookcase containing the *Fables* of Lachambeaudie,* the *Mystères de Paris* and Norvin's *Napoléon*;* and in the middle of the alcove, Béranger's face was smiling out of its rosewood frame!

Apart from Deslauriers and Sénécal, the other guests

were a newly qualified pharmacist, who hadn't got enough capital to set up on his own; a young man from Dussardier's firm; a wine-broker; an architect; and an insurance agent. Regimbart had been unable to come; his absence was noted with regret.

Frédéric was very warmly welcomed; everyone had heard from Dussardier how he'd spoken out at Monsieur Dambreuse's. Sénécal merely shook his hand and looked dignified.

He was standing with his back to the fireplace and haranguing the others, who were sitting smoking their pipes, on 'votes for all!'; this would lead to the victory of Democracy and the application of the Principles of the Gospel. What's more, the moment of truth was fast approaching; in the provinces there was a growing number of reformist banquets; and Piedmont, Naples, Tuscany . . . *

'That's right!' said Deslauriers, interrupting. 'It can't go on much longer!'

And he started to sum up the situation:

We'd sacrificed Holland* to get England to accept Louis-Philippe and this glorious alliance had gone up in smoke, thanks to the Spanish marriages! In Switzerland, Monsieur Guizot, following Austria's lead, was supporting the treaty settlements of 1815.* Prussia's *Zollverein** was going to be a big headache for us. The Eastern question* was not going to go away.

'There's no reason to trust Russia just because the Grand Duke Constantine* sends presents to the Duc d'Aumale! And as for policies at home, you've never seen such crass stupidity! Even the majority is divided amongst itself! In fact, to use those well-known words, wherever you look, there's "nothing, nothing, nothing"! And in response to this abject failure,' the lawyer went on, putting both hands on his hips, 'the government proclaims that *it's satisfied*!'*

This reference to a famous vote in the Chamber produced loud applause. Dussardier opened a bottle of beer; the froth splashed over the curtains but he paid no attention; he was filling pipes, cutting cake and carrying it round. He'd been downstairs a number of times to see if the punch was ready and it was not long before the mood of the party became very lively, for they all shared the same violent exasperation against the regime, a feeling based purely on their hatred of injustice; their complaints ranged from the justifiable to the utterly idiotic.

The pharmacist was moaning about the state of 'our fleet'. The insurance agent couldn't stomach Marshal Soult's two sentries.* Deslauriers was fuming against the Jesuits* who'd just set up quite openly again in Lille. Sénécal felt far more strongly against Monsieur Cousin;* he loathed his eclecticism which claimed to reach irrefutable conclusions, thereby fostering selfishness and destroying solidarity; the wine-broker, rather out of his depth in such matters, loudly pointed out that he'd failed to mention a large number of 'really monstrous things'.

'The royal coach on the *Nord* line must have cost eighty thousand francs! Who's going to foot that bill?'

'Yes, indeed!' said the shop assistant angrily, as if the money would be coming out of his own pocket.

The sharks in the Stock Exchange were the next to come under fire, then came corruption among the bureaucrats.

In Sénécal's opinion, you needed to look higher up and put the blame fairly and squarely on the royal princes, who were bringing back the habits and customs of the Regency.

'Didn't you see that, recently, friends of the Duc de Montpensier on their way back from Vincennes, drunk I expect, disturbed the workers of the Faubourg-Saint-Antoine* with their singing?'

'People even shouted: "Down with the crooks!"' said the pharmacist. 'I was there and I joined in!'

'That's the spirit! The Teste-Cubières* case has at last made the People sit up and take notice!'

'I was sorry about that case,' said Dussardier. 'It brought disgrace on an old soldier!'

'Did you know,' Sénécal went on, 'that in the Duchesse de Praslin's* house they found . . .'

The door was kicked open and in came Hussonnet.

'Greetings, noble lords!' he said, sitting down on the bed.

Nobody made any reference to his article, which he was in any case sorry about, for the Marshal had given him a severe ticking off.

He'd just been to see *Le Chevalier de maison rouge** at Dumas's theatre and he'd found it 'deadly'.

All these democrats were amazed to hear such condemnation of a drama whose whole trend or, rather, setting pandered to their most passionate beliefs. They protested. To settle the debate, Sénécal asked point blank if the play supported the cause of democracy.

'Well . . . I suppose so. But it's written in such a style . . .'

'What's style got to do with it? If it's democratic, it's a good play! It's the *idea* that's the important thing.'

And without giving Frédéric a chance to say anything:

'I was just making the point that in the Praslin affair . . .'

'And that's another hoary old chestnut. God, how tiresome!'

'And not only for you!' retorted Deslauriers. 'No less than five newspapers have been seized by the police as a result. Just listen to this.'

He produced his notebook and read:

'Since our best of republics was set up, the Press has faced 12,229 prosecutions, leading to prison sentences totalling 30,141 years for the journalists, plus the trifling sum of 7,110,500 francs in fines. Charming, isn't it?'

They all jeered and Frédéric, as excited as anyone else, said:

'*La Démocratie pacifique** is being prosecuted for its serial novel *The Women's Share*.'

'That's rich!' exclaimed Hussonnet. 'If they're going to deprive us of our share of women . . .'

'But what haven't they deprived us of!' said Deslauriers. 'They've banned smoking in the Luxembourg, banned the hymn to Pius IX . . .'*

'And they've banned the compositors' banquet!' exclaimed a cavernous voice. This voice belonged to the architect, tucked away in the shadowy alcove, who up till now hadn't uttered a word. He added that a chef had been sentenced for openly insulting the king.

'Well, he's in the soup!' said Hussonnet.

Sénécal thought this such a tasteless pun that he accused him of defending that 'three-card trickster from the Hôtel de Ville, the friend of the traitor Dumouriez'.*

'What me? Quite the opposite!'

In his view Louis-Philippe was a stick-in-the-mud with the mentality of your average National Guard shopkeeper, a man who wore a belt and braces. And putting his hand on his heart, he trotted out the familiar phrases: 'It is always a pleasure . . . Polish nationhood shall never perish . . . Our positive contribution to general prosperity . . . My family and I deeply appreciate the generosity . . .' They all roared with laughter and agreed he was a delightful chap and very witty; the sight of the punch-bowl sent up from the local wine shop made them even more enthusiastic.

The alcoholic glow combined with that of the candles quickly warmed up the room; the light from the garret shone out across the courtyard on to the side of a roof with its black chimney-stack standing up against the darkness. Everybody was talking at once, very loudly; they'd taken off their frock-coats and were clinking glasses and bumping into the furniture.

'Bring on the noble ladies, 'Od's blood!' exclaimed Hussonnet. 'Let's have a spot of *Tour de Nesle*,* local colour and lashings of Rembrandt, stap me!'

Busily stirring the punch, the pharmacist broke into loud song:

> 'I've two great oxen in my byre,
> Two great white oxen . . .'*

Sénécal put his hand in front of the man's mouth: he couldn't bear rowdiness and the tenants were looking out of their windows, surprised at the unusual din from Dussardier's rooms.

This nice young man was feeling happy and said it reminded him of their earlier get-togethers on the quai

288

Napoléon, though there were some absentees, 'Pellerin, for instance . . .'

'We can do without him!' retorted Frédéric.

Deslauriers enquired after Martinon.

'What's become of that interesting young gentleman?'

Frédéric immediately launched a vicious attack on the 'gentleman's' intelligence, character, bogus elegance, in fact everything about him. A typical example of the jumped-up country bumpkin; the new middle classes weren't a patch on the old landed gentry. As he made these assertions, the supporters of democracy all nodded approvingly, as if they belonged to the last category and were on familiar terms with the former. They were delighted with Frédéric. The pharmacist even compared him with Monsieur d'Alton-Shée,*who defended the People in spite of being a peer.

It was time to go; there were hearty handshakes all round and, being fond of both Frédéric and Deslauriers, Dussardier accompanied the pair of them. As soon as they were in the street, the lawyer seemed to have something on his mind and after a short pause:

'So you really do bear Pellerin a big grudge?'

Frédéric frankly admitted it.

But the painter had removed his picture from public display. People shouldn't fall out over trifles! What was the point of making an enemy?

'He gave way to a passing fit of temper, which could be forgiven in a man who hadn't a penny! You can't understand what that's like!'

After Deslauriers had gone back up to his flat, Dussardier refused to let Frédéric go; he even urged him to buy the portrait. In fact, realizing that Frédéric was not going to be intimidated, Pellerin had got round the two of them to use their influence and persuade him to buy the thing.

Deslauriers broached the matter again: the artist's claims weren't unreasonable.

'I feel sure that maybe for five hundred francs . . .'

'Oh, all right then, he can have 'em!' said Frédéric, handing over the money.

The picture was brought round that very evening. It

seemed to him even more appalling than when he'd first seen it. Through too much reworking, the shadows and half-tones had gone all muddy and looked murky against the highlights, which were still very bright in parts and clashed with the overall effect.

In retaliation for having bought the painting, Frédéric criticized it mercilessly. Deslauriers took the comments at their face value and approved Frédéric's attitude; he was still nursing the ambition of gathering a band of supporters together under his leadership; he was one of those people who enjoy getting their friends to do things they wouldn't care to do themselves.

Meanwhile Frédéric had refrained from calling on the Dambreuses since his return; he was short of funds; he'd have to offer endless explanations; and he was still not able to make up his mind. Perhaps he was right? Everything seemed in a state of flux at the moment, not excluding that coal-mining venture; he ought to drop that sort of company. In the end, Deslauriers persuaded him not to go ahead; hatred was making him virtuous. Anyway he was happier to see Frédéric remain a second-rater; in that way he'd stay down at his own level and have more in common with him.

Mademoiselle Roque's purchase had been badly bungled. Her father wrote about it, giving the fullest details and ending with a joke: 'Sorry if I'm making you work like a nigger!'

Frédéric's only course was to call on Arnoux again. He went up to the warehouse. There was no one to be seen; as the business was collapsing, the employees were showing the same lack of interest as the owner.

He walked along the shelves laden with pottery which ran all the way down the middle of the room; at the far end, near the service counter, he started to tread more heavily to announce his arrival.

The door-curtain was pulled aside. Madame Arnoux appeared.

'Good heavens, it's you! What are you doing here?'

'Yes, it's me,' she faltered, in some confusion. 'I was looking for . . .'

He noticed her handkerchief beside the desk and guessed that she'd come down to her husband's warehouse to see what was happening and no doubt to put her mind at rest about something.

'But . . . perhaps you were needing something?' she said.

'A very small thing, Madame Arnoux.'

'These assistants are quite impossible! They're never here!'

It wasn't their fault; on the contrary, he was glad it'd given him the chance . . .

She smiled ironically:

'And what about that marriage?'

'What marriage?'

'Yours!'

'Mine? There's absolutely no question of such a thing!'

She made a gesture of disbelief.

'And suppose there was, anyway? When your loveliest dreams collapse, you have to make do with second best!'

'But not all your dreams were quite so lily-white, were they?'

'What does that mean?'

'That you go to race meetings with . . . certain persons . . .'

'Damn the Marshal!' he said to himself. Then he remembered something:

'But you asked me to go and see her yourself, to help Arnoux!'

She shook her head:

'And you take advantage of that to have a good time!'

'Oh, do let's forget all this nonsense, for heaven's sake!'

'That's right, now that you're getting married!'

And she bit her lips to hold back a sigh.

'But let me tell you once again, it's not true! Can you imagine with my tastes and intellectual needs, I'd go and bury myself in the country, spend my life playing cards, keeping an eye on the builders and walking round in clogs? What would be the point anyway? They told you she's rich, didn't they? But I don't give a damn for money! Is it likely that after longing for all that's lovely, all that's loving and enchanting, an angel in human shape, and finally meeting *you*, my ideal, a vision of perfection that makes all other women non-existent . . .'

He seized her head between his hands and began kissing her eyelids, saying again and again:

'No, no, no! I'll never marry, never, never, never!'

Stunned by surprise and delight she was offering no resistance.

The warehouse door swung open; she sprang back and stood with her hand outstretched as though ordering him to keep quiet. Footsteps could be heard approaching and a voice spoke outside:

'Are you there, madam?'

'Come in!'

When the bookkeeper drew the door-curtain aside Madame Arnoux was resting her elbow on the counter and calmly twiddling a pen between her fingers.

'Good day, madam,' he said respectfully. 'I wonder if I may ask you please if I can rely on the service being ready?'

She made no reply but her tacit collusion made her flush bright scarlet, like an adulterous wife.

He came back the next day and was admitted. Anxious to press home his advantage, he immediately began to justify being with Rosanette at the Champ-de-Mars. It was the purest chance. Even allowing that she was pretty—which she wasn't—how could she possibly have interested him even for one minute when he was in love with somebody else?

'And you must know that very well, I've told you so!'

Madame Arnoux dropped her eyes.

'I'm cross with you for saying that!'

'Why?'

'Because now the most elementary common decency requires you to stop seeing me!'

He protested: his love was innocent. His past behaviour should set her mind at rest for the future; he'd promised himself never to disturb her life, never to try to pester her into accepting him.

'But yesterday my heart ran away with me!'

'We must put all that behind us, my dear boy!'

But what harm could there be if two unhappy people were prepared to share their unhappiness?

'After all, you're not happy either! Oh, I know you, I know you've not got anyone capable of responding to your need for affection and trust! I'll do whatever you ask, I swear I'll never do anything to hurt you!'

The strain was unbearable; despite himself he fell on his knees at her feet.

'Get up!' she ordered. 'Get up, I insist!'

And in the strongest terms she warned him that if he didn't obey, she'd never see him again.

'But you can't do that!' replied Frédéric. 'What will become of me? Other people want to be rich or famous or powerful but I've not trained to do anything, you're my only interest, my only riches, my only goal! My whole life, every thought I have, is centred round you, only you! I need you like I need air to breathe! Don't you realise that every atom of me is reaching upwards towards you? And that if we can't come together, my life's not worth living?'

Madame Arnoux began to tremble in every limb.

'Oh, go now, please, please go!'

She looked so distraught that he stopped; then he took a step towards her. She retreated, wringing her hands.

'Don't touch me! For pity's sake, please go!'

And he loved her so much that he obeyed.

It wasn't long before he began to feel angry with himself; he'd behaved like an idiot; within twenty-four hours he was back again.

Madame wasn't at home. He stood there on the landing, bewildered and furious with indignation. Arnoux appeared and told him that his wife had left that very morning to stay in a little rented cottage in Auteuil; they'd had to get rid of their country house in Saint-Cloud.

'It's another one of her fads! Anyway, as it suits her, and me too, incidentally, so much the better! Shall we have dinner together this evening?'

Frédéric pleaded urgent business and made his way straight to Auteuil.

Madame Arnoux couldn't repress a cry of joy; all his resentment evaporated.

He didn't mention the word love. To calm her fears he showed greater self-restraint than ever and when he asked whether he might come again she replied: 'Yes, I daresay', holding out her hand and withdrawing it almost at once.

He now began to call more and more often. He'd promise the cabbies huge tips but if the horse was slow, he'd often get impatient, jump out and breathlessly scramble on to a bus; and how scornfully he'd look at the faces of the passengers opposite him: they weren't on their way to see *Her*!

He could recognize her house from the huge honeysuckle covering one whole side of the weatherboard roof; it was a sort of Swiss chalet, painted red, with an outside balcony. There were three old Spanish chestnuts in the garden and on a mound in the middle, a thatched sun-roof supported on a tree-trunk. Below the slate walls, the straggling shoots of a badly trained vine dangled down like frayed cables. The gate-bell was rather stiff and went on ringing long after being pulled. They were always slow in coming to let him in and each time he was filled with anxiety, an indefinable dread.

Then he'd hear the flip-flop of the maid's slippers on the sand; or else Madame Arnoux would come and open it herself; one day he came upon her from behind, squatting down on the lawn looking for violets.

Her daughter's moodiness had forced her to pack her off to a convent. In the afternoons, her little boy was at kindergarten. Arnoux used to spend hours over lunch with Regimbart and his friend Compain at the Palais-Royal. There was no risk of being disturbed by any intruder.

Physical possession was out of the question, this was clearly understood. This pact, which removed all danger, made it easy for them to open their hearts to each other.

She'd talk about her early life with her mother in Chartres, her religious fervour round the age of twelve and then her passionate love of music; in her tiny bedroom overlooking the ramparts, she'd keep on singing until it was dark. He would tell her of his dreary school-days and his poetic dreams, filled with the radiant vision of a woman's face which he'd recognized the moment he'd seen her.

Usually they'd talk only about the years since they'd been seeing each other regularly. He would remind her of unimportant details, the colour of her dress on certain occasions; who had called on a particular day; what she'd said on some other occasion; and she would reply in amazement:

'Oh yes, I remember that!'

Their tastes and opinions were identical; the person listening would often exclaim:

'Me too!'

And the other one would take up the refrain:

'Me too!'

And there were never-ending outbursts against Fate.

'Why was Providence so unkind! If we'd met! . . .'

'If only I'd been younger!' she used to sigh.

'No, if only I'd been just a little older!'

And they had visions of life together, full only of love, a love rich enough to people any desert, a life of transcendental joys, free of trials or tribulations, where time would vanish in an endless outpouring of feeling, glowing with a radiance as sublime as the stars in their heavens.

Almost always they stayed upstairs, in the open; the softly rounded tree-tops in their autumnal yellow stretched out unevenly to the pale horizon; or they would walk to a pavilion at the end of the avenue where the only furniture was a grey canvas day-bed; the mirror was mottled with black spots; the walls gave off a musty odour; and they would stay there, blissfully happy, talking about themselves or other people or anything that came into their heads. Sunbeams shining through the shutters would sometimes produce a pattern of shadow like the strings of a lyre from the ceiling down to the flagstones; in the shafts of light specks of dust could be seen swirling round. She enjoyed slicing through them with her hand and Frédéric would catch hold of it gently, and study the tracery of her veins,

295

the grain of her skin; for him each of these fingers was more like a person than a thing.

She gave him a pair of her gloves and, the week after, her handkerchief. She called him Frédéric and he called her Marie, a name he adored, one expressly meant, he said, to be whispered softly in a moment of ecstasy, the very sound of which seemed to evoke drifting incense and piles of roses.

They would now settle beforehand which day he'd come and she would set off in advance and meet him on the way, as if by accident.

Lost in that carefree state peculiar to the blissfully happy, she never did anything to excite his love. All that season she wore a brown silk house-gown with velvet trimmings in the same colour, a loose-fitting garment which matched her gentle gestures and her serene and sober expression. She was indeed approaching the high summer of her sex, a time to ponder and to love, when mellowness lends a woman's eyes a more thoughtful glow, when depth of feeling blends with experience of life, and as their bloom fades, their whole being becomes a cornucopia of beauty in harmony. Never had she felt milder, more forbearing. Certain that she'd never weaken, she thought her misfortunes had given her the right to indulge her feelings. Anyway, it was such a novel and pleasant sensation! What a gulf between Arnoux's vulgarity and Frédéric's adoration!

He used to tremble at the thought that one word might lose him every advantage which he imagined he'd gained, for though an opportunity can come again, an act of foolishness is irreparable. He didn't want to have to take her, he wanted her to give herself. The certainty of being loved was a foretaste of possessing her; in any case, the spell under which she held him stirred his heart more than his senses. It was a blissful state of suspense, a feeling of elation so powerful that the possibility of achieving complete happiness now never entered his head. But once away from her, he was racked by lust.

It was not long before their conversations became punctuated with lengthy pauses. At times when their eyes met, a sort of bashfulness would bring a blush to their cheeks. Their care in hiding their love made it all the plainer and the stronger it grew the more constrained their behaviour became. The lie they were living exacerbated their feelings: the scent of damp leaves filled them with delight; the east wind distressed them; they would become irritable for no reason at all; they had gloomy forebodings; a footstep, a creaking panel would fill them with guilty terror; they felt they were being impelled towards a bottomless pit, in an atmosphere heavy with thunder; and when Frédéric could no longer hide his feeling of grievance, she'd blame herself:

'I know I'm behaving badly, that I seem to be trifling with your affections! You must stop seeing me!'

At this he'd repeat all his protestations of love and each time she'd listen to them with joy in her heart.

The complications of New Year's Day, together with her return to Paris, temporarily put a stop to their meetings. When he came back, his behaviour seemed subtly bolder. She kept going out to issue instructions and in spite of his pleadings, she held open house for all her middle-class friends. During these visits, there would be talk of such subjects as Léotade,* Monsieur Guizot, the Pope, the Palermo uprising* and the banquet in the 12e *arrondissement*,* which was causing a certain amount of concern. Frédéric relieved his feelings by running down the government; his nerves were by now so much on edge that he, like Deslauriers, was hoping for a complete upheaval. For her part Madame Arnoux was becoming depressed. Her husband was behaving more wildly than ever; he was keeping one of his factory workers, the one known as the 'Bordeaux woman'; Madame Arnoux herself told Frédéric about this. He tried to make capital out of it: 'Arnoux was being unfaithful to her.'

'Oh, I'm not bothered about that very much!' she said.

Frédéric took this remark as proof of how close their own relationship was. Was Arnoux suspicious of them?

'No, not now!'

She told him that one evening he'd left them by themselves and then crept back to eavesdrop, but as they were talking about nothing in particular, since then he'd not had any further misgivings.

'And he's right, isn't he?' commented Frédéric bitterly.

'Oh, no doubt!'

It would have been safer not to have used that expression.

One day when he called at the usual time, she wasn't at home. He felt betrayed.

On other occasions he was annoyed to see flowers he had brought her standing in a tumbler of water.

'Where should I have put them?'

'Not there anyway. But they'd be less cold there than if you'd been wearing them next to your heart!'

Some time later he reproached her for going to the Italian Opera the night before, without having informed him in advance. Other people would have seen her, admired her, perhaps loved her. Frédéric was using these suspicions purely in order to harass her and pick a quarrel; he was beginning to hate her: it was only fair that she should share some of his misery!

One afternoon in the middle of February he found her in a highly emotional state: Eugène was complaining of a sore throat; however the doctor had said it wasn't anything, a bad cold or a touch of the 'flu. Frédéric was astonished to see how feverish the boy looked. Nevertheless, he reassured his mother and quoted the example of several little lads of his age who'd recently been suffering similar complaints and soon recovered.

'Honestly?'

'Yes, of course, honestly!'

'Oh, you're so kind!'

She clutched his hand. He held on to it tightly.

'Oh, please let me go!'

'What's the matter? You were only catching hold of my hand because I was comforting you! You accept me for that sort of thing but you become suspicious as soon as I mention love!'

'Oh, you poor dear, I don't doubt your love!'

'Why can't you trust me? It's as if you think I'm a dreadful man capable of taking advantage . . .'

'Oh no!'

'If you could only prove that!'

'What proof do you want?'

So he reminded her how once they'd gone out for a walk together one foggy evening, at dusk. What ages ago that seemed! But what was there to prevent her from showing herself holding his arm in public, without any fear on her part or any ulterior motive on his, all by themselves, with no one around to pester them?

'All right then!' she said boldly, with a look of determination which for a moment took him completely by surprise.

Quickly he went on:

'Shall we say I'll be waiting for you at the corner of the rue Tronchet and the rue de la Ferme?'

'Oh, my goodness, Frédéric . . .' Madame Arnoux said uncertainly.

Without giving her time to think, he added:

'Next Tuesday then?'

'Tuesday?'

'Yes, between two and three o'clock.'

'All right!'

Coyly she looked away; Frédéric pressed his lips on the nape of her neck.

'You mustn't do that,' she said. 'You'll be making me have second thoughts!'

Women are known for their fickleness; he drew back in fright; then, as he was going out, whispered gently, as if the matter was now settled:

'Till next Tuesday!'

Discreetly, with a look of resignation in her lovely eyes, she hung her head.

Frédéric had a scheme.

He was hoping, if it was wet or else too sunny, he could take her into a doorway and once there, entice her indoors. The problem was to find a suitable house.

So he set off in search and half-way down the rue Tronchet saw a notice in the distance announcing: 'Furnished rooms.'

Recognizing what he was after, the man at the reception immediately showed him a bedroom and dressing-room on the mezzanine floor, with two exits. Frédéric took it for a month and paid in advance.

Then he went into three different shops to find the most exclusive perfume and cosmetics, buy a piece of bone-lace to replace the awful red cotton counterpane, and choose a pair of blue satin slippers; he was only restrained from making further purchases by the fear of appearing vulgar. He carted the stuff back to the room and with greater devotion than if decorating an altar proceeded to shift the furniture around, drape the curtains himself, put heather on the mantelshelf and violets on the chest of drawers; he wished he could have paved the whole room in gold.

'It's tomorrow,' he kept saying to himself, 'yes, it's tomorrow, I'm not just dreaming.'

He could feel his heart pounding wildly in anticipation; then, when everything was ready, he went off with the key in his pocket as if Lady Luck, asleep there, might try to escape.

At home a letter from his mother was awaiting him.

'Why have you stayed away so long? Your behaviour is beginning to appear ridiculous. I realize that you feel some hesitation over the marriage but do think carefully!'

And she spelt the matter out: forty-five thousand francs a year. What was more, 'people are beginning to talk' and Monsieur Roque was expecting a definite answer. As for the young lady, her situation was really embarrassing. 'She's very much in love with you.'

Frédéric flung the letter down without bothering to read it to the end and opened another one, from Deslauriers:

'The *pear** is ripe, old chap! We're relying on you, as you promised. We're meeting at the place du Panthéon at first light tomorrow. Go into the Café Soufflot. I want to have a word with you before the march begins.'

'I know all about their protest marches, thanks very much! I've got a more attractive appointment!'

By eleven o'clock next morning Frédéric had left the house. He wanted to cast a final eye over his preparations;

300

and, who knows, by some chance or other, *She* might turn up early. As he came out of the rue Tronchet, he heard a great hubbub coming from behind the Madeleine; he went along to take a look and at the far end of the square, on the left, he saw men in smocks mingling with respectably dressed middle-class citizens.

A manifesto had appeared in the papers calling on all subscribers to the reform banquet to meet there. Almost immediately the Ministry had posted notices banning it. The previous evening, the parliamentary opposition had decided to give up the idea but, unaware of this decision by their leaders, the patriots had gone ahead with the meeting, accompanied by a large number of interested spectators. A short while before, a student deputation had called on Odilon Barrot* and was now at the Ministry of Foreign Affairs. No one knew whether the banquet would take place, whether the government would carry out its threats, or whether the National Guard would put in an appearance. Feelings were running high both against Parliament and the government. The crowd was growing larger every minute. Suddenly the stirring strains of the 'Marseillaise' rang out.

It was the students' procession arriving, marching in step in double rank and in good order, bare-handed, but with angry faces and chanting intermittently:

'Long live Reform! Down with Guizot!'

Frédéric's friends were bound to be amongst them; they'd recognize him and take him along with them. He quickly took cover in the rue de l'Arcade.

When the students had marched twice round the Madeleine, they went off down towards the place de la Concorde, crammed with people who, in the distance, looked like a field of fluttering black ears of corn.

At the same moment, to the left of the church, a troop of infantry formed up in battle order.

However, the groups refused to move on and so finally plain-clothes police grabbed hold of the most provocative members of the crowd and unceremoniously hauled them off to the police station. Frédéric watched indignantly but made no move: they might have picked him up with the others and he'd have let Madame Arnoux down.

Shortly afterwards the helmets of the Municipal Guard* came on the scene; they were flailing around with the flats of their swords, on horseback. One horse fell; they rushed to its rescue and as soon as the guardsman had remounted, they all rode off.

Everything was still. The drizzle which had wet the asphalt had stopped. A balmy west wind was sweeping away the clouds.

Frédéric began to patrol the rue Tronchet, looking backwards and forwards.

At last two o'clock struck.

'Ah, it's time!' he said to himself. 'She'll be leaving her house and on her way here'; and a few minutes later: 'She'd have had time to be here by now.' Until three o'clock he endeavoured to stay calm. 'No, she's not late. Just be patient!'

With nothing better to do, he kept on looking into the few shops in the street: a bookshop, a saddler's, a mourning outfitters. Soon he was familiar with every book, every sort of harness and every kind of material. Seeing him going up and down in front of their establishments, the shopkeepers were at first surprised and then so frightened that they put up their shutters.

No doubt something had held her up and she was feeling as miserable as he was! But it wouldn't be long before they'd both be so happy! Because she was bound to come, that was sure! 'After all, she gave me her word!' But an unbearable feeling of distress was creeping over him.

On an absurd impulse, he went into the lodging house, as if thinking she might be there. At that very moment she could be coming down the street. He dashed out. Not a soul! Once again he began to pound his beat.

He kept gazing at the cracks between the paving stones, the lamp-posts, the spouts of the drain-pipes, the numbers over the doors. The most trivial objects were becoming his companions or, rather, mocking bystanders; the dull uniformity of the house-fronts seemed merciless. He could feel himself crumbling into hopelessness. The echo of his footsteps was hammering into his brain.

When his watch said four o'clock, he went dizzy and was gripped by a sense of dread. He tried reciting poetry, doing some sort of calculation or other. No good! He was obsessed by the image of Madame Arnoux. He felt an urge to rush away and meet her. But which way should he go and not risk missing her?

He went up to a street messenger and pressed five francs into his hand to go to Jacques Arnoux's place in the rue Paradis and enquire 'if Madame Arnoux was at home'. Then he resumed his post on the corner of the rue de la Ferme and the rue Tronchet in order to be able to keep an eye on both at the same time. Looking down the street, he could see massed groups of people lurching confusedly to and fro on the boulevard. From time to time he picked out the plume of a dragoon or a woman's hat; he strained his eyes to recognize her. A smiling little street urchin with a marmot asked him for a tip.

The velvet-jacketed messenger returned: 'The porter hadn't seen her go out.' What could be detaining her? If she was ill, they'd've said so! Had she had a caller? What could be easier than to say she wasn't at home! He rapped his forehead:

'How idiotic of me! It's the rioting!'

This obvious explanation calmed his anxiety. Then suddenly: 'But there's no rioting in her district!' And a horrible doubt struck him: 'Suppose she's not going to come? Suppose she gave her word just to get rid of me? No, I can't believe it!' No doubt she was being prevented by some strange accident, one of those quite unpredictable things? In that case she'd have written. He sent the man from the lodging house over to the rue Rumford to find out if there was a letter for him.

No letter had been left. This lack of news reassured him. He was trying to read omens in the random number of coins in his hand, in the expressions on the faces of the passers-by, in the colour of the horses; when the result was unfavourable, he tried to ignore it. He was overcome by fits

303

of rage against Madame Arnoux and hurled insults at her under his breath. He felt weak and faint and, a minute later, a burst of hope: she was going to appear, she was standing there, just behind him. He'd spin round: no one! Once, about thirty yards away, he caught sight of a woman of her height and wearing similar clothes. He ran towards her; it wasn't Madame Arnoux. Five o'clock struck. Half past five! Six o'clock. She hadn't come.

The night before, she'd had a dream: she'd been standing in the rue Tronchet for a long time waiting for something indefinite but important and, without knowing why, was afraid of being seen. But a nasty little dog was nipping at the hem of her dress and wouldn't go away. He kept coming back again and again, barking louder and louder all the time. She woke up. The barking went on. She strained her ears. It was coming from her son's bedroom. Not waiting to put anything on her feet, she rushed out to see: it was the little boy himself coughing. His hands were burning hot, his face flushed, and his voice had a strange rasp. With every minute he was having greater difficulty in breathing. She remained bending over and watching him till daybreak.

At eight, the drummer from the National Guard came to tell Monsieur Arnoux that his fellow guardsmen were expecting him. He quickly got dressed and left, promising to call straightaway on their doctor, Monsieur Colot. At ten o'clock, as Colot hadn't come, Madame Arnoux sent her maid round: the doctor was away in the country and his locum was out on his rounds.

Eugène was holding his head sideways on the bolster with his nostrils dilated and a permanent frown on his face; the poor little boy was going paler than his sheets and each time he drew in his breath, which was becoming increasingly sharp and rapid, almost metallic, his larynx gave a whistling sound. His cough sounded like one of those jarring pieces of clockwork inside yapping toy cardboard dogs.

Madame Arnoux rushed frantically over to the bell-pull, calling for help and shouting:

'A doctor! Fetch a doctor!'

Ten minutes later an old gentleman wearing a white necktie and with well-trimmed whiskers appeared. He asked a large number of questions concerning the habits, age and temperament of the young patient, examined his throat, put his ear to his back and wrote out a prescription. The old fellow's cool manner was quite hateful. He smelt of embalming. She'd have liked to hit him. He said he'd be back that evening.

Soon the dreadful coughing fits began again. Sometimes the little boy would jerk bolt upright, his chest muscles twitching, and when he breathed in, his stomach hollowed out as if he was gasping for air after a race. Then he would fling his head backwards on to the pillow with his mouth wide open. With infinite care Madame Arnoux kept trying to persuade him to take sips of the ipecacuanha and kermes syrup but he would moan feebly and push the spoon away. He seemed incapable of speaking above a whisper.

From time to time she consulted the prescription again; the arcane medical names of the drugs were frightening; had the chemist made a mistake? Monsieur Colot's locum arrived.

He was young and seemed diffident, a beginner who didn't conceal his reaction. For fear of doing the wrong thing, he hesitated at first and eventually prescribed ice-packs. It took a long time to get the ice. The bladder holding it burst. They had to change the boy's nightshirt. All these disturbances brought on a fresh and more devastating attack.

The little lad started to tear the packs off his neck as if trying to remove the blockage which was stifling him; he kept clawing at the wall, clutching the curtains of his bunk and looking for somewhere to prop himself up to help him to breathe. His face now had a bluish tinge; his whole body was bathed in cold sweat and seemed to have shrunk. His terror-stricken eyes were fastened on his mother. He threw his arms round her neck and desperately clasped her; she held back her sobs and in a broken voice lovingly tried to comfort him:

'Yes, my love, my little angel, my precious little boy!'

305

Then he'd grow calm, for a while.

She went and fetched some toys, his Punch, a collection of pictures, and spread them out on his bed to amuse him. She even tried to sing.

She began a song which she used to sing when cradling him in her arms and wrapping him in his swaddling clothes as a baby, on that selfsame tapestry nursing chair. But a shudder ran through his whole body, like a gust of wind whipping up a wave; his eyes were bulging; she thought he was about to die and turned away in order not to watch.

A moment later she felt strong enough to look back; he was still alive. The hours dragged on slowly, interminably, in gloom and despair; she was now measuring the minutes by the gradual stages of his death throes. His spasms of coughing flung him forward as though breaking him in half; finally he spewed up a strange object which looked like a small parchment scroll. What could it be? She imagined he must have brought up a piece of his gut. But he was breathing easily and regularly. This apparent remission scared her more than anything else; she was standing there staring, with her arms dangling, when Monsieur Colot came in. In his opinion the child was out of danger.

At first she failed to understand and asked him to repeat what he'd said. Wasn't it just one of those comforting formulas used by doctors? Monsieur Colot went off with a look of satisfaction on his face. Then she felt as if the bonds constricting her heart had suddenly burst.

'Out of danger! Is that really possible?'

Suddenly, with pitiless clarity, the thought of Frédéric sprang into her mind. It was a warning from Heaven; but in His infinite mercy, the Lord hadn't wanted her punishment to be too cruel. But what just retribution He would exact if she persisted in her love! No doubt her son would be jeered at because of her; Madame Arnoux had a vision of him as a young man wounded in a duel and being carried away dying on a stretcher. She rushed over to the little chair and with all the strength she could muster, lifted her soul up to God, offering Him the sacrifice of her only lapse, the first passionate love she had ever felt.

Frédéric had gone back home. He sat in his armchair, too prostrated even to abuse her. He dozed off and in his nightmare, still standing on the pavement, he could hear the rain falling.

Next day, a coward to the end, he again sent a messenger boy to Madame Arnoux.

Either because she never got the message or else because there was too much to explain in a note, he received the same reply as before. This insolence was the last straw! In a burst of pride and anger, he swore never even to feel desire again and his love vanished like a leaf swept away in a storm. He felt relieved, a sort of stoical joy, followed by the need to do something violent. He went out and roamed the streets.

Men from working-class suburbs were going by armed with guns and old swords, a few wearing red caps and all of them singing the 'Marseillaise' or 'Les Girondins'.* Here and there a National Guardsman could be seen hurrying off to his headquarters in his town hall. In the distance, drums were beating. There was fighting at the Porte-Saint-Martin. Everywhere you could sense a feeling of high spirits and aggression. Frédéric continued his walk. All this activity in the big city was raising his own spirits and opposite Frascati's, seeing the Marshal's windows, on a wild, youthful impulse, he dashed across the boulevard.

The double carriage gate was just being shut and the maid Delphine was writing on it in charcoal: 'We've handed over all our weapons.'

'Oh, sir, Madam's in a dreadful state!' she exclaimed. 'She sacked the groom for being insolent and she thinks we're all going to be looted! She's scared stiff, particularly as the gentleman's gone.'

'Which gentleman?'

'The prince!'

Frédéric went up to the boudoir. The Marshal appeared in her petticoat, with her hair hanging down her back and looking completely distraught.

'Oh, thank you, you've come to my rescue! That's the second time! But you never come to claim your reward!'

'I really do apologize!' said Frédéric, clasping her round the waist with both hands.

'What's the matter? What are you doing?' stammered the Marshal, not only surprised but flattered.

He replied:

'I'm following the trend! I'm a reformed character!'

As he kissed her, she laughed, and still laughing, let herself be tumbled backwards on to her divan.

They spent the afternoon watching the people in the street from their window.

Then he took her out to dinner at the Trois-Frères-Provençaux. The meal was long and delicious. As there were no cabs, they came back on foot.

The news of a change in government had made Paris change too. Everyone was cheerful; people were strolling around and the Chinese lanterns on every floor made the scene as bright as day. The soldiers were trudging back to their barracks, looking sad and harassed. They were being greeted with shouts of: 'Up the infantry!' They went on their way without making any response. The officers of the National Guard on the other hand were bursting with enthusiasm, waving their swords about and shouting: 'Up the reform!' Each time they heard that, the lovers went into fits of laughter; Frédéric was cracking lots of jokes, in fine form.

They walked up the rue Duphot and came to the boulevards. The houses were festooned with fairy lights. In the streets below there was a seething, shadowy mass of people and the occasional glint of bayonets. The hubbub was deafening. The crowd was so dense that there was no question of taking the direct way home. As they were going into the rue Caumartin, they heard a sudden crackling like an immense piece of silk being ripped apart. It was the shooting incident on the boulevard des Capucines.

'Just a few of the middle classes being put down,' commented Frédéric casually, for there are times when the least cruel of men feels so detached from his fellows that he wouldn't blink an eyelid if the whole human race were wiped out.

The Marshal's teeth were chattering as she clung to his arm. She announced that she couldn't move another step. So, in order to savour his hatred of Madame Arnoux and desecrate her memory to the full, he took Rosanette to the same hotel rooms which he'd got ready for the other woman.

The flowers were still fresh. The lace cover was on the bed. He took the little slippers out of the wardrobe. Rosanette was greatly touched by such loving solicitude.

At about one o'clock, she was woken by rumbling sounds in the distance and saw him with his head buried in his pillow, sobbing.

'What's the matter, my love?'

'It's because I'm so happy,' replied Frédéric. 'I've been wanting you for such a long time!'

PART THREE

CHAPTER I

Frédéric was awakened by the rattle of gunfire and, in spite of Rosanette's objections, insisted on going out to see what was happening. The sound had come from the direction of the Champs-Elysées but on his way there, at the corner of the rue Saint-Honoré, he met some men in smocks who called:

'No, not that way! The Palais-Royal!'

Frédéric followed them. The iron railings of the Church of the Assumption had been torn down. Further along he noticed three paving stones lying in the middle of the roadway, presumably the beginnings of a barricade, and then bits of broken bottle and coils of wire to impede the cavalry. Suddenly a young man dashed out of a side-street, pale-faced, with flowing shoulder-length black hair, wearing slippers and a sort of tight-fitting jersey with coloured spots, and carrying a long infantry rifle. He bounded away like a tiger as if in a trance. Now and again there came the thud of an explosion.

Seeing the five bodies of those killed on the boulevard des Capucines being carried through the streets in a cart the night before had changed the people's mood; and as equerries came and went at the Tuileries and Monsieur Molé*left to form a cabinet but failed to return and Monsieur Thiers was busily trying to put together another one and the king was quibbling and shilly-shallying, eventually giving overall command to Bugeaud*only to prevent him from exercising it, the uprising, as though controlled by a single hand, was becoming organized and extremely menacing. Inpassioned speeches were being spouted to the crowd on street corners; peals of bells rang out furiously, sounding the alarm from the churches; lead bullets were being cast and cartridges rolled; the trees on the boulevards, the public urinals, benches, railings and street gas lamps had been torn down or overturned; by morning, Paris was covered with barricades. Resistance was short-lived; the National Guard was joining in everywhere and by eight o'clock the people of Paris found themselves, peacefully or through force, in full control of five barracks, almost all the town halls and the most important strategic points. Gently, of its own accord, the monarchy was melting away. Now the command post of the Château d'Eau*was under attack to release fifty prisoners, who in fact weren't there.

Frédéric was forced to stop at the entrance to the square, which was full of armed groups; the rue Saint-Thomas and the rue Fromenteau were held by companies of regular infantry. The rue de Valois was blocked by an enormous barricade; the smoke floating over the top of it thinned out a little; men were running towards it, wildly waving their arms; they disappeared and the firing started up again. Inside the command post invisible defenders returned their fire; the windows were protected by oak shutters pierced with loop-holes; and the monumental three-storied building with its two wings, its fountain on the first floor and small doorway in the centre, began to be pitted with white bullet-holes. Its front terrace and the three steps leading up to it were deserted.

A man in a Phrygian cap and wearing a cartridge pouch over his woollen jacket was standing beside Frédéric, arguing with a woman in a headscarf. She was saying:

'Oh, come back, do come back!'

'Leave me alone!' the man replied. 'You can look after the lodge perfectly well yourself. I ask you, citizen, is it fair? I've always done my bit, in 1830, in '32, '34 and '39! Today there are people fighting and I've got to fight too! Off you go!'

The portress finally gave way to his objections and those of a National Guard standing beside them, a friendly, ingenuous-looking forty-year-old gentleman with a fringe of blond beard. In the thick of the mob he was talking to Frédéric, loading and firing his gun as he did so, in the matter-of-fact tone of a gardener among his plants. A young lad in an apron was trying to wheedle some caps out of him to use in his own weapon, a fine sporting gun, given him by a 'gent'.

'Help yourself from the pouch on my back,' said the older man. 'And take cover, you'll be getting yourself killed!'

The drums were sounding the attack. There was a burst of shouting and cheering and the crowd surged to and fro. Caught between two solid blocks of people, Frédéric was unable to move; indeed, he was fascinated and enjoying himself enormously. The wounded falling all around him and the dead lying on the ground didn't seem really dead or wounded. It was like being at a show.

In the middle of the turmoil, above the heads of the crowd, an old man* in a black coat appeared, riding on a white horse with a velvet saddle; in one hand he was holding an olive branch, in the other a piece of paper, and he was waving both of them in the air, very determinedly. Eventually, in despair of making himself heard, he rode off.

The regular troops had made themselves scarce and the post was now defended only by Municipal Guards. A wave of attackers boldly made towards the front steps; they were mown down; others followed; the door shuddered under the resounding blows of iron bars; the guards stood firm. But a barouche stuffed with hay and blazing like some giant torch was dragged up against the walls; firewood, straw and a cask of spirits were hastily tipped on. The fire darted along the stones; the building started puffing out smoke like a huge solfatara; enormous flames roared out between the pillars of the balustrade on the flat roof. National Guardsmen had occupied the first floor of the Palais-Royal and shots were coming from every window in the square; bullets whistled through the air and the water from the burst fountain mingled with the pools of blood on the ground; people were sliding about in the mud on pieces of clothing, military caps and weapons. Frédéric felt something soft underneath his foot: it was the hand of a sergeant in a grey greatcoat lying face down in the gutter. Fresh groups of workers were arriving all the time, urging the fighters on. The firing was intensifying. The wine merchants had opened their shops and people kept breaking off for a smoke and a pint of beer before going back to fight. A stray dog was howling. This made people laugh.

Frédéric felt a jolt and with a death-rattle, a man collapsed against his shoulder with a bullet lodged in the base of his spine. Frédéric was furious: perhaps that shot had been aimed at him; and he was just about to hurl himself into the fray when a National Guardsman stopped him:

'Don't waste your time! The king's just left. If you don't believe me, go and see for yourself!'

Frédéric relaxed. The place du Carrousel appeared quiet. The Hôtel de Nantes was still standing in its usual isolation and the houses behind the dome of the Louvre, opposite the long gallery to the right, and the stretch of uneven open land leading to the stallholders's shacks, looked as if they were floating in the grey air; murmurs of distant sounds seemed to be blending in the mist; but at the far end of the square, a garish light was spilling through a gap in the clouds and making the front windows of the Tuileries stand out sharply in white. On the ground near the Arc de triomphe,* a horse lay dead. Behind the railings, people stood talking in groups of five or six. At the open palace doors, servants were letting the public in.

In a little entrance hall downstairs, bowls of white coffee had been laid out. A few of the sightseers laughingly sat down while others remained standing, among them a cabdriver who grabbed a jar full of caster sugar with both hands, looked furtively around and greedily began to eat, sticking his nose into the neck of the container. At the foot of the main staircase, a man was signing his name on a list. Frédéric recognized him from the back:

'Good Lord, Hussonnet, it's you!'

'Yes indeed,' replied the Bohemian. 'I'm presenting myself at court. Isn't this tremendous fun!'

'Shall we go upstairs?'

They made their way up to the Hall of the Marshals. The portraits of these illustrious men were all intact except for

Bugeaud, who'd been stuck through the stomach. There they stood, leaning on their swords, in front of a gun-carriage, in awesome attitudes utterly inappropriate to the situation. A large clock showed twenty past one.

Suddenly the strains of the 'Marseillaise' rang out. Hussonnet and Frédéric peered over the banisters. It was the Paris People. In one long, irresistible, bellowing thrust, they stormed up the stairs in a wild flurry of bare heads, helmets, red caps, bayonets and shoulders, so impetuously that people were swamped in the swarming mass which kept streaming on like a rip-tide. On reaching the top, they spread out and the singing died down; the only sound now was the clumping of shoes and the babble of voices. The crowd was inoffensive and quite content just to look; but now and again the lack of elbow room would cause some-one's arm to shatter a window-pane or else a vase or a statuette would topple off a console table on to the floor. The wainscoting groaned under the strain. All around were faces, flushed and pouring with sweat.

'Heroes don't smell very sweet!' remarked Hussonnet.

'God, you're infuriating!' retorted Frédéric.

They found themselves propelled willy-nilly into a large room with a red velvet canopy. On the throne underneath, a proletarian was sitting; he had a black beard, an open-necked shirt and the stupidly cheerful look of a pot-bellied Chinese figurine. Other people were clambering up on the dais to take his place.

'What a myth!' said Hussonnet. 'Behold the sovereign people!'

The throne was picked up and carried precariously across the room.

'Od's bodikins, how she sways! Methinks the vessel of state is pitching in a mighty strong sea! Look how she's dancing around!'

It was being carried over to a window where it was flung out amidst boos and jeers.

'Poor old thing!' said Hussonnet as he watched it fall into the gardens, where it was quickly seized and taken along to the Bastille to be burnt.

There was a frenzied explosion of joy as if the throne was going to be replaced by an era of happiness without end; and not so much in a mood of revenge as with a determination to show its right of ownership, the People smashed and tore up mirrors and curtains, chandeliers and torch-holders, tables, chairs and stools, the entire furnishings, down to albums of drawings and even embroidered work-baskets. They'd won, so wasn't it up to them to have some fun? And so the riffraff decked itself out in fine lace and cashmere; gold fringes were wrapped round the sleeves of smocks, ostrich feathers were flaunted on blacksmiths' heads, Legion of Honour ribbons found their way round the waists of prostitutes. Everyone was gratifying their personal whims; some were dancing, others drinking. In the queen's bedroom a woman was plastering her hair with pomade; a couple of keen card-players were having a game behind a screen; Hussonnet drew Frédéric's attention to a fellow smoking his clay-pipe on a balcony; and the general uproar was becoming more and more deafening, with the endless sound of china and glass smashing as it hit the floor, tinkling like the strips of a glass harmonica.

Their rage now took a more ominous turn. With obscene curiosity they rummaged in all the closets, prying into every nook and cranny, leaving not a single drawer unopened. Hardened criminals thrust their arms into the princesses' beds and rolled all over them, to console themselves for not being able to rape their occupants. Others with more sinister faces prowled silently round in search of loot; but there were too many people about. Through the open doors of the suites of rooms, all that could be seen was a milling mass in a cloud of dust against the gilt. The heat was growing more and more stifling; everyone was panting for breath and to avoid suffocating, the two men left.

Motionless, with wide staring eyes, a common whore was standing on a pile of clothing in the ante-room, posing, horrifyingly, as the Statue of Liberty.

Hardly had they stepped outside than a platoon of Municipal Guards in greatcoats came up, lifted their police caps, revealing their balding heads, and made a deep bow to the People. At this mark of respect the ragged heroes puffed out their chests and Hussonnet and Frédéric couldn't help feeling a certain glow of pleasure themselves.

They made their way back to the Palais-Royal in an exultant mood. In front of the rue Fromanteau the bodies of dead soldiers were lying on piles of straw. They passed close by them without blinking an eyelid, feeling proud to be taking such things in their stride.

The Palais-Royal was crammed with people. In the inner courtyard, seven bonfires were burning fiercely; pianos, chests of drawers and clocks were hurtling out of the windows. Fire-hoses were spurting water roof-high. Some hooligans were trying to cut them with swords. Frédéric urged a Polytechnician to intervene but he didn't understand, and in any case seemed stupid. All around, in both galleries, the populace had 'liberated' the cellars and was indulging in a drunken orgy. Wine was flowing in buckets, soaking everybody's feet. Young louts were reeling about yelling and drinking out of bottles with broken-off tops.

'The people!' exclaimed Hussonnet. 'Let's get out of here, this lot disgusts me.'

All along the Galerie d'Orléans, wounded men lay on the ground on mattresses, with dark red curtains as blankets; local housewives were supplying them with soup and bandages.

'Say what you like,' said Frédéric. '*I* think the People are terrific!'

The main vestibule was filled with an angry surging mass, with men trying to force their way upstairs to complete the havoc; on the steps, National Guardsmen were struggling to hold them back. The pluckiest of them all was a light infantry officer, bare-headed, dishevelled, with his leather equipment torn to shreds. His shirt had rucked up round his waist between his trousers and tunic and he was grappling furiously in the thick of the fight. From a distance Hussonnet, who had sharp eyes, recognized Arnoux.

They walked down to the Tuileries to get some fresh air and for a few minutes sat on a bench with their eyes closed, too weak and bemused to utter a word. All around knots of passers-by were gathering and talking together. The Duchesse d'Orléans had been named Regent;* it was all over and people were enjoying that euphoria that comes from something brought to a speedy conclusion, when servants appeared at all the attic windows of the Tuileries, ripping up their livery jackets and tossing them down into the garden to demonstrate rejection of their allegiance. They were booed and disappeared.

Frédéric and Hussonnet noticed a powerfully built young man wearing a red tunic hurrying along under the trees, with a rifle over his shoulder and wearing a cartridge belt round his waist; a handkerchief was tied round his forehead below his cap. He turned his head: it was Dussardier. He flung himself into their arms, too breathless with delight and exhaustion to say more than:

'Oh, my two old pals, how wonderful!'

He'd been on the go solidly, for two whole days. He'd worked on the barricades in the Latin Quarter, fought in the rue Rambuteau, rescued three dragoons, got into the Tuileries with the Dunoyer column, gone to the Chamber of Deputies and then on to the Hôtel de Ville.

'That's where I've just come from! Everything's fine! The People are on top! The workers and middle classes are falling into each others' arms! Ah, if only you knew what I've seen! What a splendid lot! How wonderful it all is!'

Then, not noticing they were unarmed:

'I was sure you'd be taking part! It was pretty hard going for a while but that doesn't matter now!'

A drop of blood was trickling down his cheek. They asked him about it.

'Just a scratch from a bayonet, nothing to worry about!'

'But you ought to get it seen to!'

'Nonsense, I'm tough, what's the odds! The Republic's been proclaimed and now everyone's going to be happy! Some journalists talking near me a moment ago were saying we're going to liberate Poland and Italy! Do you realize there'll be no more kings? The whole world will be free, absolutely free!'

He swept his eyes over the whole horizon and flung out

317

his arms in a gesture of triumph. But he saw a long line of men running along the terrace beside the Seine.

'My goodness, I was forgetting, they've captured the forts, I must go and join them! So long!'

Brandishing his rifle, he turned and shouted:

'Long live the Republic!'

Sparks and huge spiralling clouds of black smoke were spewing out of the palace chimneys. In the distance the peals of bells sounded like the bleating of sheep. The victorious insurgents were letting fly with their guns in all directions. Unwarlike though he was, Frédéric was electrified by the enthusiasm of the crowd; he felt his Gallic blood pounding. Voluptuously he sniffed the turbulent air full of the reek of gunpowder; yet at the same time the heady fumes of universal love, an overpowering feeling of tenderness, were setting him quivering as if the heart of all mankind was beating inside him.

Hussonnet yawned and said:

'I suppose it's about time for me to go and enlighten the masses.'

Frédéric went along with him as far as his mailing office, close to the Stock Exchange, and started composing a report on the events for the Troyes newspaper, a set-piece couched in rhapsodical terms, and signed it. Then they had dinner together in a tavern. Hussonnet was looking thoughtful; the vagaries of the Revolution were outstripping his own.

After coffee, when they went down to the Hôtel de Ville, his irrepressible sense of fun had again taken over: he clambered over the barricades like a mountain goat and when challenged by the sentries cracked bawdy patriotic jokes.

They heard the Provisional Government proclaimed in the flickering light of torches; eventually, dropping with exhaustion, Frédéric got home at midnight.

'Well,' he said to his man as he helped him undress, 'are you pleased?'

'Yes, sir, I daresay, but I can't abide seeing all that mob marching in step!'

When he woke up next day, Frédéric's first thought was for Deslauriers and he hurried round to see him, only to learn that he'd just left to take up an appointment as government commissioner* somewhere in the provinces. The previous evening he'd managed to gain access to Ledru-Rollin* and by urging the claims of graduates had bullied him into letting him have a job, a mission. He was due to notify his address next week, the porter said.

After this Frédéric went round to the Marshal's, where he got a cool reception: she resented having been left in the lurch. After his repeated reassurance that peace had now been restored, her resentment evaporated. Everything was quiet now and she'd got no reason to be scared; he kissed her and she declared her support for the Republic, as the Monsignor Archbishop of Paris had already done, speedily followed, with a miraculous display of enthusiasm, by judges and public prosecutors, the Conseil d'État, the Institut, the Marshals of France, Changarnier,* Monsieur de Falloux,* all the Bonapartists, all the Legitimists and a fair number of Orléanists.

The monarchy had fallen so suddenly that, once their initial shock had subsided, the middle classes felt a sort of surprise at still being alive. The summary execution of a few looters, shot out of hand, seemed a clear act of justice. For a month the phrase of Lamartine went the rounds, about the red flag 'having only been carried round the Champ-de-Mars, whereas the tricolour* . . . etc. etc.'. So all parties closed ranks and went for cover behind it, each with its eyes firmly on its own particular colour and fully determined to rip the other off as soon as they had the upper hand.

Since all business was temporarily suspended, idle curiosity and nervousness drove people out on to the streets. Their casual dress tended to minimize class differences; any hatred was kept in the background and hope to the fore; the crowd was all sweetness and light. Faces glowed with pride at having achieved hard-won ·rights. There was a festive mood of carnival and camp-fires; it was fun living in Paris in those early days.

The Marshal would take Frédéric's arm and they'd stroll round the streets. She was amused to see everybody wearing rosettes in their buttonholes, flags hanging from every window, garish notices stuck on every wall; from time to time she'd drop a coin or two in the collection boxes for the wounded, placed on chairs in the middle of the streets.

Then she'd stop in front of the caricatures of Louis-Philippe as a confectioner, a circus performer, a dog or a leech. But she was rather scared of Caussidière's men* with their sashes and swords. Sometimes there were people planting a Tree of Liberty, with church dignitaries joining in the ceremony, and giving their blessing to the Republic, surrounded by their retinue of gold-braided assistants. The masses found this all very right and proper. The commonest sight was a deputation for this, that or the other, going to lay their claim at the Hôtel de Ville, for every trade or industry was expecting the government to provide an immediate cure for its ills. True, there were some who went to offer advice or congratulations or simply to call in and see the way things were being run.

One day round the middle of March, as he was crossing the Pont-d'Arcole on an errand for Rosanette in the Latin Quarter, Frédéric saw a column of individuals with long beards and wearing queer-looking hats marching towards him, led by a black man beating a drum, a former artist's model; and the banner fluttering in the breeze and bearing the inscription 'Artists' was being carried by none other than Pellerin.

Making Frédéric a sign to wait, he came back five minutes later; he had some time to spare because the government was at that moment meeting the stonemasons. He was going, together with his colleagues, to ask for the creation of an 'Arts Workshop', a sort of exchange, where they'd debate questions of aesthetics and produce superb works of art because they'd be pooling their genius. Paris would soon be covered with monumental buildings which he'd be decorating; he'd even started work on a figure depicting the Republic. One of his comrades came to fetch him, because there was a deputation of poulterers hard on their heels.

'How stupid!' grumbled a voice in the crowd. 'Nothing but humbug all the time! Never any real action!'

It was Regimbart. He made no attempt to shake hands but seized the chance to ventilate his grievances.

The Citizen spent his days roaming the streets, tugging at his moustache, rolling his eyes, eagerly lapping up and passing on gloomy news. His only watchwords were: 'Look out, we're being outflanked!' and 'The Republic's being double-crossed, for Christ's sake!'. He was unhappy about everything and especially that 'we hadn't got back our natural frontiers'. The mere mention of Lamartine* made him shrug his shoulders. He considered Ledru-Rollin 'not up to the job', described Dupont (de l'Eure)* as an old fogey, Albert* as an idiot, Louis Blanc as a Utopian, Blanqui* as an extremely dangerous man; and when Frédéric asked him what ought to have been done, he squeezed his arm in a vice-like grip and replied: 'Take over the Rhine, damn it!'

And he accused the forces of reaction.

They were beginning to drop their masks. The looting of the châteaux of Neuilly and Suresne,* the fire in the Batignolles, the disturbances in Lyons, every act of violence, every grievance, was being exaggerated at the moment, not forgetting Ledru-Rollin's circular,* the compulsory exchange rate, the fall of State Bonds to sixty francs and finally that crowning injustice, the last straw, the ultimate outrage, the forty-five centime tax increase!* And over and above all that, there was Socialism! Although such theories, which were about as modern as skirts for women, had for the last forty years been the subject of enough discussion to fill whole libraries, they had shocked the middle classes as much as if the sky had fallen in; their indignation sprang purely from their hatred of any new idea as such, a loathing which later becomes its title to fame and always makes it superior to its opponents, however second-rate it is.

Property now achieved the respectability of Religion, on

the same plane as God himself. To attack it was sacrilege, almost as bad as cannibalism. In spite of the most humane legislation ever seen, the bogy of '93 reared its head and every syllable of the word 'republic' vibrated like the thud of the blade of the guillotine, which didn't prevent people from despising it for its weakness. For want of a strong leader, France began to be alarmed and cry out like a blind man without his stick, or a little child who's lost its nanny.

No one was trembling in his shoes more than Monsieur Dambreuse. This new situation threatened his wealth but, above all, it made nonsense of everything he stood for. Such a good system and so sensible a king! Were such things possible? The world was going to rack and ruin! The day after the Revolution, Monsieur Dambreuse sacked three of his servants, sold his horses, bought a soft hat for wearing in public, and even had thoughts of growing a beard; meanwhile, he lurked at home, painfully absorbing the newspapers most hostile to his own views and so prostrated that even jokes about Flocon's pipe* failed to raise a smile.

As a supporter of the ex-king, he was scared of popular reprisals against his estates in Champagne; then Frédéric's laborious hotchpotch of an article for the Troyes paper fell into his hands and he assumed that this young friend of his was a very influential person who might, if not help, at least protect him. So one morning, accompanied by Martinon, Monsieur Dambreuse called on him.

He was, he said, just dropping in for a little chat. All in all, he was quite happy about the way things were going and heartily supported 'our wonderful slogan: Liberty, Equality and Fraternity, having always been a republican at heart'. If, under the previous regime, he'd voted for the government, it was simply in order to hasten its demise. He even angrily attacked Monsieur Guizot, 'who's landed us in a fine mess, we must admit!' On the other hand, he'd great admiration for Lamartine, 'who'd shown outstanding qualities, upon my soul, when he referred to the red flag . . .'

'Yes, I know,' said Frédéric.

Next he spoke of his sympathy for the workers.

'I suppose, when all's said and done, we're all workers, more or less!'

His broadmindedness even stretched to acknowledging that Proudhon* was logical, 'my word yes, very logical!'. Then, with the impartiality of a man whose mind rose above any pettiness, he mentioned the exhibition at which he'd seen Pellerin's painting. He'd found it very original, full of fine touches.

Throughout all this Martinon was chiming in with approving comments of his own; he, too, felt it was up to them to 'throw in their lot with the Republic, unhesitatingly'; and he talked about his father, a 'tiller of the soil', and of his own 'peasant background'; he was a 'man of the people'.

The conversation soon came round to the elections for the Constituent Assembly and the candidates in the Fortrelle constituency. The opposition candidate hadn't got a hope.

'You ought to stand yourself,' said Monsieur Dambreuse. Frédéric demurred.

'Why on earth not? He'd get the votes of the extreme left, because of his personal opinions, and of the conservatives, because of his family. 'And perhaps,' the banker added with a smile, 'thanks a little to my own influence.'

Frédéric objected that he wouldn't know how to set about it. Nothing simpler, just get your name put up to the patriots in the Aube by a club* in the capital. All you needed to do was not to trot out the standard confession of faith you could hear any day of the week but to read out a serious statement of principles.

'Bring it along to me, I know what suits the locals. And let me say again that you could be rendering a great service to your country, to us all and to me personally!'

At times such as these people should help one another and if Frédéric needed something for himself or any of his friends . . .

'Thank you very much indeed, Monsieur Dambreuse!'

'And of course it works both ways!'

The banker was undoubtedly a good sort; Frédéric

323

couldn't resist thinking over his advice; before long his brain was spinning at the dazzling prospect.

The great figures of the Convention* floated before his eyes. A magnificent new dawn was surely breaking. Rome, Vienna and Berlin were in revolt; the Austrians had been kicked out of Venice; the whole of Europe was in ferment. It was time to hurl oneself into the fray and perhaps help events along; he was also greatly attracted by the clothes which, it was said, the Deputies would be having. He could already see himself wearing a tricolour sash and a waistcoat with lapels. The illusions fostered by these longings grew so strong that he confided them to Dussardier.

This nice young fellow was as enthusiastic as ever.

'Of course you must! Go ahead and put your name forward!'

Nevertheless Frédéric consulted Deslauriers. The lunatic opposition which was obstructing the government commissioner in his provincial district had made him more liberal. He wrote back straightaway encouraging him.

However Frédéric felt the need for more confirmation and informed Rosanette of his idea, one day when Mademoiselle Vatnaz was there.

Vatnaz was one of those Parisian spinsters who every evening, after giving their lessons or trying to sell their little drawings or find a publisher for their scribblings, come home with mud-bedraggled petticoats, prepare their own solitary meal, put their feet on a foot-warmer and then, by the light of a smoky lamp, dream of love, a family, a home, wealth, everything they haven't got. So, like many others, she'd welcomed the Revolution as a chance to get her own back and was indulging in frantic socialist propaganda.

For Vatnaz the emancipation of the proletariat was possible only through the emancipation of women. She wanted equal opportunities for employment, affiliation orders enforceable by law, a new legal system and the abolition, or at least 'a more intelligent regulation', of marriage. Every Frenchwoman was to be obliged to marry a Frenchman or adopt an old man.* Wet nurses and midwives would be civil servants; a committee should be set up to evaluate works written by women; there should be women's publishers, state-run women's engineering colleges, a women's National Guard, everything for women! And since the government was failing to recognize their rights, they'd have to meet force with force. Ten thousand women citizens armed with rifles would make the Hôtel de Ville tremble in its shoes!

Frédéric's candidature seemed to favour such ideas. She encouraged him: He had an appointment with fame! Rosanette was delighted by the idea of having a man who'd be addressing the Chamber.

'And I expect they'll be able to fix you up in a good job!'

Thoroughly weak as always, Frédéric allowed himself to be swept away on the tide of universal lunacy. He wrote out his speech and took it round to Monsieur Dambreuse.

At the sound of the front door, a window curtain was drawn aside and a female figure appeared. He didn't have time to see who it was; but in the entrance hall he was halted in his tracks by a picture, by Pellerin, standing, no doubt temporarily, on a chair.

It represented the Republic, or Progress, or Civilization, in the shape of Jesus Christ driving a train through a virgin forest. Frédéric examined it for a moment before exclaiming:

'How obscene!'

'Yes, isn't it?' said Monsieur Dambreuse coming in at that moment and imagining Frédéric was referring not to the painting but to the doctrine it was glorifying. At the same instant Martinon arrived and they went into the study. Just as Frédéric was taking his sheet of paper out of his pocket, Mademoiselle Cécile suddenly appeared.

'Is aunty here?' she enquired innocently.

'You know very well she isn't,' retorted the banker. 'Never mind, make yourself comfortable, my dear girl!'

'No thanks, I'm going!'

She'd hardly left when Martinon seemed to have mislaid his handkerchief.

'I've left it in my overcoat pocket, excuse me a second!'

'Well!' said Monsieur Dambreuse.

He was obviously not taken in by this stratagem and seemed even to be condoning it. Why? But Martinon was quickly back and Frédéric began his speech. Even by the second page, where Frédéric deplored the excessive influence of financial interests, the banker was looking extremely put out. Next Frédéric turned to reforms and advocated free trade.

'What? But really . . . !'

Not hearing him, Frédéric proceeded: he demanded a levy on unearned income, progressive taxation, European federation, education for the masses, the widest possible encouragement of the arts.

'What harm would there be if the country provided pensions of one hundred thousand francs a year to men like Delacroix and Hugo?'

The speech ended with an exhortation addressed to the upper classes:

'Those of you who are rich shouldn't hoard your wealth: give generously and keep on giving!'

He stopped and remained standing while his audience sat in frozen silence. Martinon's eyes were popping out of his head; Monsieur Dambreuse had gone as pale as a sheet. Finally, hiding his feelings behind a tight-lipped smile:

'What a perfect speech!' and went on to praise its form, to avoid having to say anything about its content.

Such virulence from an inoffensive young man frightened him, above all because he saw it as a symptom. Martinon tried to reassure him: the conservatives would soon be making their come-back; a number of towns had already sent the Provisional Government's representatives packing; the elections weren't due till 23 April, there was plenty of time; in a word, Monsieur Dambreuse would have to stand as candidate for the Aube himself. From that time on, Martinon never left his side; he became his secretary and looked after him as solicitously as a son.

Frédéric arrived at Rosanette's very pleased with himself. Delmar was there and told him he'd 'definitely' be standing for the Seine constituency in the elections. In a poster appealing to the 'People', whom he proceeded to address with the utmost familiarity, the actor boasted how well he understood them, that he'd 'borne the cross of artistic endeavour' to achieve their salvation and thus become flesh of their flesh, their ideal; in fact, he really was convinced that he carried immense weight with the masses, so much so that some while later, in some minister's office, he volunteered to quell a riot single-handed and when asked how he intended to set about it, replied:

'Have no fear! I'll just show my face!'

To take him down a peg, Frédéric told him he had similar plans, and once he'd made sure that his future colleague had set his sights on the provinces, the showman declared he was at his service to take him round the clubs.

They visited them all or nearly all, the red and the true blue, the fanatical and the sedate, the puritanical and the raffish, the mystical and the boozy, the ones advocating regicide and those denouncing profiteering grocers; and, in all of them, tenants blasted landlords, smocks attacked frock-coats and the rich ganged up against the poor. Several of them were demanding compensation for ill-treatment by the police, others were begging for money to finance inventions; or else there were plans to set up Fourierist communes, projects for district department stores, schemes to provide universal happiness. Now and again a flash of intelligence lit up this fog of stupidity or there'd be a sudden burst of mud-slinging, a point of law summed up in an oath, flowers of rhetoric spouted by some shirtless hooligan wearing his sword-belt slung over his bare shoulder. Sometimes, too, a gentleman would be speaking, an aristocrat talking deferentially of working-class concerns; he'd not washed his hands, so that they'd look like the horny hands of a manual labourer; he'd be recognized by some patriot, righteous members of the club would catcall him and he'd leave, inwardly seething with rage. To be accepted you always had to speak disparagingly of lawyers and trot out expressions like 'grist to the mill', 'social problem' and 'workshop' as often as possible.

Delmar never missed a chance of getting up on his hind legs and when he'd run out of words, he'd resort to posing with one hand clenched on his hip and the other thrust into his waistcoat, suddenly swivelling his head to show off his profile. There'd be a burst of applause from Mademoiselle Vatnaz ensconced at the back of the hall.

In spite of the low standard of oratory, Frédéric was loath to chance his luck: these people all seemed too unfriendly or uncouth.

But Dussardier went to spy out the lie of the land and announced that there was a club in the rue Saint-Jacques called, promisingly, the Club de l'Intelligence. And he'd bring some of his pals along.

He brought along the ones he'd invited to his party: the bookkeeper, the wine-broker and the architect; Pellerin also came along; Hussonnet might be there later; and on the pavement outside the entrance, Regimbart had posted himself with two other characters, the first his trusty friend Compain, a rather dumpy, pock-marked little man with bloodshot eyes, the second an extremely long-haired individual with a black monkey-face whom he knew only as: 'a patriot from Barcelona'.

They made their way along a tree-lined path and were ushered into a large room, probably a joiner's workshop. Its walls still smelt of fresh plaster. Four oil lamps hanging parallel shed a very poor light. On a platform at the far end was a desk with a bell on it and, below, a table for use as a rostrum with two lower ones on each side for the secretaries. There was a large audience consisting of old hack painters, shabby assistant schoolmasters and unpublished authors. Here and there among the rows of grubby-collared over-coats, you could glimpse a woman's bonnet or a worker's overall. The back of the hall was in fact crammed with workers who had doubtless come for want of anything better to do or had been brought along by the speakers, to applaud as required.

Frédéric was careful to sit between Dussardier and Regimbart, who the moment he sat down planted both hands on his stick, rested his chin on them and closed his eyes. At the other end of the room Delmar was standing, dominating the gathering.

328

Sénécal appeared at the chairman's desk.

The kind-hearted Dussardier had thought this would be a pleasant surprise for Frédéric. In fact it was quite the opposite.

The crowd showed considerable deference towards its chairman. On 25 February he had been one of those who'd immediately demanded the setting up of employment schemes and at the Prado* next day he had spoken in favour of attacking the Hôtel de Ville. Since everyone in the public eye modelled himself on somebody or other, copying Saint Just or Danton or Marat, he himself was attempting to look like Blanqui, who modelled himself on Robespierre. His black gloves and cropped hair gave him a stiff, formal and extremely respectable appearance.

He opened the proceedings by reading the Declaration of the Rights of Man and of the Citizen, the usual act of faith. Then someone vigorously struck up Béranger's 'Souvenirs du peuple'.*

Other people shouted:

'No, not that one!'

'La Casquette!' the patriots started yelling from the back.

And they all sang in chorus the poem of the day:

'Off with your hat to the worker's cap!
Down on your knees to the working man!'

A word from the chairman restored silence. One of the secretaries proceeded to report on the correspondence:

'Some young men have written to inform us that every night they burn a copy of the *Assemblée nationale** in front of the Panthéon and urge patriots to do likewise.'

'Well done! Agreed!' the crowd responded.

'The Citizen Jean Jacques Langreneux, a printer in the rue Dauphine, would like to see a monument erected to commemorate the Thermidor martyrs.'*

This was greeted with applause, though some members of the audience leaned sideways to ask their neighbours who these martyrs were.

'Michel-Évariste-Népomucène Vincent, a former second-ary school teacher, would like the European democracies to adopt a uniform language. It might be possible to use a dead language, for instance a modernized form of Latin.'

'No, not Latin!' exclaimed the architect.

'Why not?' a junior assistant schoolmaster wanted to know; and the two gentlemen engaged in an argument in which others joined, each determined to show how brilliantly clever he was. This quickly became so tedious that many people started to leave.

A little old man wearing green spectacles perched beneath a prodigiously high forehead now demanded to raise an important issue.

It was a paper concerning tax assessment and the statistics poured out in an unending stream. The audience started to express their impatience first by muttering and talking amongst themselves; he remained unperturbed; then they began to hiss and whistle. Sénécal called the meeting to order; the speaker went grinding on. To stop him they were forced to jog his elbow. The old fellow seemed to come out of a trance; calmly pushing up his spectacles he said:

'Oh, I'm sorry, citizens, so sorry! Please forgive me, I'll sit down!'

This abortive operation disconcerted Frédéric, who had his speech written out in his pocket, though he would have done better to speak impromptu.

Finally, the chairman announced that they'd now move on to the substantive business of the day, the important question of the elections. There would be no discussion of the main republican lists. However, the Club de l'Intelligence certainly had the same right as any other to draw up its own list, 'with all due respect to the Hôtel de Ville bigwigs', and citizens seeking a mandate from the people could put forward their claims.

'Off you go!' said Dussardier.

A man in a cassock with frizzy hair had already raised his hand. He started gabbling that his name was Ducretot, that he was a priest and an agricultural scientist, the author of a book on manure. He was referred to a horticultural club.

Next a patriot in a smock hoisted himself on to the rostrum; he was broad-shouldered, with a large, gentle face and long black hair; he was an authentic man of the people. He cast his eye with almost sensuous delight round the room, threw back his head and finally, flinging out his arms:

'My dear brethren, you have spurned Ducretot and rightly so; but this was not through lack of religion, for we are all religious here!'

Open-mouthed, some members of the audience lapped this up ecstatically, like neophytes under instruction.

'Nor was it because he was a priest, for we too are priests! The working man is a priest, like the founder of socialism, He who is the Master of us all, the Lord Jesus Christ!'

The time had come to inaugurate the Kingdom of God! The Gospels led directly to the glorious Revolution! First slavery had been abolished and now the proletariat! After the Age of Hatred, the Age of Love would begin!

'And the corner-stone and foundation of this new edifice is Christianity!'

'Are you having us on?' shouted the wine-broker. 'Where did you unearth this sanctimonious rubbish-monger?'

This intervention produced pandemonium. Almost everybody stood up on their benches, shaking their fists and yelling: 'Atheist! Aristocrat! Scum!' while the chairman kept ringing his bell amid cries of 'Order! Order!', but undaunted and fortified moreover by the three 'coffees' imbibed before coming, the wine-broker continued to thresh about in the middle of the others shouting:

'What do you mean, aristocrat? Me? You must be mad!'

When he was eventually allowed to speak, he explained that there would never be any peace as long as there were priests around and since saving money had just been mentioned, there was one splendid way to do that, by doing away with the churches, the sacraments and eventually any religion whatsoever.

Someone objected that he was going very far.

'Yes, I am going very far, but when a ship has been suddenly caught in a storm . . .'

Before he could finish his comparison, another man piped up:

331

'All right then but that means knocking down, like any slapdash builder . . .'

'That's an insult to bricklayers!' screamed a citizen covered in plaster; and, refusing to be persuaded that no provocation was intended, he began cursing and swearing, clinging to his seat and trying to pick a fight. It took no less than three men to eject him.

Meanwhile the pious worker was still standing on the rostrum. When the two secretaries told him he should get down, he complained of being deprived of his rights.

'You'll not stop me from shouting: love everlasting for our beloved Fatherland, love everlasting for our beloved Republic as well!'

At this moment, Compain uttered:

'Citizens!' he said, 'Citizens!'

And having by continual repetition of 'Citizens!' obtained relative silence, he rested his two red stumps of hands on the rostrum, bent forward and, blinking his eyes:

'Citizens, I think that calves' head deserves far wider consideration!'

Thinking they'd misheard, no one said a word.

'Yes! Calves' head!'

There was a sudden screech of laughter from three hundred throats. At the sight of all these faces convulsed with mirth, Compain started back:

'What? You don't know about calves' head?'

The laughter erupted into hysterics. People were holding their sides; some were even collapsing on to the floor under their seats.

Completely intimidated, Compain retreated towards Regimbart and tried to persuade him to leave.

'No, I'm staying until the end,' said the Citizen.

This remark encouraged Frédéric, but as he looked towards his friends on both sides for support, he became aware of Pellerin standing in front of him on the rostrum. The painter started off in a bullying tone:

'I'd like to know where the candidate for Art is in all this! I'm someone who's actually painted a picture!'

332

'Who needs pictures?' snarled a thin man with red spots on his cheeks.

Pellerin complained that he was being interrupted.

But the other man went on darkly:

'Shouldn't the government by now have decreed the abolition of prostitution?'

This immediately got the audience on his side; he launched into a virulent attack on corruption in big cities.

'It's a crying scandal! All those well-to-do middle-class clients of the Maison d'Or ought to be nabbed as they come out and spat on! If only the government itself didn't aid and abet loose living! But the toll-keepers treat our sisters and daughters so indecently!'

From the back of the hall a voice piped up:

'It's good fun, though!'

'Kick him out!'

'They're squeezing taxes out of us to subsidize debauchery! Take the huge sums actors get!'

'This is where I come in!' exclaimed Delmar.

He elbowed his way through and leapt on to the rostrum, where he struck his favourite attitude and declared that such accusations were despicable and filled him with revulsion. He pointed out the civilizing mission of the actor. Since the stage was the centre of education, indeed of the whole nation, he would vote for the reform of the theatre and, to start with, get rid of managers and special privileges.

'Yes, put a complete stop to all that sort of nonsense!'

His performance was inciting the crowd and subversive proposals came flying from all sides.

'Down with colleges! Down with the Academy!'

'Down with the government commissioners!'

'No more Matric!'

'Down with university degrees!'

'No, let's keep those,' said Sénécal, 'but they'll be granted by universal suffrage, by the only proper judge, the People!'

But there were more important issues. First, the rich must be cut down to size! And he depicted them wallowing in crime under their gilded ceilings while the starving poor

333

cultivated all the virtues in their wretched attics. The applause was so deafening that he had to break off and stood there for a few minutes with closed eyes and head thrown back as if revelling in the anger he was arousing.

Then he began again in a hectoring, dogmatic tone as if every word had the force of law. The state must take over the banks and insurance companies. The right of inheritance must be abolished and a welfare fund set up for all workers. Other measures would follow but these would do for the present; and, returning to the elections:

'We need new blood, citizens whose hearts are pure, whose hands are clean! Would anyone like to come forward?'

Frédéric stood up. There was a buzz of approval from his friends. But Sénécal put on his Fouquier-Tinville look and started to cross-examine him: he wanted to know his name, given name, antecedents, career, way of life.

Frédéric bit his lips and replied briefly. Sénécal enquired if anyone had any objections to his candidacy.

'No! No!'

He had, though. Everybody leaned forward and listened intently. This prospective candidate hadn't handed over a certain amount, which he'd promised, to set up a democratic institution, to wit, a newspaper. Moreover, on 22 February, despite adequate forewarning, he'd failed to report at the place du Panthéon.

'I can vouch for his presence at the Tuileries!' exclaimed Dussardier.

'Can you vouch that he was at the Panthéon?'

Dussardier hung his head. Frédéric hadn't spoken. His shocked friends were watching him uneasily.

'Can you at least give us the name of some patriot prepared to guarantee your principles?' Sénécal went on.

'I will!' said Dussardier.

'That's not good enough! Anyone else?'

Frédéric turned towards Pellerin; the painter waved his arms about as if to say: 'What's the good of me, my dear chap, they've just turned me down, damn it all!'

Frédéric nudged Regimbart.

'Yes, yes, you're quite right, it's time for me to say something, here goes!'

Regimbart stepped up on to the platform.

'Citizens!' he said, pointing to the Spaniard who had followed him, 'allow me to introduce to you a patriot from Barcelona!'

The patriot made a deep bow, rolled his silver-grey eyes like a robot and then, placing one hand on his heart:

'*Ciudanos! Mucho aprecio el honor que me dispensáis, y si grande es vuestra bondad, mayor es vuestra atención.*'

'I demand the right to speak!' shouted Frédéric.

'*Desde que se proclamó la constitución de Cadiz, ese pacto fundamental de las libertades españolas, hasta la última revolución, nuestra patria cuenta numerosos y heroicos mártires.*'

Frédéric made another effort to make himself heard:

'Surely, citizens . . .'

The Spaniard ploughed on:

'*El martes próximo tendrá lugar en la iglesia de la Magdalena un servicio fúnebre.*'

'It's quite absurd! Nobody can understand!'

This remark infuriated the crowd.

'Out! Out!'

'Do you mean me?' asked Frédéric.

'Yes, you!' said Sénécal loftily. 'Out you get!'

He got up to go, pursued by the voice of the Catalonian:

'*Y todos los españoles desearían ver allí reunidas deputaciones de los clubs y de la milicia nacional. Una oración fúnebre en honor de la libertad española y del mundo entero será pronunciada por un miembro del clero de Paris en la sala Bonne-Nouvelle. Honor al pueblo francés que llamaría yo el primero pueblo del mundo sino fuese ciudano de otra nación!*'

'Aristocrat!' yelled a lout shaking his fist at the exasperated Frédéric as he made a hurried exit into the courtyard.

He blamed himself for being so public-spirited, ignoring the fact that, after all, the accusations levelled at him were justified. What a disastrous idea this candidacy had been! But what utter idiots they were! He compared himself to people like that and the thought of their stupidity soothed his wounded pride.

335

He felt an urge to go and see Rosanette; after so much ugliness and pretentiousness, her casual easy-going ways would help him relax. She knew he had been due to be introduced to a club that evening but when he went in, she didn't ask him a single question.

She was sitting beside the fire unstitching the lining of a dress. He was surprised to see her doing that sort of work.

'Good Lord, what are you up to?'

'I'm mending my old clothes, as you can see!' she replied curtly. 'It's all the fault of your republic!'

'*My* republic?'

'You're not trying to suggest it's mine, are you?'

And she started to blame everything that had occurred in France over the last two months on the Republic, accusing it of causing the Revolution, bringing people to ruin, leading the wealthy to clear out of Paris and reducing her to dying, sooner or later, in a public hospital.

'It's all very fine for you to talk, with your private income! And incidentally, the way things are going, you won't be enjoying that much longer!'

'That may well be,' retorted Frédéric. 'It's always the most public-spirited who get least credit. If one didn't have the consolation of a clear conscience, the blackguards you have to rub shoulders with would make you think twice about being unselfish!'

'Did you say unselfish? So it sounds as if our dear little Frédéric has been turned down, has he? A good job too! That'll teach you to go round making patriotic donations. Oh, don't lie to me! I know you gave them three hundred francs because your Republic's like a kept woman, it needs supporting! Well, have a good time with her, old boy!'

This barrage of idiocy was turning Frédéric's earlier disappointment into deep frustration.

He had retreated to the far end of the room. Rosanette pursued him:

'Look, have a bit of common sense, a country's like a household, it needs someone in control or else everybody will just look after number one! In the first place, we all know that Ledru-Rollin's up to his ears in debt! And as for

336

Lamartine, how can one expect a poet to know anything about politics? Oh, it's all very well to shake your head and imagine you're brighter than the rest, but it's true all the same! Yet you spend your time quibbling and no one can get a word in edgeways! Look at Fournier Fontaine, for instance, the owner of the Saint-Roch stores. Do you know the losses he's made? Eight hundred thousand francs! And Gomer, the proprietor of the packing company across the street, another one of your republicans, who keeps bashing his wife over the head with the fire-tongs and who's drunk so much absinthe that they're going to have to put him away in a home for incurables. That's what your republicans are like! A republic with interest rates of twenty-five per cent! Oh yes, it's something you can be proud of!'

Disgusted by this woman who'd suddenly exposed herself as so fatuous as well as so common in her language, Frédéric took himself off; he even felt a faint revival of his revolutionary fervour.

Rosanette grew more disgruntled every day. Vatnaz's enthusiasm got on her nerves, for her missionary zeal had given her an irrepressible urge to hold forth and catechize all the time; being better at such things than Rosanette, she could completely demolish her with her arguments.

One day she came in seething, because Hussonnet had been indulging in smutty remarks at the women's club. Rosanette said she approved his conduct and even threatened to dress up as a man and go along to 'give them all a piece of her mind', and a good hiding into the bargain.

At this moment Frédéric arrived.

'You'll come along and lend a hand, won't you?'

And ignoring him, the pair of them launched into a violent squabble, one taking the side of the conventional housewife, the other the ardent feminist.

According to Rosanette, women were born exclusively for love or to bring up children and run a home.

In Vatnaz's view, a woman had her role in the State. In olden days the women of Gaul were law-makers, Anglo-Saxon women as well; squaws took part in pow-wows. Civilization was a joint creation. Every woman ought to

337

take part, until eventually selfishness gave way to brother-hood, individualism to association, and small holdings to large farms.

'Oh, I see you've become a farming expert now!'

'Why not? Anyway we're talking about the future of the human race!'

'Why don't you concentrate on your own?'

'That's my business!'

They were losing their tempers. Frédéric stepped in. Vatnaz was growing heated and even going so far as to support communism.

'What rubbish!' said Rosanette. 'How could that ever happen?'

The other woman quoted the example of the Essenes, the Moravian Brethren, the Jesuits in Paraguay, the family of the Pingons* near Thiers in Auvergne; and as she was waving her arms about a great deal her watch chain got caught in a gold sheep pendant attached to her other trinkets.

Suddenly Rosanette went as white as a sheet.

Mademoiselle Vatnaz was busily disentangling her jewellery.

'No need for all your fuss,' said Rosanette. 'I can recognize your politics now.'

'What do you mean?' said Vatnaz, colouring up like a schoolgirl.

'Ho-ho, you know quite well what I mean!'

Frédéric was at a loss. Obviously something had just occurred between them which was more important and more personal than socialism.

'And even if it was true,' Vatnaz continued undaunted, drawing herself up to her full height, 'it's only on loan, my dear girl, it's surety for a debt.'

'Oh, I'm not pretending *I* haven't got any! But for a few thousand francs, that's a bit of a tall story! At least I borrow, I don't go round robbing people!'

Mademoiselle Vatnaz gave a forced laugh.

'I'll swear it, cross my heart!'

'Careful not to scratch yourself, your fingers are a bit claw-like!'

The old maid raised her right hand and held it poised in front of her face:

'But some of your friends find them quite attractive!'

'Must be Andalusians fond of castanets!'

'Slut!'

The Marshal gave a deep bow:

'How charming!'

Mademoiselle Vatnaz made no reply. Beads of sweat stood out on her temples. She kept her eyes fixed on the carpet. Her breast was heaving. Finally she made for the door and slammed it behind her.

'Good-night! You've not heard the last of this!'

'I can hardly wait!'

Her pent-up feelings finally burst out: quivering like a leaf, Rosanette collapsed in tears on to her divan. She was stammering abuse: what the hell did she care about Vatnaz's threats! All things considered, maybe she was the one owed money by that bitch! It was just because of the gold sheep pendant, which had been a present; and through her sobs she blurted out Delmar's name. So she loved that showman?

'In that case why did she settle on me?' Frédéric asked himself. 'Why did he come back? What's forcing her to stay with me? What's the sense in all this?'

Rosanette was still weeping gently, lying on her side on the edge of the divan with her head cradled in both hands; and she looked such a delicate, feckless, suffering little creature that he went over and softly kissed her on the cheek.

She started to tell him how fond she was of him; the prince had recently left and there was nothing to stand in their way. But she was . . . temporarily . . . in a bit of a fix. 'You saw the other day I was having to re-use my old linings.' It was goodbye to any coaches now! And that wasn't the lot: the upholsterer was threatening to repossess her bedroom and drawing-room furniture. She didn't know which way to turn.

Frédéric felt tempted to say: 'Not to worry, let me pay.' But the lady might not be telling the truth. He'd learned from experience. He confined himself to comforting words.

Rosanette's fears came true: she was obliged to return the furniture and give up her fine flat in the rue Drouot. She took another one on the fourth floor in the boulevard Poissonière. Her old boudoir provided enough knick-knacks to give her three rooms quite a cosy look. She had Chinese blinds, an awning over the terrace, a second-hand carpet still as good as new in her drawing-room, and pink silk pouffes. Frédéric contributed generously to these purchases; he was experiencing all the pleasure of a newly married man finally having a home and wife of his own; and as he liked it there very much, he'd go there almost every evening and stay the night.

Coming out of the front hall one morning, he saw a National Guard shako on the third floor making its way upstairs. Where was it heading? Frédéric waited. The wearer was continuing to come up, looking slightly downwards; he raised his eyes; it was our friend Arnoux. The situation was crystal-clear; they both blushed at the same time, equally embarrassed.

Arnoux was the first to recover his wits.

'She's better, isn't she?' he enquired, as if Rosanette hadn't been well and he'd come to find out how she was progressing.

Frédéric clutched at the lifeline.

'Yes, indeed! Anyway that's what her maid says', implying that he hadn't been allowed in.

They stood eyeing each other uncertainly; which of the two would back down? Once again Arnoux cut the Gordian knot.

'Ah well, I'll drop in again some other time. Where are you going? I'll come along with you.'

And down in the street, he chatted away as naturally as ever. Doubtless he wasn't the jealous sort or else too good-natured to be angry.

In any case, he was preoccupied by the fate of the country and was now never out of uniform. On 29 March, he had defended the offices of *La Presse*.* During the invasion of the Chamber of Deputies he had shown quite outstanding courage; and he'd taken part in the banquet offered to the Amiens National Guard.*

Hussonnet was always on duty with him, making the most of his bottle of wine and his cigars; but being irreverent by nature, he enjoyed contradicting him and making disparaging remarks about the lousy style of government decrees, Louis Blanc's Luxembourg Commission, the Vesuvians, the Tyroleans,* everything, not excluding the carnival float representing Agriculture and drawn by horses instead of oxen, with an escort of ill-favoured girls. For his part Arnoux stood up for the government and had dreams of a merger of all the parties. Meanwhile, his business ventures were all turning sour; he was not greatly troubled.

Frédéric's relationship with the Marshal hadn't upset him in the slightest; it gave him a clear conscience in cutting off the allowance which he had started making her again after her prince's departure. He pleaded hard times, explained how sorry he was, and Rosanette bore him no ill will for pulling out. Monsieur Arnoux now looked upon himself as her 'fancy man'; this made him feel younger and increased his self-respect. He had no doubt Frédéric was subsidizing the Marshal and thought the whole business 'a good lark'; he even managed to cover his tracks and if they met, he'd let Frédéric have a clear run.

Frédéric was hurt at having to share her and his rival's tact seemed to him to be carrying a joke too far. But if he lost his temper, he'd be forfeiting any chance of going back to *Her*; and it was also his only source of news about her, for the pottery dealer would, as a matter of course or perhaps with malice aforethought, often bring his wife into the conversation and even ask him why he'd stopped calling on her.

Having run out of excuses, Frédéric assured him that he had in fact called several times without success. Arnoux believed him implicitly; he'd often say to her how wonderful it was that their friend wasn't there and she'd invariably replied that she'd been out each time he'd called; thus, instead of conflicting, their two lies corroborated each other.

The young man's meekness and his own enjoyment at hoodwinking him endeared him to Arnoux all the more; he treated him with an almost impudent familiarity, not out of contempt but because he trusted him. One day he wrote saying that he'd have to be out of town for twenty-four hours on an urgent matter of business and asking him to take over his guard duty. Frédéric was afraid to refuse and reported at the Carrousel command post.

He found himself having to put up with the company of National Guardsmen! Apart from one man whose job was purging undesirable elements in the force, who was something of a wag and drank like a fish, all the others seemed as thick as two planks. The main topic of conversation was the replacement of cross-belts by ordinary ones. Others were infuriated by the National Workshops. Someone asked: 'Where's it all going to end?' and in reply the man who'd been so abruptly addressed could only gape as if on the edge of a precipice and repeat: 'Yes, where's it all going to end?' A more enterprising guardsman exclaimed: 'Things can't go on like this, we must put a stop to it!' Remarks like this persisted till nightfall and Frédéric was bored to tears.

At eleven o'clock he was greatly surprised to see Arnoux appear and explain that as his business was completed, he'd hurried back to relieve him.

This business had, in fact, been pure invention on his part in order to spend twenty-four hours undisturbed with Rosanette; but the dear man had greatly overestimated his capabilities; fatigue had induced a fit of remorse. He thanked Frédéric and invited him to join him for supper.

'It's very kind of you but I'm not hungry. What I need is my bed!'

'All the more reason to have lunch with me later on! What a milksop you are! You can't go home now, it's too late and too risky!'

Frédéric caved in yet again. Arnoux's brothers-in-arms,

who weren't expecting to see him, made a great fuss of him, mainly the man responsible for purges. They were all so fond of him; and, nice chap that he was, he said how sorry he was not to see Hussonnet. But he did need a spot of shut-eye, just a couple of minutes.

'Get down here beside me,' he said to Frédéric as he stretched out on his camp-bed without removing his equipment, even keeping his rifle, for fear of an alert, something strictly against regulations. Then, after mumbling a few stray words: 'My darling, my little angel!', he quickly dropped off to sleep.

The talking stopped and gradually silence reigned in the guardroom. Tormented by fleas, Frédéric looked around. Half-way up the yellow-painted wall was a long shelf for the knapsacks which formed a series of little humps, while the lead-grey rifles were stacked in a row underneath. The guardsmen's snores echoed round the room; their paunches were dimly discernible. A bottle stood on the stove, beside some plates. There were three cane-seated chairs round the table, on which a pack of cards was spread out. In the middle of the bench was a drum with its strap hanging down. A draught of warm air from the doorway was making the oil lamp smoke. Arnoux was sleeping with his arms sprawled out, and as his rifle was placed butt down, at an angle, the end of its barrel was poking up under his armpit. Frédéric was alarmed.

'Oh no, there's no danger, I'm mistaken. But suppose something did happen to him?'

In a second, an endless series of images flashed through his mind: he saw himself sitting in a post-chaise with *Her*, at night; then, beside a broad river, on a summer's evening, and in the light of a lamp, at home—their home. He was even planning their housekeeping budget and domestic arrangements, already anticipating and appreciating his happiness. And for this to become reality, the only thing needed was for the rifle to be cocked! Anyone could touch it with his toe and it would go off; just an accident, that's all!

Frédéric lingered over this idea like an author working

343

on a scenario; and he suddenly felt that it was on the point of being translated into action, that he was going to have a hand in it and that he wanted it to happen. Panic gripped him but mingled with his dread there was a feeling of pleasure which, to his horror, seemed to be taking over and making his scruples all melt away; his sense of reality was being swallowed up in these wild day-dreams; only a dreadful tightness in his chest made him still conscious of himself.

'How about a spot of white wine?' said the purger, waking up.

Arnoux sprang out of bed and, the white wine having been duly consumed, insisted on taking over Frédéric's guard duty.

After that he took him off to a meal at Perly's in the rue de Chartres and feeling the need to restore his strength, ordered for himself a couple of meat courses, a lobster, a rum omelette, a salad, etc., washed down with an 1819 Sauterne and a Romanée '42, not forgetting some champagne and a few liqueurs.

Frédéric let him go ahead; he was embarrassed that the other man might read his earlier thoughts on his face.

With his eyes boring into his, Arnoux was leaning right across the table resting on both elbows as he talked of his secret fantasies.

He wanted to lease all the railway embankments along the North Line to grow potatoes on; or organize a giant cavalcade on the boulevards in which he'd present the 'celebrities of the day'. He'd hire out all the window space which, at an average of three francs apiece, would return a fat profit. In a word, he was dreaming of bringing off a vast business coup by acquiring a monopoly in something. This didn't mean he lacked principles; he disapproved of outrageous or improper conduct, talked about his 'dear old father' and every evening, he said, religiously examined his conscience before 'lifting his soul to his Maker'.

'A drop of curaçao?'

'If you like.'

As for the Republic, everything would turn out all right

344

in the end; in fact, he was the happiest man in the world; forgetting his discretion, he began to make glowing references to Rosanette's attributes, even comparing her with his wife: 'Rosanette's in a different class, old boy! You can't imagine lovelier thighs!'

'All the best!'

Frédéric clinked glasses. To humour Arnoux, he'd drunk rather too much; what's more the bright sunlight was rather dazzling; as they walked side by side up the rue Vivienne their epaulettes rubbed together in true brotherhood.

Back home, Frédéric slept till seven o'clock, after which he went round to the Marshal's. She was out with someone. Maybe with Arnoux? At a loose end he sauntered along the boulevard but found it impossible to get further than the Porte-Saint-Martin because of the crowds.

Large numbers of destitute workers left to fend for themselves had taken to coming along here every evening, no doubt to take stock of the situation, and waiting for a signal. In spite of the law against public gatherings, these 'Clubs of Despair' were growing in a frightening manner and many middle-class people would come to watch every evening out of bravado, because it was the thing to do.

Suddenly, a couple of yards away, Frédéric caught sight of Monsieur Dambreuse with Martinon; he turned to go because he felt put out because Monsieur Dambreuse had got himself selected as electoral candidate. But the banker hailed him:

'A word in your ear, dear sir! I owe you an explanation!'

'I'm not asking you for one!'

'Please do listen to what I have to say!'

He was in no way to blame. They'd begged him, in a sense forced him, to act like that. Martinon immediately sprang to his defence: the people of Nogent had sent a deputation to see him.

'And in any case I considered myself a free agent, in view of the fact . . .'

They were thrust apart by a sudden crush of people on the pavement. A few moments later Monsieur Dambreuse resurfaced, whispering to Martinon:

345

'Thanks for helping me a moment ago! I'll see you don't suffer for it!'

The three of them stood with their backs to a shop in order to talk more comfortably.

There were occasional shouts of: 'Long live Napoleon! Long live Barbès! Down with Marie!'* The huge throng of people were talking very loudly and all these voices rebounding from the houses sounded like surging waves in a harbour. Every so often the talk would give way to the strains of the 'Marseillaise'. In the carriage-gate porches, mysterious-looking men were peddling sharp-pointed walking sticks. Sometimes two individuals would exchange winks as they passed and then quickly make off. The pavements were crammed with groups of onlookers and the roadway was packed solid with people, while the police kept swarming out of side-streets and just as suddenly withdrawing into them. Here and there were little flags looking like tiny flames. Cabbies sitting perched up on their seats would wave their arms in the air and drive off. All this commotion made the oddest sight imaginable.

'Wouldn't Mademoiselle Cécile have been amused by all this!' exclaimed Martinon.

'You know very well my wife doesn't like my niece coming out with us,' replied Monsieur Dambreuse with a smile.

He was unrecognizable; for the last three months he'd been shouting: 'Long live the Republic!' and he'd even voted in favour of banishing the Orléans family. But now no further commercial concessions were going to be granted. He was so furious that he had even taken to carrying a cosh.

Martinon had one as well. Now that judges and public prosecutors were no longer permanent appointments, he'd given up the Bar and was even more virulent than Monsieur Dambreuse.

The banker had a particular hatred of Lamartine (because of the poet's support for Ledru-Rollin), as well as for Pierre Leroux, Proudhon, Considérant and Lamennais,* just a bunch of hotheads and socialists.

'What on earth are they trying to do? They've done away with the duty on meat and with imprisonment for debt; now they're investigating the possibility of a mortgage trading bank. Only the other day it was a national bank! And they're budgeting to give five million francs to the workers! But fortunately, thanks to Monsieur Falloux, they've put a stop to that! So goodbye to them and the best of luck!'

Indeed, on that very day, unable to continue feeding the hundred and thirty thousand men in the National Workshops, the Minister of Public Works had signed a decree calling on every male citizen between the ages of eighteen and twenty either to join the army or else to go and work on the land.

This proposal was received with indignation, for it was seen as an attempt to destroy the Republic; for them, life away from the capital would be an intolerable exile; they could see themselves dying of fever in outlandish parts! Many of them were, in fact, skilled craftsmen who regarded farming as degrading; in a word, it was a trap, an insult and a categorical denial of earlier promises. But if they resisted, force would be used, of that they were certain, and they were taking steps to forestall it.

At about nine o'clock the crowds gathered at the Bastille and the Châtelet surged up on to the boulevard. From the Porte-Saint-Denis to the Porte-Saint-Martin there was nothing but a swarming mass, dark blue, almost black, in colour, amongst which you could glimpse men with burning eyes and pale faces drawn with hunger and fired by injustice. Meanwhile, the clouds piling up in the thundery sky heightened the electric atmosphere of the vast throngs of people swirling erratically round like a heaving Atlantic breaker; and in its depths you could feel an incalculable strength, a kind of elemental energy. Then everybody started chanting: 'Lights on! Lights on!' and when a number of windows failed to light up, stones were thrown at them. Monsieur Dambreuse thought it wiser to withdraw. The two young men went with him. He was predicting major disasters: the People might invade the Chamber of Deputies again; and incidentally, but for the help of 'a very plucky National Guardsman', he might well have been killed on 15 May.

'But I was forgetting, it was a friend of yours, the owner of the ceramics factory, Jacques Arnoux.' He was being crushed to death in a mob of rioters and this splendid citizen had seized him in his arms and dragged him to safety. As a result, a sort of relationship had sprung up between them since. 'We must all have dinner together one of these days and as you see him a lot, do tell him how very fond I am of him. He's an excellent fellow and to my mind he's been grossly misrepresented. And my goodness, he's a smart chap! So all the very best and a very good-night to you!'

After leaving Monsieur Dambreuse, Frédéric went back to the Marshal's and told her grimly that she must choose between him and Arnoux. She replied soothingly that she hadn't the faintest idea what all that 'tittle-tattle' was about, that she didn't love Arnoux and he didn't mean anything to her. Frédéric was keen to get away from Paris. She raised no objection to this whim of his and the very next day they left for Fontainebleau.

Their hotel had the unique distinction of a fountain playing in the middle of the courtyard. The bedrooms opened on to a corridor as in a monastery. They were given a large room, nicely furnished with chintz curtains, and quiet, for there weren't many travellers. Leisurely gentlemen were sauntering past in front of the houses; at dusk children came out to play prisoners' base under their windows; after the recent turmoil of Paris this peacefulness surprised and soothed them.

Early next morning they visited the palace. Going in through the gate they had a view of the whole façade with its five pavilions, their steeply pitched roofs and the sweep of the horseshoe staircase at the far end of the courtyard, framed on either side by lower buildings. Seen from a distance the lichen on the cobble-stones blended with the tawny bricks and the whole palace, rust-coloured like an old suit of armour, had something coldly regal about it, a sort of melancholy military grandeur.

Eventually an attendant arrived carrying a large bunch of keys.

First he showed them the queen's apartments, the Papal Oratory, the Francis I Gallery, the small mahogany table on which the Emperor Napoleon had signed his abdication and, in one of the rooms which divide the Stags' Gallery, the spot where Christine had Monaldeschi assassinated.* Rosanette listened most attentively to this story and then turned to Frédéric:

'I daresay she was jealous, so you'd better look out!'

Next they went through the Council Chamber, the guardroom and Louis XIII's drawing-room. The windows were curtainless and the light was harsh; the window-latches and the brass legs of the console tables were tarnished and seemed rather dusty; the armchairs everywhere were hidden under coarse canvas sheets; there were Louis XIV hunting scenes over the doorways and an occasional tapestry representing the gods of Olympus, Psyche or the battles of Alexander the Great.

As she walked past the mirrors, Rosanette kept stopping to tidy her hair.

After the keep and the Chapel of Saint–Saturnin, they came to the banqueting hall.

They were dazzled by the magnificent ceiling, which was divided into octagonal panels and picked out in gold and silver, more finely engraved than any jewel; and by the immense number of paintings covering the walls, starting at the huge fireplace over which the arms of France were surrounded by crescents and quivers, along to the musicians' dais at the other end which extended the whole width of the hall. The ten arcaded windows were wide open; the pictures gleamed in the sunlight, the blue of the sky carried the ultramarine of the round arcades on and on into the distance and from the depths of the forest, whose hazy tree-tops blocked the horizon, there seemed to echo the sound of the mort blown on ivory horns and of mythological ballets of princesses and noble lords disguised as nymphs and fauns, gathering beneath the canopy of leaves; an age of violent passions, sumptuous art and the first faltering steps of science, an age whose ideal was to transport reality into a dream of the Hesperides, when kings' mistresses were likened to stars. The loveliest of all such famous women had had herself portrayed, on the right, in the shape of Diana the Huntress or even of the Queen of the Night, no doubt to assert her infernal powers beyond the grave. These symbols all confirmed her fame and something of her still remained, a dim voice and a radiance whose glow still lingered on.

Frédéric felt a sudden, indescribable sort of retrospective sensuality which he transferred to Rosanette by turning and gazing longingly at her and asking if she wouldn't like to have been that lady.

'Which lady?'

'Diane de Poitiers!'*

He repeated:

'Diane de Poitiers, the mistress of Henri II.'

All she said was:

'Ah!'

Her silence showed that she neither knew nor understood the slightest thing about it, so out of kindness he asked:

'Are you getting bored, perhaps?'

'Oh, not a bit, quite the opposite!'

And sticking her chin in the air, Rosanette cast the vaguest of glances all around and delivered herself of the statement:

'This brings back memories!'

However, her face showed that she was trying hard to be impressed and as her earnest expression made her look prettier, Frédéric forgave her.

She found the carp pond more fun and spent a quarter of an hour tossing bits of bread into the water and watching the fish dart up to snatch them.

Frédéric had sat down beside her under the lime trees, thinking dreamily of all the famous people who'd frequented these parts, Charles V, Henri IV, Peter the Great, Jean Jacques Rousseau and the 'lovely women weeping in the first-tier boxes',*Voltaire, Napoleon, Pius VII, Louis-Philippe; he could feel these restless spirits surrounding him, jostling him and these chaotic images were making him bewildered, even although he found them charming.

Finally they went down into the flower garden.

It is in the shape of a vast rectangle, giving an overall view of its broad yellow paths, its lawns, its border of box, its pyramid-shaped yews, its low shrubs and its narrow beds of grey soil thinly dotted with flowers. At its end, there's an extensive park with a canal running straight down the middle.

Royal residences have their own peculiar melancholy atmosphere which no doubt springs from the fact that they are far too large for the small number of people who live in them, from the surprising stillness which greets you after such an introductory blare of trumpets, and from their luxury, which has grown stiff with age and bears witness to the frailty of dynasties and the eternal wretchedness of all things. These emanations of bygone ages, as funereal and numbing as the scent of an Egyptian mummy, make an impression on even the unsophisticated mind: Rosanette was yawning her head off. They made their way back to their hotel.

After lunch an open carriage called for them. They drove out of Fontainebleau across a vast roundabout of intersecting roads and then, at a walking pace, along a sandy track through a wood of young pines. Now the trees became taller and the driver maintained a steady commentary: 'Here's the Siamese twins . . . the Pharamond . . . the Bouquet-du-Roi . . .' mentioning all the well-known sites and occasionally even stopping to give them time to admire them.

They drove into the tall Franchard Forest. The carriage glided over the turf as smoothly as a sleigh; the cooing of unseen doves could be heard; a waiter appeared from a café, and they got out beside a garden fence with round tables set out in front. Then, leaving the walls of a ruined abbey on their left, they made their way on foot over some large boulders and soon reached the end of the gorge.

351

On one side are outcrops of sandstone interspersed with junipers, while on the other the almost bare slopes drop away to the bottom of a little valley where the pale track of a path shows up against the colour of the heather; and in the far distance, you can glimpse the flat, cone-shaped top with a telegraph tower beyond.

Thirty minutes later they left the carriage again to walk up the Heights of Aspremont.

The track zigzags among stocky pine trees and beneath jagged rocks; this whole corner of the forest has something wild, oppressive and brooding about it; it makes you think of hermits, accompanied by giant stags bearing a fiery cross between their antlers, kneeling in front of their caves and welcoming the good old kings of France with a fatherly smile. The warm air was filled with the scent of resin and underfoot the roots were like a matted network of veins. Rosanette was almost in tears with desperation as she kept stumbling over them.

But she cheered up once more when they reached the top and discovered a sort of refreshment stall nestling under the roof of branches where they sold carved wooden souvenirs. She drank a bottle of lemonade and bought a hollywood walking stick; then, without stopping to look at the view from the top of the plateau, she followed a little boy carrying a torch into the Robbers' Cave.

The carriage was waiting for them in the Bas Bréau.

A blue-smocked artist was working at the foot of an oak tree with his paintbox on his lap. He looked up and watched them go by.

Half-way up the Chailly Hill, a sudden downpour forced them to put up the hood. The rain stopped almost at once and when they drove back into town the street cobbles were glistening in the sun.

Travellers coming from Paris told them of bloody battles in the capital. The news did not surprise the couple. Then everybody went off, the hotel resumed its peace and quiet, the gas was put out, and the lovers fell asleep to the ripple of the fountain in the courtyard.

Next day they paid a visit to the Wolf's Gorge, the

Fairies' Pool, the Long Rock and La Marlotte;* on the following day they drove around at random wherever their driver took them, without enquiring where they were and often not even bothering to pay any attention to the well-known beauty spots.

It was so cosy in their old landau with its faded blue-striped ticking upholstery on which they could sprawl as if on a sofa. The ditches choked with undergrowth slipped gently past without a stop; the tall ferns were shot through with bright sunbeams; sometimes a disused track would stretch out in a straight line ahead, covered here and there with soft tufts of grass. Cross-roads had posts in the centre with four outstretched arms in the shape of a cross; elsewhere they would see signposts slanting sideways like dead trees and tiny tracks curving off to disappear amongst the foliage, inviting exploration; and at that very moment, the horse would swerve aside and they would follow one of them, sinking into the mud; further on moss had grown on the sides of the deep ruts.

They'd imagine they were all alone, miles from anywhere; then a gamekeeper would suddenly go by carrying his gun or a group of ragged women carting loads of long faggots on their backs.

Whenever the carriage came to a halt, complete silence would reign all around, broken only by the breathing of the horse in the shafts and, very faintly, the repeated call of a bird.

In certain parts, the sun lit up the edge of the forest leaving the interior in shadow; or else it would be dimmed to a kind of half-light in the foreground and flood the purple mists in the distance with dazzling white. By noon it would be beating straight down on the all-surrounding greenery, splashing it with light, hanging drops of silver on the tips of the branches, drawing emerald stripes over the turf and casting specks of gold on the layers of dead leaves; when you threw back your head, you could see the sky through the tops of the trees. Some of them, real forest giants, looked like patriarchs or emperors; or they would join together overhead to form a kind of triumphal arch with their long trunks; others, lurching sideways at their roots, looked like columns on the point of collapse.

And then this whole array of vertical lines would open out a little and there would be huge green waves heaving unevenly towards the surface of the valleys and met by the crests of other hills towering over pale golden plains which grew paler and dimmer until they were at last lost to sight.

Standing side by side on some mound, sniffing the breeze, they could feel their souls stirring with a kind of pride in a freer life together, bubbling over with strength and an irrational joy.

In their diversity the trees offered an ever-changing scene: the smooth white-barked beeches with their round, interlacing, leafy tops; the gently flexing sea-blue branches of the ash trees; the bushy hollies standing like bronze figures in coppices of hornbeam; a row of slender silver birches drooping in elegiac poses; and the constantly sway-ing pines, as symmetrical as organ pipes, seemed to be singing. Huge rugged oaks writhed as they strained upwards from the earth, clasped together, rock-steady on their torso-like trunks, their bare arms hurling despairing appeals and furious threats at each other like a group of Titans frozen in anger. Over the stagnant pools hemmed in by brambles, there hovered something more oppressive, a sickly miasma; their lichen-covered banks where wolves come to drink were a sulphurous yellow, as though scorched by witches' footsteps; the endless croaking of frogs echoed the cawing crows circling overhead. Finally, they'd drive through monotonous clearings planted with the occasional sapling. There was a clanging of steel on rock. Half-way up the slope a gang of quarrymen were battering away at boulders. More and more of them appeared, until in the end the whole landscape was nothing but rocks, cube-shaped like houses or as flat as flagstones, propped up against each other, blending together or overhanging one another like monstrous, chaotic ruins of some vanished city no longer recognizable; but their very wildness suggested, rather, volcanoes, floods and huge unknown cataclysms. Frédéric would say they had been there since the beginning

354

of time and would remain like that until it came to an end; and Rosanette would turn away declaring 'this would drive her out of her mind' and go off to pick some heather, whose tiny purple flowers were heaped up side by side in little uneven patches; underneath the soil had collapsed, leaving a sort of dark fringe at the edge of the sand, sparkling with tiny specks of mica.

One day they found themselves half-way up a hill consisting of nothing but sand whose virgin, untrodden surface was striped with symmetrical ripples; here and there, jutting up like promontories on a dried-up ocean bed, were boulders in vaguely animal shapes—tortoises with outstretched necks, flopping seals, hippopotamuses, bears. Not a soul in sight. Not a sound. The sand was dazzling in the sun; all of a sudden in the shimmering glare, the animals seemed to be on the move. Their heads started to reel; almost frightened, they hurried away.

This solemn forest was beginning to bring them under its sway. They'd drive for hours without saying a word, abandoning themselves to the swaying of their carriage, in a sort of drugged stupor. With his arm round her waist, he'd listen to her voice against the chirping of the birds and almost with the same glance take in the black grapes on her bonnet and the berries on the junipers, the folds of her veil and the spiralling clouds; and when he bent towards her the coolness of her flesh mingled with the scents of the forest. Everything amused them and they'd draw each other's notice to anything they found quaint, cobwebs hanging down from bushes, holes full of water among the stones, a squirrel in the branches, the flight of two butterflies pursuing them; or else, twenty yards away, a gentle, noble-looking doe walking quietly along with her fawn at her side; Rosanette longed to run over and cuddle him.

Once she was very scared when a man suddenly appeared and showed her three vipers in a box. She quickly sought refuge in Frédéric's arms and he was glad that she was weak and he felt strong enough to defend her.

That night they had dinner at an inn beside the Seine. Their table was next to the window; Rosanette was sitting opposite him and he sat gazing at her dainty little white nose, her upturned lips, her lively eyes, her wavy chestnut hair parted in the middle, her pretty oval face. Her shan-tung silk dress fitted tightly over her rather sloping shoulders and her two hands emerged from its frill-less cuffs as they kept busily cutting, pouring out and reaching over the tablecloth. They were served a spatchcock chicken, an eel stew in a pipe-clay fruit dish, some rough wine, and bread that had gone hard, while their knives had jagged blades; all this enhanced the pleasure and the illusion. They almost had the feeling that they were on their honeymoon, half-way through a trip to Italy.

Before going back to their hotel they went for a stroll along the river.

The delicate blue dome of the sky rested on a tracery of trees against the horizon. Opposite, on the far side of a meadow, was the steeple of a village church and further along, on the left, a roof-top which stood out as a red patch against the meandering river, which seemed becalmed all the way along. But the rushes were slanting, the poles stuck in along the water's edge, to fasten nets to, were quivering; there were two or three old rowing boats and an eel-pot. Near the inn a girl in a straw hat was drawing up buckets from a well and each time one was on its way up Frédéric listened to the rattle of the chain with an indescribable joy.

His happiness felt so natural, so indissolubly linked to his own life and to the person of this woman, that he had no doubt he'd be happy for the rest of his days. He kept feeling the need to express his affection for her and she'd say nice things in reply and give him little taps on his shoulder, with a surprising gentleness which he found charming. In a word, he was becoming aware of a completely new kind of beauty in her which was perhaps merely the reflection of the objects around them, unless it was the hidden potential of those objects themselves which had caused this beauty to blossom.

When they were taking a rest, out in the countryside, they would relax in the shade of her parasol with his head on her lap; or they'd stretch out flat on their stomachs in the grass, face to face, peering hungrily deep into each other's eyes; and afterwards, having gratified that hunger, as they invariably did, they'd lie there in silence with half-closed lids.

Sometimes they could hear the roll of drums in the distance; it was the general alert being sounded to go and defend Paris.

'Oh yes, that'll be the riots,' Frédéric would say with pitying contempt; all this agitation seemed paltry compared to their love and eternal nature.

They would chat about everything and anything, subjects they knew by heart, people who didn't interest them, a thousand and one trivialities. She'd tell him about her maid and her hairdresser. One day she let slip her age: twenty-nine, she was getting on . . .

On several occasions she inadvertently blurted out information about herself. She'd been a 'lady shop assist-ant', made a trip to England, started to study acting; always in fits and starts, and he could never piece together a complete picture. One day when they were sitting by the edge of a meadow under a plane tree, she was more forthcoming. At the roadside below, a little girl, barefooted in the dust, was grazing a cow. As soon as she caught sight of them she came up to beg and, with one hand holding her petticoats, she stood scratching away at the black hair which framed her nut-brown face and two superb glowing eyes like a Louis XIV wig.

'She's going to be pretty later on,' said Frédéric.

'And won't she be lucky if she hasn't got a mother!' added Rosanette.

'Good heavens, what do you mean?'

'Ah yes, if only I'd never had one . . .'

She gave a sigh and started to talk about her childhood. Her parents were silk-workers in Croix-Rousse in Lyons. She'd worked for her father as an apprentice. While the poor man slaved away, his wife would abuse him and sell anything she could lay hands on to go boozing. Rosanette could still see their bedroom with the looms lined up under the windows, the stew-pot on the stove, the bed, painted in fake mahogany, standing opposite the wardrobe, and the gloomy attic where she'd slept till she was fifteen. In the end a gentleman had called, a fat man with a face the colour of boxwood, dressed in black and having a pious look. He and her mother had had a conversation, the outcome of which was that three days later . . . Here Rosanette stopped and with a bitter look said cynically:

'The job was done!'

Then, in reply to a gesture of Frédéric's:

'As he was married and afraid of being found out at home, they took me along to a private room in a restaurant and I was told I'd be a lucky girl and get a lovely present. The first thing I saw when I went in was a silver-gilt candelabra on a table laid for two. There was a mirror on the ceiling reflecting everything and the blue silk hangings on the walls made it look like a bedroom. As you can imagine, I was completely stunned, I was just a poor little slip of a girl who didn't know anything at all! But apart from being dazzled, I was scared and wanted to leave. But I stayed just the same. The only seat was a divan beside the table and when I sat down I sank into it. The heating vent in the carpet was sending gusts of hot air up at me and I sat there and didn't eat a thing, although the waiter kept urging me to. He'd poured me out a large glass of wine straight-away and my head was going round and round. I wanted to open a window but he said: 'No, miss, that's not allowed.' He went out. The table was full of heaps of things I didn't know about and I didn't fancy the look of any of them, so in the end I decided to try a jar of jam and just went on waiting. Something or other was preventing him from coming. It was very late, midnight at least, and I was dog-tired. As I was pushing one of the cushions to one side so as to lie down comfortably, my hand hit a sort of album or notebook. It was full of dirty pictures. When he came in at last, I'd gone to sleep lying on it.'

She hung her head and was lost in thought.

All around leaves were rustling; in a tangled clump of grass, a tall foxglove swayed to and fro; light was flooding over the meadows; the silence was broken by the persistent crunching of the grazing cow, now no longer to be seen.

Rosanette's nostrils were quivering as she stared intently at a spot on the ground three yards in front of her, her mind faraway. Frédéric took hold of her hand.

'How dreadful it must have been for you, my poor darling!'

'Yes,' she replied. 'More dreadful than you think. So much so that I tried to put an end to it all, but they pulled me out of the water.'

'What?'

'Oh, let's forget about it! . . . I love you and I'm happy! Give me a kiss!'

And one by one she pulled off the bits of thistle caught on the bottom of her dress.

Frédéric was thinking mainly about all the things she hadn't told him. By what stages had she managed to escape from her predicament? Which of her lovers had provided her education? What sort of life had she led up to the time he'd first gone to her house? After her last confession, he couldn't possibly go on probing; he merely asked how she'd got to know Arnoux.

'Through Vatnaz.'

'Didn't I see you once with the pair of them at the Palais-Royal?'

He mentioned the exact date. Rosanette tried to remember.

'Oh yes, that's right! I was pretty miserable at that time!'

But Arnoux had been very kind. Frédéric hadn't any doubt about that; all the same, their friend was a queer man; he had lots of shortcomings which he went on to enumerate. She agreed.

'But never mind that, you can't help being fond of the old bastard!'

'Even now?' said Frédéric.

She began to blush, half laughing, half annoyed.

'Of course not! That's all over and done with! I'm not trying to keep anything from you. And even if there was some truth in it, with him it's different! And incidentally, I don't think you're being very nice towards your victim!'

'My victim?'

Rosanette took him by the chin.

'Of course!'

And dropping into baby talk:

'Ickle boy sometimes not good ickle boy! Ickle boy go bye-byes with someone else's ickle wifey!'

'Who, me? You're imagining things!'

Rosanette gave a smile which made him unhappy because it suggested she didn't care. But then she added gently, with the look of someone begging not to be told the truth:

'Honest?'

'Absolutely!'

Frédéric gave his most solemn word that he'd never thought of Madame Arnoux, because he was too much in love with another woman.

'And who was that?'

'You, of course, you wonderful, wonderful girl!'

'Oh, don't make fun of me! You're impossible!'

He thought it was wise to make up a story of a passionate love affair, with circumstantial details. Anyway the woman concerned had made him very unhappy.

'You really don't have much luck, do you?' said Rosanette.

'Well, maybe not, I suppose,' he said, trying to raise himself in her estimation by implying he'd had quite a number of successful affairs, just as, for similar reasons, Rosanette wasn't owning up to all her lovers; in the most candid confessions, there are always reservations caused by scruples, discretion, pity. As in other people, you come across precipices and morasses within yourself that make it impossible to go any further; in any case, you feel you'd not be understood. It's hard to communicate anything exactly and that's why perfect relationships between people are difficult to find.

For the poor Marshal this was the best relationship she'd ever had. When she looked at Frédéric her eyes would often fill with tears and she'd gaze skywards or towards the horizon, as if she could see a magnificent new dawn, a prospect of bliss without end. Eventually, she confessed one day that she'd like to have a Mass said 'to bring good luck to our love'.

In that case, how was it she'd stood out against him for so long? She couldn't explain it herself. He asked the same question several times and each time she'd just give him a hug and say:

'It was because I was scared of loving you too much, darling!'

On Sunday morning, Frédéric read in the paper a list of wounded that included Dussardier. He gave a cry and showed it to Rosanette, saying he'd have to go to Paris at once.

'What for?'

'To see him and look after him, of course!'

'But I hope you're not intending to leave me, are you?'

'You can come with me!'

'And get caught in all that shemozzle? Thanks a lot!'

'But I can't . . .'

'Oh, come off it! As if there weren't nurses enough in the hospitals! And what business was it of his, I'd like to know? Everyone for himself!'

Such selfishness made him feel indignant, and guilty at not being back there with the rest. This lack of concern about the country's troubles was rather mean and middle-class. All of a sudden, his love seemed criminal. They sulked for an hour, at the end of which she begged him to wait and not tempt fate.

'Suppose you had the bad luck to be killed?'

'So what? I'd only have been doing my duty!'

Rosanette blew up: his first duty was to love her! So he didn't love her any more? The whole thing was idiotic! Heavens above, what an idea!

Frédéric asked for his bill. But getting back to Paris wasn't easy. The Leloir line coach had just left, the Lecomte berline wouldn't be going, the Bourbonnais stage-coach wasn't coming through till late that night and was likely to be full up; there was no information whatsoever.

361

After wasting a great deal of time finding out all this, he hit on the idea of using post-horses; the post-master wouldn't let him have any, because Frédéric hadn't got a passport. Finally, he hired a barouche, the one they'd been using for their drives, and they arrived at the Hôtel du Commerce in Melun at about five o'clock.

The market-place was covered with stacked weapons. The Prefect had forbidden the National Guardsmen to proceed to Paris. Those who weren't under his jurisdiction wanted to go ahead. People were shouting. The inn was in an uproar.

Rosanette was frightened and flatly refused to go any further; she again pleaded with him to stay. The innkeeper and his wife supported her. One of the men dining, a decent sort of fellow, joined in the debate: the fighting would soon be over and in any case, you had to do your duty. At this, the Marshal began weeping louder than ever. Frédéric was exasperated. He handed her his purse, gave her a quick kiss, and made himself scarce.

When he reached Corbeil, they told him at the railway station that the insurgents had cut the line at various points and his driver refused to take him any further; his horses, he said, were 'all in'.

However, he did help Frédéric to get hold of a rickety old cabriolet which for sixty francs—excluding tip—agreed to take him as far as the Porte-d'Italie. But a hundred yards short of the toll-gate, the cabby made him get out and turned tail. As Frédéric was walking along the road, suddenly his way was barred by a sentry with his bayonet. Four men grabbed him, yelling:

'We've got one of them! Look out! Search him! Terrorist pig!'

He was so stunned that he allowed himself to be dragged off to the guardroom at the junction of the boulevard des Gobelins, the boulevard de l'Hôpital, the rue Godefroi and the rue Mouffetard.

The ends of these streets were blocked by four immense barricades made of piled-up flagstones; here and there torches were spluttering; through the clouds of dust he could make out the regular infantry and the militiamen of the National Guard, black-faced, wild-eyed and scruffy. They had just captured the square and executed a number of men by firing squad; they were still very angry. Frédéric explained that he'd come from Fontainebleau to help a wounded friend who lived in the rue Bellefond. At first no one would believe him; they inspected his hands and even sniffed his ears to make sure he didn't smell of gunpowder.

Frédéric stuck to his story and eventually convinced a captain who told two riflemen to take him to the guardroom at the Jardin des Plantes.

They walked up the boulevard de l'Hôpital. The strong breeze invigorated him. They turned into the rue du Marché-aux-Chevaux. On the right was the large mass of the Jardin des Plantes while on the left the whole front of the Hôpital de la Pitié was glowing as if on fire; shadowy figures darted across the brightly lit windows.

The two riflemen left Frédéric and another man escorted him as far as the École polytechnique.

The rue Saint-Victor was in complete darkness with not a single gas jet or light in the houses. Every ten minutes you could hear the call: 'Sentries, on guard!' breaking the silence and re-echoing like a stone falling into a pit.

Occasionally there came the tramp of approaching feet; it would be a patrol, at least a hundred strong; a murmur of voices, a vague clink of metal, the confused mass would swing past in step, and the sounds melted away into the gloom.

In the middle of the crossroads, a dragoon was sitting motionless on his horse. From time to time an orderly galloped past at speed, then silence would fall again. In the distance came the menacing dull rumble of gun-carriages trundling over cobbles, a sound so different from anything normal that your heart leapt into your mouth; it seemed almost to magnify the silence, deep though it was, a pitch-black silence of the grave.

The guardroom at the École polytechnique was packed with people. The doorway was blocked with women asking to see their son or husband. They were told to go to the

Panthéon, which had been converted into a morgue. Nobody would listen to Frédéric. He persisted, swearing his friend was at death's door and expecting him; finally they let him have a corporal to take him up to the town hall of the 12e *arrondissement* at the top of the rue Saint-Jacques.

The place du Panthéon was full of soldiers lying on straw pallets. Day was breaking; the camp-fires were being put out.

In this district the aftermath of the uprising was awesome. The street surfaces had been churned up from end to end; on the wrecked barricades were the remains of buses, gas-pipes and cart-wheels; the scattered black puddles were presumably blood. Where the plaster of the houses, riddled with projectiles, had flaked off, you could see their framework underneath; shutters dangled down like limp rags, held on by a nail. Where staircases had collapsed, the doors opened on to empty space and you could see into bedrooms with their wallpaper hanging in shreds. Sometimes quite fragile objects had survived; Frédéric caught glimpses of a clock, a parrot's perch, some engravings.

At the town hall the National Guardsmen were indulging in endless gossip about the deaths of Bréa and Négrier,* of the Deputy Charbonnel and the Archbishop of Paris.* It was said that the Duc d'Aumale had landed in Boulogne, Barbès had escaped from Vincennes, artillery was being brought up from Bourges, and help was pouring in from the provinces. Around three o'clock the good news came in that some of the parliamentarians amongst the rioters were with leaders of the Constituent Assembly.

There was general rejoicing and as he still had twelve francs left, Frédéric sent out for a case of wine, hoping to secure his release. All of a sudden they thought they heard the sound of rifle fire. Their drinking stopped; they eyed the stranger suspiciously; he might be Henri V.

To avoid any responsibility, they had him taken to the town hall of the 11e *arrondissement* where he was detained till nine o'clock before being released.

He dashed down towards the quai Voltaire. An old man stood in his shirt-sleeves at an open window; as he looked up at the sky, he was crying. The Seine was flowing peacefully. The sky was all blue; in the trees of the Tuileries gardens birds were singing.

As Frédéric was making his way across the Carrousel, a bier happened to be passing. The guard immediately presented arms and the officer in charge brought his hand up to his shako and said: 'All honour to the gallant dead!' This phrase had become almost mandatory and seemed always to be spoken solemnly and with feeling. An angry group was accompanying the bier and shouting:

'We'll avenge you! We'll avenge you!'

Carriages were driving along the boulevard and in the doorways women were shredding linen. Meanwhile, the uprising had been put down, or nearly; a proclamation by Cavaignac to this effect had just been posted. At the top end of the rue Vivienne a squad of security police* appeared. The middle-class onlookers burst into enthusiastic applause; they waved their hats, cheered, danced around, tried to embrace them and offer them drinks, while ladies showered them with flowers from their balconies.

At ten o'clock, to a background of the boom of cannon subduing the Faubourg-Saint-Antoine, Frédéric finally reached Dussardier's garret. He found him lying on his back, asleep. A woman tiptoed out of the next room: it was Mademoiselle Vatnaz. She took Frédéric aside and explained how Dussardier had been wounded.

On the Saturday, a street urchin wrapped in a tricolour flag had been standing on top of a barricade in the rue de la Fayette and shouting to the National Guard:

'Are you prepared to shoot at your brothers?'

As they kept coming on, Dussardier had dropped his rifle, pushed his way through, jumped up on to the barricade, and with a well-directed kick brought the young insurgent down and taken his flag. Dussardier had been found under the rubble with a brass slug in his thigh and extracting it had involved excising the wound. Mademoiselle Vatnaz had come round that same evening and stayed ever since.

She was competently preparing everything needed to

dress the wound, helping him to drink, flitting here and there like a little mouse, attending to his slightest wish and gazing at him with eyes brimming over with affection.

For the next fortnight Frédéric made a point of calling round every morning; one day when he was saying how devoted Vatnaz was, Dussardier gave a shrug:

'That's not true! It's self-interest!'

'Do you think so?'

'Yes, of course!' he replied without offering any further explanation.

She showered him with kindness, even bringing him newspapers with glowing reports of his exploit. These reports seemed to make him uncomfortable; he even confessed to Frédéric that he had misgivings: maybe he should have been on the other side, with the workers; after all, they had been given loads of promises which hadn't been kept and the men who'd just crushed their uprising loathed the Republic; and they'd treated them dreadfully harshly, too. The nice young fellow was tormented by the thought that perhaps he'd been fighting against a just cause.

Imprisoned in the Tuileries, under the Orangerie terrace, Sénécal was not suffering from any such qualms.

There were nine hundred of them all huddled together in their filth, black with gunpowder and clotted blood, shivering with fever and screaming with rage; and when some of them happened to die, no one came to remove their bodies. Sometimes, at the sound of a sudden explosion, they'd imagine they were all going to be shot, hurl themselves against the walls and fall back, numbed with pain, feeling they were living through some nightmare of doom and delirium; the lamp hanging from the ceiling vault looked like a bloodstain; tiny green and yellow flames produced by the noxious gases in the cellar were darting all around. For fear of an epidemic, a commission of enquiry had been set up but hardly had its chairman set foot on the top step that he recoiled in horror at the stench of excrement and corpses. Whenever the prisoners went up to the ventilator, the National Guardsmen in charge would poke their bayonets in at random, indiscriminately, to prevent them from shaking the grating.

By and large they were merciless. The ones who'd taken no part in the actual fighting were particularly anxious to demonstrate their keenness; people were panic-stricken and blindly settling old scores against newspapers, clubs, mobs, ideologies, everything that had been infuriating them for the last three months; and though victory had come, the principle of equality, as if punishing its supporters and mocking its opponents, now appeared as the triumphant law of the jungle, with everything reduced to the same level of bloodthirsty degradation, in which fanatical self-interest vied with the frenzy of the poor and under-privileged, the gentry proved as ferocious as the rabble and the cotton night-cap of the middle classes no less hideous than the Red Cap. The public mind was disturbed, as though after some cataclysm. Some intelligent people remained fools for the rest of their lives as a result.

Old Roque had become very brave, almost foolhardy. Having come to Paris with the Nogent contingent on the 26th, instead of going back home with them, he'd joined the section of the National Guard camped in the Tuileries and was delighted to be put on guard duty in front of the Orangerie terrace. At least he had that scum under his thumb there! He was overjoyed at their defeat and their utter squalor and he couldn't refrain from abusing them.

One of them, a youth with long fair hair, put his face at the bars of the window and asked for some bread. Monsieur Roque ordered him to be quiet but the young man went on moaning pitifully:

'Bread!'

'What makes you think I've got any?'

Other prisoners, unshaven and with bloodshot eyes, crowded up to the tiny cellar window, elbowing each other and screaming:

'Bread! Bread!'

Indignant at seeing his authority flouted, old Roque put his rifle to his shoulder, to scare them. The prisoners were surging forward and pushing the young man up towards

367

the ceiling, squeezing the breath out of him. He flung his head back and again shouted:

'Bread!'

'Here you are then!' said old Roque and pulled the trigger.

There was a dreadful howl and then nothing; beside the bucket something white was left lying.

After this, Monsieur Roque went back to the apartment block he owned in the rue Saint-Martin in which he had kept a small flat for himself. The damage inflicted on the front part of his property by the mob had contributed not a little to making him so angry. Now that he looked at it again, it didn't seem quite as bad as he'd thought. His recent exploit had calmed him down; somehow it had evened the score.

The door was opened by his daughter herself. The first thing she said was that she'd become anxious when he'd been away so long and scared something might have happened to him, perhaps being wounded.

This proof of daughterly love touched old Roque. He expressed surprise that she'd come without Catherine.

'I've sent her out on an errand,' replied Louise.

She enquired after his health and various odd matters; then, casually, asked if he'd run into Frédéric, by any chance.

'Not a sign of him!'

She had made the trip to Paris solely on his account. They heard a step in the passage.

'Excuse me!'

She slipped away.

Catherine hadn't been able to find Frédéric. He'd been away for several days and his close friend Monsieur Deslauriers was now living in the country.

Louise came back trembling like a leaf and unable to speak. She was holding on to the furniture.

'What's the matter? What's wrong with you?' her father exclaimed.

She made a sign that there was nothing wrong and forced herself to be calm.

The caterer from over the road brought them some supper. But old Roque had suffered too great a shock. 'He couldn't get it down'; and over dessert he nearly fainted. They quickly fetched a doctor who prescribed a pick-me-up; then, as soon as he was in bed, Monsieur Roque demanded as many blankets as possible to make him sweat. He was sighing and groaning.

'Oh, thank you, Catherine, that's kind of you! Kiss your poor old father, my pet! Oh, all these revolutions!'

And when his daughter was telling him off for having made himself ill because of her, he replied:

'Yes, you're right! But I can't help it. I'm too soft-hearted, that's my trouble!'

CHAPTER II

Madame Dambreuse was sitting in her boudoir between her niece and Miss John, listening to Monsieur Roque talking about the hardships of his military life. She was biting her lips and seemed to be in pain.

'Oh, it's nothing, it'll go off,' adding amiably: 'We'll be having to dinner someone you know, Monsieur Moreau.'

Louise gave a start.

'And a few close friends, including Alfred de Cisy.'

She went on to say a few approving words about his manners, his looks and above all his morals.

Madame Dambreuse was being less untruthful than she expected; the viscount was thinking of getting married; he had told Martinon so, adding that he was sure Mademoiselle Cécile would like him and that his parents would accept her. He would hardly have dared make such an admission if he hadn't received favourable reports as to the size of her dowry. Martinon suspected Cécile was Monsieur Dambreuse's illegitimate daughter and it would probably have been a good bet to ask to marry her, on the off-chance; but such a bold step did involve risks and Martinon had up till now avoided committing himself; in any case he couldn't see any way of ditching her aunt. Cisy's statement had put an end to his hesitation and he'd made his request to the banker who, seeing no objection, had just informed his wife.

Cisy came in. She stood up and said:

'You've been neglecting us . . .' and sharply told Cécile, in English, to shake hands with him.

At that moment Frédéric came in.

'Ah, I've caught up with you at last!' exclaimed old Roque. 'I've been round to your place with Louise three times this week!'

Frédéric had been studiously avoiding them. He explained that for some time he'd been spending every day with a friend who'd been wounded. And anyway he'd been tied up with lots of things for quite a while now. He was trying to concoct something plausible. Fortunately other guests arrived: first of all the diplomat Paul de Grémonville, whom he'd briefly glimpsed at the dance, then the industrialist Fumichon, who'd shocked him one evening by his fanatical conservatism. They were followed by the old Duchesse de Montreuil-Nantua.

At this moment two loud voices were heard in the entrance hall.

'I'm positive of it!' one of them was saying.

'Dear lady, dear lady, please, please don't get so excited!'

It was the old lady-killer Monsieur de Nonancourt, looking mummified in cold cream, and Madame de Larsillois, the wife of one of Louis-Philippe's Prefects. She was trembling like a leaf because she'd just heard a barrel organ playing a polka which was a signal used by the insurgents. Many of the middle classes were imagining similar things; it was thought that there were men in the catacombs waiting to blow up the Faubourg-Saint-Germain;* muffled sounds could be heard coming from cellars; suspicious things were taking place at windows.

Everybody did their best to reassure Madame de Larsillois: order had been restored; nothing to be afraid of any more! 'Cavaignac has rescued us!' People were exaggerating the horrors of the uprising, as if it hadn't been horrible enough as it was. The socialists had had a good twenty-three thousand convicts on their side—at least!

No one doubted for a moment that food supplies had been poisoned, and security police tied between two planks and sawn in half, that there were banners urging looting and arson.

'And more than that!' added the Prefect's wife.

'Oh my dear!' said Madame Dambreuse in shocked modesty, with a warning glance towards the three girls.

Monsieur Dambreuse emerged from his study with Martinon; she turned away to greet Pellerin who was coming over towards her. The painter was casting furtive glances at the walls. The banker drew him on one side and explained that he'd had to put the revolutionary picture away for the time being.

'I quite understand,' said Pellerin, whose views had changed since his rebuff in the Club de l'Intelligence.

In the politest of whispers, Monsieur Dambreuse added that he could be expecting further commissions from him in the future.

'But please excuse me . . . Oh, my dear fellow, what a pleasure!'

Facing Frédéric, there stood Monsieur and Madame Arnoux.

His head spun. All that afternoon Rosanette had been getting on his nerves with her admiration for the military. His old love revived.

The butler announced dinner. With a glance Madame Dambreuse indicated to the viscount that he was to take Cécile in; to Martinon she said in an undertone: 'You worm!', and they all filed into the dining-room.

Beneath the leaves of a pineapple plant, in the middle of the table, a John Dory was lying with its jaws threatening a haunch of venison and its tail brushing a spiny pyramid of crayfish. There were also pyramids of figs, pears, grapes and huge cherries, the whole array of early season fruit for the Paris market piled up in antique Meissen fruit-baskets; posies of flowers were interspersed between the gleaming silver; the room was bathed in a milky light from white silk blinds drawn down over the windows; the air was cooled by two fountains in which lumps of ice were floating; the meal was served by tall footmen in knee-breeches. After the recent shocks everything seemed to be returning to normal; once again people were able to enjoy those things they'd been afraid of losing. Nonancourt summed up everyone's feeling when he said:

'Ah, let's hope those republican gentlemen are going to allow us to eat our dinner undisturbed!'

'Notwithstanding their ideas of universal brotherhood!' added old Roque wittily.

These two pillars of society were seated to the right and the left of Madame Dambreuse, who was facing her husband, with Madame de Larsillois and the diplomat on one side of him and the old duchess next to Fumichon on the other. Then came the painter, the pottery dealer and Mademoiselle Louise; and, thanks to Martinon, who had commandeered Frédéric's seat next to Cécile, the latter found himself beside Madame Arnoux.

She was wearing a black barège silk dress, a gold hooped bracelet and, as on the first occasion he had dined at their home, something red in her hair, this time a sprig of fuchsia twined in her chignon. He couldn't refrain from saying:

'What a long time it's been since we last met!'

'Yes, hasn't it,' she replied coldly.

Speaking softly, to make his question sound less presumptuous:

'Have you thought of me occasionally?'

'Why should I?'

Frédéric was hurt by these words.

'Well, I suppose perhaps you're right, in a sort of way.'

Then, quickly having second thoughts, he swore that not a day went by without his being devastated by memories of her.

'I don't believe a word of what you say, Monsieur Moreau!'

'But you do know how I love you?'

Madame Arnoux made no reply.

'You know I love you.'

Still she said nothing.

'All right then, to hell with you!' said Frédéric to himself.

He looked up and saw Mademoiselle **Roque** at the other end of the table.

She had thought it would be smart to dress all in green; it clashed violently with her particular shade of red hair. The buckle of her belt came too high, her collar made her look neckless; no doubt her dowdiness had been partly to blame for Frédéric's lukewarm greeting. She was scrutinizing him curiously from a distance; sitting beside her, Arnoux was vainly showering her with compliments and, getting no response, gave up the attempt and turned his attention to the general conversation which at that moment was concerned with the pineapple desserts served at the Luxembourg Palace.*

According to Fumichon, Louis Blanc had a large mansion in the rue Saint-Dominique and was refusing to let rooms to workers.

'What I find amusing,' said Nonancourt, 'is Ledru-Rollin going shooting on Crown lands.'

'He owes a jeweller twenty thousand francs,' added Cisy, 'and they even claim . . .'

Madame Dambreuse cut him off.

'It's very naughty of a young man like you to be getting so excited over politics. You ought to be ashamed of yourself. Now start talking to your neighbour instead!'

The serious-minded guests now set about the newspapers. Arnoux defended them. Frédéric joined in, describing them as purely commercial concerns like any other. Reporters—he claimed to know quite a few—were generally idiots or humbugs; he poured scorn on his friend's generous sentiments. Madame Arnoux did not see that this was his way of getting his own back on her.

Meanwhile the viscount was cudgelling his brains to find a way to sweep Cécile off her feet; first, he displayed his aesthetic sense by criticizing the shape of the decanters and the engraving on the knives. Then he moved on to his stables, his tailor and his shirt-maker; finally, he broached the subject of religion and gave it to be understood that his religious observances left nothing to be desired.

373

Martinon was being far more workmanlike; in a monotonous drone, without ever taking his eyes off her, he made flattering remarks about her beaky profile, her mousy hair and her dumpy hands. The ugly duckling was squirming with pleasure under this flood of praise.

As everybody was talking at the top of their voices, no one could hear a word. Monsieur Roque was saying that France needed to be governed with a rod of iron; Nonancourt was even sorry that capital punishment had been abolished for political crimes. They ought to have exterminated that whole bunch of blackguards.

'And they're cowards too,' said Fumichon. 'I can't see anything brave about sheltering behind a barricade!'

'And talking of that, tell us about Dussardier,' said Monsieur Dambreuse, turning towards Frédéric.

The plucky young clerk had now become a hero like Sallesse, the Jeanson brothers, the Péquillet woman* and others and Frédéric needed no urging to tell the whole story of his friend; some of the glory rubbed off on him.

This naturally led them on to describe various acts of heroism. The diplomat maintained that it wasn't difficult to face death; take people involved in duels . . .

'The viscount can tell you all about that,' said Martinon.

The viscount went bright red. All the guests were watching him and Louise, more surprised than anyone, whispered:

'What's it all about?'

'He got cold feet in a duel with Frédéric,' replied Arnoux in an undertone.

'Do you know anything about all this, Mademoiselle Roque?' enquired Nonancourt quickly and passed the information on to Madame Dambreuse, who bent slightly forward to peer at Frédéric.

Without waiting for Cécile to ask, Martinon informed her that it was a matter concerning someone quite unmentionable. The girl shrank back in her chair as if to avoid any contact with such a Don Juan.

The conversation resumed; excellent claret was going the

rounds and the party was becoming extremely lively. Pellerin had a grudge against the Revolution because of the Spanish collection, now gone for good; as a painter this was what he felt most sad about. Monsieur Roque turned towards him:

'Aren't you the man who's painted a very remarkable picture?'

'Possibly! Which one are you referring to?'

'One of a lady . . . well . . . dear me . . . of a lady rather scantily dressed, with a purse, and a peacock in the background?'

It was Frédéric's turn to go scarlet. Pellerin was trying to turn a deaf ear.

'But it must be by you because it's got your name at the bottom and writing on the frame confirming it belongs to Monsieur Moreau.'

While waiting at Frédéric's place, old Roque and Louise had seen the Marshal's portrait. The old boy had even taken it to be 'a Gothic painting'.

'No,' replied Pellerin curtly. 'It's the portrait of a woman.'

'And a woman who's very much alive, eh, Cisy?' said Martinon.

Cisy didn't know which way to look and his embarrassment made the shabby way he must have behaved over the portrait perfectly plain. As for Frédéric, the model could only have been his mistress; this was the inference which people inevitably drew, as the expressions of all those present clearly proved.

'All those lies he was telling me!' said Madame Arnoux to herself.

'That explains why he left me!' thought Louise.

Frédéric fancied that these two stories might damage his reputation and when they'd all gone into the garden he tackled Martinon.

'Nonsense, it'll be a help! Press on, old chap!'

What did that mean? And anyway, why all this solicitude, so unlike him? Without further explanation, he went off to the far end where the ladies were sitting. The men had gathered round Pellerin, who was expounding his ideas. The most favourable form of government for an artist was an enlightened monarchy. He was disgusted by modern times, if only because of the National Guard; his ideal was the Middle Ages and Louis XIV; Roque complimented him on his views and even admitted that they upset all his prejudices against artists. But, attracted by Fumichon's voice, he very soon went off.

Arnoux was trying to argue that there are two kinds of socialism, one good and one bad; the industrialist couldn't detect any difference between them and when the word 'property' was mentioned, he became almost hysterically angry.

'Property's a law of life, part of the natural order of things. Children are attached to their toys, aren't they? And every race in the world, every animal shares my view; if it could speak, even the lion would describe itself as a landowner! Take my case, for instance: I started with a capital of fifteen thousand francs and do you know, gentlemen, for thirty years, I'd be up at four in the morning, day in, day out! I had a devil of a job to make my fortune! And now people are coming along and telling me it's not mine, that my money doesn't belong to me, that property is theft!'

'But Proudhon . . .'

'Don't talk to me about Proudhon! If I had him here now, I reckon I'd wring his neck!'

And he would have been as good as his word, for particularly after the liqueurs, Fumichon didn't know what he was doing; his apoplectic face looked all ready to explode like a shell.

'Evening, Arnoux!'

It was Hussonnet, bouncing in over the lawn.

The Bohemian was bringing Monsieur Dambreuse the first page of a pamphlet entitled *The Hydra*, defending the interests of a reactionary group, and the banker introduced him as such to his guests.

Hussonnet amused them first of all by claiming that tallow merchants were paying three hundred and ninety-two street urchins to shout: 'Lights on!' every night; next, by ridiculing the principles of 1789, the emancipation of the blacks and left-wing orators; he even launched into a skit on *Prudhomme* on a barricade*, perhaps because he felt childish envy of these well-to-do middle-class people who'd just had such a good dinner. The parody made little appeal. Their faces fell.

Anyway this was no time for joking, as Nonancourt pointed out by reminding them of the killing of Monsignor Affre and General Bréa. These deaths were still very much in everyone's mind. They started to discuss them. Monsieur Roque gave his view that there had never been anything so sublime as the way the archbishop had died; Fumichon thought that the general's death had been even more noble; and instead of being content merely to express sorrow at the two murders, they launched into an argument as to which was the more shocking. They then proceeded to draw another analogy between Lamoricière and Cavaignac, with Monsieur Dambreuse enthusing over Cavaignac and Nonancourt over Lamoricière. In fact, not one of those present could possibly have seen either of them in action, except Arnoux; this didn't prevent them from passing categorical judgements about their operations. Frédéric refused to comment, admitting that he'd taken no part in the fighting. The diplomat and Monsieur Dambreuse gave approving nods. Fighting the rioters had meant support for the Republic and the result, though satisfactory, had strengthened the republican cause. They'd eliminated the losers; now they were longing to do the same with the winners.

As soon as they had gone into the garden, Madame Dambreuse had told Cisy off for being so inept; then, seeing Martinon, she sent him away and enquired from her future nephew why he'd been making fun of the viscount.

'I hadn't got any reason.'

'And it all seemed meant to show Monsieur Moreau in a good light. What was in your mind?'

'Nothing at all. Frédéric's a charming fellow. I'm very fond of him.'

'So am I! I'd like to have a word with him. Go and bring him over here.'

After a few banalities, she started making some slightly derogatory remarks about her guests, implying that she thought more highly of him. Frédéric craftily took care to be rather disparaging about the other women, thereby flattering her. But it was her 'at home' day and she kept having to go away to welcome the lady guests who were arriving; then she came back to her seat and it so happened that, where they were sitting, no one could overhear their conversation.

She showed herself lively, earnest, wistful and full of common sense. She took little interest in current affairs; there was a whole range of things of more lasting concern; she complained of poets distorting the truth; then she looked up at the sky and asked him the name of a star.

There were two or three Chinese lanterns hanging in the trees, swaying to and fro in the breeze; coloured rays of light flickered over her white dress. As usual she was sitting rather far back in her armchair, with her footstool in front of her, giving a glimpse of the tip of a black satin shoe; every so often she'd stress a point by raising her voice and sometimes even laugh.

These flirtatious antics were lost on Martinon, who was busy with Cécile; but they had a powerful effect on the little Roque girl who was talking to Madame Arnoux, the only one among all these women who didn't seem stuck-up. She had gone over to sit beside her and felt a sudden impulse to open her heart to someone:

'Isn't Frédéric Moreau a good talker?'

'Do you know him?'

'Oh yes, very well, we're neighbours, he used to play with me when I was only a little girl.'

Madame Arnoux looked long and hard at her, with the unspoken question: 'You don't happen to be in love with him by any chance?'

The girl's eyes gave the frank answer: 'Yes, I am!'

'So you see quite a lot of him?'

'Oh no, only when he visits his mother. He hasn't been

back for ten months and yet he'd promised to come more regularly.'

'You mustn't put too much reliance on what men say, my dear.'

'But he's never tried to lie to me!'

'Unlike what he's done to others!'

Louise felt a shiver down her back: 'Perhaps he's made her a promise, too?' Her face screwed up in a spasm of hatred and suspicion.

Madame Arnoux felt almost frightened and wished she could take back what she'd said. Neither spoke.

Frédéric was sitting opposite them on a folding chair and they were both watching him, one discreetly out of the corner of her eye, the other open-mouthed, unashamedly. Madame Dambreuse said:

'Do turn round so that she can see you.'

'Who do you mean?'

'Monsieur Roque's daughter, of course!'

And she teased him about the love of that 'little girl up from the country'. He protested and tried to laugh it off:

'How can you possibly imagine such a thing! That little ugly duckling!'

All the same, he did feel enormously flattered. His mind went back to that earlier evening when he'd gone away, humiliated and sick at heart. He puffed out his chest; he felt at home here, almost on his own ground, as if all this, including the Dambreuse mansion, belonged to him. The ladies had gathered round him in a semi-circle to hear what he was saying and to show how clever he was, he put forward the suggestion of reintroducing divorce and making it so easy that every couple could break up and come together again indefinitely, as often as they liked. There were horrified protests; other women were whispering; little bursts of chatter were coming from the shadows under the wall covered in clematis. It was like the cheerful cackling of a bunch of hens. He continued to expound his theory with the self-assurance that springs from the knowledge that you've made a hit. A footman brought a trayful of ices into

379

the arbour. The men came over. They were talking about the arrests.*

Frédéric could now settle his account with Cisy. He hinted at the likelihood that the latter might be had up as a Legitimist. The other man protested: he'd never left his room. His opponent pointed out all the odds against him. Even Dambreuse and de Grémonville were amused; they proceeded to congratulate Frédéric; but what a pity that he wasn't employing his talents in the defence of law and order; on parting, they shook him warmly by the hand: from now on, he could rely on their support. Finally, as everyone was leaving, the viscount made Cécile a deep bow:

'It's been a great privilege. Good-night, Mademoiselle.'

She replied curtly: 'Good-night!'

But she gave Martinon a smile.

In order to pursue his discussion with Arnoux, old Roque suggested going along with him and 'your lady wife', since they lived in the same direction. Louise and Frédéric were walking on ahead. She'd clutched hold of his arm and as soon as they were some distance away from the others:

'Oh, at last we can talk! I've had such a miserable evening! Aren't those women spiteful! And so condescending!'

He tried to stand up for them.

'And for a start you might have spoken to me when you came in, since you haven't been to see me for a year!'

'It's not as long as that,' said Frédéric, glad to be able to correct her on one detail and ignore any others.

'All right! It seemed a very long time to me, that's all! But during that awful dinner party, you seemed to be almost ashamed of me! Oh, I realize I'm not as attractive as they are!'

'You're wrong,' said Frédéric.

'Really and truly? You promise you don't love any of them?'

He gave his word.

'And you only love me?'

'Good Lord, yes!'

380

This assurance made her more cheerful. How she'd like them to slip away and walk around together all night.

'I was so terribly worried down there in Nogent. They kept talking of nothing but barricades the whole time. I could see you collapsing on the ground all covered in blood! Your mother was in bed with her rheumatics. She didn't know anything. I had to bottle it all up inside myself! In the end, I couldn't stand it any longer so I brought Catherine along with me!'

She told him about how she'd managed to get away, the journey, and the lie she'd told her father.

'He's taking me back home in two days' time. Come round tomorrow evening, sort of accidentally, and then you can ask him if we can get married.'

Any thought of marriage had never been further from Frédéric's mind. What was more, Mademoiselle Roque seemed to him rather a silly little person. What a contrast with a woman like Madame Dambreuse! He could look forward to quite a different sort of future! Now that he was certain of this, today wasn't the time to commit himself to such an important decision, on a sudden sentimental impulse. He must be businesslike; and he'd seen Madame Arnoux again, too. All the same, Louise's forthrightness embarrassed him. He replied:

'Have you really thought carefully about that suggestion?'

'What do you mean?' she cried, stunned by surprise and indignation.

He said it would be madness to get married at the moment.

'So you don't want me?'

'You don't understand me!'

He launched into a complicated rigmarole to make her realize that there were most important considerations standing in the way, that he had a whole pile of business matters to attend to, that his financial situation was highly precarious and finally, as she kept summarily dismissing all these arguments, that the political situation was quite inappropriate. The sensible thing was to wait a little while; things would undoubtedly straighten themselves out, at least he hoped they would; and having run out of reasons, he suddenly pretended that he'd forgotten that he ought to have been at Dussardier's a couple of hours ago.

Then, having said good-night to the others, he vanished down the rue Hautefeuille, doubled back round the Gymnase Theatre to the boulevard and dashed up the four flights of stairs to Rosanette's.

The Arnouxs left old Roque and his daughter at the beginning of the rue Saint-Denis and continued home without saying a word; he was exhausted by having talked so much while she was overcome by such a terrible weariness that she even had to support herself on his shoulder.

He was the only man who'd shown any decency of feeling that whole evening and she felt very well-disposed towards him. He, however, was feeling rather aggrieved towards Frédéric.

'Did you see his face when the question of that portrait came up? Haven't I been telling you that he's her lover? You wouldn't believe me!'

'Yes, I realize I was wrong!'

Arnoux pressed home his advantage.

'I bet he even gave us the slip a moment ago to nip round and see her! He's with her now, believe you me! He sleeps there!'

Madame Arnoux had pulled the hood of her cape right down over her face.

'You're shivering!'

'I'm cold,' she replied.

As soon as her father was asleep, Louise went into Catherine'd bedroom and shook her by the shoulder.

'Quick, get up. Do hurry! And go and fetch a cab.'

Catherine replied that there wouldn't be one at that time of night.

'So you'll come along with me yourself, then?'

'Where to?'

'Frédéric's.'

'Out of the question! Why?'

To talk to him; it couldn't wait; she needed to see him at once.

382

'What are you thinking of? Going to someone's house like that in the middle of the night! Anyway, he'll be asleep.'

'I'll wake him up!'

'It's not the right thing for a young lady to do!'

'I'm not a young lady! I'm his wife! I love him! Come along, get your shawl!'

Catherine stood beside her bed, thinking. Finally she said:

'No, I don't want to go.'

'All right, then, don't! I'll go by myself!'

She crept stealthily downstairs; Catherine rushed after her and caught up with her on the pavement. Vainly protesting, she followed Louise, still fastening up her jacket. It seemed a very long way; she was complaining about her old legs.

'And anyway, I haven't got your excuse, for heaven's sake!'

Then her heart softened.

'You poor dear! You've only your Katie left, haven't you?'

Her qualms kept coming back.

'Ah, it's a fine thing you're making me do! Supposing your Dad wakes up? Let's hope nothing terrible happens!'

In front of the Variétés Theatre they were stopped by a National Guard patrol. Louise hastily explained she was going with her maid to fetch a doctor from the rue Rumford. They let them through.

At the corner of the Madeleine, they met another patrol and when Louise offered the same explanation, one of the guards said:

'One of those nine-months illnesses, is it deary?'

'No foul language in the ranks, Gougebaud!' exclaimed the captain. 'On you go, ladies!'

In spite of his warning, witticisms continued to fly.

'Have a good time!'

'My regards to the doctor!'

'Look out for the big bad wolf!'

'They will have their little joke,' said Catherine. 'It's because they're young!'

Eventually they reached Frédéric's house. Louise jerked hard at the bell, several times. The door was half-opened and in reply to her query, the porter said:

'No!'

'But he must be in bed?'

'I said no! He's not been sleeping here for the last three months!'

And the little window of the porter's lodge slammed down like a guillotine. They were standing under the archway in the dark. An angry voice shouted:

'And now be off with you!'

The outer door reopened and they went out.

Louise had to sit down on the corner-post. Covering her face in her hands, she wept her heart out. Day was breaking; carts were going by.

Catherine helped her to walk back, kissing her and making all sorts of comforting remarks drawn from her experience. You oughtn't to let yourself get so upset over sweethearts; there were as many fish in the sea as ever came out.

CHAPTER III

When Rosanette's enthusiasm for the security police had died down, she became more charming than ever and little by little Frédéric took to living with her.

The nicest part of the day was the morning on the terrace. In her loose cambric housecoat, she'd slop around, stockingless, in her slippers, cleaning out the canary cage, putting more water into the goldfish bowl and doing some gardening, with a fire-shovel, in a box filled with soil in which nasturtiums were climbing up a wall-trellis. Then they would both lean over the balcony and watch the carriages and passers-by together, enjoying the sun and making plans how to spend the evening. They would go out but never for more than two hours at the most; after that they'd go to some sort of show, sitting in stage-boxes; and, clutching a large bunch of flowers, Rosanette listened to the music while Frédéric whispered funny stories or loving words in her ear. Other times, they would hire a barouche and take a drive in the Bois-de-Boulogne, even staying out half the night. They would finally come back via the Arc-de-Triomphe and the main avenue, sniffing the night air, with the stars above and the gas-lights all in line like a double rope of pearls glittering in front of them as far as the eye could see.

Whenever they went out, Frédéric always had to wait for her; she would spend a great deal of time arranging the two ribbons of her bonnet under her chin and stand smiling at herself in her wardrobe mirror. Then she'd slip her arm through his and force him to look at the two of them together.

'What a nice couple we make, side by side like this! Oh, I could gobble you up, my pet!'

She owned him; he was her thing. This gave her face a sort of permanent glow while at the same time she seemed more soft and tender, her figure more rounded; however, he could feel a change in her even though he was unable to define it.

One day she told him that she had an important piece of news for him: friend Arnoux had recently set up one of his former female factory hands in a linen-draper's shop and he was going there every evening and spending a lot of money; only a week ago, he'd even presented her with a suite of rosewood furniture.

'How did you hear about that?' asked Frédéric.

'Oh, I'm absolutely certain!'

Delphine had been making enquiries, on her instructions. So she must be fond of Arnoux to be so concerned about his affairs! He merely replied:

'How does that affect you?'

Rosanette seemed surprised by his question.

'But the swine owes me money! Isn't it sickening to see him supporting sluts!'

Then, with a spiteful look, she added jubilantly:

'And incidentally she's making a complete bloody fool of

385

him! She's got three other fellows in tow, and a good job too! If she can squeeze his last penny out of him, I'll be absolutely delighted.'

And indeed, the long-suffering Arnoux, like any infatuated man in his dotage, was letting himself be exploited by 'the woman from Bordeaux'.

His factory was no longer operating and his business affairs were in such a mess that to put them on their feet again he'd first of all thought of opening a café with music where they'd sing nothing but patriotic songs and which, with a government grant, would have become a propaganda centre and a source of profit. Changes in government policy had put all this out of the question. He now had dreams of starting up a large factory to manufacture military headgear but he lacked the necessary capital.

He was having no better luck in his home life. Madame Arnoux was proving less amenable, sometimes even a trifle rough, towards him. Marthe always took her father's side and this increased the tension; his family life was becoming thoroughly unpleasant. He would often leave in the morning, spend the day roaming around trying to forget, and end up having dinner in some country inn, moodily brooding.

Frédéric's continued reluctance to call on them was disrupting his habits and one afternoon he went round to beg him to come and see him, as he had done in the old days. Frédéric promised he would.

The thought of calling on Madame Arnoux again scared him: he felt he'd betrayed her. But he was behaving in a thoroughly cowardly way. He could think of no excuses. Sooner or later, he'd have to do it! So one evening he set off.

It was raining and he'd just gone into the Jouffroy Arcade when, in the light of the shop windows, he was approached by a fat little man wearing a cap. Frédéric immediately recognized Compain, the speaker whose proposal had caused so much hilarity at the club. He was leaning on the arm of an individual decked out in a red Zouave cap; he had a very long upper lip, a jaw concealed by a goatee beard, an orange complexion, and he was gazing at him with eyes oozing emotion.

Compain must have been proud of him, for he said:

'You must meet this splendid chap, he's a friend of mine, a boot-maker and a patriot! How about a drink?'

Frédéric politely declined and the other man immediately launched into a violent attack on the Rateau motion,* a put-up job by the aristocrats. They'd have to start '93 all over again and put a stop to this sort of caper. Then he asked after Regimbart and a few other equally famous people such as Masselin, Sanson, Lecornu, Maréchal and a certain Deslauriers, implicated in that business of carbines recently intercepted in Troyes.

All this was news to Frédéric. Compain had no further information. As he was leaving, he said:

'See you soon, specially as you're a member of the club.'

'Which club?'

'The calves' head!'

'Which calves' head?'

'You will have your little joke, won't you!' replied Compain digging him in the ribs.

And the two terrorists vanished into a café.

Ten minutes later Frédéric had stopped thinking about Deslauriers and was standing on the pavement in front of a house in the rue Paradis gazing up at the light of a lamp behind the curtains on the second floor.

Finally he went upstairs.

'Is Arnoux in?'

'No, but please come in.'

She flung open a door:

'It's Monsieur Moreau, madam.'

She stood up, paler than her collar. She was trembling.

'To what do I owe . . . the honour of this . . . unexpected visit?'

'No special reason, apart from the pleasure of seeing old friends again!'

He sat down.

'And how is the dear man?'

'Very well indeed! He's not in at the moment.'

'Oh, of course! Still his old evening jaunts, a spot of relaxation!'

'Why shouldn't he? After working out figures all day, the mind needs a little rest!'

She even praised his capacity for hard work, which annoyed Frédéric. He pointed to a piece of blue-braided black material on her lap:

'What's that you're doing?'

'I'm altering a jacket for my daughter.'

'And I don't see her, by the way; where is she?'

'At boarding school,' replied Madame Arnoux.

Tears came into her eyes which she held back, busily applying herself to her sewing. He had tactfully picked up a copy of *L'Illustration* on the table beside her.

'Cham's cartoons are very funny, aren't they?'

'Yes.'

They both fell silent again.

A sudden gust of wind and rain rattled the windows.

'What weather!' said Frédéric.

'Yes, isn't it, and it's very kind of you to have come out on such a dreadfully wet night.'

'Oh, I don't mind at all! I'm not like some people who I dare say fail to keep their appointments because of it!'

'What appointments?' she asked innocently.

'Don't you remember?'

She gave a shiver and dropped her eyes.

Gently, he put his hand on her arm.

'You made me terribly, terribly unhappy, I can tell you!'

She replied with a sort of wistfulness:

'But I was afraid for my little boy!'

She told him about young Eugène's illness and how worried and distressed she'd been that day.

'Oh, thank you! Thank you, you've put my mind at rest! And I love you as much as ever!'

'But that's not true, it can't be!'

'Why not?'

She gave him a cold look.

'How about that other woman, the one you parade at

388

race meetings? The woman whose portrait you've got! Your mistress!'

'Oh, all right then!' exclaimed Frédéric. 'I admit I've behaved very badly! But just hear me out!' If he'd taken up with that woman, it was sheer desperation, like committing suicide. Anyway, he'd taken his own guilty feelings out on her and made her very unhappy. 'Can't you understand I was out of my mind with misery?'

He saw her lovely face turn towards him; she stretched out her hand. They closed their eyes in ecstasy, cradled on a gentle, endless wave of joy. Then they stood close, gazing into each other's face.

'Could you ever have imagined I'd stopped loving you?'

Fondly she whispered:

'No, in spite of everything, I knew at the bottom of my heart that it wasn't possible and one day the obstacles between us would go away!'

'Me too! And I was longing to see you so desperately!'

'One time', she went on, 'I passed right beside you in the Palais-Royal.'

'Really?'

He told her how overjoyed he'd been to see her at the Dambreuses'.

'But how I hated you when I went away that night!'

'You poor boy!'

'My life's so miserable!'

'Mine too! I wouldn't mind so much if it was just the worries and heartache and humiliations, all the things a wife and mother has to put up with. We've all got to die some day, haven't we? But it's being so lonely which is terrible, not to have anyone . . .'

'But you've got me!'

'Yes, that's true!'

Her chest heaved. A sob broke from her lips and lovingly she flung open her arms. They held each other tightly, in a lingering kiss.

A floorboard creaked. There was a woman beside them. Madame Arnoux recognized Rosanette and stood glaring at her in surprise and indignation. Finally Rosanette spoke:

'I've come to see Monsieur Arnoux on a matter of business.'

'Well, he's not here, as you can see.'

'Oh yes, so I can,' the Marshal replied. 'Your maid was right. Do forgive me!'

Then, looking at Frédéric:

'What are you doing here, my pet?'

For Madame Arnoux these words were like a slap in the face; she blushed scarlet.

'I've already told you he's not here!'

The Marshal had been running her eyes round the room. She turned to Frédéric:

'Well, let's go home, shall we? I've got a cab waiting downstairs.'

He pretended not to hear.

'Oh, do come along!'

'Yes, you mustn't miss your chance, do go!' said Madame Arnoux.

They left; leaning over the banisters, she watched them going downstairs; a shrill, heart-rending laugh pursued them from above. Frédéric pushed Rosanette into the cab, sat down opposite, and didn't open his lips during the whole journey.

It was he himself who'd brought this outrageous action and its appalling consequences down on his own head. He'd suffered a shameful, a crushing, humiliation and his happiness was in ruins. She'd been his for the taking and now she'd slipped out of his grasp for ever. And it was that woman, that bitch, that whore, who was to blame! He wanted to strangle her; he could scarcely breathe. When they reached home, he flung down his hat and tore off his necktie.

'Well, you must admit that really was a low-down trick!'

She faced him defiantly, hands on hips.

'Well, what about it? Where's the harm in that?'

'The harm? So you've been spying on me!'

'Is it my fault? Why do you want to have your fun with respectable married women?'

'That's got nothing to do with it! I refuse to let you insult her!'

'How did I insult her?'

He was at a loss for an answer; then, more angrily than ever:

'How about that other time at the Champ-de-Mars?'

'Oh God, do stop boring us with your old fancy women!'

'You bitch!'

He raised his fist.

'Don't you dare! I'm going to have a baby!'

Frédéric recoiled.

'You're lying!'

'Take a look at me, then!'

She held a light up to her face.

'Do you know about that sort of thing?'

Her skin was strangely puffy and covered in tiny yellow blotches. Frédéric didn't deny the obvious truth. He went over to open a window, took a few paces up and down the room, and slumped into an armchair.

This was a calamity: first of all, it would prevent any possibility of their parting for the time being and further upset all his plans. In any case, the thought of becoming a father seemed to him something unthinkable and grotesque. But why? Supposing, instead of the Marshal . . . ? And he fell into a day-dream which became almost hallucinatingly real: he could see a little girl there, on the hearthrug; she looked a bit like Madame Arnoux and himself, with brown hair, a white skin, dark eyes and strongly marked eyebrows, her curls tied with a pink bow! (Oh, how he would have loved her!) And he seemed to hear her voice saying: 'Daddy! Daddy!'

Rosanette, who had just got undressed, came over to him and seeing a tear on his eyelids, solemnly kissed him on the forehead. He stood up and said:

'Don't worry, we're not going to kill the little mite!'

This remark started her chattering: as it was obviously going to be a boy, they'd call him Frédéric and they must begin buying clothes for him. She was so happy that his anger turned to pity. He asked why she'd called on Arnoux.

It was because Vatnaz had that very day presented her with a long overdue IOU and she'd gone round to Arnoux's to get some money.

'I'd have given you it!' said Frédéric.

'It was simpler to go and pick up what I was owed and let that other woman have her thousand francs.'

'Is that all you owe her, at least?'

'Certainly!'

At nine o'clock the following evening, the time suggested by the porter, Frédéric called on Mademoiselle Vatnaz.

Stumbling over the furniture which cluttered up the entrance hall and guided by the sound of voices and music, he opened a door and found himself pitched into the middle of a party. In front of a piano being played with a great deal of loud pedal by a bespectacled young woman, Delmar was declaiming a piece of humanitarian verse about prostitution in the solemn cavernous voice of a bishop which boomed out over her powerful sostenuto. The wall was lined with a row of women dressed largely in black, unrelieved by collars or cuffs. Half a dozen men, all intellectuals, were scattered around on chairs. Slumped in one armchair was a former writer of fables—a complete wreck—and the acrid smell of a couple of lamps mingled with the aroma of mugs of chocolate littering the card-table.

With an oriental scarf draped round her hips, Mademoiselle Vatnaz was standing at one corner of the fireplace, while opposite her, on the other side, was Dussardier. He looked slightly embarrassed at being in such a position. This sort of arty society intimidated him, anyway.

Had Vatnaz ditched Delmar? Possibly not, yet she did seem jealous of the nice young clerk and when Frédéric asked if he might have a few words with her, she motioned to him to come with them into her bedroom. When he produced the thousand francs, she asked for the interest as well.

'It's not worth the trouble,' said Dussardier.

'Nobody asked your opinion!'

Frédéric was pleased to see such cowardly behaviour from such a brave man; it justified his own. He took the

IOU and never mentioned the incident at Madame Arnoux's again. But from that time on he was conscious of all the Marshal's shortcomings. She had incorrigibly bad taste, was incredibly lazy, and so abjectly ignorant that she considered Dr Des Rogis very famous and was proud to see him and his wife in her house 'because they were married'. She lectured Mademoiselle Irma about Life and bullied the poor little creature, who was endowed with a thready voice and under the protection of a former Customs and Excise officer, 'a real gentleman' and an expert at card tricks. Rosanette used to address him as 'my big sweetie-pie'. Nor could Frédéric stand her constant use of stupid expressions like 'Pull the other one!', 'Get lost!' or 'It has always been a mystery . . .' etc. etc. And every morning, she'd insist on dusting off her knick-knacks with a pair of old white gloves! Above all, he was revolted by the way she treated her maid, whose wages were always in arrears and whom she even used to borrow money from. On the days when they were settling their accounts, they'd bicker like a couple of fishwives and then make it up with hugs and kisses. He was beginning to become depressed at having to spend so much time with her and it was a relief when Madame Dambreuse's parties started again.

At least she was fun! She knew all about society intrigues, which ambassadors were due for a move, the names of the fashion designers, and if she did happen to utter a platitude, it was so conventionally phrased that you could take it ironically or as sheer politeness. You should have seen her surrounded by a score of people all chatting, never neglecting a single one of them, eliciting the replies she wanted and ignoring all the awkward ones! She could make a simple piece of information sound like an intimate secret; her slightest smile could set you dreaming. In a word, her charm was as subtle and indefinable as the exquisite perfume which she normally wore. In her company Frédéric experienced the pleasure of discovering something new every time and yet she was always as unruffled as the limpid sheen on a sheet of water. But why was she so cold towards her niece? At times, indeed, she'd throw very odd glances in her direction.

As soon as the question of her marriage had been mooted, she'd objected to her husband that the 'dear child's health wasn't up to it' and whisked her away to take the waters at Balaruc. On their return, new pretexts were discovered: the young man hadn't got a proper job, this 'deep love' of his somehow lacked conviction; nothing would be lost by waiting. Martinon agreed to wait. He was behaving more than nobly. He praised Frédéric to the skies, he even instructed him how to get into Madame Dambreuse's good books and hinted that, through her niece, he had inside knowledge of her aunt's feelings.

As for Monsieur Dambreuse, far from appearing jealous, he was showing his young friend every consideration, consulting him on various matters, and even expressing concern about his future, so much so that when old Roque's name came up one day, he whispered into his ear, with a crafty look:

'You did the right thing there!'

And in the whole household there was not a single person who wasn't absolutely charming to him—Cécile, Miss John, the servants and the porter. He would desert Rosanette and go round there every evening. Her impending motherhood was making her more earnest, even a little sad, as if she was worried about something. Each time he enquired, she invariably replied:

'You're mistaken, I'm perfectly all right!'

In fact, there had been *five* IOUs and, not daring to tell Frédéric since he'd paid the first one, she'd gone to see Arnoux who'd promised her in writing a third share of his profits from the Gaslight Company of the Languedoc (a stupendous project!), but asked her not to take up her shares before the next shareholders' meeting, a meeting which kept being postponed from week to week.

Meanwhile the Marshal needed money. She'd have died rather than ask Frédéric. She didn't want any from him. That would have spoilt their love. True, he was subsidizing the household expenses; but the monthly hire of a little

394

carriage, plus other indispensable sacrifices now that he'd become a regular guest of the Dambreuses, were preventing him from doing anything more for his mistress. Two or three times when he came home unexpectedly, he thought he caught a glimpse of male backs slipping through doors, and she often used to go out without saying where. Frédéric made no attempt to pry. One of these days he'd make up his mind, one way or the other. He was dreaming of a different sort of life which would be more fun—and more honourable.

This ideal made him more tolerant towards the Dambreuses' establishment. Their house was a private offshoot of the rue de Poitiers* and he met there the great M.A., the famous B, the profound C, the eloquent Z, the stupendous Y, the old stars of the centre left, the shining knights of the right, the stalwart middle-of-the-roaders, all the timeless stock of theatrical puppets. He was astounded by the appalling quality of their talk, their pettiness, their cattiness and their insincerity; all these people, having voted for the Constitution, were now making every effort to demolish it; and they were frantically active, launching manifestos, pamphlets, biographies—Fumichon's, written by Hussonnet, was a masterpiece. Nonancourt was in charge of propaganda in the provinces, Monsieur de Grémonville was working on the clergy, and Martinon was rallying the younger members of the middle classes. Everyone was exercising whatever talents he might possess, even Cisy himself who, his mind now set on serious matters, would drive round all day in a cab running errands for the party.

Monsieur Dambreuse was their weathercock, constantly indicating the most recent changes in direction; Lamartine was never mentioned without quoting the comment of one of the rioters: 'Give your harp a rest!' He now saw Cavaignac as nothing but a traitor. The President, whom he'd admired for three whole months, was beginning to go down in his estimation; he didn't have 'enough drive'; and as he always needed a saviour, his allegiance, ever since the Conservatorium of Arts and Crafts incident,* had settled on Changarnier: 'Thank God Changarnier . . . Let's hope

Changarnier ... Oh, nothing to fear as long as Changarnier ...'

But their highest praise was reserved for Monsieur Thiers and his book attacking socialism,* in which he had shown that he was not just a writer but a thinker. They considered Pierre Leroux ludicrous: he quoted bits of the *Encyclopédie*＊ in the Chamber! They made jokes about the Fourierists' tail.* They applauded *'La Foire aux idées'*＊ and compared it to Aristophanes. Frédéric was there with the rest of them.

Political logorrhoea and good food were beginning to blunt Frédéric's sense of right and wrong. However second-rate he might think these prominent persons, he was still proud to know them and secretly longed to gain the respect of this well-to-do middle-class society. A mistress like Madame Dambreuse would set him up nicely.

He started to go through the prescribed ritual.

He made sure of meeting her when she went for a walk and never failed to call and pay his respects at her theatre box; knowing what time she went to church, he'd lie in wait, in a melancholy posture, behind a pillar. Drawing her attention to anything of special interest, a concert, books or magazines to borrow, involved a continual exchange of little notes. Apart from his regular evening visit, he would sometimes call towards the end of the day and with ever-increasing enjoyment he'd go through the main gate, across the courtyard, through the entrance hall and the two drawing-rooms until he finally came to her boudoir, as private as the grave and as cosy as an alcove, where you would bump against softly padded furniture amidst all sorts of scattered objects: dainty little chiffonniers, screens, trays and bowls of ivory, tortoiseshell, lacquer or malachite, expensive knick-knacks, frequently replaced, some of them simple—three pebbles from Étretat used as paperweights, a Friesian bonnet hanging on a Chinese screen—yet they were all in harmony; you were even struck by an overall grandeur, perhaps because of the height of the ceiling, the opulence of the door-curtains and the long silk fringes floating round the gilt rungs of the stools.

She was almost always to be found sitting on a tiny two-seated sofa close to the plant-stand adorning the window recess, or perched on the edge of a large pouffe on casters. He would direct his most persuasive compliments at her while she looked at him with her head slightly on one side and a smile on her lips.

He would read her pages of poetry, as soulfully as possible, in order to touch her heart and arouse her admiration. She would cut him short with a disparaging comment or a practical observation; and always their conversation would revert to the everlasting topic of Love! They wondered what caused it, if women were more susceptible to it than men, and what differences there were in that respect. Frédéric would try to express his views without being indelicate or trite. It would develop into a sort of contest, sometimes pleasant, sometimes tiresome.

Sitting at her side he never felt the surge of ecstasy that had projected him, body and soul, towards Madame Arnoux, nor yet the wild gaiety of his early days with Rosanette; but he lusted after her as something difficult and out of the ordinary, because she was rich and pious and had a title; he imagined her possessing feelings as refined and exquisite as her lace, wearing amulets on her bare skin, demure and depraved.

He turned for help to his former love and retailed to Madame Dambreuse feelings inspired by Madame Arnoux, his tender longings, his disquiet, his dreams. She accepted all this like someone accustomed to such things, not rejecting him but not yielding an inch. His efforts at seduction proved as fruitless as Martinon's efforts to get married: to eliminate her niece's prospective husband, she accused him of being after her money, even getting her husband to put him to the test by informing the young man that as an orphan of poor parents, Cécile had no dowry and no expectations.

Martinon didn't believe him and, either because he felt too committed to withdraw or else through one of those acts of foolish obstinacy that turn out to be a stroke of genius, replied that his fifteen thousand francs a year would be enough. The banker was touched by such unexpected altruism, promised Martinon the caution money for a post as district tax collector, and undertook to get him the job. So in May 1850, Martinon married Cécile. There was no wedding ball and the young couple left for Italy the same evening. Next day, Frédéric called on Madame Dambreuse. She seemed paler than usual and sharply contradicted him on a couple of trivial matters. Anyway, all men were selfish.

But there were some who were loyal and affectionate, if only himself.

'Rubbish! As bad as the rest of them!'

Her eyes were red; she was crying. Then, making an effort to smile:

'Do forgive me, I'm behaving badly! I just had a sad thought!'

He couldn't make head or tail of all this.

'Anyway, she's not as tough as I imagined!' he thought to himself.

She rang for a glass of water, took one gulp and then sent it back, complaining that her servants were hopeless. To cheer her up, he jokingly offered to take over the job himself, claiming that he could hand round plates, dust furniture, announce visitors, in fact be her servant or rather her lackey, although the latter were no longer in fashion. He'd have enjoyed standing at the back of her carriage in a hat plumed with cock feathers.

'And I'd follow you on foot very grandly, with a little dog in my arms!'

'You're very cheerful!' said Madame Dambreuse.

Wasn't it idiotic, he went on, to take everything seriously? There was enough trouble in the world already without trying to create more. Nothing was worth being unhappy about. Madame Dambreuse raised her eyebrows, vaguely signifying her agreement.

This conformity of views encouraged Frédéric to become bolder. He'd learned from his earlier miscalculations. He went on:

'Our grandfathers knew more about how to live. Why

shouldn't we follow our impulses?' After all, in itself, love wasn't all that important.

'What you're saying is quite immoral!'

She had gone back to sit on her sofa. He perched himself on the edge against her feet.

'Don't you realize I'm just pretending? You see, to please women you either have to be carefree and play the fool or else be tragic and passionate. When you say to them quite simply that you love them, women laugh at you. For me, the exaggeration they expect degrades the idea of real love. So these days, no one knows how to express their love, particularly to those women . . . who are . . . very clever . . .'

She was gazing at him through half-closed eyes. He leaned towards her and lowered his voice.

'Yes, you intimidate me! Perhaps I'm offending you? . . . I'm sorry, I didn't mean to blurt all this out! It's not my fault! You're so lovely!'

Madame Dambreuse closed her eyes; his easy victory surprised him. In the garden, the tall trees, which were gently quivering, grew calm; the sky was streaked red with long, still bands of cloud; the whole universe seemed in abeyance. Vague memories of similar evenings and similar silences stirred in his mind . . . Where had that been?

He knelt down, clasped her hand and swore to love her for ever. As he was leaving, she beckoned him back and whispered:

'Come back for dinner! We'll be all alone!'

As he went downstairs, it seemed to Frédéric that he was no longer the same man; he was bathed in a balmy hothouse warmth and felt sure he was poised to break into the lofty world of upper-class adultery and high intrigue. To make his mark there, all he needed was a woman like that. No doubt she was restless and hungry for power; having married a second-rater, to whom she'd been of enormous help, she must feel the need for someone strong, whom she could guide? Nothing was impossible now. He felt capable of riding a hundred miles or working night after night and never feeling tired. His heart was bursting with arrogance.

On the pavement in front of him a man in an old greatcoat was walking along with a bowed head, in such a hangdog manner that Frédéric turned round to look at him. It was Deslauriers. As he was hesitating, Frédéric flung his arms round his neck.

'It's you! What's happened to you, you poor old chap?'

And he hauled him off to his house, plying him with questions.

First, the ex-government commissioner told about all his trials and tribulations. As he'd been preaching the brotherhood of man to the conservatives and respect for law and order to the socialists, the former had tried to shoot him and the latter to string him up. After June, he'd been unceremoniously sacked. He'd launched into a conspiracy, an arms deal in weapons which had been seized in Troyes. He'd been released for lack of firm evidence. The action committee had sent him to London, where he'd been involved in a brawl with his fellow members in the middle of a banquet. When he got back to Paris . . .

'Why didn't you come and see me?'

'You were never at home! Your porter used to put on a mysterious air, so I didn't know what to think, and anyway I wasn't keen on turning up as a failure.'

He'd gone the rounds of the supporters of democracy, offering his help as a writer, a speaker or a canvasser; they'd all turned him down; people didn't trust him; and he'd sold his watch, his library and his linen.

'I'd just as soon kick the bucket on the hulks on Belle-Isle* with Sénécal!'

Frédéric, who was at that moment in the process of adjusting his necktie, did not seem greatly put out by this news.

'Oh, so they've deported our good friend Sénécal, have they?'

Deslauriers was running his eyes enviously over the walls; he replied:

'Not everyone has your good luck!'

'You'll have to forgive me,' said Frédéric, not noticing the inference, 'I'm dining out. We'll get something for you to eat; order whatever you feel like! You can even have my bed.'

Deslauriers was disarmed by such open-handed generosity.

'Your bed? But . . . wouldn't that put you out?'

'Not a bit, I've got other beds to sleep in!'

'Oh, I see.' The lawyer laughed. 'Where are you going for dinner?'

'Madame Dambreuse's.'

'And . . . are you . . . perhaps . . . ?'

'Don't be so nosey!' said Frédéric with a smile which confirmed his friend's suspicions.

He glanced at the clock and sat down again.

'Well, that's how it is! And you mustn't despair, you old champion of the People!'

'Heaven forbid! Others can have a go at defending them!'

As a result of what he'd had to put up with in his allotted district, a coal-mining area, the lawyer loathed the workers. Each pit had set up its own provisional government, issuing him with orders.

'And everywhere their whole attitude was charming—in Lyons, Lille, Le Havre or Paris! Following the example of the manufacturers who want to keep out foreign goods, those fine gentlemen demand a ban on workers from England, Germany, Belgium and Savoy! As for their intelligence, what good was their famous guild system during the Restoration? In 1830 they joined the National Guard without even having gumption enough to take it over! And after '48, didn't the corporations reappear, each flying its own banner? They even wanted people's representatives of their own who'd have represented nobody but themselves! Just as the beetroot lobby doesn't worry about anything but beetroot! Oh, I've had my bellyful of all that bunch, kowtowing to Robespierre's guillotine, Napoleon's jack-boot, Louis-Philippe's umbrella,* a rabble who'll swear undying allegiance to anyone who'll toss them a crust of bread to fill their guts. Talleyrand's* always attacked for being venal but the messenger boy downstairs would sell his country for a few sous if he was promised three francs per message! What a fiasco! We ought to have been able to set the whole of Europe on fire!'

'You lacked the vital spark!' Frédéric replied. 'You were always just tradesmen and shopkeepers and the best of you were nothing but jumped-up schoolmasters! As for the workers, they've got a right to complain because, apart from the million francs they got from the Civil List—a blatant bit of boot-licking that was, by the way—the only thing you ever gave them was words, words and still more words! The boss continues to hold on to the pay-book and even in law the wage-earner is inferior to the employer, because his word won't be accepted. In fact, the Republic seems to me to have run out of steam. Who knows, perhaps progress can only be achieved by an aristocracy—or by one man? Initiative always comes from above! The masses aren't yet grown up, whatever people claim.'

'You may be right,' said Deslauriers.

Frédéric, who'd benefited from all the time he'd spent in the Dambreuse mansion, was of the opinion that the man in the street wanted nothing better than peace and quiet and that the odds were all on the conservatives. However, that party needed new blood.

'If you were to put yourself up, I'm sure . . .'

He stopped short in mid-sentence. Deslauriers realized why and ran both hands over his forehead; then suddenly:

'But how about you? There's nothing to stand in your way! Why shouldn't you become a Deputy?' Because of a double election, there was a vacant seat going in the Aube. Monsieur Dambreuse, who'd been re-elected,* held a different constituency. 'Would you like me to arrange it?' He knew lots of innkeepers, schoolmasters, doctors, lawyers' clerks and their employers. 'And you can get a peasant to believe anything you like!'

Frédéric felt his ambitions reawakening.

Deslauriers added:

'You ought to get me a job in Paris, you know!'

'Oh, that won't be difficult, through Monsieur Dambreuse!'

'And talking of coal-mines,' the lawyer went on, 'what's

become of that big merger? That's the sort of job that would suit me! And I could be useful to them and still keep my independence.'

Frédéric promised to take him round to see the banker in the next couple of days.

Dining alone with Madame Dambreuse was an exquisite experience. She sat opposite him on the other side of the table, smiling across a basket of flowers under the hanging lamp; and as the window was open, they could see the stars. They said very little, doubtless not trusting themselves, but as soon as the servants had their backs turned, they would purse their lips in a kiss. He mentioned his idea of standing for Parliament. She approved and even undertook to enlist Monsieur Dambreuse's help.

Later in the evening, a few friends dropped in to congratulate and condole with her; she must be sorry to have lost her niece? Anyway, it was all very well for the newly-weds to go off on their honeymoon, it was later on that trouble develops and children start coming! Nor was Italy all that people made it out to be, either! However, they were at an age when you still have illusions and everything was more wonderful on your honeymoon in any case! In the end, the only guests left were Monsieur de Grémonville and Frédéric. The diplomat was not keen to leave but finally, at midnight, he stood up. Madame Dambreuse signalled to Frédéric to do the same and rewarded him for obeying with a pressure of her hand, sweeter than everything else.

On seeing him arrive, the Marshal exclaimed out loud in delight. She'd been expecting him since five o'clock; he made the excuse of having had unavoidable business on Deslauriers's behalf. His face was radiating such an aura of triumph that Rosanette was quite dazzled.

'Perhaps it's your evening dress that suits you so well but I've never seen you looking more handsome! Oh, aren't you handsome!'

Carried away by her emotions, she made a vow to herself never to go to bed with anyone else, whatever happened, even if it meant dying in a garret!

Her pretty eyes were glistening and sparkling so passion-ately that Frédéric pulled her down on to his lap, saying to himself delightedly:

'Aren't I a bastard!'

CHAPTER IV

When Deslauriers called on Monsieur Dambreuse, the latter had been contemplating reviving his big coal-mining scheme. But this type of large-scale merger was frowned on and people were up in arms against monopolies, as if you didn't need huge amounts of capital for such projects!

Deslauriers knew all about this question, having just read Gobet's work and Monsieur Chappe's* articles in the *Journal des mines* for that very purpose. He was able to point out that the law of 1810 gave the concession holder an inalienable right; what's more, you could give the operation a democratic slant: banning coal-mining mergers was an infringement of the basic principle of association!

Monsieur Dambreuse handed over some notes for him to draw up a report. As for the remuneration for his work, he made promises which were all the more generous for being unspecific.

Deslauriers gave Frédéric an account of the interview; he'd also seen Madame Dambreuse downstairs as he was leaving.

'Congratulations, old boy! Good for you!'

Then they discussed the election. They'd have to work something out.

Three days later, Deslauriers brought him a handwritten note intended for publication in the newspapers; it was, in fact, a personal letter from Monsieur Dambreuse support-ing their friend's candidacy. With the recommendation of a conservative and the strong support of a Red, it was bound to succeed. How had the financier come up with such a load of rubbish? The lawyer had quite unblushingly taken it upon himself to show it to Madame Dambreuse who'd liked it very much and undertaken to see to the rest.

Although this move took him by surprise, Frédéric

agreed to it and then, since Deslauriers was intending to get in touch with Monsieur Roque, he explained how matters stood between himself and Louise.

'Tell them anything you like, say I've got business problems which I'll be able to straighten out. She's young, she can afford to wait!'

Deslauriers set off and Frédéric thought himself very smart. In any case, he felt extremely contented and smug: possessing a rich woman was an unmitigated pleasure; his personal feelings were in perfect harmony with the circles in which he moved. Life was a bed of roses.

His keenest pleasure came perhaps from watching Madame Dambreuse surrounded by people in her drawing-room. Her decorum brought other attitudes of hers to mind: while she was coolly chatting, he would recall her inarticulate cries of passion; he was delighted to hear tributes being paid to her virtue; he saw them as redounding on himself; sometimes he felt an urge to shout: 'But I know her better than you! She belongs to me!'

Their relationship soon became generally recognized and accepted; Frédéric spent the whole winter tagging along with her in society.

Nearly always he'd arrive early to see her come in wearing a sleeveless dress, carrying a fan, and with pearls in her hair. She'd stand for a second in the doorway, blinking, looking to see if he was there. She'd take him home in her carriage; rain would be lashing against the windows, the shadowy figures of passers-by struggling along in the mud; and in a daze, locked in each other's arms, they would look out on all this with quiet disdain. On various pretexts he'd manage to stay on in her bedroom for a good hour.

Madame Dambreuse had given herself largely out of boredom; but it was her last try, it mustn't be wasted; she wanted love with a capital L. She began showering Frédéric with every possible token of adulation and affection.

She sent him flowers; she embroidered a chair for him; she gave him a cigar-holder, a writing desk, a thousand and one everyday articles, so that he could do nothing without being reminded of her. At first he was charmed by these delicate attentions but soon he came to take them for granted.

She would take a cab, pay it off at the entrance to an alleyway, slip out at the other end and then, wearing a double veil and creeping along close to the wall, reach the street where Frédéric was looking out for her; quickly he'd seize her arm and take her back to his house. His two servants had gone for a stroll, the porter was out on an errand, there was nothing to fear! And she would heave a sigh of relief like someone returning from exile. Their good luck made them bolder and they met more and more frequently. One evening she arrived suddenly on the scene in full evening dress. Surprises like that could be risky; he remonstrated with her for being so indiscreet. Worse still, he found her unattractive; her low-cut dress showed too much of her flat chest.

He now realized something which he'd been hiding from himself: sexually, he felt let down; he still put on a great show of passion but in order actually to feel it, he had to think of Rosanette or Madame Arnoux.

This atrophy of his emotions left his mind quite clear; he was keener than ever to make his mark in society. He had a wonderful stepping-stone, he might as well make use of it.

One morning about the middle of January, Sénécal came into his study and in reply to Frédéric's exclamation of surprise explained that he was now Deslauriers's secretary and in fact bringing a letter from him. It contained good news but criticized him for his neglect: he'd got to come down.

The prospective Deputy said he'd be there in a couple of days.

Sénécal did not express any views as to the candidacy. He talked about himself and the state of the country; it was a shambles but he was delighted, because things were heading for communism. For one thing, the government itself was showing the way by taking more and more things under its control every day. Even Property hadn't escaped scot-free under the 1848 Constitution, despite the latter's shortcomings: on the grounds of public interest, the State could now appropriate whatever it thought fit. Sénécal was all in favour of Authority; Frédéric noted that his views were an exaggerated version of the ones he himself had voiced to Deslauriers. The republican even virulently attacked the incompetence of the masses.

'In defending the rights of the minority, Robespierre had Louis XVI brought to trial by the National Convention and saved the People.* The end justifies the means. Dictatorship is sometimes inevitable. Long live tyranny, as long as it's a benevolent one!'

Their discussion went on for a long time and just as Sénécal was leaving, he confessed (and this was perhaps the real purpose of his mission) that Deslauriers was becoming very impatient at Monsieur Dambreuse's continued silence.

However, Monsieur Dambreuse was a sick man. As a friend of the family, Frédéric had access to his house and saw him every day.

The capitalist had been badly affected by the dismissal of Changarnier.* That same evening he had a burning sensation in his chest and difficulty in breathing, which made it impossible for him to remain lying down. Leeches brought immediate relief; the dry cough disappeared, his breathing became easier and a week later, as he was drinking some beef-tea:

'Ah, that's better! But I was heading for that long journey of no return . . .'

'You wouldn't have gone without me!' exclaimed Madame Dambreuse, implying that she wouldn't have wanted to survive him.

He made no reply but his eyes rested on her and her lover with an odd smile, resigned, indulgent, ironical, even with a hint of derision, a quiet relish.

Frédéric wanted to go down to Nogent; Madame Dambreuse was against it and he kept packing and unpacking his bags according to the fluctuations in the patient's health.

Suddenly Monsieur Dambreuse started to bring up vast quantities of blood. On consultation, the 'cream of the medical profession' could offer no fresh ideas. His legs were becoming swollen and he was growing weaker. He'd asked several times for Cécile to come and see him; she was at the other end of the country with her husband who had just been appointed district tax-collector a month ago. He gave express instructions that she must be sent for. Madame Dambreuse wrote three letters which she showed him.

She wouldn't rely on the sister of mercy and didn't leave his bedside for a second, refusing to lie down herself. The visitors signing their names at the porter's lodge enquired after her admiringly. The passers-by were awed by the quantities of straw lying in the street under the windows.

At five o'clock on 12 February he began expectorating frightening quantities of blood. The doctor on duty warned of the danger; they hurriedly summoned a priest.

While Monsieur Dambreuse was confessing, his wife stood gazing at him with a look of curiosity from a distance. After this, the young doctor blistered him and waited.

The furniture was casting uneven patches of shadow round the room. Frédéric and Madame Dambreuse were watching the dying man from the foot of the bed. In a window recess the priest and doctor were talking in an undertone; the nun was on her knees mumbling prayers.

Finally the death rattle began; his hands were growing cold, his face started to turn pale. From time to time he would draw a very deep breath; they were becoming less and less frequent; a few mumbled words came from his lips; his eyes turned, he gave a tiny gasp and his head fell back sideways on to the pillow.

For a minute, no one stirred.

Madame Dambreuse went over and calmly and naturally, like a dutiful wife, closed his eyes.

Then she flung out her arms and twisting her body as if to restrain a spasm of despair, she left the room, supported by the doctor and the nun.

Fifteen minutes later, Frédéric went up to her room.

It was full of an indefinable scent given off by all the dainty objects in it. A black dress was spread out in the middle of the bed, making a strong contrast with the pink coverlet.

Madame Dambreuse was standing on one side of the

fireplace. While he didn't imagine she'd be grief-stricken, he did think she might be a little sad and so, with some concern in his voice, he asked:

'Are you feeling all right?'

'Me? Perfectly!'

As she turned her head, she noticed the dress and examined it; then she told him to make himself comfortable.

'Do smoke if you want. It's my house now!'

And with a deep sigh:

'Heavens above! What a relief!'

Frédéric was astonished at this exclamation. He kissed her hand and said:

'But all the same, we were never caused any trouble.'

This reference to the freedom they'd enjoyed in carrying on their affair seemed to offend Madame Dambreuse.

'You don't seem to have any idea of all the favours I did him or the agonies I went through!'

'Really?'

'Of course I did! How could I ever feel secure when I always had his bastard daughter round my neck? A girl he brought here five years after our wedding and who but for me would certainly have made him do something silly!'

She explained how her affairs stood: by their marriage settlement, she'd retained control of her own property, which amounted to three hundred thousand francs, while Monsieur Dambreuse had contracted to settle a pension of fifteen thousand francs a year on her and ownership of their house should he predecease her. But shortly afterwards, he'd made a will leaving everything to her and, as far as she could judge at the moment, she estimated this to amount to more than three million francs.

Frédéric's jaw dropped.

'So it was worth all the trouble, wasn't it? And anyway, I contributed towards it! I was defending myself against Cécile who wanted to deprive me of what was mine by rights!'

'Why didn't she come to see her father?' asked Frédéric.

409

Madame Dambreuse threw him a glance and said sharply:

'I've no idea! Sheer heartlessness, I expect! Oh, I know what she's like. She'll not get a penny out of me!'

She hadn't really caused any trouble, since her marriage, anyway.

'Oh, her marriage!' exclaimed Madame Dambreuse with a sneer.

She was annoyed with herself for having been so kind to that silly stuck-up girl, who was selfish, hypocritical and jealous. 'Just like her father!' She was becoming more and more scathing; she didn't know any man so utterly dishonest, quite ruthless, incidentally, and with a heart of stone, a 'bad, bad man!'

Even the wisest of people can blunder and in this spiteful outburst, Madame Dambreuse had done just that; Frédéric sat in an armchair opposite her, shocked and pondering.

She stood up and perched herself delicately on his lap.

'You're the only *really* good man! You're the only man I love!'

Looking at him, her heart overflowed and a nervous reaction brought tears to her eyes. She whispered:

'Will you marry me?'

At first he thought he must have misheard; all this wealth was bewildering. She said again, more loudly:

'Will you marry me?'

Finally he replied with a smile:

'Do you really need to ask?'

Then, feeling a pang of conscience and to make amends, he volunteered to keep watch over the dead man himself. But being ashamed of this pious sentiment, he added offhandedly:

'Perhaps it would look better.'

'Yes, perhaps it would,' she agreed. 'We must think of the servants!'

The bed had been dragged completely out of its recess; a nun was at its foot and a priest, a different one, tall and thin, with a fanatical Spanish look, at its head. On the bedside table, which was covered in a white napkin, three wax candles were burning.

Frédéric took a chair and looked at the dead man.

His face was straw-coloured and there were specks of blood-flecked foam marking the corners of his mouth. He had a silk handkerchief tied round his skull, a knitted waistcoat, and a silver crucifix resting on his chest between his folded arms.

And so that troubled life had reached its end! Think of all the departments and offices he'd called on, all the rows of figures he'd worked out, the reports he'd listened to, the shady deals he'd put through! Think of that smoke-screen of lies and smirks and the bowing and scraping! After all, he'd welcomed, with open arms, Napoleon, the Cossacks, Louis XVIII, 1830, the workers, one regime after another, and his respect for authority was so great that he'd have paid to sell his own conscience!

But he was bequeathing the Fortrelle estate, three factories in Picardy, the forest of Crancé in the Yonne, a farm near Orléans and a considerable portfolio of stocks and shares.

And once more Frédéric mentally calculated this man's wealth; but now it'd be his! First he thought of 'what people would say', then of a present for his mother, of the horses and carriages he would own, of an old coachman, a family retainer, whom he'd take on as his house porter. The livery would be changed, of course. He'd turn the large drawing-room into his study. By knocking down three walls on the second floor, there was no reason why he shouldn't have a picture gallery. Downstairs, it might be possible to fit in a Turkish bath. As for that unpleasant office of Monsieur Dambreuse's, what could be done with that?

The priest kept blowing his nose and the nun tending the fire, rudely interrupting these visions, but reality confirmed them: the corpse was still there. His eyelids had reopened and, despite being covered in a murky, glutinous film, his pupils had an enigmatic look that was unbearable. Frédéric felt that he was somehow passing judgement on him and he almost felt remorseful, for he'd never had any reason to complain about the man, quite the opposite, for he . . . 'Oh, come on, he was a miserable old rogue!' He was scrutinizing his face, trying to harden his heart and inwardly shouting:

'Well, what's wrong? Was it I who killed you?'

In the meantime, the priest was reading his breviary and the nun quietly snoozing; the candlewicks were growing longer.

The rumble of carts on their way to the Central Markets went on for two hours; the window-panes grew paler; a cab went by; and then a bevy of she-asses trotting along on the cobbles, the noise of hammering, the cries of itinerant traders, bugle calls, all these sounds blended to make up the many voices of Paris as she awakes.

Frédéric set out on his various errands. First, he drove to the town hall to notify the death; next, having obtained the official certificate from the doctor concerned, he went back to the town hall to tell them which cemetery the family wanted and to make arrangements with the undertakers.

The assistant produced a drawing and a programme, the first showing the various grades of funeral, the second, complete details of the proceedings. Did they want a hearse with a gallery or one with plumes, ribbons on the horses, egrets for the footmen, a monogram or coat of arms, funeral lanterns, a man to carry the regalia, and how many carriages? Frédéric splashed out: Madame Dambreuse had told him to spare no expense.

Then he went off to the church.

The curate in charge of funerals began by criticizing the way the undertakers operated; for instance, an official to carry the regalia was quite superfluous; it would be better to have lots of candles! They agreed on a low Mass, with music. Frédéric signed the contract, which included an undertaking to pay all charges.

Then he went to the Hôtel de Ville to buy a site. A plot six feet by three cost five hundred francs. Did he want it for fifty years or in perpetuity?

'Oh, in perpetuity!' said Frédéric.

He was taking the matter seriously and giving himself a lot of trouble. In the courtyard of the Dambreuse residence, a monumental mason was waiting to show him plans and estimates for Greek, Egyptian or Moorish graves but the architect of the house had already conferred with the mistress on the subject; and on the hall table, there were all sorts of prospectuses relating to the cleaning of mattresses, disinfecting of bedrooms and various methods of embalming.

After dinner he went back to the tailor's to arrange mourning for the servants and then had one final errand, because he'd ordered kid gloves and they should have been floss silk.

When he arrived next morning at ten o'clock, the large drawing-room was already filling up and as they all greeted each other with long faces, nearly everybody said:

'And to think I saw him only a month ago! Ah well, it's something we've all got to face up to!'

'Yes, but let's try to put it off as long as possible!'

Then they'd give a smug snigger and begin talking about totally unconnected matters. Finally, the master of ceremonies, wearing the traditional evening dress, with knee-breeches, a cloak, white mourning strips on his cuffs, a rapier and a cocked hat tucked under his arm, made a bow and uttered the ritual words:

'Gentlemen, if you please.'

They set off.

The weather was bright and mild and it was flower market day in the place de la Madeleine. The canvas stalls were flapping in the breeze which was billowing round the edges of a huge black flag over the front porch. Monsieur Dambreuse's escutcheon figured on it in three places, on a velvet square; *left arm sable sinistrorse or clenched fist argent*, with the coronet of a count and the motto *Par toutes voies.**

The pall-bearers carried the heavy coffin up the steps and everybody went in.

The six side-chapels, chancel and chairs were all draped in black. On the catafalque below the chancel, the light of the tall candles blended into a single yellow glow; spirit lamps were burning in candelabra in both corners.

The chief mourners took their seats in the sanctuary, the rest in the nave. The service began.

With few exceptions the congregation was so ignorant of religious matters that every so often the master of ceremonies had to signal when to stand up, when to kneel and when to sit down again. The organ and two double basses alternated with the voices; in the intervals of silence, the priest could be heard mumbling at the altar; then the instruments and singers took over again.

The light coming from the cupolas overhead was dim but through the open door a bright beam of daylight streamed in over all the bared heads; half-way up the nave, in mid-air, hung shadow, shot through with reflections from the gilt of the groins and of the pendentives and foliage decorating the capitals of the columns.

To relax, Frédéric listened to the *Dies Irae*; he was gazing at the congregation and trying to make out the paintings representing the life of Mary Magdalen, which were set too high. Fortunately, Pellerin came and sat down beside him, immediately launching into a long dissertation on the frescos. The bell rang. They left the church.

The draped hearse, adorned with ostrich feathers and drawn by black horses with beribboned manes, plumes on their heads and decked out in silver-embroidered trappings hanging down to their hooves, made its way towards the Père-Lachaise cemetery. Their driver wore riding boots and a cocked hat with a long piece of black crepe dangling down behind. The four pall-bearers were all prominent people: one of the Treasurers of the Chamber of Deputies, a member of the Departmental Council of the Aube, someone representing the coal-mining companies and Fumichon, as a friend. The deceased's barouche and a dozen mourning carriages followed while, behind them, the invited mourners filled the middle of the boulevard.

Passers-by kept stopping to look at all this; women climbed on to chairs with their babies in their arms; men enjoying a glass of beer came over to the café windows with a billiard cue in their hands.

It was a long journey and just as at banquets, where guests start off by being reserved and then relax, the mourners did not take long to become less inhibited. Conversation centred on the refusal of the Chamber to grant extra funds to the President. Monsieur Piscatory had been too outspoken, Montalambert 'superb, as usual', and Messieurs Chambolle, Pidoux, Creton and, in fact, the whole committee would perhaps have been better advised to follow Messieurs Quentin-Bauchard and Dufour.*

The discussion continued in the rue de la Roquette, where there are rows of shops with nothing to see except coloured glass chains and little black discs covered in gold characters and patterns, so that they look like china shops and caves full of stalactites. However, at the cemetery gates, all conversation stopped instantly.

The graves—pyramids, broken columns, temples, dolmens, obelisks, Etruscan vaults with bronze gates—stood amongst trees. In some of them, you could catch a glimpse of a sort of funeral boudoir with rustic chairs and folding stools. Tattered cobwebs dangled from the little chains of the urns; the bunches of satin ribbon and the crucifixes were covered in dust. Everywhere, between the pillars of the balustrades and on the graves, were wreaths of Everlasings, candlesticks, vases, flowers, black discs picked out in letters of gold, plaster statuettes of little boys and girls, or little angels suspended on brass wire; a number of them even had a zinc roof over them. Enormous cables of spun glass, entwined like long boa constrictors, black and white and bright blue, reached from the top of the steles to the foot of the flagstones, glittering in the sun among the black wooden crosses; the hearse was proceeding along the main avenues, which were cobbled like city streets. Now and then, the axles of the carriages would rattle. With their dresses trailing in the grass, kneeling women were quietly talking with their departed. Whitish plumes of smoke drifted up from the leafy green yew trees: discarded floral tributes and other rubbish were being burnt.

415

Monsieur Dambreuse's grave was close to Manuel's and Benjamin Constant's.* At that point the ground slopes sharply away; the tops of the evergreens are at ankle-level, beyond them are factory chimneys, and still further on, the metropolis.

The speeches gave Frédéric a chance to admire the scenery.

The first one was on behalf of the Chamber of Deputies, the second of the Departmental Council of the Aube, the third of the Mining Company of Saone-et-Loire, the fourth of the Farmers' Association of the Yonne; and there was one more, on behalf of a philanthropic society. Finally, as everyone was leaving, a stranger began to read a sixth speech on behalf of the Antiquarian Society of Amiens.

All the speakers seized the opportunity to inveigh against socialism, which had led to Monsieur Dambreuse's death. It was the spectacle of anarchy together with his devotion to the principle of order which had brought him to an early grave. They praised his enlightened understanding, his honesty, his generosity and even his failure to speak when representing the people in the Chamber, for though he may have had no gift for oratory, he did, instead, have those sound qualities, far, far more valuable . . . and so on and so forth . . . with all the obligatory phrases: 'Untimely death . . . boundless sorrow . . . that other homeland . . . not farewell but until we meet again in a better world . . .'

The stony earth fell on Monsieur Dambreuse; he was gone and the world would never concern itself with him again.

They did still go on talking about him a little as they left the cemetery and their comments did not lack candour. Hussonnet, who had to report the funeral in the newspapers, went so far as to parody all the speeches; after all, old Dambreuse had been one of the most notorious 'palm-greasers' of the previous regime. Then, these pillars of society were driven away in their mourning carriages to see to their own business affairs; thank God, the ceremony hadn't been too long!

Frédéric was tired and went back home to his own place.

When he arrived at the Dambreuse residence the following day, he was told that 'Madame was working in the study downstairs'. The cardboard boxes and drawers were all open, in a jumble; ledgers were strewn all round the room; he nearly tripped over a bundle of rolled-up documents labelled 'Bad debts' and picked it up. Buried in a big armchair, Madame Dambreuse couldn't be seen.

'Where are you? What's wrong?'

She leapt to her feet.

'What's wrong? I'm ruined, do you realize, ruined!'

The solicitor, Monsieur Adolphe Langlois, had asked her to call at his office and had shown her a will made by her husband before their marriage, leaving everything to Cécile. The other will had disappeared. Frédéric went very pale. Perhaps she hadn't looked thoroughly?

'Have a look yourself!' said Madame Dambreuse, pointing to the room.

The two strong-boxes had been hacked wide open by a cleaver; she'd turned the desk inside out, rummaged through the wall cupboards, shaken the door mats; suddenly, she uttered a shrill cry and rushed over to a corner where she'd just spied a little box with a brass lock; she opened it: nothing!

'The dirty rat! When I think how devotedly I looked after him!'

She burst into tears.

'Perhaps it's somewhere else?'

'No, it was there, in that strong-box, I saw it quite recently! It's been burnt, I'm certain!'

One day, at the beginning of his illness, Monsieur Dambreuse had gone downstairs to sign some documents.

'And that's when he did it!'

Completely overcome, she collapsed on to a chair. A mother mourning over an empty cradle is not more pitiful than Madame Dambreuse gazing on her dismembered strong-boxes. Indeed, in spite of its squalid motive, her grief seemed so genuine that he tried to comfort her by pointing out that, all things considered, she wouldn't be poverty-stricken.

'Yes I shall, because I shan't be able to make you a *really* wealthy man!'

She'd be left with only thirty thousand francs a year, apart from the house which was worth eighteen to twenty, perhaps.

Although for Frédéric this was affluence, he could not help feeling disappointed. Goodbye to all those dreams of the grand life he was going to lead! In all decency, he had to marry Madame Dambreuse. He thought for a minute and then said lovingly:

'But I'll still have you!'

She flung herself into his arms and he held her tight, with a feeling of tenderness not unmixed with a certain admiration for himself. Madame Dambreuse had stopped crying and looked up at him with her face glowing with happiness and clutching his hand, exclaimed:

'Oh, I knew I could rely on you! I was sure of it!'

The young man didn't enjoy hearing her take for granted an action which he considered noble.

She took him up to her bedroom and they started to make plans. Frédéric must now set about furthering his career. She even offered some valuable advice concerning his candidacy.

First of all, he must keep two or three phrases of political economy handy. He should develop some speciality, such as horse-breeding, for example, publish a few papers on questions of local concern, always have the odd post-office or tobacco shop licence up his sleeve, and do lots of little favours for people. Dambreuse had been perfect at that sort of thing; for instance, he'd once stopped with a coachload of his friends at a country cobbler's and bought a dozen pairs of shoes for his guests and an absolutely appalling pair of boots for himself—which he'd worn like a hero for a good fortnight. This anecdote restored their good humour; she recovered her youthful charm and wit and regaled him with a few more stories.

She approved of his idea of going down to Nogent at once. They bade each other a fond farewell and on the doorstep she whispered to him once more:

418

'You do love me, don't you?'

'For ever and a day!' he replied.

At his house, a messenger was waiting for him with a pencilled note informing him that Rosanette was about to give birth. He'd been so busy during the last few days that he'd forgotten all about it. She'd gone into a special clinic in Chaillot.

Frédéric took a cab and set off there.

At the corner of the rue Marbeuf he saw a notice in big letters announcing 'Nursing Home and Maternity Hospital under the management of Madame Alessandri, qualified midwife from the School of Midwifery, author of various publications etc.' Then, halfway down the street, on a very small door, was a further notice, with no reference to maternity, just 'Madame Alessandri's Nursing Home', and listing her qualifications.

Frédéric gave a loud knock on the door.

A saucy-looking maid showed him into the reception-room furnished with a mahogany table, garnet-red plush armchairs and a clock under a glass dome.

Madame Alessandri appeared almost at once. She was a tall, slim, well-bred woman of forty, with dark hair and fine eyes. She informed Frédéric that the mother had had a successful confinement and showed him up to her room.

Rosanette gave him a wonderful smile and in a breathless whisper, as if overcome by a wave of emotion, pointing to a cradle cot next to her bed:

'It's a boy, look over there!'

He pulled the curtains aside and beheld a yellowish-red object lying among bedclothes; it had an unpleasant smell and was emitting loud wails.

'Give him a kiss!'

To hide his repulsion, he said:

'Isn't there a risk of hurting him?'

'No, go ahead!'

So, very gingerly, he kissed his child.

'Doesn't he take after his dad!'

And in a burst of tenderness he'd never seen before, she hung her arms weakly round his neck.

He remembered Madame Dambreuse and felt he was a monster to betray this poor little child of nature who was so sincere in the way she loved and suffered. For several days he stayed with her until evening.

She was happy in this house, so discreet that even the front shutters were kept constantly closed; her room, decorated in pale chintz, looked out on to a large garden. Madame Alessandri, whose only weakness was dropping the names of all the famous doctors who were her close friends, surrounded her with every care and attention. Her female companions, almost all unmarried country girls, were very bored as no one came to visit them; Rosanette realized that they envied her and was proud to tell Frédéric so. They had to converse in whispers, however, as the partitions were thin; everybody eavesdropped, albeit through a constant background of piano music.

Just as he was finally about to leave for Nogent, he received a letter from Deslauriers.

Two new candidates were now standing, one conservative, one Red; any third candidate, whatever his views, wouldn't stand an earthly. It was Frédéric's own fault, he should have struck while the iron was hot, got moving and come over before. 'You didn't even go to the Agricultural Show!' The lawyer blamed him for not having any press contacts. 'If only you'd taken my advice earlier, we'd have had our own newspaper!' He kept harping on this point. Anyway, lots of people, who'd have voted for him to oblige Monsieur Dambreuse, would now be dropping him. One such was Deslauriers himself; having nothing further to hope for from the capitalist, he was going to ditch the man who'd been backed by him.

Frédéric took the letter round to Madame Dambreuse.

'You don't seem to have gone to Nogent?' she said.

'Why do you say that?'

'Because I saw Deslauriers three days ago.'

Knowing of her husband's death, the lawyer had shown her some notes on the coal-mines and offered his services as business manager. This seemed odd to Frédéric; and what was his friend up to down in Nogent?

Madame Dambreuse enquired how he'd been spending his time since their last meeting.

'I've not been well,' he replied.

'You might at least have let me know.'

'Oh, there was no point'; anyway he'd had a lot of disruptions, appointments and callers.

From this time on, he led a double life, religiously spending the night at the Marshal's and the afternoons with Madame Dambreuse, so that he barely had an hour to himself in the middle of the day.

The baby was in the country, at Andilly.* They went to see him every week.

The wet nurse's cottage was at the end of the village, at the rear of a little farmyard which was as gloomy as a well, with straw on the ground, hens all over the place, and a vegetable barrow under the Dutch barn. The first thing Rosanette did was to rush over and smother him in kisses and then dash around in a frenzied sort of way, trying to milk the cow, munching farmhouse bread, sniffing at the manure and wanting to pick up a little bit of it in her handkerchief.

Then they would go for long walks; she'd visit the nurseryman's, tear off branches of lilac dangling down over walls, shout 'Gee up, Neddy!' to the donkeys drawing a cart, and stop to gaze through the iron gates at the lovely gardens; or else the nurse would take the baby, put him down in the shade of a walnut tree, and the two women would spend hours in boring and inane chatter.

Nearby, Frédéric would be gazing at the patches of vine on the sloping ground, with the odd clumps of trees here and there; the dusty tracks looked like dirty grey ribbons and the scattered houses provided the occasional splash of red and white amongst the greenery; sometimes the long horizontal trail of smoke from a train would stretch out like a giant ostrich plume with its feathery tail drifting away skywards.

Then he'd turn round to look at his son. In his mind's eye he could see him as a young man; he'd be a companion for him; yet maybe he'd be stupid, and surely unhappy;

he'd always have the handicap of being illegitimate. It would have been better for him never to have been born; and with an inexplicable feeling of foreboding, he'd mutter sadly: 'Poor little lad!'

They often missed the last train and then Madame Dambreuse would tell him off for being unpunctual. He made up some story or other.

He had to do the same with Rosanette. She couldn't understand how he managed to spend all his evenings: if a message was sent to him at home, he was never there! One day when he did happen to be at home, they both turned up almost simultaneously. He got the Marshal out of the room and hid Madame Dambreuse, explaining that he was expecting his mother.

He soon discovered that lying was fun: he'd repeat to one of them the promises he'd just made to the other, send them identical bunches of flowers, write to them both at the same time and then make comparisons between the two. Always present in his mind there was a third woman and the impossibility of having *Her* justified his duplicity, which added a spice of variety to his pleasure; and the more he'd deceived one of them, the more she loved him, as if each woman's love was excited by the other's, like a kind of competition in which each was trying to make him forget her rival.

'Just see how wonderfully I trust you!' said Madame Dambreuse to him one day. She unfolded a sheet of paper informing her that Monsieur Moreau was cohabiting with a certain Rose Bron.

'Would that perhaps be the lady at the races?'

'How absurd!' he retorted. 'Let me see it!'

The letter was written in capitals and unsigned. In the beginning Madame Dambreuse had accepted that particular affair as a cover for their own adultery, but as she had become more passionately involved, she insisted that he give her up, something which Frédéric claimed he'd done a long time ago. Now, after he'd finished reassuring her yet again, she looked at him, blinking her eyes in which there lurked the sharp glint of a dagger wrapped in muslin, and said:

'Well, and how about the other one?'

'Which other one?'

'The wife of that pottery manufacturer.'

He gave a scornful shrug. She didn't insist.

But a month later, during a discussion on honesty and straight dealing, when, as a precautionary measure, he slipped in a good word for his own standards of conduct, she said:

'Yes, that's true, you are honest. You've stopped going to see her.'

With the Marshal in mind, Frédéric stammered:

'Who do you mean?'

'Madame Arnoux.'

He insisted on being told where she'd got that piece of information. It was from her second dressmaker, Madame Regimbart.

And so she knew all about his life and he didn't know anything about hers!

However, in her dressing-room he'd come across a miniature of a gentleman with long moustachios: was he the same man concerning whom he'd once heard a rumour of suicide? But there was no way for him to find out more about him! In any case, what was the point? Women's hearts are like those little cabinets with lots of secret drawers, one inside the other; you give yourself a great deal of trouble, break your nails and, in the end, discover a withered flower, a few specks of dust—or a blank.

And perhaps he was scared, too, of finding more than he'd bargained for.

She made him refuse invitations when she couldn't go with him, kept him tied to her apron-strings and was afraid of losing him; yet in spite of this ever-increasing intimacy, there were sudden glimpses of enormous gulfs between them in their judgement of a person or of a work of art, matters of little importance.

She played the piano with steely accuracy. Her spiritualism (she believed in the transmigration of souls) didn't

423

prevent her from keeping a remarkably sharp eye on her expenses. She was high-handed with her domestic staff and had a heart of flint when it came to the ragged poor.

Her everyday language bristled with expressions of naïve self-interest: 'What's that got to do with me? That would be very sensible of me, wouldn't it? There's no need to!', which showed up in a thousand and one obnoxious little ways, impossible to define exactly. She would have eavesdropped outside doors; she surely lied to her confessor. She asserted her authority by demanding that Frédéric should go to church with her. He obeyed, and carried her prayerbook.

The loss of her legacy had changed her considerably and her strained look, which people interpreted as grief at her husband's death, made her interesting. She continued as before to do a great deal of entertaining. Since Frédéric's electoral fiasco, she had hopes of a diplomatic post in Germany for them, so the first thing to be done was to follow current trends of ideas.

There were some who wanted a new Napoleonic empire, others, a return to the Orléans, others, the Comte de Chambord; but everyone was agreed on the urgency of decentralization, for which various methods were put forward, such as cutting Paris up into a mass of villages by means of large arterial roads, transferring the seat of government to Versailles, moving the principal state institutions of higher education down to Bourges,* doing away with libraries, putting major-generals in charge of everything; and country people came in for very high praise, since illiterates naturally had more sense than anyone else! There was rampant hatred on all sides: hatred directed at primary school teachers and wine-merchants, the philosophy classes* in schools, the teaching of history, novels, red waistcoats,* long beards, any kind of independence or expression of individuality, for it was essential to 'reassert the principle of authority', no matter on whose behalf or who was exercising it, as long as it was tough and uncompromising! Conservatives were now talking the same language as Sénécal. Frédéric was completely puzzled and in his old mistress's house he was forced to listen to the same talk from the very same men!

The drawing-rooms of prostitutes—their importance dates from this time—provided a sort of neutral ground where reactionaries of different colours could come together. Hussonnet, who was engaged in a smear campaign against the celebrities of the day (an excellent method of restoring Order), had egged Rosanette on to set up her own 'at home', like any other woman; he'd report them in the papers; and as a start, he brought along a man of substance, Fumichon; then others began to drop in—Nonancourt, Monsieur de Grémonville, our friend the former Prefect, de Larsillois, and Cisy, now an agricultural scientist, a votary of Lower Brittany and more of a Christian than ever.

In addition, there were the Marshal's ex-lovers such as the Baron de Comaing, the Comte de Jumillac and a few more. Frédéric found their unceremonious behaviour offensive.

To assert his position as master of the house, he stepped up their style of living: they took on a groom, moved into new premises, and acquired new furniture. This expenditure was useful inasmuch as it made his marriage appear less disproportionate to his financial situation. The latter was deteriorating at a frightening rate as a result; and Rosanette had no idea of all this!

Being at heart a middle-class housewife who had come down in the world, she adored domesticity, a cosy home life; yet she was glad to have her 'visiting day', would refer to those in a similar position to her own as 'those women!', wanted to be 'a society lady'—and thought she was. She asked Frédéric to stop smoking in her drawing-room and tried to get him not to eat meat on Friday as 'this sort of thing wasn't done'.

In fact she was belying her own function: she was becoming prim and always put on a slightly wistful look before going to bed, on the same principle as they plant cypresses outside tap-rooms.

He found out the reason: she was dreaming of wedding bells—so that made two of them! Frédéric was exasperated.

What's more, he hadn't forgotten the time when she turned up at Madame Arnoux's and still bore her a grudge for holding out so long against him.

All the same, he did try to discover who her lovers had been. She denied them all. He became obsessed by a sort of jealousy and was irritated by all the gifts she'd received and was still receiving; yet even while becoming more exasperated by her true nature, he felt attracted to her by a fierce animal lust, a momentary aberration of the senses which eventually turned to hatred.

He came to dislike everything about her—her voice, her language, her smile and above all her eyes, that eternally limpid and inane feminine gaze. There were times when this got on his nerves so much that he would have stood by and cheerfully watched her die. But how could he get angry with her? She was maddeningly sweet and gentle.

Deslauriers again appeared and explained that he'd been staying on in Nogent to negotiate the purchase of a solicitor's practice. Frédéric was glad to see him back: what a remarkable fellow he was! He invited him along to form a threesome.

The lawyer used to dine at their house from time to time and whenever small disagreements arose, he always took Rosanette's side, until on one occasion Frédéric made it obvious how glad he'd be to get rid of her by saying:

'All right then, go to bed with her if you feel like it!'

About the middle of June, she received a writ from a bailiff, Maître Athanase Gautherot, requiring her to reimburse the sum of four thousand francs owed to Mademoiselle Clémence Vatnaz; in default, he would come round next day to distrain.

In fact, of the four earlier IOUs, only one had been paid, any money she might have received in the interim having gone towards other needs . . .

She rushed round to see Arnoux; he was now living in the Faubourg-Saint-Germain and the porter didn't know the street. She drove round to a number of friends, failed to find anyone and returned home in despair. She didn't want to say anything to Frédéric, terrified that any fresh trouble might damage her marriage prospects.

Next morning, Maître Athanase Gautherot arrived with two acolytes, one of them with a sly cadaverous face which seemed green with envy, the other wearing a detachable collar, very taut trouser-straps and a black taffeta finger stall on his forefinger; both were revoltingly grubby, with dirty collars and coat-sleeves half-way up to the elbow.

On the other hand, the man in charge was extremely personable; he began by apologizing for his unpleasant errand while at the same time running his eye round the room, 'full of very pretty things, my word!' He added: 'Quite apart from those that can't be seized.' He signalled to his two myrmidons to go into the next room.

He became even more complimentary. How could anyone possibly imagine that so . . . charming . . . a person had not got a friend to stand by her! A forced sale was a real disaster! It's something you never recover from. He tried to frighten her and then, seeing how shocked she was, he suddenly adopted a benign tone. He was a man of the world, he'd had dealings with all those ladies; and as he listed their names, he was scanning the frames hanging on the walls. They were pictures provided in earlier days by the kindly Arnoux, sketches by Sombaz, water-colours by Burrieu, three landscapes by Dittmer. Rosanette obviously hadn't any idea of their value. Maître Gautherot turned towards her:

'Look here, to show what a nice chap I am, let's make a deal: you let me have those Dittmers and I'll settle everything. Is that all right with you?'

At that moment Frédéric, who'd been briefed by Delphine and had just seen the two minions, came in, still with his hat on and looking grim. Maître Gautherot resumed his dignified air and as the door had been left open:

'Keep going, gentlemen! Note it all down! In the second room we have: one table, oak, with two leaves, two sideboards . . .'

Frédéric interrupted him to ask whether there wasn't some way of preventing the seizure.

427

'Certainly! Who paid for the furniture?'

'I did.'

'Very well then, lodge a claim, that'll hold things up anyway.'

Maître Gautherot quickly finished making his inventory, entered an injunction against Mademoiselle Bron in his report and left.

Frédéric made no recriminations; he was gazing at the muddy marks left by the two assistants on the carpet. He said to himself:

'We must get hold of some money!'

'Good Lord, how stupid of me!' exclaimed the Marshal.

She rummaged in a drawer, took out a letter and rushed round to the offices of the Languedoc Gaslight Company to arrange the transfer of her shares.

An hour later she was back: they had been disposed of to someone else! After scrutinizing the sheet of paper bearing Arnoux's written promise, the clerk had told her: 'This document isn't a legal transfer and the company can't recognize it.' In a word, he'd sent her about her business and she was almost speechless with rage: Frédéric must go off at once to clear this matter up with Arnoux.

But Arnoux might well imagine that this was an indirect way of getting back the fifteen thousand francs he'd lost over the mortgage, and laying a claim against a man who'd been his mistress's lover seemed a dirty trick to play. He decided to try an alternative, and having got Madame Regimbart's address from the Dambreuses' house, he sent a messenger round to find out which café was currently favoured by the Citizen.

It was a small one in the place de la Bastille where he'd spend all day, in the corner on the right at the back, more or less part of the furniture.

After progressing in stages from a small coffee dash to a grog to a port and orange to a mulled wine and even to water with a dash of red wine, he had gone back to beer and every half-hour he would utter the words: 'Same again!', having reduced his vocabulary to a bare minimum. Frédéric asked him if he ever ran across Arnoux.

428

'No!'

'Really? Why not?'

'An idiot!'

As it could have been politics that had caused the rift, Frédéric thought it might be diplomatic to enquire after Compain.

'What an oaf!'

'How do you mean?'

'His calves' head!'

'Oh, do tell me what that's all about!'

'Sheer rubbish!'

There was a long pause. Frédéric asked:

'So he's changed his address?'

'Who?'

'Arnoux.'

'Yes. Rue de Fleurus!'

'What number?'

'Do you take me for a pal of the Jesuits?'

'The Jesuits?'

The Citizen flared up.

'That bastard got money out of a patriot I introduced him to and he's set up as a dealer in rosaries!'

'I can't believe it!'

'Go and see for yourself!'

It was absolutely true; Arnoux had had a stroke and turned religious; in any case, he'd 'always been a religious man, at heart', and with his typical blend of mercantile instinct and infantile optimism, had decided to save his soul, and his bank balance, by trading in religious articles.

Frédéric had no difficulty in finding the shop, which bore the sign: YE GOTHICK ART SHOPPE: *Ecclesiastical restoration and decorative articles. Polychrome statuary. Magi, incense, etc. etc.*

On each side of the shop-window there stood a gaudy wooden statue painted in gold, vermilion and cerulean blue: a Saint John the Baptist, complete with sheepskin, and a Saint Geneviève carrying roses in her apron and a distaff under her arm; then some plaster casts: a nun teaching a little girl, a mother kneeling beside a cot, three

429

schoolboys at the Communion table. The prettiest thing was a sort of wooden shed representing the inside of Christ's crib with the ox and the ass and the child Jesus lying sprawling on some straw—real straw. There were shelves filled from top to bottom with dozens of medals, all sorts of rosaries, scallop-shaped holy water stoups, and portraits of ecclesiastics of glorious memory, including Cardinal Affre and the Holy Father, both smiling and looking very splendid.

Arnoux was dozing at the counter with his head hanging forward. He had aged terribly and even had a ring of pink pimples round his temples, highlighted by the reflection of the sun from the gilt crosses.

Frédéric felt sad to see the wreck he'd become but out of loyalty to the Marshal, he stifled his qualms and was just about to go up to him when Madame Arnoux appeared at the back of the shop. He beat a hasty retreat.

'I wasn't able to contact him,' he said when he got home.

In spite of his promises to write off at once to his solicitor in Le Havre, Rosanette went off the deep end: she'd never seen such a weak, spineless creature; other people were living like lords while she had to put up with every sort of hardship.

Frédéric was thinking of poor Madame Arnoux and picturing the appalling drabness of *her* home. He'd sat down at his secretaire and Rosanette was continuing to nag at him in her shrill voice.

'Oh, for God's sake shut up!'

'Perhaps you feel like taking their side, do you?'

'All right then, yes, I do!' he exclaimed. 'Why do you have your knife in them all the time?'

'And why don't you want them to fork out? You're afraid of hurting that ex-mistress of yours, be honest!'

He'd have liked to bash her over the head with the clock; words failed him; he didn't answer. Pacing up and down the room, Rosanette went on:

'I'm going to put the police on to your friend Arnoux. Oh, I don't need any help from you!' and pursing her lips: 'I'll seek advice elsewhere!'

Three days later, Delphine burst into the room.

'Oh madam, there's a man with a glue-pot, I'm scared!'

Rosanette went through into the kitchen and saw a villainous-looking individual with a pock-marked face, a withered arm, more than half tipsy and mumbling incoherently.

It was Maître Gautherot's bill-sticker. The objection to the distraint had been overruled and the sale would be going ahead as arranged.

For the effort involved in climbing the stairs, he first of all demanded a 'wee drop' and then, as an additional favour, made a touching appeal for some theatre tickets, being under the impression that 'Madame was an actress'. He then spent several minutes blinking mysteriously and eventually came out with the offer, for a couple of francs, to tear off the corner of the notice he'd already stuck on the door downstairs which, in an exceptionally strict application of the law, specifically mentioned Rosanette by name; the full extent of Vatnaz's animosity was obvious.

She had in the past been a soft-hearted creature, and actually written to Béranger for advice over an unhappy love affair. But the rough-and-tumble of life had made her bitter; she had in turn been a piano teacher, run a cheap restaurant, contributed to fashion magazines, sublet flats, consorted with women of easy virtue as a dealer in lace, in which capacity her contacts had made it possible for her to oblige a large number of people, including Arnoux. She had also previously worked in a firm where her job was to pay the girls employed there. For each of these work-girls, there were two pay-books, one of which she always held. To oblige one of the girls, called Hortense Baslin, Dussardier had been looking after her account and one day he was at the cash-desk when Mademoiselle Vatnaz presented that girl's pay-book for 1,682 francs, which the cashier handed out. But the day before, Dussardier had noted down only 1,082 francs in Baslin's book. He invented a pretext to ask for it back and then, to cover up the whole matter of the theft, told her he'd lost it. The girl in all innocence repeated his lie to Madamoiselle Vatnaz; anxious to find out exactly how things stood, she asked the young clerk about it, as casually as she could. He merely replied: 'I've burnt it'; and that was an end to the matter. She left the firm shortly after, not convinced that the pay-book had been destroyed and believing that Dussardier still had it.

Hearing that he'd been wounded, she had raced round to his room intending to get it back but, failing to discover anything in spite of the most thorough search, she'd developed a great respect for this young man who was so upright, so gentle, so heroic and so strong—a respect which soon turned to love. At her age, a windfall like this was unhoped for and she flung herself on him like a man-eating tigress, abandoning literature, socialism, 'comforting doctrines and generous Utopias', the lectures she was giving on the *Desubordination of Women*, everything, even including Delmar; and finally, she proposed to Dussardier that they should get married.

Although they'd become lovers, he wasn't in love with her in the least. Moreover, he'd not forgotten her theft. And anyway, she was too rich. He turned down her proposal. She began to cry and confessed she had a dream: they'd open a ready-made dress shop together; she had just enough capital and by next week it would be four thousand francs more. She told him about her lawsuit against the Marshal.

Dussardier was distressed because of his friend. He remembered the cigar-case he'd been offered at the police station, the evenings he'd spent in the quai Napoléon, so many pleasant chats, the loan of so many books, Frédéric's hundreds of little acts of kindness. He begged Vatnaz to withdraw her suit.

She laughed at him for being so soft-hearted and showed an inexplicable depth of hatred for Rosanette; in fact her only reason for wanting lots of money was to have the pleasure, one day, of running her over in her carriage.

Dussardier was appalled at such sheer fiendishness; he ascertained the exact date of the sale and left. The very next morning, he called on Frédéric. He looked embarrassed:

'I've come to apologize to you!'

'What for?'

'You must think I've got no sense of gratitude, as she's my . . .' He had difficulty in finding words. 'Oh, I shan't be seeing her again, I'm not going to stand by and see that sort of thing happen.' And realizing that Frédéric was looking at him completely at a loss:

'It's true that in three days' time they're going to sell up your mistress's furniture, isn't it?'

'How do you know that?'

'Vatnaz told me herself! But I'm afraid of offending you . . .'

'How could I be offended by a friend like you?'

'Oh yes, that's true, you're so kind-hearted!'

Gingerly he held out a small leather wallet; it held his entire savings: four thousand francs.

'What's that? Oh no, I couldn't possibly . . .'

'I knew I'd hurt your feelings,' said Dussardier, almost breaking down.

Frédéric grasped his hand. The nice young man said violently:

'Do take it! Just to please me! I feel so hopeless! And isn't everything finished anyway? When the Revolution came I thought we'd be happy. Can you remember how wonderful it all was, how we all felt free to breathe? But now we've sunk even lower than before!'

He stared at the floor.

'Now they're killing our Republic just as they killed the other one, the Roman Republic! And poor Venice and Poland and Hungary!* It's obscene! First they cut down the Trees of Liberty, then they restricted the right to vote, shut down the clubs, reintroduced censorship and handed education over to the priests,* until such time as they bring back the Inquisition! Why not? There are some conservatives who'd like to see the Cossacks* back! When newspapers attack capital punishment, they're banned, Paris is stiff with bayonets, sixteen *départements* have declared a state of emergency, and once again they've turned down an amnesty!'*

He clutched his forehead with both hands and then flung out his arms, obviously in extreme distress.

'But if only people would make the effort! If people were sincere, we could get on all right together! But they're not! And you can see the workers are as bad as the middle classes! In Elbeuf recently, they refused to help put out a fire! There are some swine who call Barbès an aristocrat! They want to put up Nadaud* for the presidency to bring the People into disrepute—a bricklayer, I ask you! And there's no remedy, no way out, everybody's against us. I've never done anybody any harm and yet I have a sick feeling in my stomach! If it goes on like this, it'll drive me mad! I'd like to get killed! I'm telling you I don't need the money! You can let me have it back, for heaven's sake, it's a loan!'

In the end, having no other choice, Frédéric reluctantly accepted the four thousand francs. There was no further danger from Vatnaz.

Shortly afterwards, however, Rosanette lost her case against Arnoux and obstinately insisted on appealing.

Deslauriers did his utmost to get it into her head that Arnoux's promise was neither a gift nor a legal transfer; she refused even to listen and said the law was unfair; it was because she was a woman—men always stood up for each other! All the same, she eventually followed his advice.

He was making himself so much at home at Rosanette's that on a number of occasions he brought Sénécal round to dinner. Frédéric found this sort of unmannerly behaviour unpleasant; while he was advancing him money and even letting him use his own tailor, the lawyer was passing on his old frock-coats to the socialist, whose means of support were unknown.

However, Deslauriers would have liked to oblige Rosanette. One day she was showing him her twelve shares in the China Clay Company, the concern which had led to Arnoux's being fined thirty thousand francs. He said:

'But that's crooked! How wonderful!'

She had the right to sue him and force him to reimburse his creditors. She could prove, in the first place, that he had joint responsibility for all the company's debts, since he'd presented personal debts as consolidated liabilities; and further that he'd misappropriated company assets.

'All this makes him guilty of fraudulent bankruptcy under arricles 586 and 587 of the Trade Practices Code and you can rest assured we'll get him behind bars, my sweet!'

Rosanette flung her arms round his neck. Next day, he sent her round to his former employer, since he couldn't handle the case himself, because he had to be in Nogent; in any emergency, Sénécal could get in touch with him.

His alleged negotiations for the purchase of a solicitor's practice were a blind; he was spending his time at Monsieur Roque's, where he had begun not only by singing his friend's praises but by copying his ways and expressions as far as he could, thereby gaining Louise's confidence; he ingratiated himself with her father by abusing Ledru-Rollin.

Frédéric's failure to return to Nogent was caused by the fact that he was moving in high society; and bit by bit, Deslauriers revealed that he loved someone, that he had a child, and that he was keeping a woman of dubious character.

Louise was shattered and Madame Moreau, too, was highly indignant. She could see her son sinking into unspeakable depravity; it offended her deep respect for propriety and she took it almost as a personal disgrace. Then, suddenly, there was a different look on her face and when asked about her son, she would reply slyly:

'Oh, he's doing very well!'

She knew of his marriage with Madame Dambreuse.

They'd fixed the date and he was even beginning to break the news gently to Rosanette.

Around the middle of autumn, she won her case over the China Clay shares; Frédéric learned this from Sénécal when he met him outside her door, hot foot from the hearing.

Monsieur Arnoux had been found guilty of complicity in fraud and the ex-schoolmaster seemed so overjoyed that Frédéric cut him short and said he'd pass the message on to

Rosanette himself. He went in with an irritated look on his face:

'Well, you'll be happy now!'

She took no notice.

'Take a look here!'

She showed him her child lying in his cradle beside the fire. She'd found him looking so poorly at the nurse's that morning that she'd brought him back with her to Paris.

His arms and legs had gone terribly thin and his lips were covered in white spots, forming what looked like tiny clots of milk inside the mouth.

'What did the doctor say?'

'Oh, the doctor! He says that the journey had made . . . whatever he said it was . . . something ending in itis . . . worse. Anyway, it's thrush. Have you ever heard of that?'

Frédéric promptly replied: 'Of course I have!' and added that it was nothing.

But in the course of the evening, he was frightened to see how weak the child looked and by the way these bluish spots were spreading; they looked like mould, as if life was already deserting the poor little body and leaving only something for fungus to grow on. His hands were cold; he couldn't even drink and the wet nurse—a different one whom the porter had been able to find by chance from an agency—kept saying:

'He looks in a bad way to me, a very bad way!'

Rosanette stayed up all night.

In the morning, she went to fetch Frédéric.

'Come and see. He's stopped moving.'

And indeed he was dead. She took him up, holding him tight and calling him all sorts of pet names, covering him in kisses and tears, frantically spinning round and round, tearing out her hair and shrieking; then she flopped down on to the divan where she sat with her mouth open and floods of tears pouring from her glazed eyes. After that she lapsed into a complete state of apathy and everything in the room became still; the furniture had been knocked over; two or three towels were lying around. It struck six. The night-light went out.

All of a sudden Rosanette said tenderly.

'We'll not let him go, shall we?'

She wanted to have him embalmed. There were many reasons against this; the best one, to Frédéric's way of thinking, was that it just wasn't practical with such young children. A portrait would be better. She accepted the idea. He scribbled a note to Pellerin which Delphine hurried round to deliver.

The painter lost no time in coming, hoping that his promptness would remove memories of his earlier conduct. The first thing he said was:

'Oh, the poor little angel! What a tragedy!'

But gradually the artist in him took over and he pointed out that there was nothing to be done with such dark-rimmed eyes and livid face. It was a regular still-life and would require a lot of skill. He kept murmuring all the time:

'Dear me, it's not easy, it's not easy at all!'

'All we need is a good likeness,' objected Rosanette.

'Oh, don't worry about the likeness. Realism's a lot of rot! It's the *spirit* that one's painting. Just leave it to me. I'll try to work out how it should look.'

He put his left hand to his forehead, stuck his elbow out to the right and pondered.

'Ah, I've got it! A pastel! Using coloured half-tints, almost flat, you can get a wonderful effect of relief, just along the edges!'

He sent the maid off to fetch his box of pastels and then, with a chair beside him and his feet resting on another one, he set to work, with broad strokes, as calmly as if he'd been copying a plaster cast. He kept praising Correggio's little Saint Johns, Velasquez's pink Infanta, Reynold's milky flesh tints, the refinement and elegance of Lawrence, especially his treatment of the long-haired child on Lady Gower's lap.

'Is there anything more charming than those tiny tots! A mother and child is perhaps the epitome of everything sublime, as Raphael proved in his Madonnas.'

Unable to contain her feelings, Rosanette left the room. Pellerin immediately said:

'Well, have you heard about Arnoux?'

'No, what?'

'I suppose it was bound to come to that in the end?'

'But what is it?'

'It's quite possible . . . excuse me a sec.'

He stood up to lift the tiny corpse's head a trifle.

'You were saying . . . ?' said Frédéric.

The painter squinted, to check his proportions; then:

'I was saying it's quite possible that by now friend Arnoux is in clink!'

And smugly:

'Just take a look at that! Haven't I got it to a T?'

'Yes, wonderful. But what's this about Arnoux?'

Pellerin laid down his pastel.

'As far as I can gather, he's being sued by a man called Mignot, a close friend of Regimbart—what a mug that fellow is, isn't he? A prize idiot! Do you know, only the other day . . .'

'Look, we're not concerned with Regimbart!'

'Oh yes, that's right. Anyway, yesterday Arnoux had to find twelve thousand francs or else he's a goner!'

'Oh, surely it can't be that bad!' said Frédéric.

At that moment Rosanette came back into the room. She had red patches under her eyes as if she had been using bright red eye-shadow. She sat down beside the sketch and watched. Pellerin made a sign that he wasn't going to say any more, because of her. Frédéric ignored him.

'All the same, I can't believe . . .'

'I'm telling you that I saw him at seven o'clock yesterday evening in the rue Jacob. He'd even got his passport with him, just in case, and he was talking of catching the boat from Le Havre, with all his brood.'

'What! With his wife?'

'Of course! He's too much of a family man to go off and live by himself.'

'And you're absolutely sure?'

438

'Of course I am! How on earth could he lay hands on twelve thousand francs?'

Frédéric paced two or three times round the room, breathing heavily and biting his lips. Then he picked up his hat.

'Where are you going?' asked Rosanette.

He made no reply and disappeared.

CHAPTER V

Twelve thousand francs or he'd never see Madame Arnoux again! Up to now, he'd always been hoping against hope: after all, wasn't she his heart's blood, the very breath of life? For a few minutes he stood there on the pavement, agonized, wondering what he could do, though still relieved to have got away from that other woman.

Where could he find the money? From personal experience, he knew how tricky it was to lay hands on cash at a moment's notice, on whatever terms. Only one person could help him: Madame Dambreuse! She always kept a fair amount of cash in her bureau. He went round and came straight to the point.

'Can you let me have twelve thousand francs?'

'What for?'

It was confidential; someone else was involved. She asked who it was. He was adamant; so was she. In the end, she told him bluntly she wouldn't hand over a penny without knowing the reason. Frédéric went very red. One of his close friends had stolen some money and it had to be returned that very day.

'Who is it? Come on, out with it, what's his name?'

'Dussardier!'

He flung himself at her feet and begged her not to tell anyone.

'Who do you think I am?' said Madame Dambreuse. 'Anyone would think you were the culprit! Stop being so tragic. Here you are, here's your money and much good may it do him!'

He rushed round to Arnoux's shop; he wasn't there, but

439

he was still living in the rue Paradis, because he had two establishments.

At the rue Paradis, the porter swore that Arnoux hadn't been there since the day before and as for Madame, he daren't say. Frédéric dashed upstairs and put his ear to the keyhole. Eventually the door was opened. Madam had left with the master. The maid didn't know when they'd be back; she'd been paid up to date and she was leaving too.

Suddenly a door creaked.

'Is someone there?'

'Oh no sir! It's the wind.'

He went away. Such a sudden disappearance was rather mysterious, all the same.

Could Regimbart, a close friend of Mignot's, throw any light on the matter? Frédéric drove round to his house in the rue de l'Empereur in Montmartre.

His house had a tiny side-garden with an iron panel set in the gate. The white house-front was set off by a terrace with three steps leading up to it. From the pavement outside you could see into the two ground-floor rooms, a drawing-room with dresses draped over all the furniture, followed by the workroom for Madame Regimbart's dress-making assistants. These girls were all convinced that the master was engaged on most important work, with most important connections, a man of the utmost distinction. When he went along the passage, his hat with the turned-up brim, his long solemn face and his green frock-coat filled them with such awe that they'd stop working; and he never failed to drop them a word of encouragement or a flowery compliment; and later on in life these little working girls would be unhappy in their marriages because they still saw him as their ideal.

But none of them loved him as much as Madame Regimbart, an intelligent little person whose trade provided him with his livelihood.

As soon as Monsieur Moreau had given his name, she came bustling in; she'd learnt what he meant to Madame Dambreuse from the latter's servants. Her husband 'had just that minute come in'; and as he followed behind her,

Frédéric admired the spick and span house, with its large areas of lino everywhere. For a few minutes he waited in a sort of office where the Citizen would withdraw when he wanted to think.

His welcome was less uncouth than usual and he explained about Arnoux. The former ceramics manufacturer had got round the patriot Mignot, who held a hundred shares in *Le Siècle*, by persuading him that the management and editorial staff needed replacing, for the good of Democracy, and on the pretext of putting forward this view at the next shareholders' meeting, had asked him for fifty shares, which he'd pass on to reliable friends who would support his motion; Mignot wouldn't be held responsible and wouldn't put anyone's back up; then, having achieved his aim, he'd see to it that Mignot got a good job on the staff, five or six thousand a year at least. Mignot had handed over the shares, which Arnoux had promptly sold and set up shop with a partner to sell religious articles. Mignot had objected, Arnoux had hummed and hawed; finally the patriot had threatened to take legal action for false pretences if he didn't return the shares, or their equivalent, fifty thousand francs.

Frédéric was looking distraught.

'And that's not the lot,' Regimbart went on. 'Mignot, who's not a bad sort of chap, agreed to take just a quarter. So, more promises from the other man, sheer humbug, of course. To cut a long story short, Mignot demanded that he hand over twelve thousand francs, without prejudice to the remainder, within twenty-four hours.'

'But I've got them!' said Frédéric.

Slowly the Citizen turned and stared at him.

'You must be joking!'

'Excuse me, I've got them here in my pocket. I wanted to hand them over to him . . .'

'Well I'm blowed! You don't let the grass grow under your feet, do you? Anyway, you're too late. He's started proceedings and Arnoux's done a bunk!'

'By himself?'

'No, with his wife. Someone saw them at the station in Le Havre.'

Frédéric went deathly pale. Madame Regimbart thought he was going to faint, but, recovering, he managed to ask a few more questions about the episode. Regimbart felt sorry about it: after all, it wasn't doing the cause of Democracy much good. Arnoux had always been a dissolute and disorderly fellow.

'A regular scatter-brain! He burnt the candle at both ends! He could never resist a bit of skirt! But it's not him I feel sorry for, it's his poor wife!' The Citizen admired virtue in the fair sex and had a high opinion of Madame Arnoux. 'How she must have suffered!'

Touched by his sympathy, Frédéric shook him effusively by the hand, as if he'd just done him a great favour.

'Did you see everybody you wanted?' enquired Rosanette when Frédéric reappeared.

He hadn't had the courage, he replied; he'd been roaming the streets trying to forget.

At eight o'clock, they went into the dining-room but sat facing each other in silence, now and then heaving a deep sigh and pushing away their plates. Frédéric drank some spirits. He felt quite broken, a crushed and shattered man, conscious only of being immensely tired.

She went and fetched the portrait. The blobs of yellow, red, green and indigo-blue clashed violently, making the whole thing look hideous, even grotesque.

In any case, the dead baby had become unrecognizable. The violet tinge of his lips was emphasizing the whiteness of his skin; his nostrils were even more pinched and his eyes more sunken; his head was resting on a blue taffeta pillow surrounded by camellia petals, autumn roses and violets; this had been the chambermaid's idea and they had both reverently arranged him like that. On the mantel-shelf there were silver-gilt candlesticks standing on a coarse lace covering and interspersed with palm-sprigs; in the two vases at each end, aromatic Turkish pellets were burning; this all formed, together with the crib, a sort of makeshift altar. Frédéric was reminded of the time when he'd watched over Monsieur Dambreuse's body.

Every quarter of an hour or so, Rosanette would draw the curtains aside to gaze at her child. She could see him, a few months hence, becoming a toddler, then going to school and playing prisoners' base in the middle of the playground; and then, as a young man of twenty; so, in her intense grief, she became a mother many times over; and each imaginary son she invented was one she had lost . . .

Frédéric was sitting in the other armchair, not moving; he was thinking of Madame Arnoux.

No doubt she would be in a train looking out of the carriage window, watching the countryside slip past in the direction of Paris, or else on the deck of a steamer, as when he'd first met her; but this time, the ship was sailing away, on and on towards lands from which she'd never return. Then he saw her in the room of some inn, with her luggage spread round on the floor, tattered wallpaper, doors rattling in the wind. And what would become of her after that? A schoolmistress perhaps . . . a lady companion . . . a chambermaid? She'd be exposed to all the perils which beset anyone who is destitute. Being powerless to know her fate was torture. He should have stopped her from leaving or gone after her. He was her real husband, wasn't he? And as he reflected that he'd never see her again, that it was all over, that she was lost forever, he could feel his whole being disintegrating; the tears which had been building up inside him since the morning overflowed.

Rosanette noticed them.

'Ah, you're crying too! It's frightful, isn't it?'

'Yes, it's frightful!'

He hugged her tight and they sobbed together.

Madame Dambreuse was also sobbing as she lay flat on her face on her bed, holding her head in her hands.

During her visit that evening to try on Madame Dambreuse's first dress since going out of mourning, Olympe Regimbart had told her of Frédéric's call and even that he'd brought along twelve thousand francs, all ready to give to Monsieur Arnoux.

Then that money, her money, had been to prevent the departure of that other woman, in order to hang on to his mistress!

Her first reaction had been rage and a determination to send him packing like a lackey. She sobbed her heart out and then calmed down; it would be better to keep it to herself and say nothing.

Next day Frédéric brought back the twelve thousand francs.

She told him to keep them in case the need arose again and questioned him very closely about this man. What could have led him to commit such a breach of trust? Some woman, she supposed! Women can lead you to commit any crime!

Frédéric was disconcerted by this banter. He felt very remorseful about wrongfully accusing Dussardier but reassured because Madame Dambreuse could never learn the truth.

However, she persisted in this vein and enquired again about his 'little friend' the following day; then she asked about the other one, Deslauriers.

'Is he reliable as well as intelligent?'

Frédéric couldn't speak too highly of him.

'Ask him to call on me one morning, will you? I'd like to consult him on a business matter.'

She had discovered a bundle of old papers containing some of Arnoux's bills of exchange, formally declared as having been dishonoured, which Madame Arnoux had endorsed; they were the bills that had led to Frédéric's lunchtime call on Monsieur Dambreuse on an earlier occasion and though the banker had refrained from taking legal action to recover the debts, he'd got the commercial court to record a conviction, not only against Arnoux but also against his wife; she was unaware of this, since her husband hadn't thought fit to tell her.

She had a weapon! Madame Dambreuse was in no doubt as to that; but her own solicitor might perhaps advise her not to proceed; she'd prefer a stranger and she remembered that impudent young devil who'd offered his services.

In all innocence, Frédéric delivered her message. The lawyer lost no time in calling on her, delighted to establish contact with so grand a lady. She informed him that, as her niece was inheriting the estate, this was an additional reason for collecting these debts, which she'd then reimburse; she was anxious to heap coals of fire on the heads of the Martinon couple.

Deslauriers realized that there was something fishy behind all this and as he examined the bills, ideas started running through his head. Madame Arnoux's signature brought back vivid memories of her and of how she'd grossly insulted him. Since he'd got the chance to get even with her, why not take it?

He therefore advised Madame Dambreuse to put these irrecoverable debts up for auction; they'd be bought by an undercover man who'd proceed to take legal action; he undertook to provide the man.

Towards the end of November, as he was passing through Madame Arnoux's street, looking up towards her windows, Frédéric saw a notice fastened to the door announcing, in large print:

'Sale of a valuable collection of furniture, comprising kitchen utensils, personal and table linen, shifts, lace, skirts, underwear, French and Indian cashmere shawls, Érard piano, two oak Renaissance chests, Venetian mirrors, Chinese and Japanese porcelain.'

'It's their furniture!' Frédéric exclaimed to himself; the porter confirmed his suspicions but he didn't know at whose instigation the sale was being held; the auctioneer might be able to enlighten him.

At first the official receiver wouldn't give him the name of the debtor forcing the sale; Frédéric insisted. It was a certain Sénécal, a business broker; and Maître Berthelmot even obliged by lending him his copy of the *Petites Affiches*.*

When he arrived back at Rosanette's, he flung it down on the table.

'Read that!'

'What about it?' she asked, so unmoved that he felt revolted.

'Oh, that's right, pretend you're innocent!'

'I don't understand.'

'It's you who's getting Madame Arnoux sold up!'

She reread the notice.

'There's no mention of her name.'

'So what! It's her furniture, you know that as well as I do!'

'What's that got to do with me?' said Rosanette with a shrug.

'What's it got to do with you? You're getting your own back on her, that's what! You can't stop persecuting her! Didn't you even have the nerve to call on her, you, a worthless little tart, on the most charming, the most saintly, the best woman in the world. Why are you so dead set on wrecking her life?'

'I promise you you're mistaken!'

'Oh, come on! As if you haven't put Sénécal up to it!'

'That's stupid!'

He flew into a rage.

'You're lying, you bitch, you're lying! You're just jealous! You had her husband convicted! You've already had dealings with Sénécal and he loathes Arnoux as much as you do, so you've ganged up together! I saw how delighted he was when you won your case over the China Clay Company. You don't deny that, do you?'

'But I promise you . . .'

'Oh, I know all about your promises!'

Frédéric gave her a list of her lovers, by name, with circumstantial details. Rosanette shrank back, looking paler and paler.

'That surprises you, doesn't it? Because I turned a blind eye, you thought I really was blind. But now I've had a bellyful. Liars and cheats like you aren't worth dying for. When they become too foul, the only thing to do is to get right away from them, it'd be sinking too low to punish them!'

She was wringing her hands.

446

'Oh God, what's got into you to make you change like this?'

'Just you!'

'And all because of Madame Arnoux,' exclaimed Rosanette in tears.

He said frigidly:

'She's the only woman I've ever loved!'

This scathing remark cut off her tears.

'That just shows your good taste! Middle-aged, muddy complexion, waist like an elephant and eyes like saucers—empty saucers at that! Why not go after her, since you've got a weakness for that sort of thing!'

'Good, I was hoping you'd say that!'

Completely taken aback by such extraordinary behaviour, Rosanette did not move, even when the door closed behind him. Then she sprang after him and caught up with him in the hall. She flung her arms round his neck.

'You're mad, quite mad! It's ridiculous! I love you!' Now she was begging him: 'Oh God, for the sake of our baby!'

'Own up that you did it!' said Frédéric.

Once again she protested her innocence.

'You won't own up?'

'No!'

'All right then, it's goodbye for ever!'

'Please listen!'

Frédéric turned to face her.

'If you knew me better, you'd know I'd never go back on what I've said!'

'Oh no! You'll come back all right!'

'Not in a thousand years!'

He slammed the door violently behind him.

Rosanette wrote to Deslauriers telling him she needed his help immediately.

He turned up one evening five days later. When he heard that he'd left her:

'Is that all? What's all the fuss?'

At first she'd thought that he might be able to persuade him to come back to her but now it was obviously hopeless.

447

She'd learned from his porter of his imminent marriage to Madame Dambreuse.

Deslauriers read her a lecture and seemed remarkably relaxed and full of fun. As it was very late, he asked if he could spend the night on the sofa. Next morning, he went back to Nogent, warning her that he didn't know when they'd be meeting again as there might shortly be a big change in his life.

Two hours after his return, the town was in an uproar. It was said that Monsieur Frédéric was going to marry Madame Dambreuse. In the end, unable to bear the suspense, the Auger sisters drove round to Madame Moreau's; she proudly confirmed the news. Old Roque nearly had a fit; Louise shut herself up in her room. There was even a rumour that she'd gone mad.

Meanwhile Frédéric was unable to conceal his depressed state. Madame Dambreuse was more attentive than ever and took him out for a drive every afternoon, no doubt trying to cheer him up. On one such drive, since they were passing through the place de la Bourse, she suggested going into the Auction Rooms.

It was 1 December, the very day that Madame Arnoux's sale was due to be held. Remembering the date, he said he wasn't keen; the noise and the crowds of people made it really unbearable. She merely wanted to take a quick look. The brougham pulled up; he had to follow her.

In the courtyard there were wash-stands minus their basins, armchair frames, old baskets, bits of broken china, empty bottles, mattresses and men in smocks or grubby frock-coats, grey with dust, uncouth-looking, some carrying canvas bags on their shoulders, all talking in separate groups or else calling out to each other boisterously.

Frédéric pointed out how unpleasant it would be to go any further.

'What nonsense!'

They went upstairs.

In the first room on the right, gentlemen with catalogues were examining pictures; in another room, a collection of Chinese weapons was being sold; Madame Dambreuse decided to go downstairs again. She was looking at the numbers over the doors and led him to the far end of the passage towards a room crammed with people.

He immediately recognized the two whatnots from *L'Art industriel*, her work-table, all her furniture! It was spread out on the floor at the far end, stacked in a pile sloping right up to the ceiling, while on the other sides, carpets and curtains hung from the walls. Beneath them were tiers of seats occupied by dozing old men. On the left, standing behind a sort of counter, was the auctioneer in white necktie, flourishing a little gavel. Beside him a young man was busily writing and down below, a sturdy young fellow, a mixture of commercial traveller and ticket tout, was calling out the articles being offered; three porters were bringing them along to a table surrounded by second-hand and old clothes dealers, sitting in rows. Members of the public were moving around in the background.

When Frédéric came in, the petticoats, scarves, handkerchiefs and even the shifts were being passed round from hand to hand for scrutiny; every so often, they'd be tossed over to someone else and something white would suddenly flash through the air. Next her dresses were sold, then one of her hats with a broken feather dangling down, then her furs, then three pairs of bootees; seeing all these relics of her doled out in bits and pieces, where he could still vaguely sense the shape of parts of her body, seemed to him like a sort of atrocity, as if vultures were tearing pieces off her corpse. The atmosphere in the room reeked of other people's breath, making him feel sick. Madame Dambreuse offered him her smelling salts; she was finding it extremely entertaining, she said.

They produced the bedroom furniture.

Maître Berthelmot would mention a price, which was then loudly repeated by the crier; the three porters waited impassively till the hammer fell before removing the article into the next room. And so, one after the other, he saw the things disappear: the large blue floral carpet over whose camellias *Her* tiny feet used to brush as she walked towards him, the small tapestry wing-chair where he would always

449

sit facing *Her* whenever they were alone; the two fire-screens, whose ivory had been made the softer by the touch of *Her* hands; a velvet pincushion still bristling with pins. With each article, he felt as if a piece of his own heart was being taken out; the monotonous repetition of voices and gestures was making him tired, numbing his mind, dissolving him into a deathly state of torpor.

His ear caught the crackle of silk; Rosanette was touching him.

She had learned about the sale from Frédéric himself. Once she had partly recovered from her distress, it had occurred to her that she might turn it to advantage, so she'd come to take a look at the other woman, looking herself triumphant in skin-tight gloves, flounced skirt and white satin waistcoat, with pearl buttons.

He went white with anger. She looked at the woman beside him.

Madame Dambreuse had recognized her and for a minute they eyed each other from head to foot, painstakingly, searching for the weak spot, the blemish, one possibly envying the other's youth, the other upset by the impeccable stylishness and aristocratic simplicity of her rival.

Finally, Madame Dambreuse turned away with a smile of unutterable scorn.

The crier had opened a piano—*Her* piano! He stood in front of it and played a scale with his right hand, offered the instrument for twelve hundred francs before coming down to one thousand, eight hundred . . . seven hundred . . .

Madame Dambreuse was laughingly making fun of the 'old crock.'

The second-hand dealers were now looking at a little casket with medallions and silver clasps and corners, the very same one which he'd seen the first time he'd dined in the rue de Choiseul and which had later turned up at Rosanette's before finding its way back to Madame Arnoux's; during their chats, his eyes had often looked at it; it was one of his most treasured memories. His heart was

450

full to overflowing; then, all of a sudden, he heard Madame Dambreuse say:

'Look, I'm going to buy that.'

'But it's nothing remarkable,' he said.

On the contrary, she thought it was very pretty. The crier was pointing out its fine quality:

'A real jewel of the Renaissance! Just eight hundred francs, gentlemen! Almost entirely solid silver! With a little polishing it'll look a treat!'

And as she was pushing her way through the crowd:

'What a very odd idea!' said Frédéric.

'Why, are you annoyed?'

'No, but what can one do with that sort of knick-knack?'

'Who knows? Keep love-letters in it, maybe?'

She threw him a glance which made the reference quite obvious.

'All the more reason not to pry into dead people's secrets.'

'I didn't think she was as dead as all that.' She added loudly: 'Eight hundred and thirty francs!'

'You're doing something that's not right,' Frédéric muttered.

She was laughing.

'And you know, my dear, this is the first favour I've ever asked you.'

'And do *you* know you're not going to make a very agreeable husband?'

Someone had raised the bidding. She held up her hand:

'Nine hundred francs!'

'Nine hundred I'm bid!' repeated Maître Berthelmot.

'Nine hundred and ten . . . fifteen . . . twenty . . . thirty!' yelled the crier, jerking his head as he looked round the room.

'Prove to me that I'm marrying a reasonable woman.'

He urged her gently towards the door.

The auctioneer was continuing:

'Come along, gentlemen, nine hundred and thirty francs, have I a bid at nine thirty?'

Madame Dambreuse had reached the doorway. She stopped and called out loudly:

'One thousand francs!'

A thrill ran round the room.

'One thousand francs I'm bid, gentlemen! Any advance on one thousand? At one thousand? All done?'

He rapped the desk with his ivory gavel.

She passed up her card, they handed down the casket which she stuffed into her muff.

Frédéric felt an icy cold pierce his heart.

Madame Dambreuse had continued to hold on to his arm; she didn't dare to look him in the face until they reached her carriage waiting in the street.

She sprang into it like an escaping thief and when she had sat down, turned towards Frédéric, who was standing there with his hat in his hand.

'Aren't you coming?'

'No, Madame Dambreuse!'

He bowed stiffly, shut the carriage door, and made a sign to the coachman to drive on.

His first feeling was one of elation; he'd recovered his independence and he was proud to have avenged Madame Arnoux by making this enormous financial sacrifice for her sake. Then he was amazed at what he'd done and felt overcome with weariness.

Next morning, his manservant told him the news. A state of emergency had been decreed, the National Assembly dissolved and a number of the people's representatives held in Mazas.* These public affairs left him unmoved; he was too worried about his own concerns.

He wrote off to a number of tradesmen cancelling purchases relating to his wedding, which now seemed to him rather a shabby speculation, and he felt loathing for Madame Dambreuse who had almost made him behave so shabbily. Any thought of the Marshal had been completely driven from his mind, he'd even stopped worrying about Madame Arnoux. Left high and dry amid the wreckage of his dreams, sick at heart, grief-stricken and disconsolate, he felt hatred for the artificial society in which he'd suffered so much; he was yearning for the fresh green of grass, the peace and quiet of the country, a sleepy existence in the shelter of the roof under which he'd been born, amid people who were simple at heart. On Wednesday evening, he at last went out.

There were many people standing around in groups along the boulevard. From time to time a patrol would scatter them and after it had gone by, they'd gather again. People were speaking out freely, shouting jokes and insults against the soldiers, but not doing anything.

'Good God, isn't anyone going to fight?' Frédéric asked a worker.

The man in the smock replied:

'We're not so stupid as to get ourselves killed for the sake of the toffs! Let them look after themselves!'

And one of the 'toffs' scowled towards the worker and grunted:

'Socialist scum! Perhaps this time we could finish them off for good!'

Frédéric couldn't understand such stupidity and resentment. It increased his disgust for Paris and two days later he took the early train to Nogent.

Soon the houses disappeared and the countryside spread out. Alone in his carriage, with his feet resting on the seat, he sat running over in his mind the recent events and his whole past. He thought of Louise.

'Ah, now she really did love me! I was wrong not to seize my chance of happiness . . . So what? Let's forget about it!'

Then five minutes later:

'But who knows? . . . Why not? . . . later on . . . ?'

His eyes and his dreams were becoming lost in dim horizons.

'She was rather simple and countrified, almost a child of nature—but how kind-hearted she was!'

The nearer he came to Nogent, the closer he felt her coming towards him. As the train passed through the meadows of Sourdun, he could glimpse her as in the past, cutting rushes beside the pools under the poplars. They were arriving; he got out.

He leant over the wall of the bridge to look once more at the island and garden where they'd strolled one sunny day and, feeling dazed by the journey and the fresh air, in a sort of euphoria brought on by the weakness resulting from his recent shocks, he said to himself:

'Perhaps she's gone for a walk. Supposing I were to meet her!'

The bell of Saint-Laurent was tolling and in the square in front of the church there was a group of poor people gathered round a barouche—the only one in the district, which was used for weddings—when suddenly in the middle of a stream of gentlemen in white ties who poured out of the church door, a bridal couple emerged.

Frédéric thought he must be suffering from hallucinations but it was sober reality: Louise was standing there, shrouded in a flowing white veil from her red hair down to her heels; and there was Deslauriers!—resplendent in a Prefect's uniform, a blue coat embroidered in silver. What was it all about?

He hid round the corner of a house until the wedding procession had gone past. Then, battered and defeated, he sheepishly made his way back to the station and took the train to Paris.

His cabby assured him that the barricades had been set up from the Château d'Eau to the Gymnase Theatre and drove him round via the rue du Faubourg-Saint-Martin; at the corner of the rue de Provence, Frédéric got out and walked down to the boulevards.

It was five o'clock and drizzling. There was a crowd of middle-class bystanders on the pavement in front of the Opéra: the houses opposite were all closed up with nobody at the windows. Leaning over their horses' necks, dragoons with drawn swords were galloping along at full speed occupying the whole width of the boulevards; as they rode past, the plumes on their helmets and their large white cloaks billowing behind them stood out against the flare of

454

the gas lamps swirling in the mist. The crowd stood watching in terrified silence.

In between cavalry charges, squadrons of police came up to force people back into the side-streets.

But on the steps of Tortoni's, conspicuous in the distance by reason of his great height, one man stood stock-still like a caryatid, refusing to move: Dussardier.

A policeman marching in front, with his cocked hat pulled down over his eyes, threatened him with his sword.

At this the other man took a step forward and started shouting:

'Long live the Republic!'

With arms spread wide, he fell crosswise on to his back.

There was a scream of horror from the crowd. The policeman swung his eyes all around him; the crowd recoiled and Frédéric's jaw dropped: it was Sénécal.

CHAPTER VI

He travelled.

Chilly awakenings under canvas; dreary mail-packets; the dizzy kaleidoscope of landscapes and ruins; the bitter taste of friendships nipped in the bud: such was the pattern of his life.

He came home.

He went into society. He had more affairs but the ever-present memory of his first love made them insipid; in any case, desire had lost its edge, the very springs of feeling had dried up. His intellectual ambitions had also faded. Years passed, and he came to terms with his mental stagnation and the numbness in his heart.

One evening, towards the end of March 1867, as dusk was falling, he was sitting by himself in his study when a woman came in.

'Madame Arnoux!'

'Frédéric!'

She gripped his hands and led him gently towards the window, gazing at him and repeating:

'It's him! It's really him!'

In the half-light, under the little black lace veil hiding her face, he could distinguish only her eyes.

She placed a small garnet-red velvet wallet on the edge of the mantelshelf and sat down; they faced each other, smiling, unable to find words.

Finally, he started asking her lots of questions about herself and her husband.

They'd settled in the wilds of Brittany, so as to live cheaply and pay off their debts. Arnoux was a sick man; he looked old now. Her daughter was married, living in Bordeaux, her son on garrison duty in Mostaganem.* Then she looked up at him:

'But now I've seen you again! Oh, I'm so happy!'

He made a point of telling her that when he'd heard about the disaster which had overtaken them, he'd hurried round to see them.

'Yes, I know!'

'How do you know?'

She'd caught sight of him in the courtyard and hidden.

'Why did you do that?'

Hesitantly, in a voice that trembled, she said:

'I was afraid! . . . yes . . . afraid of you . . . and myself!'

This revelation filled him with a kind of shocked delight. His heart was pounding. She went on:

'Forgive me for not having come before.' And pointing to the little garnet-red wallet with its gold palm-leaf decoration: 'I've embroidered it specially for you and put in it the money that was meant to be guaranteed by the building land at Belleville.'

Frédéric thanked her for her present but told her she ought not to have taken all that trouble.

'No, that's not why I'm here! I was anxious to come and see you and then I shall go back to Brittany!'

She talked about the place where she was living.

It was a low single-storied building with a garden full of huge box trees, and a double avenue of chestnuts going right up to the top of the hill from where you could see the sea.

'I go and sit up there on a bench that I call Frédéric's bench!'

Then she began to look at the furniture, the knick-knacks, the pictures, greedily, so as to be able to carry them away in her mind's eye. The Marshal's portrait was half hidden behind a curtain but her attention was attracted by its whites and golds which stood out against the shadow.

'Isn't that someone I knew?'

'Impossible,' said Frédéric. 'It's an old Italian painting.'

She confessed that she'd like to go for a stroll round the streets, holding his arm.

They went out.

Now and again her pale face stood out in profile against the bright shop-fronts and then once more was wrapped in shadow; they went slowly on their way, amidst the carriages, the crowd and the noise, intent only on themselves, deaf to everything, like a couple walking side by side in the country, over a bed of dead leaves.

They reminisced over days gone by, the dinner parties at the time of *L'Art industriel*, Arnoux's little quirks, the way he used to tug at the points of his collar, smear wax on his moustache, and other more personal and significant matters. How delighted he'd been the first time he heard her sing! How lovely she was on her name-day in Saint-Cloud! He reminded her of the little garden in Auteuil, evenings at the theatre, a meeting on the boulevard, former servants, her black maid.

She was amazed at his memory. However, she said to him:

'At times, your words come back to me like a distant echo, the sound of a bell carried on the wind, and when I'm reading about love in a book, you seem to be there with me.'

'You made me feel everything they criticize as being far-fetched in that sort of book,' he said. 'I can understand men like Werther who aren't put off by Charlotte's sand-wich-making.'*

'Oh, you poor dear man!'

She sighed and then after a long pause:

457

'Never mind, we shall really and truly have loved each other!'

'But without ever being lovers!'

'Perhaps it's better that way,' she said.

'Oh no, it's not! We'd have been so happy!'

'Yes, I think so, with the sort of love you felt!'

And it must have been very strong to survive such a long separation.

Frédéric asked how she'd discovered he loved her.

'It was one evening when you kissed my wrist between my cuff and my glove.* I said to myself, he loves me, he loves me! But I didn't dare find out if that was true. Your discretion was so charming, so adorable, a kind of involuntary confession of your lasting devotion for me.'

He had no regrets. He felt repaid for all he'd suffered in the past.

When they'd gone back to his room, Madame Arnoux took off her hat. In the light of the lamp on the pier table, he saw her hair was white. It was like a punch over the heart.

To hide his disappointment, he sat down on the floor at her knees and, stroking her hands, began to caress her with words:

'For me, the world revolved around you, around your slightest movement. My heart used to be stirred like dust under your feet. You seemed to me like a moonlit summer's night, full of scents and soft shadows, whiteness and infinity; for me your name represented the joys of the flesh and of the spirit, I would keep on repeating it to myself, trying to kiss it with my lips as I spoke. I just couldn't imagine anything beyond that, only Madame Arnoux with her two children, exactly as you were, loving, responsible, dazzlingly beautiful and so kind! That picture blotted out all the others. Not that I even thought of them, for deep down inside me, I could always see your wonderful eyes and hear the music of your voice!'

She listened entranced to these adoring words for the woman she'd once been. Intoxicated by his own rhetoric, Frédéric was beginning to believe what he was saying. With her back to the lamp Madame Arnoux bent over him; he could feel her breath gently caressing his forehead and the vague contact of her whole body through her clothes. Their hands clasped; the tip of her bootee was sticking out a little from under her dress; he felt faint. He said:

'The sight of your foot is disturbing me.'

She blushed and sprang to her feet. Then, standing stock-still and in a strange tone, like a sleepwalker:

'At my age! Frédéric! No woman has ever been loved like I have! Why worry about not being young? I don't care! I despise all the women who come up here!'

'Oh, there aren't very many,' he said kindly.

Her face lit up. She asked him if he'd be getting married.

He swore he never would.

'Really? Why not?'

'Because of you!' said Frédéric taking her into his arms and holding her tightly.

She stayed there, leaning backwards, looking up at him with her lips parted, and then suddenly pushed him away with a look of despair. As he begged her to answer, she lowered her eyes and said:

'I wish I could have made you happy!'

Frédéric suspected Madame Arnoux of having come to give herself to him and once again felt a wild, frantic surge of lust more violent than ever. Yet he had an indefinable feeling of repugnance, a sort of terror of incest. And there was something else, too, a fear of revulsion later on. And how inconvenient it would be! So, out of caution and from a desire not to tarnish his ideal, he turned away and began to roll a cigarette.

She looked at him wonderingly.

'Oh, I don't know anyone like you, anyone at all, you're so kind and considerate!'

It struck eleven.

'So soon!' she said. 'At quarter past I must go.'

She sat down again but kept her eyes on the clock; he continued to smoke as he walked up and down. Neither could find anything to say. There comes a moment during leave-taking when the loved one is no longer with us.

Finally, when the hand had moved beyond twenty-five past, she slowly gathered the ribbons of her hat.

'Goodbye, Frédéric, my dear, dear Frédéric! I'll never see you again. This is the last thing I'll ever do, as a woman. But I'll always be with you in spirit! And may God bless you and keep you all the days of your life!'

She kissed him on the forehead like a mother.

But she seemed to be looking around for something and asked for a pair of scissors.

She loosened her comb and all her white hair came tumbling down.

Savagely she hacked off a long lock at the roots.

'Keep it! Goodbye!'

When she'd left, Frédéric opened his window. On the pavement, Madame Arnoux signalled to a passing cab. She got in. It drove off.

And that was that.

CHAPTER VII

Towards the beginning of that winter, Frédéric and Deslauriers, reconciled yet again, were sitting chatting by the fireside, fated by their natures to be perpetually meeting and feeling drawn towards each other.

One of them briefly explained how he'd fallen out with Madame Dambreuse who'd then found a second husband, an Englishman.

The other man, without saying how he'd come to marry Mademoiselle Roque, revealed that one fine day his wife had run off with a singer, making him the laughing stock of his prefecture. His attempt to live this down by fanatical devotion to his government duties had led to trouble and he'd been sacked. After that, he'd been put in charge of a colonization project in Algeria, been secretary to a Pasha, chief editor of a newspaper, an advertising agent, and ended up as legal adviser to an industrial firm.

As for Frédéric, after squandering two-thirds of his fortune, he'd settled down to a humdrum middle-class life.

They exchanged information about their friends.

Martinon was now a senator.

Hussonnet had got a senior job where he had control of all the theatres and the whole of the Press.

Cisy was steeped in religion, the father of eight children, and living in his ancestral home.

After going in for Fourierism, homeopathy, table-turning, Gothic art and humanitarian painting, Pellerin had become a photographer and he could be seen on posters all over Paris, wearing evening dress, with a huge head and a diminutive body.

'And what about your pal Sénécal?' asked Frédéric.

'I've no idea, he's disappeared. And how about your great passion, Madame Arnoux?'

'She must be in Rome with her son, who's a lieutenant in a light cavalry regiment.'

'And her husband?'

'He died last year.'

'Well, well,' said the lawyer.

Then, rapping his forehead:

'And talking of her, who did I meet in a shop the other day but our good old Marshal, holding the hand of a little boy she's adopted. She's the widow of someone called Oudry and she's got very fat, huge in fact. What a come-down, she used to be so slim.'

Deslauriers didn't hide the fact that he'd taken advantage of her despair to undertake a personal inspection of her slimness.

'As you'd given me permission to, of course.'

This confession was meant to make up for omitting to mention he'd chanced his arm with Madame Arnoux; as it hadn't come off, Frédéric wouldn't have been too put out.

Although rather annoyed at his disclosure, Frédéric pretended to laugh it off; thinking of the Marshal led him on to Vatnaz.

Deslauriers hadn't ever met her, any more than lots of others who used to go to Arnoux's; but he did remember Regimbart very well indeed.

'Is he still alive?'

'Just about. Every evening without fail, he totters along

461

bent double past all the cafés from the rue de Gramont to the rue Montmartre, just an empty ghost of a man.'

'And how about Compain?'

In a jubilant voice, Frédéric asked the former commissioner of the Provisional Government to explain the mystery of the calves' head.

'It's an English import, a parody of the ceremony which the Royalists used to celebrate on 30 January: Independents* organized an annual banquet when they ate calves' head and drank red wine out of calves' skulls to toast the extermination of the Stuarts. After Thermidor* some Terrorists set up a similar sort of club, which goes to show that stupidity is very catching.

'You seem to have calmed down a lot in your politics.'

'It's age,' replied the lawyer.

And they went back over their lives.

They'd both been failures, the one who'd dreamed of Love and the one who'd dreamed of Power. How had it come about?

'Perhaps it was lack of perseverance?' said Frédéric.

'For you maybe. For me, it was the other way round, I was too rigid, I didn't take into account a hundred and one smaller things that are more crucial than all the rest. I was too logical and you were too sentimental.'

Then they blamed it on their bad luck, the circumstances, the times in which they'd been born.

Frédéric went on:

'It's not what we expected to become, back in Sens, when you wanted to write a critical history of philosophy and I was going to write a grand medieval novel about Nogent on a subject I'd found in Froissart: "How Sir Brokars de Fenestrange and the Bishop of Troyes assailed Sir Eustache d'Ambrecicourt". Do you remember?'

And as they exhumed their youth, at every sentence they kept saying:

'Do you remember?'

They could see the school playground, the chapel, the parlour, the fencing room at the foot of the stairs, the faces of masters and pupils, a certain Angelmarre from Versailles,

462

who used to cut his trouser-straps out of old boots, Monsieur Mirbal and his red whiskers, the two teachers of geometrical and free-hand drawing, Varaud and Suriret, who were at daggers drawn, and the Pole, the fellow countryman of Copernicus, with his planetary system made out of cardboard, an itinerant astronomer whose lecture fee was a free meal in the dining-hall; and that dreadful booze-up, on an excursion, their first pipe, Speech Day, the thrill of the holidays . . .

It was in the course of the summer holidays in 1837 that they'd paid a visit to the Turkish woman.

Her real name was Zoraïde Turc and many people thought she was a Muslim, an actual Turk, thus adding to the poetic charm of her establishment, which was situated down at the water's edge, behind the ramparts; even in high summer, there was shade round the house, which could be recognized from its goldfish bowl standing on the window-sill, next to a pot of mignonettes. Young women in white bed-jackets with rouged cheeks and long ear-rings would tap on the window-pane as men went by and at night would stand in the doorway, gently humming in husky voices.

This den of vice projected an amazing aura throughout the whole district. People would refer to it indirectly as 'that place you know', 'a certain street', 'below the bridges'. Farmers' wives in the neighbourhood used to tremble for their husbands, middle-class ladies were terrified for their maids, because the Deputy Prefect's cook had been caught there; and, needless to say, it was the secret obsession of every adolescent.

So one Sunday, while everyone was at Vespers, Frédéric and Deslauriers, having previously got their hair curled, picked some flowers in Madame Moreau's garden, left by the back way over the fields, took a roundabout path through the vineyards, came back via the fishery and slipped down to the Turkish woman's house, still clasping their large bouquets.

Frédéric held his out like a sweetheart offering flowers to his bride-to-be. But the heat, fear of the unknown, a vague

463

feeling of guilt, and even the thrill of seeing, at one glance, so many women at his disposal, upset him so much that he went very pale and stood rooted to the spot, unable to speak. The women were all laughing, amused by his embarrassment; thinking they were making fun of him, he turned tail and fled; and since he was holding the money, Deslauriers was obliged to follow him.

They were seen leaving the house; the scandal this aroused still lingered on three years later.

They told each other the story at great length, each filling in the details left out by the other, and when they'd reached the end:

'Ah, that was our best time!' said Frédéric.

'Could be? Yes, that was our best time!' said Deslauriers.

1830 July	Republican-led uprising in Paris forces abdication of Charles X. With support of Thiers, Lafayette, and Laffitte, Louis-Philippe, Duc d'Orléans, proclaimed King of the French under a more liberal constitutional Charter. Thwarted republicans form anti-monarchical secret societies.
1831	Anti-clerical working-class riots in Paris and first of several uprisings of Lyons silk-workers put down.
1832	The Duchesse de Berry (Charles X's daughter-in-law) makes futile attempt to restore her son the Duc de Chambord, the Legitimist Pretender (Henri V). Anti-monarchical riots at funeral of a republican general.
1833	Secret republican Société des Amis du Peuple suppressed; Société des Droits de l'Homme formed.
1834	Failed uprising in Lyons; Paris uprising ruthlessly repressed by order of interior Minister Thiers; massacre of the rue Transnonain (p. 253).
1835	Fieschi's attempted assassination of the king. September Laws muzzle the Press (p. 62).
1836	Louis Napoleon (Napoleon I's nephew and Bonapartist pretender) makes abortive coup. *La Presse* and *Le Siècle* (popular democratic newspapers) founded (pp. 115, 173, 341).
1839	Major insurrection, organized by the extreme revolutionary Société des Saisons, captures the Paris Hôtel de Ville but is crushed. Ringleaders (left-wing republican Barbès, the terrorist Blanqui, Austen, Steuben) imprisoned on Mont-Saint-Michel. Little further organized republican activity but criticism in Press and in books continues. Socialist Louis Blanc publishes *L'Organisation du travail* asserting the right to work.

| 1840 | Louis Napoleon makes another failed coup. Socialist Proudhon publishes *Qu'est-ce que la propriété?* (*What is property?* His answer: Property is theft).
	Diplomatic defeat of France over Egyptian-Turkish conflict (pp. 62, 285). Guizot (conservative centre-right) replaces Thiers as virtual head of government until 1848.
1841	*La Revue indépendante* founded by humanitarian socialist Pierre Leroux and republican feminist George Sand.
1842	Cabet publishes *Voyage en Icarie* (p. 148).
1845	Ledru-Rollin (radical parliamentary leader) becomes leading republican on death of Godefroi Cavaignac (brother of General Cavaignac, see under 1848).
1846	Attempted assassination of king by Lecomte. The Spanish marriages (p. 151) and the Pritchard affair (p. 31). Harvest failure in large areas of France (p. 150).
1847	The Duc d'Aumale (the king's fourth son) accepts Algerian surrender. Lamartine publishes *Les Girondins* (p. 252). Financial scandals involving government officials. As political meetings are banned, campaign of banquets seeking electoral reform is launched.
1848 February and March	Demonstrators in favour of final banned banquet fired on. Fighting breaks out; the king abdicates; Second Republic proclaimed, with Provisional Government including Ledru-Rollin, Lamartine, Flocon (editor of extreme left-wing republican newspaper *La Réforme*). National Workshops to counter unemployment set up but soon unable to cope with increasing number of workless. Louis Blanc made chairman of government commission on labour relations sitting in the Luxembourg Palace. Clubs of all factions (including a *Club des Femmes*, see pp. 324, 337) proliferate.
April and May	Constituent Assembly to draw up new constitution elected by universal male suffrage and contains mainly moderates. Provisional Government replaced by an Executive Commission.

	15 May: Assembly invaded by left-wing revolutionary mob; its attempt to dissolve it and set up a new government fails.
June	Assembly votes to close National Workshops; ensuing working-class insurrection crushed with heavy bloodshed by War Minister General Cavaignac and General Lamoricière (both fresh from North Africa); Cavaignac given dictatorial powers. Louis Blanc takes refuge in England; Barbès, Blanqui, and Albert (former working-class representatives in the Provisional Government) arrested. Many clubs and newspapers closed.
December	Louis Napoleon, with support of Thiers and reactionary rue de Poitiers Committee (p. 395), is elected President of the Second Republic under the new constitution.
1849 May	Constituent Assembly dissolves itself (p. 387, Rateau motion); a new, strongly right-wing Legislative Assembly elected.
June	French expeditionary force despatched to help crush the newly established Roman Republic; republican demonstration against this action put down (see note to p. 395 on Conservatorium also note to p. 433 on Roman Republic).
1850	Reaction continues (p. 433).
1851 2 December	Louis Napoleon seizes power in military coup with little opposition (pp. 452–5).

EXPLANATORY NOTES

3 *quai Saint-Bernard*: on the Left Bank, beside the Jardin des Plantes (the Paris Zoo).

Nogent-sur-Seine: small town about sixty miles south-east of Paris, in the Aube *département* (chief city Troyes).

13 *Conseil d'État*: see note to p. 109.

Madame Lafarge: just sentenced to life imprisonment for poisoning her husband.

Guizot's latest book: Guizot was an historian as well as a politician.

14 *Cygne de la Croix*: means Swan of the Cross; sounds like *Signe de la Croix* (Sign of the Cross).

trafficker in men: who supplies, at a price, substitutes for those unlucky in the draw for military service liability.

15 *Third Form*: three years before university entrance exam.

Jouffroy . . . Scottish school: Jouffroy (1796–1842) popularized in France the 'common-sense' *Scottish school* of Reid (1710–96) and Stewart (1753–1828), which influenced *Laromiguière* (1756–1837) and *Cousin* (1792–1867), both contemporary eclectic philosophers, i.e. wishing to combine what they thought best in a variety of philosophies. The seventeenth-century idealist and religious thinker *Malebranche* is the odd man out.

Froissart . . . Brantôme: *Froissart*, fourteenth-century chronicler; *Commynes*, late fifteenth-century memorialist; *L'Étoile*, chronicler of the sixteenth-century wars of religion; *Brantôme* (1540–1614), a memorialist, best known for his scandalous (and perceptive) *Vie des dames galantes*.

17 *Werther . . . Lélia*: *Werther* (1774), Goethe's immensely popular story of a young man's desperate love for an older married woman, ending in suicide; *René* (1801) by Chateaubriand, also featuring a tragic lover; *Lara*, a verse tale by Byron about a mysterious—and tragic—chieftain; *Lélia* (1833), the passionate heroine of a novel by George Sand (1804–76); *Franck*, the romantic lover in Musset's play *La*

468

Coupe et les lèvres (*Twixt Cup and Lip*, 1833). Sand, an ardent feminist and later humanitarian socialist, had a tempestuous affair with Musset.

20 *Rastignac*: Balzac's quintessential careerist features in many of his *Comédie humaine* novels; one of his best coups was a rich marriage with a former mistress's daughter (cf. Martinon's coup with Madame Dambreuse's niece).

Catholic and Satanic poets: *Catholic*, e.g. Chateaubriand's seminal *Génie du Christianisme* (1801), Victor Hugo's early poetry, a good number of Lamartine's maudlin and pious love poems mourning the death through tuberculosis of his beloved Elvire. *Satanic*, e.g. the early poetry of Théophile Gautier, the morbid writings of the so-called 'little Romantics', strongly influenced by Byron and preoccupied with crime and evil, anything to outrage the staid and philistine middle classes. Some of Flaubert's early writings were frenetic in this way.

Mirabeau: a great Revolutionary politician who, like others of Deslauriers's heroes (e.g. Camille Desmoulins, p. 123), finished on the guillotine. Is there a hint of death wish in some characters?

rue Coq-Héron: terminus, on the Right Bank, of the Nogent–Paris stage-coach.

21 *rue d'Anjou*: smart address on the Right Bank, near the Madeleine Church, and handy for chic funerals. Frédéric's final Paris address won't be far away and his first address (p. 23), near the Tuileries, is also quite smart. The young man always has Right Bank pretensions, though in the beginning he cannot afford to eat there (p. 26).

27 *Saint Just*: a keen member of the high-principled and bloodthirsty Committee of Public Safety during the 1793 Terror.

28 *the Odéon*: large state theatre on the Left Bank, now the Théâtre de France.

Revue des deux mondes: founded in 1829, a major cultural periodical. Hugo and Sand were contributors.

Collège de France: a prestigious quasi-independent institution of higher education dating from the sixteenth century.

29 *quai Napoléon*: now the quai aux Fleurs on the central Île-de-la-Cité. Frédéric is discriminating.

the Panthéon: a neo-classical building near the Sorbonne, a mausoleum for 'great Frenchmen'.

30 *National Guard*: formed originally in 1789 to maintain public

order, the middle-class National Guard militia (they had to provide their own uniforms, weapons, and equipment) was being won over to the need for electoral reform.

Humann's scheme: this Minister of Finance instituted in 1841 a census with a view to reorganizing French taxation; fear of higher taxes led to riots.

Louis XI . . . Benjamin Constant: a humorous time-gap: *Louis XI*, late fifteenth-century, *Constant* (1767–1830), an active liberal writer and politician under the Restoration, 1815–30.

Frédérick Lemaître in Robert Macaire: this full-blown Romantic actor took the part of the bandit Robert Macaire in the comic sequel of that title to the earlier melodrama *L'Auberge des Adrets* (1823).

English:Hussonnet addresses the poor fellow in English!

Artaxerxes: this Persian king (464–25 BC) welcomed and honoured the exiled Athenian general and statesman Themistocles, an earlier enemy of his country.

Customs Union: protectionism against foreign competition is a most important—and still highly topical—issue in the novel; see, for example, pp. 150, 172, 207, 326, 401. Hussonnet's typically scatter-brained remark may be alluding to the customs union (*Zollverein*, p. 285) of certain German states set up under Prussian leadership in 1833.

31 *secret societies*: see Historical Sketch for 1830, 1833, 1839; their uprisings had been brutally repressed and their continued existence must have been in doubt. After the Revolution of Feb. 1848, they were revived in the form of public political clubs (see note to p. 323).

Zachariae and Rudorff: eminent German jurists. Flaubert had studied law, with limited success and enthusiasm.

Pritchard: a missionary and British consul in the French protectorate of Tahiti had been expelled on the grounds of anti-French activity; in the interests of the *entente cordiale* with Great Britain, Guizot had incurred unpopularity (and the scornful nickname Lord Guizot) by agreeing to pay compensation for the expulsion.

32 *Marseillaise*: under a monarchy, this was a provocatively revolutionary song.

470

Béranger's house . . . Voltaire's: Béranger was a composer of epicurean and political popular songs and was against the monarchy; the banker *Laffitte*, liberally inclined, had helped finance the 1830 Revolution against Charles X; *Chateaubriand*, the Romantic author of *René* and *Atala*, also had liberal leanings; a visit to *Voltaire*, as proposed by the relentlessly humorous Hussonnet, would have been difficult, as he'd been dead some sixty years.

September troubles: riots roused by Humann's proposals.

39 *louis*: a gold coin worth twenty francs; Arnoux pays well.

Cherubini's portrait . . . Beaux-Arts: this famous composer's portrait was by Ingres; the historical painter Delaroche decorated the *lecture theatre*.

Institut: the *Institut* groups the five official *Académies* (Fine Arts, Sciences, etc.), including the prestigious French Academy.

40 *Boucher*: eighteenth-century court painter, fond of painting plump pink females.

Faubourg-Poissonnière: cheap district, on the way to the traditional artists' quarter of Montmartre.

41 *Callot*: flourished under Louis XIII (1610–43); his engravings of the horrors of war influenced Goya.

Phidias and Winckelmann: the Greek sculpted a good deal of the Parthenon decoration; the eighteenth-century German archaeologist and aesthetician was a lover of classical art. Pellerin's clutter of morbid, exotic Romantic paraphernalia may add power to his words but they give the lie to his 'classicism'. Surrounded by inconsistent characters, Pellerin outdoes the lot.

42 *Le National*: a liberal political newspaper founded by Thiers in 1830; later was to nominate some members of the Provisional Government after the February Revolution; Marrast was its editor (see also note to p. 64).

47 *rue de Choiseul*: a good address near the *grands boulevards*; his later ones aren't so good, except for a brief sojourn in the aristocratic Faubourg-Saint-Germain (p. 426).

51 *daspachio . . . Lipfraoli*: the provincial Frédéric is, as so often, confused; his soup must be the Spanish gazpacho, his 'extraordinary wine' is doubtless a French approximation to the German Liebfraumilch.

471

56 *Stabat Mater*: first performed in Jan. 1842; Flaubert often fixes dates in this indirect way.

60 *Dreux . . . Pradier*: *Dreux*, a fashionable horse painter—Frédéric would have done better to steer clear of horses, as we shall see later; Flaubert knew *Pradier*, who sculpted graceful, fleshy nudes.

62 *new Bastilles*: in the wake of the anti-British uproar occasioned by France's backing the wrong side in the Egyptian-Turkish conflict (see Historical Sketch for 1840), Thiers had revived an earlier plan of providing Paris with a defensive ring of fortifications which suspicious republicans saw as being a sinister plot to build 'new Bastilles' to suppress the working man.

the September Laws; *Pritchard*: *Lord Guizot*: for September Laws, see Historical Sketch for 1835; for Pritchard and Lord Guizot, see note to p. 31 under Pritchard.

63 *Regency*: the Regency of Louis XV's minority (1715–23) was a period of considerable licence at the court.

64 *Rhine frontier*: Regimbart is a dyed-in-the-wool *patriote*, an extreme Revolutionary; he wants to extend France's eastern frontier up to the Rhine, as during the Revolution. The term *patriote* recurs frequently.

École polytechnique: a state institution run on military lines, including uniforms, to produce civil and military engineers, (cf. Polytechnician on p. 316).

Marrast: a journalist (Flaubert disliked journalists) who had been editor of *La Tribune* (mouthpiece of the suppressed Society of the Rights of Man), was now editor of *Le National*, and became President of the Provisional Government in 1848. Flaubert greatly admired Voltaire.

65 *de Staël . . . Poland*: Madame de Staël (1766–1817) was a most distinguished writer and critic who fostered Romanticism in France by introducing the French to German literature; but for republican zealots, Poland's struggle for independence in 1830 and later would make an ode to Poland, of whatever literary quality, a far more important work.

66 *'Toujours lui . . . de l'Arnoux'*: a parody of Hugo's poem 'Lui' from his exotic collection *Les Orientales* (1829).

72 *Trois-Frères-Provençaux*: a very well-known and expensive restaurant in the Palais-Royal.

79 *Marquise d'Amäégui*: this so-called Andalusian noble lady (she comes in a poem entitled *L'Andalouse* written by Alfred de Musset) has, oddly enough, a Basque name and comes, in fact, from Barcelona!

81 *Dumersan*: a prolific playwright of the period; the ugly actor Odry (p. 91) took comic roles in his plays; Flaubert's detailed authenticity is remarkable.

95 *Garde-Meuble*: a warehouse for state furniture on the corner of the rue de Rivoli and the rue Royale, close to the place de la Concorde.

96 *Orsay Debating Society*: an association of lawyers meeting in the Paris law-courts to practise their skills.

105 *Atala . . . d'Automne*: *Atala* (1801), a Chateaubriand tear-jerker: unhappy love ends in suicide in virgin forests of exotic Louisiana; *Cinq-Mars* (1826), an historical novel of conspiracy ending in disaster in the reign of Louis XIII; *Les Feuilles d'automne* (1831), poetry of melancholy nostalgia by Victor Hugo (who hadn't yet reached the great age of thirty!).

Letourneur's: this was an eighteenth-century translation.

109 *Conseil d'État*: Frédéric is expecting to be welcomed with open arms into this prestigious supreme French judicial body which advises on and interprets government laws and decrees and acts as a sort of ombudsman between the State and private citizens; ludicrous arrogance.

112 *Charenton*: Frédéric wakes up in the Paris suburb best known for its mental hospital . . .

115 *Le Siècle*: a liberal constitutional paper which became republican in 1848.

Le Charivari: founded 1832, this satirical periodical had amongst its contributors the author and caricaturist Henri Monnier, who created the archetypical self-satisfied, pompous, and banal petty bourgeois Joseph Prudhomme (p. 377), and the caricaturist Cham (p. 388).

119 *laddikins*: Arnoux is from Marseilles, a city traditionally supposed, by Frenchmen from further north, to contain a high proportion of imaginative braggarts. Flaubert is making him use his patois baby-talk.

120 *Prescription*: positive prescription is a claim based on long use or use for a prescribed period.

121 *the Gauls . . . the Arabs*: the historian Thierry (1795–1856) had the theory that the Franks, as late arrivals in France, were exploiting the original Celtic Gauls. The Turkish Empire at that time contained many Arab peoples (e.g. Syria, which then included Lebanon and Palestine).

Poland: another reminder of Poland's subjugation by her neighbours.

try again: failure in this examination excluded any hope of an academic career; his stubborn adherence to abstract principles changes his whole life.

Véfour's: next door to the *Trois-Frères-Provençaux*; Frédéric is living in grand style.

122 *become Deputies*: the property qualification for a parliamentary candidate was higher than that for an elector, itself high enough to restrict the electorate to about 250,000. Adult male suffrage brought in after the 1848 Revolution raised it to 9 million.

Mondor: an extremely rich and unsavoury seventeenth-century Frenchman, appropriately named: *mont d'or* means a mountain of gold.

124 *That terrible Assembly . . . forceful stride*: Barthélemy (1796–1867) published these lines praising the 1793 Terror under the *Convention* (see note to p. 324) in 1832 in *Nemesis*, his satirical periodical in verse.

131 *A Postilion of Longjumeau*: a character from a comic opera by A. Adam (1803–56), composer of the ballet *Giselle*.

132 *the Porcherons*: in eighteenth-century Paris (nostalgic Frédéric!) this was a locality midway between the centre and Montmartre devoted to pleasure—drinking, dancing and the rest—where the rich could watch the poor, e.g. licentious soldiery, having a good time.

Ambigu . . . le Pêcheur: the *Ambigu* was one of several 'little theatres', usually on the boulevards, offering light entertainment, such as vaudevilles, ballet, light comedy, etc; the Délassements (pp. 96, 254) and the Gymnase (p. 153) were two others. *Gaspardo* was a melodrama by a certain Bouchardy.

136 *Grassot*: a comic actor of the period.

474

Celuta: the heroine of *Les Natchez*, Chateaubriand's sequel to *Atala*, with a cast of Red Indians in exotic Louisiana.

140 *rue Rumford*: a brand-new street in the smart 8ᵉ *arrondissement*.

141 *Father Coeur*: a fashionable preacher; he later made Affre's (p. 192) funeral oration.

148 *patriots all*: i.e. extremely militant revolutionaries.

Social Contract: Jean-Jacques Rousseau (1712–78) believed that man is born free and naturally good but is corrupted by society. In *Du contrat social* (1762) he said that man should, willingly, surrender this freedom to the sovereign will of the People, in a social contract.

Revue indépendante: see Historical Sketch for 1841.

Mably . . . Louis Blanc: *Mably*, an eighteenth-century thinker and historian influenced by Rousseau; *Morelly*, an early utopian communist thinker, also of the eighteenth century; François Marie Charles *Fourier* (1772–1837) had a strong belief in the goodness of the instincts (particularly the sexual urge) and proposed the setting up of communities (*phalanstères*) in which men and women, bound together in love and harmony, would all share the fruits of their joyful labour; the Comte de *Saint-Simon* (1760–1825) thought that equality and prosperity would result from giving chief power in the State to industrialists and scientists; his followers included at one time George Sand (also influenced by Fourier) and Pierre Leroux (1797–1871; see pp. 194, 396), both writing in *Le Globe*; Auguste *Comte* (1798–1857), a former secretary to Saint-Simon, a graduate of the École polytechnique (see note to p. 64) and a mathematician, was the founder of a positivist philosophy of sociology in which metaphysical speculation was barred and the study of society was to be reduced to scientific laws based on careful observation and logical deduction; later religio-mystical elements crept in: Étienne *Cabet* (1788–1856), a non-violent communist, published his utopian novel *Icarie* in 1842; all goods are jointly held, everyone is equal and good; *Louis Blanc* (1811–82), see p. 194 and note.

150 *the Buzençais murders*: in riots provoked by harvest failure and food shortage, landlords had been killed and their murderers executed in the town of Buzençais in the Indre *département*.

475

Malthus: Thomas Robert Malthus (1766–1834); in his *Essay on the Principle of Population* (1798) he advocated birth control.

151 *the Spanish marriages*: in October 1846 the Duc de Montpensier, a son of Louis-Philippe, married a sister of the Queen of Spain who at the same ceremony married an Italian Bourbon prince. British disquiet at this strengthening of Bourbon family links—Louis-Philippe was himself married to a Sicilian Bourbon princess—and particularly at the possible unification of the French and Spanish crowns, brought *entente cordiale* to an end.

the Rochefort frauds: dishonest administration at the naval base of Rochefort which the government was suspected of trying to cover up.

the new chapter at Saint-Denis: the chapter of the Basilica of Saint-Denis, a northern suburb of Paris, which had charge of the royal tombs there, was to be reorganized.

La Mode: a Legitimist paper; the shape of things to come for Cisy.

152 *cut a piece . . . on a Gros*: this had happened to battle paintings by these artists—arguably the most suitable for such treatment?

153 *Barbès*: see Historical Sketch for 1839 and June 1848.

Poland . . . Lafayette: the Marquis de Lafayette had fought in the American War of Independence, helped draw up the Rights of Man during the French Revolution, and played an important part in establishing the July Monarchy. Hussonnet is suggesting that this liberal politician is mistaken in considering Poland anything more than a geographical expression; one of the journalist's more absurd paradoxes.

Poniatowski: a Polish prince (1763–1813), one of Napoleon's Marshals, drowned while covering the Imperial Army's retreat from Moscow. The Poles in Saint-Marceau would be refugees from foreign repression.

Saint Bartholemew's Day: this massacre on 24 Aug. 1572 was unlikely to have been considered any sort of a joke by the many Huguenots murdered then and certainly not by the Pope who struck a medal to commemorate the event. Flaubert found many points of similarity between religious dogmatism and the intolerant political dogmatism here voiced by Sénécal.

476

the League: the Roman Catholic Holy League formed four years after the Massacre, in 1576.

Lola Montez: the expensive actress/mistress of King Ludwig I of Bavaria (1786–1868).

154 *new physiologies*: a physiology was a collection of studies depicting some aspect of life, a profession, etc., with anecdotes, sketches of people, little scenes. Balzac wrote some; but the vogue had passed; Cisy, as one might expect, is out of date.

161 *Creil*: a small town about thirty miles north of Paris.

168 *Les Treize*: a fictional élite society of adventurers and aristocrats invented by Balzac.

170 *General Foy*: one of Napoleon's generals and, after 1815, a liberal politician; Dambreuse is hedging his bets two or even three ways.

172 *Hôtel Lambert*: in this seventeenth-century aristocratic house charity fêtes were given in support of Polish independence, a cause unlikely to have a wide appeal to Dambreuse's upper-class guests.

173 *Genoude . . . Le Siècle*: Genoude was editor of the Legitimist *Gazette de France*; he hoped that a broader suffrage would help the Pretender, Henri V. *Le Siècle*, see note to p. 115.

La Reine Margot: the heroine of this Romantic drama by Dumas senior, which showed various dirty deeds of the royal Valois family and their associates, was Marguerite de Valois, la Reine Margot (1553–1615), wife of Henry IV.

174 *Duc de Nemours*: the second son of Louis-Philippe who, like his brother the Duc d'Aumale, had fought in Algeria.

Monsieur Thiers . . . witty remark: Adolphe Thiers (1797–1877), originally a journalist, founder of *Le National* (see note to p. 42), played, with Lafayette, a decisive role in establishing the July Monarchy; he was Minister of the Interior during the brutal repression of the 1834 Paris uprising and the rue Transnonain massacre (p. 253); he lost favour in 1840, moved to the centre left, supported the 1848 Revolution, was elected to the Constituent Assembly; then moving to the right, he became leader of the so-called 'party of order' and a prominent member of the rue de Poitiers group (see note to p. 395). He was still alive when the novel

477

was published and became first President of the Third Republic in 1871. The 'witticism' mentioned was perhaps his answer when asked whether any writers should be part of the deputation to the island of Saint Helena in 1840 to bring the Emperor's ashes back to Paris: 'Certainly not! I want to be sure it's a properly dignified occasion.'

incompatibility . . . assassination attempted in April '46: Thiers' speech maintained that holding government office was incompatible with being a parliamentary Deputy. See Historical Sketch for assassination attempt.

181 *Lesurques*: executed in 1794 for a crime he had not committed.

185 *Henri IV*: this friendly French King (1553–1610) was often depicted in history books giving piggy-backs.

186 *Antony*: eponymous hero of a drama by Dumas senior in which passionate love is thwarted by bastardy and ends tragically.

193 *Phrygian bonnet*: the emblematic Revolutionary cap.

the Civil Code: the French code of law based on Roman law, drawn up under Napoleon I.

194 *Lycurguses*: Lycurgus was the traditional, possibly legendary, legislator of pre-Hellenic Sparta.

Wronsky: this Pole had served in the Russian army, settled in France, and wrote scientific (so-called) and philosophical works in a mystical vein.

Enfantin: Prosper Enfantin (1796–1864), follower of Saint-Simon (see note to p. 148), had given the movement a religious twist (hence the nickname Father) and set up religious communities; his preaching included emancipation of the flesh and this landed him in gaol.

Leroux: Pierre Leroux (1797–1871) was also originally a Saint-Simonian; see Historical Sketch, 1841, and p. 395.

Louis Blanc: became a socialist Deputy after 1848; see Historical Sketch for 1839 and February and June 1848.

195 *École normale*: élite higher education institution designed to produce university and secondary school teachers.

202 *Raimondi*: an Italian Renaissance engraver, a friend of Raphael.

217 *Phèdre . . . Desgrieux*: all passionate and unhappy lovers:

Phèdre, from Racine's tragedy; *Dido*, Queen of Carthage, deserted by Aeneas; *Desgrieux*, from Prévost's *Manon Lescaut* (1731).

221 *Bou-Maza*: a captured chieftain brought to Paris.

224 *snail*: the occupant of this tiny vehicle fitted into it like a snail in its shell.

226 *demi-fortunes*: the last in this impressively cosmopolitan list of vehicles is a four-wheeler drawn by a single horse, economical transport for the not-so-wealthy.

229 *Ozäi*: first performed at the Paris Opera in April 1847.

Edgar Quinet and Mickiewicz: *Quinet* held the Chair of Southern European Languages and Literature and was critical of Roman Catholicism, especially the Jesuits. The lectures of *Mickiewicz*, the Polish writer and patriot, holder of the Chair of Slavonic Languages and Literature, had aroused republican demonstrations.

Maistre: Joseph de Maistre (1754–1821), a fiery supporter of monarchy and the Pope, vehemently anti-Revolutionary.

Sainville: an expert in grotesque facial contortions.

231 *Baucher . . . d'Aure*: Baucher advocated indoor riding school techniques, while the count supported the freer, outdoor, English methods.

234 *the Salon*: the official annual Paris painting exhibition, where Rosanette had hoped to see her portrait in the Main Hall.

236 *Drouillard and Bénier*: the first involved electoral bribery by a banker, the second, embezzlement by a senior official.

Japanese kris: If Frédéric (or Flaubert) thought a kris was Japanese, he was wrong; it is a Malaysian dagger.

Godefroi Cavaignac: see Historical Sketch for 1845.

238 *Père et Portier*: a vaudeville first performed in May 1847.

Saintonge: a former French county, bordering on and north of the Gironde.

239 *savate*: a French form of boxing using the feet.

Rodolphe . . . de Paris: *Les Mystères de Paris*, an immensely popular serial novel published in the early 1840s by Eugène Sue (1804–57), proponent of social and democratic reform; the character *Rodolphe*, mysteriously disguised, frequents the underworld on humanitarian missions—an unlikely role for

Cisy, who is silly, soppy, and, like many of the characters in this novel, lacking in self-knowledge.

241 *Sophie Arnoux*: Cisy is either trying to be funny or is completely fuddled; how could he otherwise confuse Marie Arnoux with Sophie Arnould, a notoriously loose-living eighteenth-century singer?

243 *La Fougère*: author of a book on sword-fighting; an expert in feints.

249 *Croix-Catelan . . . Bagatelle*: the *Croix-Catelan* is a monument in the Bois to commemorate the assassination of a medieval troubadour of that name there; *Bagatelle* is an eighteenth-century château and gardens nearby.

252 *Dulaure . . . Girondins*: Dulaure was an important figure in Revolutionary French politics from 1792–1799; the Baron de *Barante* (1782–1866) served under Napoleon, the Restoration, and Louis-Philippe; he was a liberal; the *Girondins* were a moderate right-wing party of the French Revolution, many of whom were guillotined during the 1793 Terror under the Convention (see note to p. 323); *Lamartine*'s book on them was widely read. Frédéric is trying, unsuccessfully, to stimulate Dussardier's critical faculties.

Chalier: leader of the extreme left wing (Jacobins) of Lyons; he was guillotined in 1793.

Société des Familles: one of the most active of the socialist revolutionary secret societies in the 1830s.

Alibaud: had attempted to assassinate the king in 1835.

253 *rue Transnonain*: all the occupants of a house, including women and children, had been butchered.

254 *Carpentras*: for some obscure reason the inhabitants of this southern French town were the butt of nineteenth-century humorous magazines (e.g. *Le Charivari*, p. 115 and note) as being dull and stupid.

255 *Don Basilio*: in Beaumarchais's *Barbier de Séville*.

257 *Xavier lectures*: founded by the Jesuits, a sort of Roman Catholic Workers' Educational Association.

260 *Desolmes . . . of 1791*: the republican *Desolmes* had translated *Blackstone*'s famous *Commentaries of the Laws of England*; the *Bill of Rights* of 1689 established the British constitutional

monarchy; *Article 2* of the French Revolutionary *Constitution of 1791* spoke of the inalienable Rights of Man.

261 *carbonaro*: member of a secret association of liberals in the early 1820s who aimed to overthrow the French Bourbon monarchy; they took their name from an earlier Italian society which had the same aim for their own country.

Arabs: we must remember that the French were at the time completing their conquest of Algeria.

280 *tombac*: a sort of tobacco sometimes mixed with marijuana or opium.

284 *Lachambeaudie*: a Saint-Simonian and a friend of Blanqui and Enfantin; Lachambeaudie's *Fables populaires* were published in 1839.

Napoléon: Norvin's book on Napoleon dates from 1827.

285 *Piedmont, Naples, Tuscany*: there was political unrest throughout Italy.

Holland: at the London Conference of 1830, when Louis-Philippe had just accepted the Crown, France had agreed, with England, to recognize Belgium's independence from the Dutch.

Switzerland . . . of 1815: France and Austria backed the Roman Catholic cantons which were seeking independence; the supporters of a federal union of all the Swiss cantons won the day.

Zollverein: see note to p. 30.

the Eastern question: in the 1841 settlement of the conflict between Egypt and the Ottoman Empire, the former, which had had French support, had been forced to give up Syria and other territories to the Turks.

Constantine: the Czar's second son.

it's satisfied: these *well-known words* were in reply to a rhetorical question: 'What has the government done since 1840?' The government had expressed itself 'satisfied' after Guizot had defended the administration against charges of bribery and corruption.

286 *two sentries*: considered too extravagant to guard the residence of the War Minister Soult, a former Napoleonic Marshal.

the Jesuits: Jesuit schools had been officially banned in 1845.

Cousin: Victor Cousin was not only an eclectic philosopher (p. 15) but the director of the École normale (see note to p. 195) and thus an élitist member of the 'Establishment'.

Faubourg-Saint-Antoine: a working-class suburb.

Teste-Cubières: a financial scandal involving the Minister of Works, Teste, and a former War Minister, General Cubières.

Duchesse de Praslin: a high-society scandal: the duchess was stabbed to death and the duke committed suicide before he could be brought to trial; popular rumour had it that he had been allowed to get away.

287 *Le Chevalier de Maison Rouge*: this play concerns an attempt by an officer of the Royal Household Guards to rescue Queen Marie-Antoinette from prison. It shows the Revolutionary Tribunal at work and also involves the Girondins (see note to p. 252).

La Démocratie pacifique: the Fourierist (see note to p. 148) paper, edited by Victor Considérant (p. 346).

Pius IX: this pope had shown liberal sympathies from which he later retreated.

288 *trickster . . . Dumouriez*: the 'trickster' Louis–Philippe, who'd cheated the republicans in 1830, had been proclaimed king from the Hôtel de Ville; during the Revolutionary period he had served in the French army with General Dumouriez, who later defected to the anti-Revolutionary forces.

La Tour de Nesle: historical drama based on the novel of the same name by Dumas senior and depicting scandalous and murderous goings-on by Queen Margaret, wife of Louis X, in the tower which stood beside the Seine on the present site of the Académie française.

I've two great . . . oxen: a song by the popular song-writer Pierre Dupont (1821–70), whose songs about peasants and workers had a great vogue at this time.

289 *d'Alton-Shée*: a former royalist who had become a republican; he was a count but, more importantly, a colonel in the National Guard (see note to p. 30).

297 *Léotade*: a Brother of the Christian Doctrine accused in February 1848 of sexual abuse and murder of a girl; he was condemned and died in gaol.

482

the Palermo uprising: after an uprising in Sicily, the king had been forced to grant a constitution.

12ᵉ arrondissement: this *arrondissement* covered what is now the students' Latin quarter (cf. p. 364); demonstrations planned to precede the banquet in favour of electoral reform had been banned.

300 *the pear*: cartoonists depicted the king with a head the shape of a pear.

301 *Barrot*: a liberal monarchist who'd been promoting the banquets.

302 *Municipal Guard*: armed mounted police.

307 *Les Girondins*: a revolutionary song by the author of the 'Marseillaise'.

310 *Molé*: the king had replaced Guizot by his personal friend the Comte de Molé, who proved unable to form a government.

Bugeaud: Marshal Bugeaud had fought in Algeria from 1840 to 1847 and was now in command of the regular troops in Paris.

311 *Château d'Eau*: so-called because of its fountain, this building in front of the Palais-Royal commanded the entrance to the Louvre Palace.

312 *an old man*: he was the former Napoleonic Marshal Gérard, about 75 years old at the time; we can appreciate an excellent example of Flaubert's striving for complete authenticity.

313 *Arc de triomphe*: this is the smaller one, in the place du Carrousel, near the Louvre.

317 *Duchesse d'Orléans . . . Regent*: she did not last long, despite Barrot's support (pp. 318, 319).

319 *commissioner*: republican commissioners were appointed to replace the Prefects and Deputy Prefects throughout France.

Ledru-Rollin: this leading radical republican had become Minister of the Interior.

Changarnier: Governor of Algeria, later commander of the National Guard and supporter of the rue de Poitiers group (see note to p. 395).

de Falloux: a royalist count, he was elected to the Constituent Assembly, produced the report which led to the closing of the National Workshops (pp. 341, 347), and drew up the Falloux education law (p. 433) in 1850.

whereas the tricolour: '. . . the tricolour had carried the name, the fame and the freedom of the Fatherland round the world.'

320 *Caussidière's men*: Caussidière was a left-wing Jacobin who had played an important role in the 1834 Lyons uprising and now became Paris chief of police; he organized a tough force of security police drawn from the younger working classes, dressing them in dashing uniforms—blue shirts, red neckties, and belts—which later greatly took Rosanette's eye.

321 *Lamartine*: now Foreign Minister in the Provisional Government.

Dupont (de l'Eure): head of the Provisional Government, more than 80 years old.

Albert: leader of a secret society and working-class member of the Provisional Government; he was deported after taking part in the riot in the Chamber of Deputies in May 1848.

Blanqui: a terrorist, secret society leader, gaoled after the 1839 Paris uprising and again after the mob invasion of the Chamber in May 1848.

Neuilly and Suresne: *Neuilly* was a royal palace, *Suresne* belonged to the Rothschilds.

Ledru-Rollin's circular: this was addressed to the commissioners, asking them where possible to appoint men of working-class origin, and to mayors, where his requests included having law officers appointed by popular vote, arranging easy credit for farmers, ensuring a fair share of capitalists' profits for the workers, and other well-intentioned but sometimes impractical and ill-timed suggestions.

compulsory exchange rate . . . tax increase: the fall in State Bonds showed that France was nearly bankrupt; hence the tax increase to 45 per cent and the exchange controls which decreed that banknotes were to be regarded as equal in value to gold of the same denomination.

322 *Flocon's pipe*: the editor of *La Réforme* had been made Minister of Trade; he always sported a pipe (cf. Churchill's cigar).

323 *Proudhon*: Pierre Joseph Proudhon (1809–65) (see Historical

Sketch for 1840) had been elected to the Constituent Assembly. He was the most influential socialist theoretician of his age, vigorously anti-capitalist and anti-authoritarian, believing that only individual moral effort could lead to a better society and rejecting any organized religion; a firm supporter of the idea of European Federation.

a club: after Feb. 1848 large numbers of political clubs came into being, replacing the banned secret societies and promoting factional interests, e.g. feminism, which made a great upsurge (p. 324).

324 *the Convention*: French Revolutionary Government from 1792 to 95; it included such famous names as Danton, Marat, Camille Desmoulins, Robespierre, and Saint Just. In addition to declaring the first French Republic, it founded the École polytechnique, the École normale supérieure and the Institut which grouped the various *Académies*.

Every Frenchwoman . . . adopt an old man: some of Flaubert's information on feminism was obtained from a pamphlet which included a Women's Political Constitution and which he has here, either unintentionally or deliberately, grossly misrepresented; the article of the constitution to which he refers merely states that any foreign women, fifteen years old or more, who married a Frenchman or adopted an old man, would be granted French citizenship rights.

329 *the Prado*: a dance-hall; the meeting was arranged by the terrorist Blanqui.

Souvenirs du peuple: this song by the popular patriotic poet celebrates the memory of Napoleon I; ironically, though it is disapproved of by this club, Napoleon I's nephew was to be elected President of the Second Republic at the end of 1848 and go on to destroy it in his coup of December 1851 (see p. 452 *et seq.*).

Assemblée nationale: a royalist paper founded in 1848 by former July Monarchy officials.

Thermidor martyrs: the 27 July 1794 (9 Thermidor, Year II in the Revolutionary calendar) marked the Convention's rejection of Robespierre and the end of the reign of Terror; the 'martyrs' were Robespierre and other terrorists, including the Public Prosecutor Fouquier-Tinville.

338 *Essenes . . . Pingons*: the *Essenes*, the Moravian Brethren and the *Pingons* are all mentioned in Cabet's *Voyage en Icarie*.

341 *La Presse*: this paper had proved too moderate for the zealots.

Amiens National Guard: they had sent a detachment to help the Paris police and National Guard in their anti-riot activities; in general, the provinces were far more conservative than Paris.

the Vesuvians, the Tyroleans: the *Vesuvians* were groups of young working-class feminists, the *Tyroleans* were Caussidière's formidable police.

346 *Napoleon . . . Marie*: the *Napoleon* is Louis Napoleon, soon to be President of the Second Republic; *Marie* was the Minister of the Interior who reintroduced laws restricting public gatherings.

Considérant and Lamennais: Victor *Considérant* was the editor of the Fourierist newspaper (p. 287); Félicité Robert de *Lamennais* (1782–1854), a Breton priest of strongly humanitarian views, considered heretical and excommunicated, was, like Considérant, a member of the Constitutent Assembly.

349 *Christine . . . assassinated*: Queen Christine of Sweden abdicated in 1654, had her lover assassinated in 1657, and died piously in Rome in 1688.

350 *Diane de Poitiers*: 1499–1566; Henri II was twenty years her junior.

351 *lovely women . . . boxes*: a reminiscence from Rousseau's *Confessions*.

353 *La Marlotte*: a hamlet near these famous beauty spots.

364 *Bréa and Négrier*: two of the six generals killed in the June uprising.

Archbishop of Paris: his name was Affre (p. 377)

365 *security police*: though recruited from the working classes, Caussidière's armed security police had sided with the middle-class National Guard.

370 *Faubourg-Saint-Germain*: an aristocratic suburb in which the Palais-Bourbon, where the Constituent Assembly held its sittings, was situated.

373 *pineapple . . . Luxembourg Palace*: hints of extravagant living on the part of the republican labour commission.

374 *Sallesse . . . Péquillet woman*: *Sallesse* was one of Caussidière's men, the *Jeansons* were National Guardsmen, and *Péquillet* worked in a military canteen.

377 *Prudhomme*: see note to p. 115 on *Le Charivari*.

380 *the arrests*: the round-up after the uprising.

387 *the Rateau motion*: the Deputy Rateau had moved that the Constituent Assembly should dissolve itself and elections be held for a new Legislative Assembly; Compain's fears were realized: the new Assembly was far more to the right.

395 *the rue de Poitiers*: the so-called 'committee' of the rue de Poitiers represented the right-wing 'party of order' which included Falloux and Thiers and supported Louis Napoleon's candidacy as president.

Conservatorium . . . incident: left-wing supporters, including Considérant and Ledru-Rollin, organized a protest demonstration against the French government's action in sending troops to help suppress the newly declared Roman Republic; the demonstration was broken up by General Changarnier, a former governor of Algeria, commander of both the National Guard and regular army forces in Paris. Protesters took refuge in the Conservatorium of Arts and Crafts but were quickly dispersed.

396 *book attacking socialism*: probably Thiers' *De la propriété*, a counter-blast to Proudhon's book on the same subject.

Encyclopédie: this eighteenth-century encyclopaedia, whose contributors included Voltaire and Rousseau, was liberal and rationalistic, attacking intolerance, injustice, and persecution.

Fourierists' tail: Fourier, always highly imaginative, would have liked mankind to be provided with a tail containing an eye, so that people could see what was happening behind their backs.

La Foire aux idées: a four-part vaudeville ridiculing socialist thinkers, performed from May to October 1849.

400 *Belle-Isle*: Barbès and Blanqui were among the insurgents held on this south Breton island.

401 *Louis-Philippe's umbrella*: umbrella-carrying was part of Louis-Philippe's middle-class image.

Talleyrand: Charles Maurice de Talleyrand (1754–1838) started in the Church, became a bishop, left the Church, and served, mainly as a diplomat, under Napoleon, during the Restoration and under Louis-Philippe; he had a profitable life.

402 *re-elected*: to the Legislative Assembly.

404 *Gobet . . . Chappe*: *Gobet* was an eighteenth-century mineral-ogist; Deslauriers's information is not very up-to-date; of the two *Chappe* brothers, who collaborated with each other, one died in 1805, the other in 1828.

407 *Robespierre . . . saved the People*: Sénécal is arguing that the majority of people don't know what's good for them; Robes-pierre, even if he was in a minority, was right to bring Louis XVI to trial.

dismissal of Changarnier: Changarnier (see note to p. 395 on Conservatorium) was a monarchist. Louis Napoleon had sacked him in Jan. 1851.

413 *left arm . . . toutes voies*: the clenched fist is unambiguous, the gold and silver very appropriate for a financier; the motto means *Using any means*.

415 *Piscatory . . . Dufour*: of these, only *Quentin-Bauchard* and *Dufour* voted in favour of the increase; however, the Comte de *Montalambert*, who had been an admirer of Lamennais, later supported the coup of Dec. 1852, whereby the President Louis Napoleon became the Emperor Napoleon III.

416 *Manuel's . . . Constant's*: Jacques Antoine *Manuel* (1775–1827), a liberal Deputy under the Restoration; *Constant*, see note to p. 30.

421 *Andilly*: a tiny village a few miles north of Paris.

424 *Bourges*: a cathedral city about 140 miles south of Paris.

philosophy classes: the classes preparing for university entrance.

red waistcoats: a garment which had symbolized keen Roman-ticism ever since Théophile Gautier had worn one at the tumultuous first night of Hugo's first Romantic historical drama in 1830, opening a new era.

433 *Roman Republic . . . Hungary*: *Roman Republic*, see p. 395 under Conservatorium of Arts and Crafts; the *Venetian* Republic was liquidated shortly afterwards by Austria which, with Russian help, also crushed the *Hungarian* independence

movement; *Poland* remained partitioned between Austria, Prussia, and Russia.

Trees of Liberty . . . over to the priests: these trees, planted to celebrate the 1848 Revolution (see p. 320) were being uprooted by order of the new Paris police chief Cartier; the right to vote had been reduced by one third, largely by introducing stricter residential qualifications (workers had to move around a good deal in search of work and became disqualified); a law of June 1849 against certain clubs had been extended; a stricter press law was introduced in July 1849; and by the law of March 1850 (*Loi Falloux*), primary education was placed under clerical supervision and clerics were allowed to open private secondary schools without the qualifications required of state school teachers.

Cossacks: these tough troops had been part of the occupying force in Paris after the fall of Napoleon.

amnesty: the amnesty for the insurgents of June 1848.

434 *Nadaud*: Nadaud was a socialist member of the Legislative Assembly who went into exile in England after Louis-Napoleon's December 1851 coup.

445 *Petites Affiches*: a long-established magazine for all sorts of buying and selling, including legal notices such as forced sales.

452 *Mazas*: a brand-new prison; Thiers, Lamoricière, Cavaignac, and Changarnier were all held there.

456 *Mostaganem*: in western Algeria, on the Mediterranean; another of the many reminders in the novel of France's important newly acquired colony.

457 *Werther . . . sandwich-making*: a further reference to this influential novel of Goethe (see note to p. 17); when Werther first sees Charlotte, she is cutting bread and butter.

458 *you kissed . . . and my glove*: ironically, the only similar action recorded in the novel is when Frédéric kisses Rosanette's wrist on the way to the fateful race meeting; another example of the interchangeability of women, who are seen in similar situations, playing similar roles, throughout the novel.

462 *Independents*: this was a name given earlier to Free Churchmen, later known as Congregationalists.

Thermidor: see note to p. 329.

The Oxford World's Classics Website

www.worldsclassics.co.uk

- Information about new titles
- Explore the full range of Oxford World's Classics
- Links to other literary sites and the main OUP webpage
- Imaginative competitions, with bookish prizes
- Peruse the Oxford World's Classics Magazine
- Articles by editors
- Extracts from Introductions
- A forum for discussion and feedback on the series
- Special information for teachers and lecturers

www.worldsclassics.co.uk

MORE ABOUT   SICS

American Literature

British and Irish Literature

Children's Literature

Classics and Ancient Literature

Colonial Literature

Eastern Literature

European Literature

History

Medieval Literature

Oxford English Drama

Poetry

Philosophy

Politics

Religion

The Oxford Shakespeare

A complete list of Oxford Paperbacks, including Oxford World's Classics, Oxford Shakespeare, Oxford Drama, and Oxford Paperback Reference, is available in the UK from the Academic Division Publicity Department, Oxford University Press, Great Clarendon Street, Oxford OX2 6DP.

In the USA, complete lists are available from the Paperbacks Marketing Manager, Oxford University Press, 198 Madison Avenue, New York, NY 10016.

Oxford Paperbacks are available from all good bookshops. In case of difficulty, customers in the UK can order direct from Oxford University Press Bookshop, Freepost, 116 High Street, Oxford OX1 4BR, enclosing full payment. Please add 10 per cent of published price for postage and packing.